Nonverbal Communication

Loretta A. Malandro

Malandro Associates, Inc.

Larry L. Barker

Auburn University

▲▲ ADDISON–WESLEY
PUBLISHING COMPANY
Reading, Massachusetts
Menlo Park, California
London•Amsterdam
Don Mills, Ontario
Sydney

Nonverbal Communication

Sponsoring Editor: *Linda Fisher*
Production Editor: *Mary Clare McEwing*

Text Designer: *Margaret Ong Tsao*
Art Coordinator: *Susanah H. Michener*
Cartoonists: *Richard Varney, Gene Warne*
Photographer: *Carolyn Brown*
Illustrator, chapter openings: *Richard Varney*

Production Manager: *Herbert Nolan*
Production Coordinator: *Sheryl Stenzel*

*The text of this book was composed in Compugraphic Palatino by Pine
Tree Composition Service, Inc.*

Library of Congress Cataloging in Publication Data

Malandro, Loretta.
 Nonverbal communication.

 Bibliography: p.
 Includes index.
 1. Nonverbal communication. I. Barker, Larry Lee,
1941–   . II. Title.
P99.5.M34   001.56   82-1771
ISBN 0-201-05336-5   AACR2

ISBN 0-201-05336-5
BCDEFGHIJ-HA-89876543

PREFACE

The area of nonverbal communication has provided an exciting and enriching opportunity for us, both in teaching and research. The more we have studied this aspect of communication, the greater our awareness and application of nonverbal skills have grown. Perhaps it was our enthusiasm that drew classes of over three hundred students—students who wanted to learn more about their own nonverbal behavior as well as the behavior of others. During our many years of teaching nonverbal communication classes we found that our students wanted much more than what was offered in the traditional textbook. They wanted examples, applications, research findings presented in an interesting way, a historical perspective, contemporary information, and complete reference lists with both traditional and nontraditional books and articles. In other words, our students have been asking for a book that is enjoyable to read—a book that will stimulate them both intellectually and emotionally. In attempting to blend the important aspects of content and process (the means by which we have presented the information), it has been our purpose to create a book that comes alive for the reader.

Specifically, we have considered the need for multiple sensory input through three important channels—kinesthetic (feeling), visual (seeing), and auditory (hearing). Lankton (1980)* presents a strong argument for the fact that information is taken in through all channels, but processed through a favored channel. Therefore, the sensory processing channel of which a person is most conscious is that person's primary representational system. For example, a student with a highly developed visual orientation might experience difficulty or frustration with a textbook that uses little or no actual visual display such as illustrations, cartoons, or photographs, or that does not graphically and visually describe a scene or event for which the reader can create his or her own visual image. A kinesthetically

*Lankton, S., *Practical Magic: A Translation of Basic Neuro-linguistic Programming into Clinical Psychotherapy.* Cupertino, California: Meta Publications, 1980.

v

oriented person might find the traditional textbook dry and boring because it provides little or no input of "feeling." For this person, the need to "experience" the material or to read stories that produce an emotional response or impact may be important. Finally, those who favor the auditory channel may respond more favorably to the traditional approach because they will most likely process the information they read and hear it in their minds. It seems clear, however, that a book should reach all people and should activate and use all channels of sensory input.

Recognizing and utilizing the various sensory channels of communication has been used in client–therapy relationships and is part of the neurolinguistic programming method. One of the important premises of this approach is that when you can match the channel that your client uses, you are making a powerful move toward greater contact and rapport. You will literally be speaking the client's language (Lankton, 1980, p. 19). Toward this end, it is our purpose to move toward greater contact and rapport by speaking the language of our readers.

We would like to express our deep appreciation to several people who helped bring this book to completion. First, we gratefully acknowledge several students, friends, and colleagues who helped author or coauthor individual chapters in the text. In each case these individuals conducted the initial research for their chapter(s) and wrote original chapter drafts. Thanks to Tally Anderson (Chapter 4); Renée Edwards (Chapter 7); Debbie Roach (Chapters 4, 10, 11); Frances Sayers (Chapter 9); Kathy Shumaker (Chapter 1); and Kittie Watson (Chapters 1 and 5). Also, thanks to Sondi Feldmaier who contributed the section on "Dance" in Chapter 11.

Other people who served as editors, reviewers, copyreaders, typists, and general project helpers deserve special recognition. Thanks to Vern Jones, Karen Graham, Cheryl Fisher, Brian Walker, Janis Andersen, Peter Andersen, Richard Cheatham, Tom Steinfatt, Dick Varney, Gene Warne, Carolyn Brown, Kevin Frese, Owen Marcus, Mindy Marshack, Dale Campbell, and Marie Henderson.

Finally, thanks to all our students in nonverbal communication classes over the past ten years who provided the basis for many of the examples and illustrations included in the text.

Tempe, Arizona   L.A.M.
Auburn, Alabama   L.L.B.
September 1982

CONTENTS

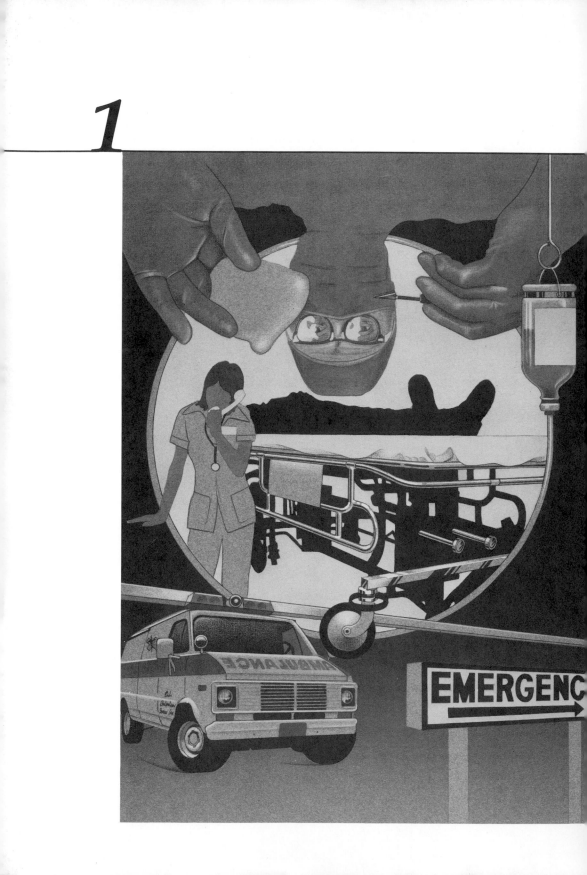

INTRODUCTION TO NONVERBAL COMMUNICATION

In the Hermie/Aggie sector, Aggie, touched by the drama on the screen, moved closer to Hermie, not so much out of desire as out of compassion for all human beings in distress. Hermie noticed the imperceptible move because a current of air wiggled and her tiny shifting measured a loud 193 on his seismograph. Dizzily encouraged by Aggie's brazen demonstration of lustful desire, Hermie decided to make his move because it was do or die. The film was spinning out whether Bette Davis liked it or not, and there wasn't much time left in which Hermie could grab a squeeze. Up in the air his right arm went in its intended journey behind Aggie's back. But in the process he miscalculated the distance involved, and thus, his hand smacked Aggie on the nose.

H. RAUCHER, *SUMMER OF '42*

1

*T*he scouting motto "Be prepared" influences people in all walks of life, yet being prepared has different meanings for different people. Being prepared can mean opening a savings account to prepare for retirement, making a religious commitment to prepare for death, buying enough groceries to prepare for surprise guests, or having a stock of birthday, anniversary, wedding, get-well, and friendship cards in your desk drawer to prepare for special occasions. Even with all the preparation that goes on in our lives, some events just cannot be prepared for in advance. Falling in love, flash floods, surprise parties, and accidents occur unexpectedly.

9:39 A.M. Darlene Masters, a thirty-two-year-old career woman, drives to Lakeside Shopping Mall to shop for baby clothes.

10:15 A.M. While paying for her purchase, Darlene suddenly feels a sharp pain.

10:20 A.M. The store manager calls for an ambulance.

10:35 A.M. An ambulance from the Lady of the Lake hospital arrives at the Mall.

10:40 A.M. Within seconds, Darlene is placed on a stretcher and wheeled to the waiting ambulance.

10:43 A.M. With siren blasting, the ambulance speeds to the hospital's Emergency Room entrance.

10:53 A.M. Darlene and the ambulance are greeted with a flurry of activity as the staff, nurses, and doctors prepare the delivery room for use.

11:25 A.M. The cries of a newborn baby girl are heard all over the emergency room.

The preceding example illustrates a variety of nonverbal messages communicated during an emergency. Even though Darlene had expected her baby to arrive a month later, her baby was on another time schedule. However, in this situation, others were prepared to deal with her emergency. By examining how Darlene's nonverbal messages influenced her interactions, you will begin to realize the important role that **nonverbal communication** behaviors play in everyday and life-or-death situations.

In this example, Darlene's physical appearance, dress, and body language played an important role in signaling the store manager to call for an ambulance. First, as you know, pregnant women have a "unique" body shape all of their own. Of course, Darlene could have been just obese or overweight, but her maternity outfit (stretch pants and a T-shirt with an arrow pointing to the word BABY) helped clarify that she was indeed pregnant and not overweight. Next, Darlene's body language suggested that something was wrong. A painful facial expression in combination with her falling against the counter clued the manager that emergency help was needed.

Another nonverbal factor that influenced this situation was the use of a siren. The ambulance's siren was intended to mobilize quick responses in others. First, motorists were signaled to pull over to give the ambulance the right of way. Second, the siren was used to warn the hospital staff that a new patient was arriving for treatment. How quickly the ambulance is driven also suggests the severity of the emergency. Slow speeds may mean that everything is under control, that the patient died, or that no one is in the ambulance, whereas high speeds tend to suggest that the situation is a matter of life or death. The ambulance attendants and hospital personnel also use other forms of nonverbal communication to send messages to others. Their clothing and equipment told the Mall shoppers that someone was in need of special care. The uniforms also labeled who was in charge by indicating distinctions between patients and staff. In addition, medical staff routinely use special hand movements to signal that a patient needs oxygen or is stabilizing, or to indicate where to apply pressure.

How individuals are perceived by others influences how they will be responded to in a given situation. The hospital staff's assessment of Darlene's moral, socioeconomic, and physical characteristics probably controlled how she was treated. Some people would have a tendency to look immediately to the fourth finger of the left hand to check for a wedding band. If there had been none, the staff may have looked negatively at Darlene for bringing an illegitimate child into the world. (They may have formed this conclusion even though today many couples choose not to wear wedding bands.) The type of clothing worn (i.e., quality, colors, fabrics, etc.) also influences where patients will be treated. Wealthier patients may be taken to private hospitals and given private rooms, while poorer ones may be taken to public hospitals. One segment from a "Sixty Minutes" documentary suggested that doctors involved in Medicare frauds estimated whether or not a patient was insured or uninsured on the basis of the patients' dress when they arrived for treatment. Finally, physical characteristics influence both the method and type of treatment given to patients. For example, if Darlene's baby was physically healthy the child would probably be given to her immediately. However, if the child was of such a weight as to be classified as "premature" or if the child had some physical deformity, "extraordinary" measures would have been taken to save her life. Moreover, the attractiveness of Darlene and her child affects hospital interactions. More attractive individuals receive better care.

The impact of nonverbal communication may not always be as obvious as in the case of Darlene, but it is clear that nonverbal communication significantly affects the behavior of others and the outcomes of many communication events. Characteristics such as your voice, body movements, gestures, spatial distancing, and touch relay important information that is often universally understood. For this reason, it is vital for you to "be prepared" to understand what you and others communicate nonverbally.

The following pages provide a perspective through which you can view information and research efforts related to nonverbal communication. These chapters will assist you in creating a general understanding of just what nonverbal communication is and how it plays an important role in your life.

PERSPECTIVES ON NONVERBAL COMMUNICATION

Does anybody really know when nonverbal communication (as a discipline) originated? Knapp (1978) traces interest in nonverbal communication to the early Greeks (400–600 B.C.). Other authors of nonverbal texts (e.g., Weitz, 1979) trace the origins to the elocutionary period in which hand and body movements were emphasized. Darwin (1872), because of his work in explaining the relationship between animal and human behavior, is also mentioned by some authors as the father of modern nonverbal communication. What we can glean from these confusing and apparently contradictory assumptions by different authors is that nobody "really knows" when nonverbal communication became a significant area of study.

Nonverbal behavior, experiences, and communication are with you, literally all of the time. Television, radio, motion pictures, records, magazines, newspapers, public speeches, interpersonal conversations, classroom interactions, and solitary daydreams all have nonverbal dimensions that affect you significantly. The ability to identify specific nonverbal behaviors that communicate effectively (or even miscommunicate) can assist you in improving your communication skills.

What Is Nonverbal Communication?

Although our primary emphasis will not be on the origins of or early research pioneers in nonverbal communication, we need to address the issue of what nonverbal communication *is*.

"I tell you, Mr. Arthur, this survey has no
way of registering a nonverbal response!"

Most authors of nonverbal communication texts choose to define
communication first and then address the nonverbal component
separately. We will follow this lead. Communication may be viewed as
a "sharing of meaning, involving the sending/receiving/encoding and
decoding of messages" (Burgoon and Saine, 1978). A somewhat more
elaborate definition suggests that communication is not only composed
of such elements as "sender," "message," and "receiver" but that it is
an interactive process, which is "dynamic, irreversible, proactive and
contextual" (Rosenfeld and Civikly, 1976). It should be pointed out that
there is considerable academic debate concerning which definition of
communication is more useful and which is more valid. Some critics

believe that all communication must be intentional. The question of intentionality will be addressed later in this chapter.

In an effort not to be drawn into the controversy concerning what is communication and what is not, we take the view in this text that it is useful to study all possible forms of verbal and nonverbal behavior and events that may influence human beings. We also elect to use a broad definition of the term "communication" in an attempt to bring the greatest possible number of approaches, variables, and ideas together to improve our understanding of nonverbal objects, events, behaviors, and processes.

Let us now turn our attention to the question *What is nonverbal communication?* If someone asked you this question, how would you answer it? Perhaps some of the following definitions would come to mind:

Nonverbal communication is communication without words.

Nonverbal communication can be viewed as occurring whenever an individual communicates without the use of sounds.

Nonverbal communication is anything someone does that someone else assigns meaning to.

Nonverbal communication is the study of facial expressions, touch, time, gestures, smell, eye behavior, etc.

To some extent each of these definitions would be valid. As a matter of fact, were you to research the topic, you would more than likely find some component of your definition in at least one nonverbal communication text. The point is that people conceive of nonverbal communication (rightfully or wrongfully) in various ways. A psychologist's orientation toward nonverbal communication is different from that of a sociologist; an interpersonal communication student's view of nonverbal communication is different from that of an organizational or mass communications student.

As a new student of nonverbal communication you may or may not be aware of (or care about) the controversy surrounding the meaning of nonverbal communication. However, as a scholar, it is important that you possess a clear and workable definition of the term "nonverbal communication." After all, you will probably agree that it is more difficult to learn about something that has never been clearly defined for you.

Dimensions of Verbal and Nonverbal Communications

With increased interest in the study of nonverbal communication, a controversy concerning how nonverbal communication should be defined has formed. Present definitions range from the "beyond-words'' definition, which explains nonverbal communication as all communication other than the spoken word (Ruesch and Kees, 1956), to more specific definitions such as the one proposed by Burgoon and Saine (1978):

> Nonverbal communication is those attributes or actions of humans other than the use of words themselves which have socially shared meaning, are intentionally sent or interpreted as intentional and are consciously received and have the potential for feedback from the receiver. (p. 9)

Definitions such as the ones presented above give only a limited picture of the various dimensions of nonverbal communication. By examining characteristics that distinguish verbal from nonverbal communication, we hope to provide you with a clearer understanding of nonverbal communication. Based on our own and other authors' distinctions (Rosenfeld and Civikly, 1976), the following dimensions of verbal and nonverbal communication will be discussed: structure versus nonstructure; linguistic versus nonlinguistic; continuous versus discontinuous; learned versus innate; and hemispheric versus nonhemispheric processing.

Structure versus nonstructure.   Verbal communication is highly structured and has formal laws or rules of grammar. In every language (French, German, Spanish, etc.), these rules help us consistently make sense out of what other people are saying. Foreigners, when learning a new language, often misuse appropriate language structures (for example, they might say ''Love I you!'' and ''See you, very nice, was it''). On the other hand, with nonverbal communication there is little or no formal structure with which to guide communication. Most nonverbal communication occurs unconsciously without a predictable sequence of events. Because there are no formal rules, we must be careful to look at all the available cues to interpret nonverbal messages correctly. Without a pattern, the same nonverbal behavior can mean different things at different times. For example, people can cry when sad, excited, happy, or for no reason at all.

Linguistic versus nonlinguistic.   Since there is no specific structure for nonverbal communication, there are few assigned symbols in the system. In some cultures, nodding your head indicates agreement, whereas in others it indicates disagreement. Although some researchers have attempted to assign specific meaning to particular facial movements (Birdwhistell, 1970), there exists no documented nonverbal language system. Some theorists would say that the only exception to this is the universal sign language of the deaf. Even the deaf, however, have unique nonverbal symbols with no assigned meanings. This is not the case in verbal communication. Verbal communication is a system of symbols that have meanings arbitrarily assigned to them.

Continuous versus discontinuous. Wiseman and Barker (1974) explain that nonverbal communication is continuous whereas verbal communication is based on disconnected units. There is no way to stop communicating nonverbally unless you leave the room, and even then your intrapersonal processes (communication within and to oneself) keep on going. Even without other people present, our bodies, emotions, and minds send continuous verbal and nonverbal messages that we must process during our waking hours. As long as your body, face, and presence are perceived by another individual or yourself, the potential for nonverbal communication exists. However, words and symbols have a definite beginning and ending point. Nonverbal messages linger on. After a heated discussion, there may be no further words exchanged, yet cold stares, angry glances, and stiff body positions suggest that the disagreement is far from resolved—at least nonverbally.

Learned versus innate. Although you learn much nonverbal communication through observation and reinforcement, you are seldom taught to communicate nonverbally. No one teaches a child to smile; however, when infants are happy, they do smile to indicate contentment. We believe that individuals are born with basic nonverbal instincts. On the other hand, it is obvious that verbal communication is learned. Although most people are born with the ability to make sounds, they do not speak a ''language'' or know how to communicate with others until they are taught how to say words, make sentences out of groups of words, and attach meaning to them. Our innate abilities to communicate nonverbally can best be explained by watching tourists in a foreign country. Initially, tourists eagerly attempt to look up words and phrases in a dictionary. Eventually, however, many tourists revert to nonverbal symbols to find food, restrooms, and motels.

By permission of King Features Syndicate Division.

Hemispheric versus nonhemispheric processing. A final characteristic involves the neurophysiological approach to nonverbal communication (Andersen, Garrison, and Andersen, 1979). This approach explains how most nonverbal stimuli such as spatial, pictorial, and gestalt tasks are processed in the right hemisphere of the brain; conversely, the majority of verbal stimuli or analytical and reasoning tasks are processed in the left hemisphere of the brain. Although neurophysiological research is continuing, the results acknowledge the differences that exist between verbal and nonverbal stimuli processing. It is important to understand the implications involved. Processing differences for verbal and nonverbal messages also suggest differences in the ability to send messages to and receive messages from others. It is possible that some individuals may not use the correct hemisphere at appropriate times and therefore confuse messages.

The foregoing has been a brief discussion of five areas of difference between verbal and nonverbal communication. These differences do not constitute an exclusive list; rather, they are included in this discussion on nonverbal communication to aid you in understanding the potential differences between verbal and nonverbal communication.

Up to this point, we have told you what is and is not nonverbal communication and how nonverbal communication differs from verbal communication. It is not the goal of this text to provide an absolute, rigid definition of nonverbal communication. Rather, we believe it is time to dismiss some of the more scholarly arguments and attempt to provide a feasible, workable definition of nonverbal communication. Based on the preceding discussion, we suggest that nonverbal communication is the process of (an) individual(s) transmitting nonverbal cues that have the potential to stimulate meaning in the mind(s) of (an)other individual(s).

With an understanding of the differences between verbal and nonverbal communication and a working definition of nonverbal communication, the next section examines variables that influence the potential of nonverbal behavior.

Distinctions between Signs and Symbols

Deciding what is and what is not nonverbal communication is a complicated problem. As mentioned earlier, there are distinct differences in the ways nonverbal communication is defined. Some authors (e.g., Dance, 1967) object to the label "nonverbal" to describe many of the variables, events, and behaviors discussed in nonverbal communication texts. Dance's contention is that communication is verbal if it is symbolic. He points out that the *experiences* can be nonverbal but that when they are translated into symbols, they become verbal.

Dance used the terms **sign** and **symbol** to explain his conception of nonverbal communication. Basically, a symbol is something that represents or takes the place of an idea, person, or object. In contrast, a sign is a natural representation of an idea, person, or object (Burgoon and Saine, 1978). The following behaviors would be signs of extreme anxiety: sweaty palms, increased heart rate, and difficulty in breathing. The symbol for this condition would simply be the word "anxiety." In other words, a symbol has a specific assigned meaning, but a sign's meaning is often inferred.

Consider the following examples and try to decide which are signs and which are symbols of nonverbal communication.

1. Susie blinking her eye.
2. Jill clicking her tongue, while her girlfriend fills her in on the latest gossip.
3. Bobby smiling because he received an "A" on his chemistry exam.
4. Jack waving at his friend at a football game.

In the first situation, all you can be sure of is Susie's behavior—blinking her eye. This may not be an example of nonverbal communication because we don't know why she's blinking her eye or if anyone has observed her blinking. However, as you will discover in Chapter 5, blinking also provides information about a person's level of concentration. If a person is observed with this idea in mind, blinking would be a form of nonverbal communication. In addition, had someone interpreted the blink as a wink, then this behavior would have been a form of nonverbal communication.

Jill, on the other hand, is already involved in communicating with her friend. The potential for response to Jill's behavior exists because there is a receiver present. Burgoon and Saine (1978) explain that a potential for response or feedback is a necessary element in determining what is and what is not nonverbal communication. In this example, Jill's friend may interpret the tongue movement as a signal of disgust or contempt at the news.

The third example contains only one individual; however, his motivation for the behavior is explained. We know that Bobby is smiling because he is happy. Bobby could be happy without smiling, but since he may want people to observe his happiness, he is smiling. Although there may not be anyone around to "see" him smile, he is still communicating happiness nonverbally.

The final example discusses two people interacting; therefore, the potential for response exists. In addition, we also know the motivation for Jack's gesture—to gain his friend's attention or to say hello. Consequently, this example is also a type of nonverbal communication.

Variables that Determine the Potential for Nonverbal Communication

Context.   The preceding examples illustrate three variables that help to determine the communicative potential of a nonverbal behavior: **context, potential for a behavioral response,** and **motivation of behavior.** The first of these variables is context. Biting your nails while alone in your bedroom may or may not indicate anxiety. In most cases, you are probably unaware that you are biting your nails and the action may simply be a behavior that has become a habit. However, if your teacher observed you biting your nails during an exam, then the behavior could be interpreted as an expression of nervousness about the test. Although you may bite your nails in either context, the action of biting your nails is interpreted differently in a context that has the potential to communicate to others. Since different situations elicit unique responses, when observing another's nonverbal cues, it is very important that you keep in mind the context of the behaviors.

Potential for a behavioral response.   Whenever the potential for a response exists, behaviors are viewed as a form of nonverbal communication. For example, a seven-year-old boy, Tommy, just bought a triple-dip ice cream cone from a park vendor. Just as he was about to take his first lick he tripped and the three dips fell to the ground. Immediately, tears welled up in his eyes and began to roll down his little cheeks. At first, you may not label this event as a form of nonverbal communication, but it is. In this case several nonverbal messages were transmitted simultaneously. As soon as the ice cream fell to the ground, the potential for a response existed. Intrapersonally, Tommy's crying provided feedback to himself and to others about his emotional state. These nonverbal behaviors also had the potential of causing others to respond. In this case, Tommy's mother saw what happened and bought Tommy more ice cream, but this time in a cup.

Motivation of behavior.   The third variable that influences the potential for nonverbal communication is the motivation of a behavior. Messages can be sent intentionally or unintentionally. In the example above, Tommy sent both intentional and unintentional messages. Intentionally, Tommy may have held three fingers up to reinforce that he wanted three scoops of ice cream. He repeated his oral message nonverbally to make sure the vendor understood what he wanted. On the other hand, Tommy unintentionally dropped the ice cream and unintentionally began to cry. Little Tommy did not want to communicate his clumsiness or his sadness to others.

It is important for you to understand the importance of intentionality in distinguishing and identifying different purposes of nonverbal behavior. McKay's (1974) discussion of goal-directed and non-goal-directed behavior helps to explain degrees of intentionality during nonverbal communication.

McKay presents four dimensions of nonverbal communication. The first is concerned with behaviors that are goal-directed (intentional) and interpreted as goal-directed (intentional). For example, during an introduction two business professionals usually shake hands with each other. This ritual, or greeting, is interpreted by both persons as purposeful because handshaking serves as a polite way of establishing relationships. Intentional messages are exchanged between the two professionals.

Other nonverbal behaviors occur unintentionally but are perceived as intentional. John accidentally bumped into a young woman at a local bar. Immediately, she turned around and said, "Watch where you're going!" The woman thought John had bumped into her purposefully. Likewise, if a person forgets to call to reconfirm an airline reservation, an airline company usually cancels the reservations. The lack of a response causes the booking agent to interpret the message intentionally. At times, previous interactions influence the ways that unintentional messages are interpreted. Sally and Doug had an argument about spending too much money on long-distance calls, so when Doug didn't call for two weeks, Sally thought he was just trying to prove his point. Doug, however, had started dating someone else and did not want to continue calling or dating Sally.

A third form of nonverbal behavior is communicated intentionally but is not interpreted as intentional by the receiver. At times, we attribute incorrect meanings to the nonverbal messages received. A group of girls with negative self-concepts decided to go to the beach during spring vacation. While en route, several carloads of guys passed them, waving and honking. The girls didn't wave back, but each time the group waved, the girls pulled over to see if something was wrong with their car. Later, when they stopped for gas, one of the drivers of the cars that had honked was also getting gas at the same filling station. Concerned about their safety, one of the girls asked the driver if he had seen something wrong with their car. He looked puzzled and said, "We were just saying hello. . . ." In this case, the girls interpreted the guys' message incorrectly. Instead of realizing that the guys were flirting, they thought something was wrong with their car. Nevertheless, an intentional message was sent, but it was perceived in an unintentional way.

Interpreted as goal-directed   Not interpreted as goal-directed

Goal-directed   Nonverbal   Nonverbal
                        communication   communication

Not goal-   Nonverbal   Nonverbal
directed   communication   behavior

Figure 1.1
Intentionality in nonverbal behavior and nonverbal communication.

A fourth nonverbal behavior is communicated unintentionally and is not perceived as intentional. Think of a time when you have caught yourself staring off into space for a few minutes. There was probably no reason for this lapse of concentration. In this context, your gaze was not intentional and would probably not be perceived as intentional by anyone else. Since the behavior was not perceived by anyone else or yourself as intentional, it was not a form of nonverbal communication.

In summary, then, it can be said that there are four dimensions to nonverbal behavior: intentional and perceived as intentional; intentional and not perceived as intentional; not intentional but perceived as intentional; and not intentional and not perceived as intentional. From these four behaviors, you can see that the three behaviors that are intentional or perceived as intentional are considered nonverbal communication.

Functions of Nonverbal Communication

In our working definition of nonverbal communication, we implied at least three functions that nonverbal communication may fulfill— complementing verbal messages, substituting for verbal messages, or accenting verbal messages. In addition to these three major functions of nonverbal communication, which will be discussed at greater length, we will also present some related functions: contradicting verbal messages, repeating verbal messages, and regulating verbal messages. Each of these six functions will be examined separately.

Complementing.   If you hug a child while saying that you are proud of his or her straight A's, the hug serves to complement or add to the meaning of your verbal message. Nonverbal cues such as tone of voice, facial expression, gestures, or distance between people often serve to complement the verbal message and add to, clarify, or reinforce the meaning. The term "complement" indicates that the behavior alone would not communicate the intended message. A complementing nonverbal message changes the meaning of the verbal message by adding additional insights or information. Recently, a new teacher asked his sixth-graders to "sit down and listen" to their daily assignments. After waiting for a moment, he repeated his request. Finally, after only a handful of students responded appropriately, he raised his voice and hit his fist on the desk. At that point, after he had reinforced and clarified his message, the students sat down and looked to their teacher attentively.

Contradicting.   At other times our nonverbal messages contradict our verbal messages. Think of a time when you have had a "forced" or artificial smile on your face. Verbally, when expressing gratitude for an unwanted present you received, you may have forced an expression of happiness. At times it is difficult to manifest consistent verbal and nonverbal behaviors, and contradictions, when perceived by others, create confusion. Others tend to believe your nonverbal messages rather than your verbal messages when there are contradictions.

Repeating.   A nonverbal restatement of the verbal message is known as "repeating." Repetition differs from complementing in that it could stand alone without the verbal message as opposed to enhancing it. Repetition is used in order to emphasize or clarify the verbal message. Think back to the last sporting event you attended. Because of spectator noise you may have found yourself holding up two fingers to tell the hot dog vendor how many you wanted, while at the same time asking for them verbally. You could have screamed to repeat "two, please," but instead you decided to repeat the message nonverbally.

Regulating.   Regulation often serves to coordinate the verbal dialogue between people. It can occur in the form of a head nod (which a speaker might use to indicate to a group member that it is his or her turn to speak) a drop in one's vocal tone to suggest the end of a thought, or a touch of a person's arm to let him or her know you have something to say. The next time you listen to a friend talk, observe how you nod your head as he or she speaks and how you let each other know who should speak next. These nonverbal messages serve to regulate the flow of communication interactions.

Children often use "substitution" cues. The finger pointing at the dog is used in place of a verbal message.

Substituting.   Substitution occurs when a nonverbal message is transmitted in place of a verbal message. For instance, substitution is used when barriers to verbal communication exist in the environment. A noisy school cafeteria might prompt you to wave at a friend instead of screaming to get his or her attention. Substitution is also used for emphasis. Picture yourself in a group of friends when your girlfriend or boyfriend decides to tell the group about your most embarrassing experience! Instead of verbally expressing your objection, you may use a substitute for words by glaring into his or her eyes until your message that you do not want the experience repeated comes through loud and clear.

Accenting.   The primary function of accenting is to emphasize a particular point in a verbal message. Although some accenting might be considered a form of complementing, the distinction lies in the placement of the nonverbal behavior. For instance, a well-skilled public speaker might pause before or after an important point in a speech. The pause would serve to highlight or accent the point that the speaker is about to make. At other times, touch is used to accent or emphasize a point. After a marital argument, Jane's husband expressed his regret and told her he loved her while holding her close and kissing her cheek.

Meaning and Nonverbal Communication

Such popular books as Julius Fast's *Body Language* (1970) have left the impression with many people that nonverbal behaviors and communication have particular undisputable meanings associated with

"B. C." by permission of Johnny Hart and Field Enterprises, Inc.

them. This text will help provide some insight into common "stereotypes" that people have concerning particular nonverbal events, behaviors, and actions. These stereotypes, however, cannot be accepted as categorically true without understanding the "total" situation and interaction. Perhaps the most useful way to approach the meaning of nonverbal communication is through the use of some rather broad "metaphors" suggested by Albert Mehrabian (1981). The following section is developed, with some adaptation, from Mehrabian's discussion of the metaphors in the recent edition of his book, *Silent Messages*.

The approach metaphor.   The **approach metaphor** is concerned with what Mehrabian (1981) refers to as immediate behaviors. In simple terms, the approach metaphor suggests that you approach or locate yourself near something or someone you like and avoid or create distance between yourself and something or someone you dislike. Mehrabian contends that the approach metaphor manifests itself as early as infancy. Children, for example, will reach for or crawl toward bright, colorful objects that they find interesting or attractive. Conversely, children will not seek objects that do not initiate interest in them or that they find aversive. Along these lines, parents attempt to encourage interests in some areas and to discourage interest in others. For example, although children are almost instinctively attracted to candy, parents warn their children to avoid strangers with candy.

The approach metaphor need not be limited entirely to nonverbal behavior; examples of the approach metaphor are clearly found in verbal communication. For example, the use of the adjective "this" as opposed to "that" is a demonstration of the difference between immediate and nonimmediate verbal language. "This" tends to suggest a psychological or physical degree of closeness that is not implied in the adjective "that."

The willingness to approach or be close to someone or something does not occur only in a physical sense. Think about someone you feel close to. Chances are that you think this person is easy to talk to and that you have a good idea of how this person feels about certain issues. This implies a ''mental closeness'' that does not require physical proximity to attain. Watch the behaviors of others sitting on benches in the parks, on public transportation, or in cars. Different messages are communicated when two people sit on opposite ends of a park bench, when a person moves to find an empty seat on a bus, or when a couple sits side by side in a drive-in theater.

There are several specific nonverbal behaviors that result from the approach–avoidance metaphor: You sit closer to someone with whom you feel positive; you are more willing to touch a person whom you approach and you are more willing to be touched by that person; in a conversation with someone you like you tend to communicate in a face-to-face position as opposed to a side-by-side position in which eye contact is more limited.

The arousal–activity metaphor. We live in an environment that is rich in stimuli, an environment that we often take for granted because we have become accustomed to certain stimuli and events, such as neon lights in a large city or the smell of fresh, clean air in the country. However, certain unique, exciting, and outstanding environments or elements within a particular environment may create an emotional reaction in you. As a result of your reaction to a particular environment, you may change or modify your behavior. It is this quality of change that results from the environment that Mehrabian describes as the **arousal–activity metaphor.** In simple terms, you are aroused by your environment and react to that arousal in either a positive or negative manner. For example, you visit a major metropolis. The environment of the city might negatively arouse you, or it might positively excite you. If you are accustomed to a large city and find it to be exciting, you may react negatively to a rural environment when you visit the country. Or think for a moment about the arousal experiences in different types of restaurants. Fast-food establishments with bright colors, hard seats, loud music or no music, and fast service encourage you to eat and run. In contrast, the finer restaurants encourage you to linger and enjoy the cuisine by using secluded seating, dim lighting, comfortable surroundings, soft music, and leisurely but ''professional'' service. People have different reactions to the same environment. For example, a child may feel high levels of arousal at the suggestion of McDonald's and get fidgety and bored during a two- to three-hour meal.

Arousal level, according to Mehrabian, is measured in three areas: the amount of change in your facial and vocal expressions, the rate at which you speak, and the volume of your speech. An example of a highly aroused person is one who is speaking with a great deal of variation in voice (pitch and tone), who is revealing emotions through facial expressions, and who is speaking loudly and rapidly. It is not unusual to see high levels of arousal at football games, pep rallys, rock concerts, and amusement parks.

The power metaphor.   The **power metaphor** is viewed as a dominance-submission dimension of communication. In other words, behaviors that give an individual dominance in a situation will result in that person's being perceived as powerful. When you visualize a powerful person, what image comes to mind? Do you think of a small, tense, watchful individual or someone who is large, relaxed, and confident? It's obvious that power and "bigness" are often associated. As a result of this association, another dimension of power is "fearlessness." Obviously, if you are stronger and larger than the people around you, you have less to fear from them than they have to fear from you. Of course, there are some behaviors that are culturally specific or even situationally specific. For example, powerful people are "allowed" to engage in greater eye-gaze behavior than less powerful people. Think of a time as a child when you were in a staring contest with another child. You did not want to be the first one to blink or look away. Either of these behaviors would have suggested that the other child was more powerful or braver than you. In some contexts, staring is not a sign of power. Staring at someone in a crowded elevator or at someone who is handicapped, for instance, is a sign of rudeness, not of power.

CLASSES OF NONVERBAL COMMUNICATION

Scholars and practitioners have identified and categorized literally hundreds of objects, behaviors, vocal characteristics, and events as forms of nonverbal communication. As we noted previously, many of these nonverbal behaviors may not technically involve intentional communication, but all have the potential to impart meaning to a receiver. The following section will identify the specific classes of nonverbal behavior and communication discussed in this text. Each class discussed relates to a chapter in the text. The description serves not only as a definition of the specific class of nonverbal communication or behavior but also as a preview of the chapters to come.

Body Types, Shapes, and Sizes

Almost everyone wants to be considered attractive. Your attractiveness can be viewed from three different perspectives. The first is how attractive others perceive you to be. The second is how attractive you perceive yourself to be. The third is how attractive you think others think you are. Each of these perceptions of your attractiveness is an important element in the development of your personality. The perception you have of your attractiveness is probably one of the most important variables in your self-concept. Your perceived attractiveness affects not only your personality but also your behavior patterns. When you are confident of your looks, you are more likely to behave in a manner that reflects feelings of confidence.

The image you have of your body is an important dimension of your perception of your attractiveness. A lack of awareness or an inaccurate image of one's body can result in body depersonalization, distortion, and/or the establishment of extreme physical boundaries around yourself. In addition to body awareness, the shape of your body can be related to certain personality characteristics. Your shape probably falls into one of the following categories: **ectomorphic,** a slender and fragile body type; **mesomorphic,** a muscular and firm body type; or **endomorphic,** a heavy and rounded body type.

Many other dimensions of your body influence your attractiveness, such as your hair color, height, and skin color. Depending upon your

Hair—long, short, curly, straight—communicates an important nonverbal message about the wearer.

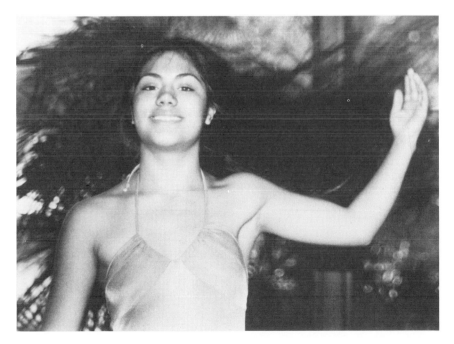

individual physical characteristics, your perception of yourself can vary from contentment to dissatisfaction.

Clothing and Personal Artifacts

The style in which you dress directly influences how others perceive you. In our culture, clothing is no longer primarily associated with the functions of protection and modesty. In today's society, clothing supplies information about yourself. Others' perceptions about how you dress may result in the formation of opinions about your social status, age, and socioeconomic level. Clothing is a powerful form of nonverbal communication that people often use to stereotype others, not only in terms of demographic characteristics but also in terms of inferred personality traits.

What type of jewelry do you wear? Do you smoke a pipe? Are you one of the many men who wear a beard? The artifacts you do or do not adorn yourself with supply an observer with clues about you. Many of the objects you wear transmit both intentional and unintentional messages. A diamond ring on the fourth finger of the left hand usually indicates that a woman is engaged or married; consequently, many single women avoid wearing diamonds on that finger so that they will not be falsely categorized. By the same token, some single women *will* wear an "engagement" or "wedding" ring just so that they will be falsely categorized and thus will be able to avoid "come-ons" from members of the opposite sex. In order to communicate more effectively, it is important to be aware of the messages your clothing and artifacts transmit to others, as well as what messages you receive from the dress of others.

Body Movement and Gestures

The study of **kinesics** (body movement, gestures, and posture) has been a major concern of researchers in psychology, communication, and many other areas of academic endeavor. Your behaviors serve very specific functions in either complementing your verbal messages or substituting for them. Researchers have divided body movements into five categories: emblems, illustrators, regulators, affect displays, and adaptors. These categories of movement will be defined in a later chapter.

Beyond the classification of nonverbal behavior, the study of posture and its relation to immediacy, status, gender differences, locomotion, and emotion is an important concern. For example, are you

Gene Warne

"The problem is your body language, Susie.
You just invite others to walk all over you."

aware of the differences in your posture when you are with a person you like and when you are with a person you don't particularly like? Do you lean toward the person you like, move in closer, and allow him or her to get closer to you? Often our posture reveals our attitudes toward people. Even gender differences reveal important information. Do you smile a great deal, cock your head, and look down with your eyes? If you do, you may be exhibiting submissive nonverbal behaviors. It's important that you realize that your behaviors will often affect the response of others. For example, submissive behaviors may encourage others to treat you as a subordinate.

Facial Expression and
Eye Behavior

Facial expressions have many universal meanings throughout the world. There are, however, certain facial expressions that tend to be culturally specific. It is not easy to manipulate facial expressions, although there are people who have learned the skill of face management and control. Facial management usually is used for one of four reasons: (1) to intensify a true emotion; (2) to deintensify a true emotion; (3) to neutralize a true emotion; or (4) to mask a true emotion. Detection of facial manipulation is difficult to the naked eye, but not impossible. To the trained eye, it is possible to distinguish sincere and natural facial behaviors from manipulated expressions.

Because of its importance to the communication process, eye behavior is studied independently from facial behaviors. Eye behavior can serve in four capacities: (1) to establish and define relationships; (2) to control channels of communication; (3) to display emotion; and (4) to reduce distractions.

Eye behavior is even more difficult to manipulate than facial expressions because much of eye behavior is involuntary. Differences in a person's sex, culture, and personality, as well as the context of the situation, also affect the use of eye movement in the communication process.

Environment

Learning about the communication potential of one's environment enables people to predict what types of behavior and emotions to expect in specific situations. How you perceive your environment influences how long you will remain there, what type of interactions will occur, and whether interaction will occur again in that environment. As mentioned earlier, fast-food restaurants are decorated with semihard seats, bright lights, and plastic decoration—an interior not conducive to lingering conversations. The logic behind this interior design is that the restaurant makes more money when there is a fast turnover of customers. Consequently, they do not want you to stay any longer than is absolutely necessary to complete your meal. Better yet, in many cases they encourage you to order your meal "to go."

The environment can be viewed in two dimensions. The first dimension is that of **macrospace,** or space that is fixed and generally out of the control of the individual. A school building and a town square are both examples of macrospaces. The second dimension of the environment is that of **microspace,** the immediate environment around an individual that he or she can control or change. Examples of microspaces are seating arrangements, table size, lighting, and room color. All of the elements within one's microspace help to determine the attractiveness of the surroundings. The type of interaction that takes place within an environment, the degree of intimacy during the interaction, and the behavior involved in the interaction are all influenced by the perceived attractiveness of that environment. This is illustrated by the elaborate "honeymoon suites" with their heart-shaped bathtubs in the honeymoon haven of the Poconos as contrasted with a traditional motel room with its standard bathtub built for persons under five feet tall.

The importance of studying one's environment was clearly illustrated during the Paris Peace Conference. Before the members of the meeting could address the matter of peace in Vietnam, the size and shape of the table had to be agreed upon by the conference members. The problem was finally solved over an eight-month period while thousands of people were being killed.

Personal Space, Territory, and Crowding

The study of proxemics, or space, is critical. Proxemic messages are communicated through the use and misuse of space. There are two types of space that deserve attention. The first type is called **human territory** and is defined as the continuous association of a person or group with a certain place. Human territory can be divided into four categories: (1) the size of the territory; (2) the importance of the territory to the "owner"; (3) the type of interaction occurring within the territory; and (4) the body territory. Territory categorized by size can range from a "spot," a small territory, to a "nucleus," a territory large enough for several people to occupy. Based on its importance to the owner, territory can be divided into primary and secondary territories and can be further divided into public, temporary, and home territories. Interactional territory has to do with the number and status of people interacting in a place. Finally, body territory is concerned with personal space and one's actual body.

One of the most important aspects in the study of territory is how people react when someone else invades or encroaches on their designated territory. Encroachment usually takes one of three forms: (1) violation of one's designated territory; (2) invasion of one's designated territory; or (3) the contamination of one's designated territory.

In addition to the type of space called human territory, there is a second type of space referred to as **personal space.** Personal space is the expanding or contracting "bubble" that surrounds and travels with an individual. The size of this imaginary bubble varies as a function of the situation, the intimacy of the relationship, and the individual's age, sex, status, and culture.

Another area in the investigation of space is concerned with what happens when there is a lack of space. "Crowding," for instance, is a psychological experience created when a person becomes aware of spatial restrictions. The importance of crowding becomes apparent when people are forced to live "on top of one another," as many must today in our large cities. Crowding can produce certain negative behaviors and may cause people to develop defense mechanisms. The potential dangers involved with overcrowding in cities generally result from these negative reactions.

Touching Behavior

People touch for many different reasons, in many different ways, and in many different places. Research indicates that all human beings need and want some form of tactile stimulation. However, the intensity and the frequency of touch that one is willing to give and accept are often determined, at least in part, by one's culture, sex, age, status, and personality.

One method of studying the effects of touch on humans is to examine touching behavior in animals and how it relates to their growth and development. Research indicates that animals need a certain degree of touch in order to grow and develop in a normal and healthy manner. Not surprisingly, similar findings for human development have also been discovered. Touch serves a variety of functions in society. Five functional categories of touch include: functional–professional; social–polite; friendship–warmth; love–intimacy; and sexual arousal.

Cultures tend to have specific norms concerning the appropriateness of the amount and type of touch. North Americans, for instance, are one of the least touch-oriented cultures in the world. If you have ever traveled to a Latin American country you may have noticed that their willingness to touch and to be touched is perhaps stronger than that with which you may be comfortable. Conversely, Latin Americans tend to find North Americans somewhat aloof because of their reluctance to touch.

The process of touch can transmit various specific messages. A tactile message may communicate an emotion or an interpersonal attitude. For example, you may grab someone with whom you are angry or stroke someone you love. One particular category of physical touch is **body contact/tie signs.** Body contact/tie signs supply information on bonds existing between two people. Examples of body contact/tie signs are a handshake, a kiss, a caress, or an embrace. Each of these touching behaviors indicates a particular bond that exists between the two people engaging in the behavior.

Voice Characteristics and Qualities

Verbal communication will not be effective if your receiver cannot understand what you are saying. A lack of verbal understanding may result from the speaker's mumbling, speaking too softly, or various other negative vocal behaviors. **Paralinguistics,** the study of all cues in oral speech other than the content of the words spoken, addresses these problems as well as other vocal behaviors.

Vocal behaviors have a greater influence on the way you are perceived than you might realize. The *way* you say what you say may be more important than the *content* of the message. The manner in which you use your voice influences the expression of feeling within the message, the receiver's perception of your socioeconomic status, and the receiver's judgment of your personality. Do you speak quickly, slowly, loudly, or softly? Your ability to persuade others is influenced by your vocal behaviors. In addition, **vocalics,** or vocal behaviors, serve to regulate conversations and assist in detecting verbal deception in communication. One of the most effective vocal behaviors is no sound at all—the pause. A pause in a conversation or a speech can be used to emphasize a point or to give the audience a chance to process what has just been said.

Taste and Smell

People in the United States are obsessed with smelling "good." The money Americans spend on products such as perfume, deodorant, toothpaste, and mouthwash reaches billions of dollars annually. Smelling "good," however, is not universally agreed upon. Often a pleasant aroma in one society is offensive in another. For example, there are certain cultures in which people, for religious reasons, bathe infrequently. Consequently, natural body odors in these cultures are accepted and probably not noticed. However, if they were to travel to the "sweet-smelling" United States and continue to bathe on an irregular basis, they might offend others by their odor. Conversely, if you were to travel to their country, covered with six different scents, your body smell might be equally offensive to them.

The study of smell, however, goes beyond the mere pleasantness or unpleasantness of a scent. **Olfactics** has proven to be useful in the field of medicine in helping to diagnose certain medical problems. Moreover, the fact that certain smells are often associated with particular environments aids in describing other environments. For example, when describing your Italian friend's home, you might say it always smells like pasta or spaghetti sauce.

Another dimension of smell is the role it plays in the taste process. Although the tongue is the principal organ involved in the tasting process, the sense of smell also plays a part in helping you taste certain foods. As you are probably aware, when you have a cold, often food does not taste as good as it usually does. Or you may not be able to taste it at all. Part of the reason for your diminished sense of taste is the fact that your nose is clogged and blocking some of the aroma that you traditionally associate with particular foods.

Culture and Time

In today's world, the necessity to be cross-culturally aware is increasing daily. We encounter people from various cultures in all aspects of our lives. As a result of this cultural diversity, we must realize and accept the fact that each culture has its own unique norms regarding proper nonverbal behavior. Acceptance of these various cultures' norms will aid in effective **cross-cultural communication.**

One of the most important cultural differences is the perception and treatment of time. An example of this difference can be found in the attitude toward arrival time throughout the world. In some cultures, arriving "on time" is viewed as impolite rather than proper behavior.

Nonverbal messages differ from culture to culture with regard to clothing, body positioning, use of touch, and use of space.

Two types of time that can be studied universally are our psychological time orientation and our biological time system.

Perception of time is not the only nonverbal behavior about which cultures differ. Certain body movements and facial expressions differ from culture to culture. Examples are to be found in types of greetings, kissing behaviors, and cultural dances.

SUMMARY

This chapter was designed to define and present a general overview of nonverbal communication. Nonverbal communication influences the behaviors of others while affecting the outcomes of communication events. Different approaches to the study of nonverbal communication have caused considerable controversy. One method of understanding nonverbal communication more effectively is through an examination of the differences between verbal and nonverbal communication. Five such distinguishing characteristics include: structure versus nonstructure, linguistic versus nonlinguistic, continuous versus discontinuous, learned versus innate, and hemispheric versus nonhemispheric processing. Based on these distinctions, nonverbal communication is defined as the process of (an) individual(s) transmitting nonverbal cues which have the potential to stimulate meaning in the mind(s) of (an)other individual(s).

Deciphering differences between verbal and nonverbal communication is often difficult. At times it helps to examine differences between signs and symbols. A sign is a natural representation of an idea, person, or object. A symbol, on the other hand, is something that represents or takes the place of an idea, person, or object. Three variables that help to determine the communicative potential of nonverbal behaviors are communication contexts, motivations of behaviors, and the potential for behavioral responses. Along this line, nonverbal behaviors are transmitted either intentionally (goal-directed) or unintentionally (non-goal-directed).

Nonverbal communication functions to complement verbal messages, substitute for verbal messages, accent verbal messages, regulate interactions, repeat verbal messages, or contradict verbal and nonverbal messages. Nonverbal behaviors also give meaning to our message exchanges through three broad metaphors. The approach metaphor is concerned with degrees of liking or disliking of people or things. The arousal–activity metaphor deals with positive and negative responses to aspects of the environment. Finally, the power metaphor refers to the degree of dominance or submission suggested through displays of nonverbal communication.

Theorists and practitioners of nonverbal communication have identified and categorized hundreds of objects, behaviors, vocal characteristics, and events as nonverbal communication. The following chapters of this text preview the major categories of nonverbal communication. These chapters include body types, shapes, and sizes; clothing and personal artifacts; body movement and gestures; facial expression and eye behavior; environment; personal space, territory and crowding; touching behavior; voice characteristics and qualities; taste and smell; and culture and time.

As you can see, the study of nonverbal communication is extremely broad and ranges from such specific and isolated behaviors as yawning to larger categories such as the voice. This text attempts to provide an understanding of the major areas of nonverbal behavior that have communication potential. Since major categories are presented, specific areas such as mime, music, learning, dance, and sign language are touched on only briefly. It is our hope that this text will provide a partial understanding of nonverbal phenomena and the role nonverbal communication plays in your daily life.

REFERENCES

Andersen, P. A., J. P. Garrison, and J. F. Andersen. "Defining Nonverbal Communication: A Neurophysiological Explanation of Nonverbal Information Processing." *Human Communication Research*, 1976, 6, 1.

Birdwhistell, R. L. *Kinesics and Context*. Philadelphia: University of Pennsylvania Press, 1970.

Burgoon, J., and T. Saine. *The Unspoken Dialogue*. Dallas: Houghton-Mifflin, 1978.

Dance, F. E. X., ed. *Human Communication Theory*. New York: Holt, Rinehart & Winston, 1967.

Darwin, C. *The Expression of the Emotions in Man and Animals*. Chicago: The University of Chicago Press, 1965.

Fast, J. *Body Language*. New York: M. Evans, 1970.

Knapp, M. L. *Nonverbal Communication in Human Interaction*, 2nd ed. New York: Holt, Rinehart & Winston, 1978.

McKay, D. M. "Formal Analysis of Communicative Processes" in R. A. Hinde, ed. *Nonverbal Communication*. New York: Cambridge University Press, 1972.

Mehrabian, A. *Silent Messages*, 2nd ed. Belmont, Cal.: Wadsworth, 1982.

Raucher, H. *Summer of '42*. New York: Dell Publishing Company, 1971.

Rosenfeld, L. B., and J. M. Civikly. *With Words Unspoken.* New York: Holt, Rinehart & Winston, 1976.

Ruesch, J., and W. Kees. *Nonverbal Communication: Notes on the Visual Perception of Human Relations.* Berkeley: University of California Press, 1956, 1971.

Weitz, S. *Nonverbal Communication: Readings with Commentary,* 2nd ed. New York: Oxford University Press, 1979.

Wiseman, G., and L. Barker. *Speech—Interpersonal Communication,* 2nd ed. New York: Chandler, 1974.

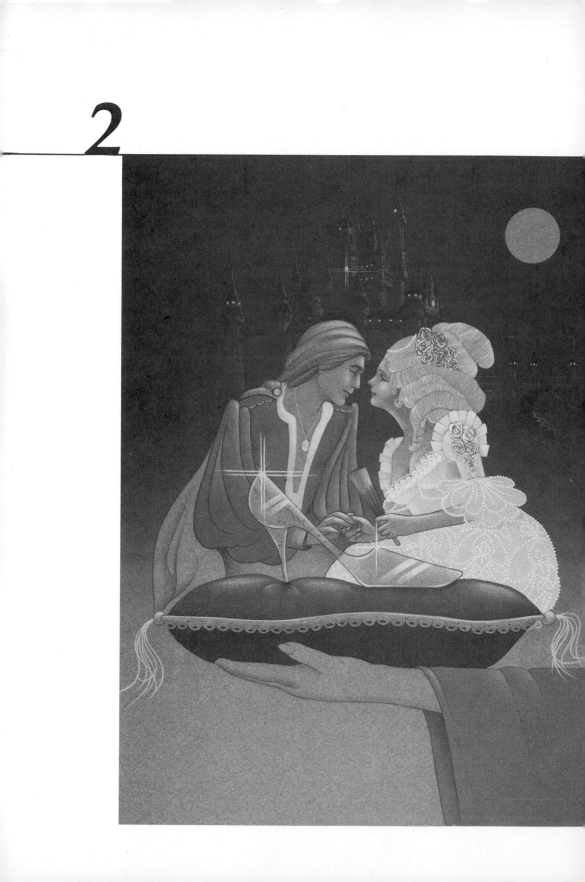

2

BODY TYPES, SHAPES, AND SIZES

I was sitting alone in a compartment of a sleeping car when a violent jolt opened the door of the adjoining washroom and an aged man, wearing a dressing gown and a cap, entered my compartment. I supposed that he had mistaken his direction when leaving the washroom, which was situated between two compartments. I arose to so inform him, when I was stupefied by recognizing that the intruder was myself reflected by the mirror in the washroom door.

SIGMUND FREUD, 1924

"**W**hen evening came, she wished to leave, and the king's son was anxious to go with her, but she escaped from him so quickly that he could not follow her. The king's son had, however, used a strategem: He had caused the whole staircase to be smeared with pitch, and when she ran down, the girl's left slipper remained behind in the sticky substance. The king's son picked it up; it was small, dainty, and golden. The next morning he went with it to his father and said to him, 'No one shall be my wife but she whose foot this golden slipper fits.'

Then the two sisters were glad, for they had pretty feet. The eldest took the shoe into her room and wanted to try it on, and her mother stood by. But she could not get her big toe into it; the shoe was too small for her. Then her mother gave her a knife and said, 'Cut the toe off; when you are queen, you will no more need to go on foot.'

Then the girl cut the toe off, forced the foot into the shoe, swallowed the pain, and went out to the king's son. Then he took her on his horse as his bride and rode away with her. They were, however, obliged to pass a grave and there, on the hazeltree, sat two pigeons who cried:

Turn and peep, turn and peep,
There's blood within the shoe,
The shoe is too small for her,
The true bride waits for you.

The king's son looked at her foot and saw how the blood was flowing from it. He turned his horse round and took the false bride home again. He said that she was not the true one and that the other sister was to put the shoe on. Then this one went into her chamber and got her toe safely into the shoe, but her heel was too large. So her mother gave her a knife and said, 'Cut a bit off your heel; when you are queen you will have no more need to go on foot.'

The maiden cut off a bit of her heel, forced her foot into the shoe, swallowed the pain, and went out to the king's son. He took her on his horse as his bride and rode away with her, but when they passed the hazeltree, two little pigeons sat on it and cried:

Turn and peep, turn and peep,
There's blood within the shoe,
The shoe is too small for her,
The true bride waits for you.

Then he looked down at her foot and saw how the blood was running out of her shoe and how it stained her white stockings.''

The above story, whispered into the ears of little children, is the well-known tale of Cinderella. Chances are that you have not heard this version, even though it is the original Grimm Brothers' fairy tale (Grimm, 1897). Most printed stories of Cinderella have been edited, and some books omit it altogether.

Whether the original or revised version, the story of Cinderella clearly reveals that the ''queen-to-be'' was selected by the smallness and daintiness of her feet. Her small feet represented the ultimate in feminine beauty, so much so that the two stepsisters were willing to mutilate their own feet in order to conform to the prevailing standards of beauty.

History records a long list of both common and uncommon ways in which women and men have suffered for beauty. In times past and in contemporary life, the body has been used as a medium for communicating messages through such channels as smell, hair, bone structure, skin color, and body shape. The following pages will contrast the historical and contemporary use and abuse of the human body and its role in communicating nonverbal messages.

A HISTORICAL PERSPECTIVE

The human body has been twisted, pulled, and pushed into a myriad of shapes for the sake of beauty and in order to be perceived as a visual symbol of group identification. The human body has been distorted by men and women in many cases in order to communicate a particular message to others, as the following examples attest.

The practice of binding the foot at infancy to inhibit growth lasted nearly a thousand years in China. The Chinese Golden Lily Foot, as it is referred to, was based on experience in horticulture, in which certain branches of a plant are sacrificed in order to feed others. It was believed that the dislocated bones in a woman's foot would produce hypertrophy of her sexual parts. The result of the foot binding was the mutilation of muscles and bones, which made walking an excruciating experience. The smallness of a woman's foot was also used to communicate wealth: The shoe of the bride-to-be was placed in the window of her family's home.

Have you ever wondered how Scarlett O'Hara in *Gone with the Wind* managed to have a seventeen-inch waistline? During this period, nature was assisted with the whalebone corset, which was strapped around the waistline of women. The beauty-conscious woman slept in the corset at night in addition to wearing it during the day. (This explains why there were many "swooning" beauties.) Waist constriction of this type (the result was referred to as the wasp waist) was also practiced by men as far back as ancient Greece and in traditional tribes such as the Papuans.

The Mayans of Mexico filed their teeth into points and placed jewels in them. Decorative body scars and tattoos were also common throughout history. In fact, anthropologists claim that no part of the body is safe from tattooing. History records that people have tattooed lips, gums, genitals, even the tip of the tongue. Everything but the eyeball has been tattooed.

Females of central Africa's Saras-Djinges tribe, at the age of four, had their lips stretched with wooden disks. Eventually their lips became as large as fourteen inches in diameter and resembled soup plates. Barely able to talk, these women could consume only liquids.

Reshaping heads has been another popular pastime. During childhood, the Congo's Mangbettu females had their heads tightly bound to produce an elongated shape. The Mayans, on the other hand, tied boards to their children's heads to flatten them. When the powdered wig was popular in France, girls' heads were laced to form ridges upon which the wig could rest. In the Burmese culture, brass or iron rings—each about one inch thick—were placed around girls' necks. With the help of the rings, the young girls' necks reached lengths of up to fourteen inches.

What are people willing to do today in order to be perceived as attractive, beautiful, or handsome? One of the most dramatic techniques for reshaping the body was ushered in during the 1960s: liquid silicone. This treatment was hailed as a salvation to the underendowed woman. Unfortunately, although breasts did grow in size with the injection of the silicone, so did the problems. The silicone began to solidify and to travel through the body, creating lumps in places that are not supposed to have any. Also, the use of plastic surgery to "remake" all parts of the body has skyrocketed during the last decade, especially by men. Body lifts, from the breasts to the derriere, help to fight gravity's downward pull. And although Americans are not binding their feet, they are putting platform heels on them in order to raise themselves anywhere from three to eight inches off the ground. The abnormal arch into which the foot is forced causes a painless type of crippling and may result in foot problems later in life.

Whether in ancient Egypt or contemporary America, the body, in all its various shapes and forms, is used to communicate important messages. The purpose of this chapter is to explore how the body communicates specific messages with regard to attractiveness, body image and appearance, and body shapes and types.

ATTRACTIVENESS

Before a large audience, a researcher was reporting her findings on the size of men's derrieres. Specifically, she claimed that women are most attracted to men with small derrieres. "Gentlemen," she told the male delegates, "you may be sitting on your greatest asset."

To what specific parts of the body are men and women attracted? In a study by Lavrakas (1975), the favorite male physique reported was the "V-look"—a medium-wide trunk or medium-thin lower trunk and thin legs. The most disliked physique was the "pear-shape"—either a thin upper trunk or a wide lower trunk. Lavrakas reported that women who saw themselves as traditionally feminine or conservative in their life-style preferred "muscle men." The more liberated women liked thinner, more linear bodies, while big women were attracted to big men. In summarizing the research findings, Lavrakas reported that the best clue to a woman's favorite male physique was the type of physique of the man who was most important to her at the time of the survey.

With the wealth of research available on attraction, it is important to determine what effect, if any, varying degrees of attractiveness or unattractiveness have in a communication context. Specifically, how does being attractive or unattractive affect interpersonal contacts with others? In searching for these answers, a series of questions must be

Richard Varney

asked. First, what are the characteristics of the "beautiful people?" Do these people actually possess the socially desirable attributes that we ascribe to them? Second, how are attractive persons perceived by others? Third, what effect does being attractive or unattractive have on the individual and on others? Does a negative body concept, for instance, affect the self-concept of an individual? These questions will be explored in the following pages.

Characteristics of Attractive People

Attractive women seem to receive differential treatment when compared with their less attractive counterparts. Attractive women receive higher grades in college courses (Singer and Lamb, 1966), are more successful in changing attitudes of male students (Widgery and Webster, 1969; Mills and Aronson, 1965), are given lighter sentences in court hearings (Sigall, 1974), and have more dates (Berscheid and Walster, 1974). But are attractive people more likable or more socially skilled than individuals of lesser attractiveness? In other words, do attractive individuals actually possess the behavioral characteristics of interacting effectively with others?

In an article entitled, "Good Looking People are Likeable Too," researchers William Goldman and Phillip Lewis (1977) provide some interesting data on the actual characteristics (rather than the perceptions) of attractive individuals. One hundred and twenty students were divided into male–female pairs. Each pair talked for five minutes and was then asked to rate one another on scales for social ease, anxiety, and likability. The three scales were combined for an overall rating, and outside observers rated each student's physical attractiveness. Findings revealed that for both men and women, attractive students were consistently considered more socially skillful and more likable than less attractive ones. The final question, which remains unanswered is "Are attractive people more socially skilled because they are treated more favorably all their lives?"

Consider yourself and the varying degrees of attractiveness that you have experienced throughout your life. Were you an attractive child, an ugly teenager, a college beauty? Most people experience an "ugly" phase in their lives, often during their teenage years. During these various phases of your life, do you remember how people responded to you? If you have had a significant life experience such as having your nose reshaped or losing twenty pounds, chances are that the response to this bodily change was very dramatic. Some people, for example, report that after a dramatic weight loss they are surprised by the fact that people seem to increase eye contact with them and maintain it for longer periods of time.

At a very early age we form a self-concept about being attractive or unattractive. This perception is difficult to change later in life.

Probably the most potent communicative value of "attractiveness" rests with the perception of others. Attractive persons, for instance, are readily stereotyped both in negative and positive ways.

Perceptions of Attractive People

Attractive and successful male movie stars such as Paul Newman, Robert Redford, Burt Reynolds, and Ryan O'Neal report facing a crisis in their careers resulting from the perceptions others had of their attractiveness. As one star said, "Even if a handsome man doesn't try to get by on looks alone, people may assume he's lazy—or nothing more than a gorgeous face." Alain Delon, the quintessential French lover, bitterly observed, "For years I've fought to make people stop believing I am just a pretty boy with a beautiful face."

Attractive persons, according to researchers Berscheid and Walster (1972), are rated higher on a wide range of socially desirable evaluations such as success, personality, popularity, sociability, sexuality, persuasiveness, and often happiness. Attractive women, the authors report, are less likely to be objects of aggressive acts and are more likely to be helped. In a follow-up study, Dion, Berscheid, and Walster (1972) reported that students predicted beautiful people would have more fulfilling lives, happier marriages, and more prestigious occupations. In all, the students in the sample viewed beauty as a guarantee of life-long happiness.

The perception of mismatched couples (i.e., an attractive partner and an unattractive partner) has been of interest to researchers Bar-Tal and Saxe (1976). They report that evaluations of males may change dramatically if they are married to someone who is very different in physical attractiveness. Among other things, unattractive men with attractive women were perceived as making more money, as being more successful in their occupations, and as being more intelligent than attractive men with attractive partners. It seems reasonable that judges assumed that an unattractive man had to have something special to offer for an attractive woman to marry him. In contrast, however, the ratings of an unattractive woman with a handsome man did not increase significantly. This research suggests that people perceive the unattractive partner as attempting to balance the scales on the financial or emotional side. It is somewhat as the advertising slogan claims: ''Avis tries harder.''

In the July 1972 issue of *Psychology Today*, readers were offered the opportunity to express their thoughts and feelings about their bodies. The response was overwhelming, with more than 62,000 readers returning the 109-item questionnaire. Some of the more interesting findings were revealed in comments that people wrote on the questionnaire. For example, most people perceived attractive individuals to have greater social desirability. One reader confessed: ''I discriminate against beautiful people, probably out of jealousy, and tend to label them shallow and egotistical'' (Berscheid and Walster, 1972).

The Effects on Behavior

Is a young accountant's corporate career potential reduced because he looks like a ninety-seven-pound weakling who gets sand kicked in his face? Does a secretary with good office skills have trouble getting a job because her face is too chubby? Does the fresh-faced college girl land the receptionist's job over the forty-five-year-old woman with sagging eyes? Do parents give less attention and affection to children with big

"Sorry, sir! But one mile over or a
thousand, it's all the same to me!!"

"Now, now, miss! There's no need for tears.
I'm sure a simple little reminder that it's 25
through here and not 55 should suffice."

Gene Warne

ears or crooked teeth? How are people who are not physically attractive
affected? Do they develop poor self-images, and do these self-images
affect their dating habits, marital plans, or career goals? Researchers
continue to conduct studies about how attractiveness affects interpersonal relationships and the development of self-esteem. Their findings

indicate that the degree of attractiveness of an individual does affect (1) persuasive ability, (2) courtship and marriage choices, and (3) interaction behavior.

Persuasion and manipulation. "Society is biased against uglies," says researcher Heckenmueller, "and somehow attractive people tend to be more persuasive or wield more influence than plain people" (1972). A few years earlier, Mills and Aronson (1965) conducted a study based on this hypothesis. They had one woman made up to look both attractive and unattractive. In the unattractive guise, she wore loose-fitting clothing, her hair was messy, make-up was conspicuously absent, a trace of a mustache was etched on her upper lip, and her complexion was oily and unwholesome looking. Not surprisingly, independent observers rated her as less persuasive than when she appeared "attractive."

The relationship between physical attractiveness of females and obtaining higher grades from college professors was investigated by Singer (1964). Forty faculty members rated 192 pictures of freshman women five times. Ratings were then compared with grade-point averages and birth order. A positive relationship between higher grade-point average and being first-born, attractive, and female was revealed. In explanation of these findings, Singer posited that first-borns engage in more exhibiting behavior and therefore professors would remember them and give them the benefit of the doubt on grades.

Does the attractiveness of an individual affect our system of justice? Specifically, do attractive defendants receive lighter sentences? Some researchers answer "yes" and report that unattractive defendants are more likely to receive longer sentences. In a study using simulated jurors, a photograph and summary sheet of facts was given to each juror. They were then asked to determine the guilt or innocence of a female defendant in a college cheating case. Although evaluations of the male jurors were influenced by the physical attractiveness of the fictitious female, the effect on female jurors was not as pronounced. Researcher Efran (1974) reported that the "physically attractive defendants were judged with less certainty and given less severe recommended punishments."

Consider how the "good guys" and the "bad guys" are depicted on television. They are markedly different in terms of attractiveness. The bad guys always seem to have obvious facial scars and are clad in dark clothing. The good guys, our heroes, are usually clean-shaven and good-looking, and they wear colors other than black. Most horror films depict the ominous creature, human or animal, as an "ugly" entity. It may be that we subconsciously label an attractive person as "good" and an unattractive person as "bad." Attractiveness, in and out of the courtroom, affects the degree to which an individual can persuade or manipulate others.

Courtship and marriage choices. Is physical attractiveness important in courtship and marriage? Current findings lean toward an affirmative response; physical attractiveness *is* an important factor. In testing this statement at a dance attended by couples matched by a computer, Walster, Aronson, Abrahams, and Rohmann (1966) found that physical attractiveness was the most important determinant of how much a date would be liked by his or her partner. In a replication of this study, Brislin and Lewis (1968), studied fifty-eight unacquainted men and women. The researchers found a strong correlation between the "desire to date again" and "physical attractiveness." Each subject was also asked whether he or she would like to date anyone else at the dance. Thirteen people were named by the subjects and all had previously, and independently, been rated as very attractive.

Attractiveness also affects marriage decisions, as indicated in an early study conducted by Baber (1939). Students were asked if they would marry a person who ranked low in such qualities as economic status, good looks, disposition, family religion, morals, health, education, intelligence, or age. Although men rejected most frequently women who were deficient in good looks, disposition, morals, and health, women did not seem to worry as much about marrying a man who lacked "good looks." Another interesting difference between men and women on this issue was revealed in a study conducted by Sigh (1964) in India. The researcher reported that men desired wives who were more physically beautiful than themselves. Women, however, wanted husbands who were equal to them in physical beauty.

In a classroom experiment that demonstrated how attractiveness affects courtship behavior, fifteen students volunteered to be blindfolded for a period of twenty-four hours. The students were blindfolded in separate rooms so they did not have the opportunity to see the participants, but they could talk to one another. The sighted observers noticed some interesting "pairing-offs" that took place. One very conservative young woman, who had previously remarked that she detested men with long hair, was talking for two hours to one of the "long-hairs" and had, in fact, made a date with him for the following night. At the conclusion of the twenty-four hours, the participants sat in a circle and removed their blindfolds. The room went silent, and they looked at one another in a fixed state of shock. One man later wrote, "When I was blindfolded, I thought that every woman I talked to was beautiful. Then when I had my eyes back, Barb, who I thought was

The blindfolded participants quickly learn how to use other channels of communication to replace the absence of sight. They begin to rely on touch and scent to determine information about another person.

tall, lean, and sensual, turned out to be five feet two, chubby, and less sensual than I perceived her to be." Another participant wrote, "I was bitterly shocked and disappointed to find that I and others judge people so much on their physical appearance. Beauty may only be skin-deep, but you have to have it to attract someone and show them you're beautiful all the way through."*

Attractiveness appears to be a very potent variable, both in court-ship behavior and marriage preferences. Being attractive or unattractive also affects how people behave in various settings toward the attractive or unattractive person.

Interaction behavior. Darren, thirteen years old, decided to lose twenty-five pounds because he was tired of being left out of games and sports. He was called names and it was especially difficult for him to make new friends. Being unattractive at any age changes the way people perceive you and, ultimately, the way they treat you, as Darren found out. Schools provide the nesting ground for the differential treat-ment of attractive and unattractive children. An unattractive child is

---

* Malandro and Barker (1972–1976) recorded personal feedback from students who par-ticipated in the blindfold experiments. These records are unpublished.

seen as a chronic problem, for example, while the same misbehavior by an attractive child is dismissed as only a temporary problem.

According to Algozzine (1976), teachers interact less frequently and less positively with the unattractive elementary school child. Peers also react unfavorably to the unattractive child. With the unattractive individual, the nonverbal responses include behaviors of avoidance (e.g., reduced eye contact, greater distance from the person) as well as the verbal response of singling out the "misfit" through namecalling or other forms of ridicule.

The attractive individual usually receives an approach response that involves nonverbal signs of interest. A recent study was conducted to determine if males exhibit different kinds of kinesic behaviors when they interact with attractive females. A subject and a female confederate (previously rated as "attractive") were told that the study was on first impressions. Findings showed that males with a low self-concept looked more at the attractive females, while males with high self-concepts looked more at both the attractive and unattractive female confederates (Fugita, Agle, Newman, and Walfish, 1977). (The findings of this study replicated a 1975 experiment conducted by Kleck and Rubenstein.)

Another interesting phenomenon involving attractiveness is the double standard of aging as it applies to men and women. Susan Sontag explains that according to social convention, aging progressively enhances a man but progressively destroys a woman. A woman is never totally accepted as she is. Her face is a "canvas upon which she paints a revised, corrected portrait of herself." Conversely, men need only have a clean face. Advertising capitalizes on the plight of women, as in the Oil of Olay ad that asks, "Is it a little scary competing with all those fresh-faced young girls out of college?" Probably thousands of middle-aged women have responded with a resounding "yes!"

The quest for attractiveness has been a theme of both historical and contemporary cultures. In Elizabethan England, hair was dyed red or saffron as a compliment to the Queen. Beauties swallowed a combination of gravel, tallow, and ashes in an effort to make their skin pale. In medieval England, elaborate headdresses required plucking the hair on the forehead and neck. Women used a mirror to aid them and did their plucking in public, an activity considered much less shocking than applying make-up ("Long-Ago Faces," *Redbook's Be Beautiful*, 1978).

Since the stakes for being attractive are so high, it is understandable why people are willing to do just about anything to reap the benefits. After all, being attractive affects not only the way people perceive you but the way they respond to you. Whether it is in the courtroom, classroom, or bedroom, being attractive seems to have definite advantages. In addition, the attractiveness of an individual communicates a message and receives a somewhat predictable response with regard to persuasive ability, dating and marriage decisions, and interaction behaviors. Some people have escaped the tyranny of "wishing" they were more attractive, while others admit they never will, as the following woman self-discloses:

> I am nearly thirty years old, a success in a field few women enter, a good speaker, conversationalist, and clown—I am happily married and feel valued by my family, but I'd chuck it all if some mephistophelean character offered me the option of the kind of long-legged, aquiline, tawny beauty praised in myth and toothpaste ads (Berscheid, Walster, and Bohrnstedt, 1973, p. 131).

BODY IMAGE AND APPEARANCE

To most people, the body is unknown and alien. As Tennessee Williams observed in *Orpheus Descending,* all of us are sentenced to solitary confinement within our own bodies. Throughout our lives we experience varying degrees of awareness and satisfaction with our bodies. The awareness and body satisfaction experienced not only affects our communication behavior with others but also our self-concept. In exploring the communicative value of the body, the areas of (1) **body awareness,** (2) **body satisfaction,** and (3) **body messages** will be explored.

Body Awareness

When was the last time you saw yourself unexpectedly in a mirror, photograph, or on film? Did you immediately recognize yourself? Or, for a moment, did you feel as if you were looking at an unknown entity? This experience of nonrecognition underscores the fact that most people simply do not know their own bodies. As a result, many people experience (1) **body distortion,** (2) **body depersonalization,** and (3) **body boundaries.**

Body distortion.   In an investigation by Traub and Orbach (1964), subjects were put in front of a special mirror that had been cleverly designed to distort the image systematically. When they were shown how to manipulate the controls for the mirror, the subjects experienced great difficulty in converting the distorted reflection back to the true image. This suggests that people have trouble "remembering" what they in fact look like. In another experiment conducted by Wolff in 1943, subjects had difficulty in identifying pictures of their own hands and pro-

Do you see yourself as you really are?

Gene Warne

files when they did not expect to be confronted by them. Look at your hands. Could you recognize them in a series of one hundred photographs? You might be able to do so if someone told you that there was a picture of your hands among the photographs. But if you were not prewarned, chances are you would not recognize your own hands.

People also experience difficulty in visualizing accurately the size of certain parts of their body. They are especially likely to overestimate head dimensions; the head feels larger than it really is (Warner, 1960). British behaviorist Andrew Szmedla claims that body distortion may be revealed in the problems an individual experiences when driving. "If you are among those otherwise eminently successful people who have inordinate difficulty parallel parking," speculates Szmedla, "the reason is that you don't honestly know how large your behind is. You have only a partially developed picture of your own body." Szmedla contends that people who are not sure how broad they are will tend to try driving their automobiles into spaces that are too narrow (Neen, 1976).

When provided with the opportunity to closely examine our bodies, we do so through a complex set of selective filters, seeing what it is we want to see. A man with a potbelly may instead focus on his broad shoulders, while a woman with a large nose may see only her eyes. Not knowing your body or not being aware of your body may be traced, in part, to the fact that body curiosity is socially discouraged. A male who spends a great deal of time in front of a mirror is often ridiculed, while the same behavior for a female is more readily accepted. Yet for both males and females, a careful study of the front and back of the body is reserved for special groups of people such as artists and doctors. Since body curiosity is socially discouraged, it is understandable that both men and women suffer from a lack of knowledge about their own bodies.

It is interesting to note that people considered ''mentally ill'' tend to exhibit more body curiosity than normal individuals. Rosenzweig and Shakow (1973) observed how schizophrenic patients acted when they were alone in a room with a mirror. From a concealed position, the researchers watched the patients as they stood directly in front of the mirror and stared with continued fascination at their own body images. As if testing how their behavior would look in the mirror image, the patients made faces for an hour in front of the mirrors. There are many different interpretations of this mirror behavior, but one perspective is that it represents curiosity about something that has for a long time been mysterious—the human body. Lack of body awareness often results in body depersonalization—a sense of strangeness concerning one's own body.

Body depersonalization.   Body depersonalization occurs when a person feels that he or she is surrendering his or her body to another person(s). In some cases, it may be the fear of this surrender that keeps people from seeking medical or dental help. The average person, even after recognizing the need for medical help, will often delay and put off indefinitely setting up an appointment. This avoidance phenomenon occurs even with physicians and other well-educated persons who have technical knowledge and know that they should not delay. When people finally decide to submit their bodies to medical examination, they will then be probed and will essentially surrender the anatomy of their bodies. During a prolonged stay in the hospital, one's body actually becomes "public property": It belongs to the hospital establishment. This feeling of body depersonalization has been reported in other institutions such as prisons or the military (Fisher, 1973).

How does body depersonalization affect our behavior? The most dramatic effect occurs in our attempt to avoid body depersonalization. Through a variety of strategies such as eating spicy foods, smoking, dancing, exercising, engaging in sports, suntanning, and resorting to plastic surgery, we try to experience body sensations. Consider your level of physical activity. If you are a student, an avid television watcher, and/or office professional, your body sits for hours, rarely moving, and becomes a passive and alien object. The absence of physical stimulation and activity over a period of time may result in an increasing depersonalization of the body. Body security and the recognition of the physical boundaries of the body constitute another important area of body awareness.

Body boundaries.   John Lilly (1972), a psychiatrist and well-known author, has experimented with the boundaries of the body in an isolation tank. Floating in complete darkness in highly salted water, which was the same temperature as his body, Lilly discovered that after awhile he could not distinguish where his body left off and the water began.

Boundaries, in general, are extremely important to people. We spend great amounts of money and energy in erecting defensive boundaries such as forts, fences, and shelters. We build **body armor** in the form of clothing and use olfactory screens such as perfume or cologne. Military and police uniforms are similarly used with the addition of chest decorations, leather gloves, boots, hats, and helmets. Kernaleguen (1968) found that college women who are most insecure about their **body boundaries** are likely to take the lead in wearing the newest clothing fashions in order to reinforce the boundaries by making them more visually vivid through the use of attention-getting clothing.

The car we drive is another example of a body boundary. When we get behind the wheel of a car, our body image actually expands to the "skin" of the car. We become the car, and the car becomes our new boundary. Seatbelts provide an excellent example. Despite the fact that statistics prove we have a much better chance of surviving an accident unscathed if we are wearing seatbelts, many people still refuse to fasten their seatbelts. Seatbelts may conflict with the driver's image of himself/herself. Neen (1976) speculates:

> You get in your Wildcat or Cougar; your body image expands. You feel speedy and omnipotent and then all of a sudden there's that seatbelt tugging at you, rubbing you around the waist, reminding you of your real and natural boundaries. The easiest way to deal with the conflict is by simply not buckling up. (pp. 94–95)

Body security, or the lack of it, may be reflected in various forms of body armor. Clothing, as already mentioned, is one form of body armor. A second type is the use of the body itself, such as crossing the arms in front of the chest. Sometimes these behaviors are used as a means of creating boundaries, and, as a result, body security.

The following section explores how body distortion, body depersonalization, and body boundaries relate to the degree of satisfaction
people have with their bodies.

Body Satisfaction

Are you satisfied with your body? If you answer "yes," then you share
the feelings of the majority of the sample of 2000 respondents who
answered a *Psychology Today* questionnaire. Most of the respondents
were satisfied with their overall appearance, but there were specific
aspects of their bodies that caused greater concern than others.
Women, according to questionnaire results, are less satisfied with their
bodies than are men (Berscheid, Walster, and Bohrnstedt, 1973).

The image you have of your body is believed to influence your self-
concept. Body cathexis, an individual's feeling of **body satisfaction** or
dissatisfaction with parts or processes of the body, plays a major role in
the development of self-concept (Richards and Hawthorne, 1971).

Body concept.   The term **body concept** refers to your perception of the
attractiveness and the abilities of your body, which has developed
through (1) your interactions with others, (2) your role in a specific
cultural and social environment, and (3) your personal experiences.
There is evidence to suggest that your body concept is related to your
self-concept (the feelings that you have about your social and psychological self). In the *Psychology Today* questionnaire on body image, the
researchers found that only eleven percent of the respondents with a
below-average body image had an above-average level of self-esteem.
This suggests a relationship between one's feelings about one's body
and one's feelings about oneself as a person.

An effect of the parental body attitude on children's body concept
was reported by Arnaud (1955). He found that children raised in a family in which one of the parents had some serious body defect were
unusually anxious about their own bodies (Arnaud, 1955). Whether
you like your body or not may also be related to whether or not your
parents like your body. According to investigators Jourard and Secord
(1955), a poor body concept may in part be the result of negative feedback received from parents who considered their child's body to be
unattractive.

Berscheid, Walster, and Bohrnstedt reported that an overwhelming
majority of respondents who had a below-average body image were frequently teased as children by their peers and parents about their appearance. Said one respondent: "My mother had a few pet names for
me such as 'prune face' and 'garbage disposal.' These comments had
more of an influence on me than anything my peers had to say."

Researchers Jourard and Secord (1955) reported that males were most satisfied when they were somewhat larger in body size than normal. Females, on the other hand, were satisfied when their bodies were smaller than normal and when their busts were larger than average. Berscheid, Walster, and Bohrnstedt conclude: "A woman's self-esteem relates to her feeling pretty and slim; a man's self-esteem relates to being handsome and having a muscular chest" (1973).

Feelings of inadequacies and a below-average body concept affect one's self-concept and ultimately one's behavior. Another area of concern is the structure of the body and what it communicates about the person.

Body structure. Have you ever wanted to cry but held it in because other people were present? The process of "holding in" an emotion is not just a figurative expression; it is a reality. We tense our muscles, for example, in an effort to stop or hold in a particular emotion. If this tensing becomes habitual, then muscle patterns become fixed and, in turn, sustain an attitude. In other words, your mind shapes your body, and your body reshapes your mind (Gross, 1976).

Psychoanalyst Alexander Lowen, in studying depression and the body, points out the connection between **body structure** and the depressed state. "The degree of depression," explains Lowen, "is a measure of how much the person has lost his self-awareness as a bodily person. When the body dies, the person dies." When a person feels "alive" the body is also "alive." Lowen (1967) explains this in more detail:

> If the body is relatively unalive, a person's impressions and responses are diminished. The more alive the body is, the more vividly does he perceive reality and the more actively does he respond to it. We have all experienced the fact that when we feel particularly good and alive, we perceive the world more sharply. In states of depression, the world appears colorless. (p. 5)

"The body never lies," claim Kurtz and Presetera (1970), authors of *The Body Reveals.* Healthy persons have a natural flow of expression. For example, in feeling sadness we usually exhibit a trembling jaw, tears, or even sobbing. To block this emotion we would tense the jaw, chest, diaphragm, stomach, and some muscles of the face and throat. This blocking or holding action halts the emotion and sets the muscles in the body. Could it be that a person whose shoulders are slumped forward is carrying the weight of the world? Or that the person with a sunken chest feels as if he or she has no energy left for life? Analyzing the body as a communicative message about a person's psychological and emotional world is the concern of many therapeutic approaches.

The manipulation of the body to relieve suffering is the concern of osteopaths and chiropractors. Gestalt therapy and psychodrama focus on the reality of body statements, although they do not involve actual physical work on the body. There are specific body-oriented approaches that involve physically manipulating the body so as to release muscle rigidity and areas of holding and tension. One such approach is structural integration, referred to as rolfing, and developed by Ida Rolf. Both Reichian therapy and bioenergetics are also grounded in psychoanalytic theory and were pioneered by Wilhelm Reich and Alexander Lowen. Judith Aston, in collaboration with Dr. Rolf, has developed an approach called "patterning" along the same theoretical perspective as rolfing. At the heart of each of these therapeutic approaches is the concept that the body is always communicating messages about the individual.

BODY MESSAGES

Attractiveness, body awareness, and body satisfaction communicate important information about an individual. Other messages of the body are communicated through body shape, height, weight, nudity, skin color, and hair. Before reading the next section, take the self-description test provided (Cortes and Gatti, 1965). This will give you some information about yourself and about the theory and research in this area. In the following pages, you will have the opportunity to score your test and interpret some of the findings.

Instructions: Circle three (3) words for each of the following statements. If the words do not fit you exactly, select the words that seem to fit most closely the way you are. Select any three words from among the twelve choices offered.*

1. Most of the time I feel:

calm	relaxed	complacent	contented
anxious	confident	reticent	impetuous
cheerful	tense	energetic	self-conscious

2. When I study or work, I seem to be:

efficient	sluggish	precise	placid
enthusiastic	competitive	determined	meticulous
reflective	leisurely	thoughtful	cooperative

---

* "Self-Description Test" from J. B. Cortes and F. M. Gatti, "Physique and Self-Description of Temperament," *Journal of Consulting Psychology*, 1965, Vol. 29, p. 434. Copyright © 1965 by the American Psychological Association. Adapted by permission of the publisher and author.

3. Socially, I am:

outgoing	considerate	argumentative	gentle-tempered
affable	awkward	shy	hot-tempered
tolerant	affected	talkative	soft-tempered

4. I am rather:

active	forgiving	sympathetic	introspective
warm	courageous	serious	cool
domineering	suspicious	soft-hearted	enterprising

5. Other people consider me rather:

generous	optimistic	sensitive	dominant
adventurous	affectionate	kind	detached
withdrawn	reckless	cautious	dependent

Instructions: Circle one (1) word for each of the following statements. If the words do not fit you exactly, select the word that seems to fit most closely the way you are.

6. I consider myself to be rather:

assertive   relaxed   tense

7. I consider myself to be rather:

hot-tempered   cool   warm

8. I consider myself to be rather:

withdrawn   sociable   active

9. I consider myself to be rather:

confident   tactful   kind

10. I consider myself to be rather:

dependent   dominant   detached

11. I consider myself to be rather:

enterprising   affable   anxious

Body Shape

What would you do if you walked into a department store at Christmas time and saw a skinny man in a Santa Claus outfit? Or a very muscular man in Santa Claus clothes wearing tight pants? Chances are you would say, ''That's not Santa Claus; after all, everyone knows that Santa is fat and jolly!'' To most people Santa has an easily identifiable body shape (fat) and a very definite temperament (jolly). His body type would be referred to as endomorphic and his temperament as viscerotonic.

Researchers, philosophers, and writers have for some time suggested that there is a relationship between body type and temperament. In 1925, Ernst Kretschmer, a professor of psychiatry and neurology, made the first known comprehensive effort to record differences in body type. In his book *Physique and Character: An Investigation of the Nature of Constitution and of the Theory of Temperament*, Kretschmer claimed that individuals who share morphological similarities could be classified into three groups. The first group exhibited the asthenic or skinny, bony, and narrow body, the second group the athletic or muscular body, and the third group the pyknic or fat body.

Researchers are not the only group to suggest that there is a relationship between **body shape** and temperament. Shakespeare, with his uncanny insight into human character, revealed his perception of body shape and temperament in his well-known play *Julius Caesar:*

> Caesar: Let me have men about me that are fat;
> Sleek-headed men, such as sleep o'nights.
> Yond Cassius has a lean and hungry look;
> He thinks too much; such men are dangerous.
>
> Anthony: Fear him not, Caesar; he is not dangerous.
> He is a noble Roman and well given.
>
> Caesar: Would he were fatter! . . .

During the 1940s William Sheldon studied body types and temperaments. He suggested that a given body type or shape corresponded to a particular temperament. The following table illustrates the relationships hypothesized.

SHELDON'S SYSTEM

Body type	*Psychological type*
Endomorph (oval-shaped body; heavy, large abdomen)	**Viscerotonic** (slow, sociable, emotional, forgiving, relaxed)
Mesomorph (triangular body shape, muscular, hard, firm, upright body quality)	**Somatotonic** (confident, energetic, dominant, enterprising, hot-tempered)
Ectomorph (fragile physique; flatness of chest; poorly muscled limbs)	**Cerebrotonic** (tense, awkward, meticulous, tactful, detached)

According to Sheldon, if you have an endomorphic physique you probably also have a viscerotonic temperament, and so on down the line. But Sheldon's method of measuring body type has been severely

Endomorph   Mesomorph   Ectomorph

Gene Warne

criticized. First, he committed a major experimental error by rating both the body builds and temperaments of his subjects himself. It was suspected that this subjective approach resulted in experimenter bias and influenced the ratings. Second, there have been reports of mathematical errors in Sheldon's computations. Although this criticism provides a sound basis for not accepting the findings of Sheldon's work as conclusive, the relationship Sheldon was investigating should not be rejected on this basis alone.

Now let's return to the self description test that you filled out earlier. This test has been used in numerous studies concerning the relationship between body types and temperament characteristics. The following description indicates how to score your test. Score your test now and compare it to the discussion of the psychological types.

Below you will find the key for the self-description test. The number "1", "2", or "3" precedes each word. Count the number of words you have selected that have the number "1" in front of them. Follow this procedure for words that have a "2" or a "3" code in front of them. The total number of words you have chosen to describe yourself should add up to twenty-one.

Example: Mike selected the words relaxed, contented, and cheerful to describe himself. Both relaxed and contented are number-one words (i.e., words that are preceded with the number one in the key) while cheerful is a number-two word. So far his score is 2/1/0.

1. (1) calm	(1) relaxed	(1) complacent	(1) contented
(3) anxious	(2) confident	(3) reticent	(2) impetuous
(2) cheerful	(3) tense	(2) energetic	(3) self-conscious
2. (2) efficient	(2) sluggish	(2) precise	(3) placid
(2) enthusiastic	(2) competitive	(2) determined	(3) meticulous
(3) reflective	(1) leisurely	(3) thoughtful	(1) cooperative
3. (2) outgoing	(3) considerate	(2) argumentative	(2) gentle-tempered
(1) affable	(3) awkward	(3) shy	(2) hot-tempered
(1) tolerant	(1) affected	(2) talkative	(1) soft-tempered
4. (2) active	(1) forgiving	(1) sympathetic	(3) introspective
(1) warm	(2) courageous	(3) serious	(3) cool
(2) domineering	(3) suspicious	(1) soft-hearted	(2) enterprising
5. (1) generous	(2) optimistic	(3) sensitive	(2) dominant
(2) adventurous	(1) affectionate	(1) kind	(3) detached
(3) withdrawn	(2) reckless	(3) cautious	(1) dependent

6. (2) assertive	7. (2) hot-tempered	8. (3) withdrawn	9. (2) confident
(1) relaxed	(3) cool	(1) sociable	(1) tactful
(3) tense	(1) warm	(2) active	(3) kind
10. (1) dependent	11. (2) enterprising		
(2) dominant	(1) affable		
(3) detached	(3) anxious		

Your Score

TOTAL	TOTAL	TOTAL	
#1 WORDS	#2 WORDS	#3 WORDS	= 21

Your temperament score is based on the number of adjectives you chose from the endomorphic (#1 words), mesomorphic (#2 words), or ectomorphic (#3 words) category. For example, if you had a score of 4 in the endomorphic category, 12 in the mesomorphic category, and 5 in the ectomorphic category, your temperament score would be 4/12/5. This would suggest, according to Sheldon, that you have a mesomorphic physique and a somatotonic temperament.

Several major questions can be explored in the research on body types and temperaments. First, what are the perceived psychological characteristics of each body type? Second, what are the actual characteristics of each body type? Third, do the actual characteristics correlate with the corresponding psychological type?

Perceived characteristics of body types.   Although there are no conclusive results on the correlation between body type and temperament,
research findings do suggest that there is a correlation between body
type and *perceived* psychological characteristics. Researchers Wells and
Siegel (1961) showed 120 adult subjects silhouette drawings of the **endomorph, mesomorph,** and **ectomorph.** The subjects were asked to rate
the silhouettes on a set of twenty-four bipolar adjective scales such as
dependent–self-reliant, fat–thin, lazy–energetic, and so forth. The
results underscored the perceived correlation between body types and
psychological characteristics. The subjects rated the endomorph as
more old-fashioned, lazier, weaker, more talkative, older, shorter
(silhouettes were the same height), more warm-hearted and sympathetic, more good-natured and agreeable, more dependent on
others, and more trusting of others. They perceived the mesomorph as
stronger, more adventurous, more masculine, more mature, more self-
reliant, younger, and taller. They saw the ectomorph as more am-
bitious, thinner, younger, more suspicious of others, more tense and
nervous, more inclined to be difficult, less masculine, more pessimistic,
and quieter. A study by Strongman and Hart (1968) reports similar findings on the perceptions of body types. A question raised by these
studies is: Do the ''perceived characteristics'' accurately reflect the actual psychological characteristics hypothesized for each body type?

Actual characteristics of body types.   Studies either replicating or partially replicating Sheldon's original ideas have examined body types in
relation to (1) the need for achievement, and (2) prediction of behavior.
Perhaps a different relationship would have been uncovered if the
study had used female subjects. Beller (1977), in her book *Fat and Thin,*
argues that fat women are not only cuddly, jovial, and loving, but sexier, too. Endomorphic women, Beller claims, are more responsive to
erotic stimulation and have greater sexual appetites. In one survey conducted in a Chicago hospital, ''fat women outscored their thin sisters by
a factor of almost two to one'' in terms of excitability.

In comparing one hundred delinquent boys (ages sixteen-and-a-
half to eighteen-and-a-half) who had been convicted in court with one
hundred nondelinquent boys of the same age, Cortes and Gatti (1965)
examined the need for achievement. Each boy looked at pictures of persons in ordinary but ambiguous situations and was asked to write a
story about each picture. The researchers found that the nondelinquent
boys had a significant and positive association between the mesomorphic (muscular) body build and the need for achievement. On the other
hand, ectomorphs demonstrated less need for achievement. In support
of their earlier hypotheses, the researchers found that eighty percent of
the mesomorphs were above average in the need for achievement,

while eighty-one percent of the endomorphs were below average. The delinquent boys had the same associations, but at a lower level of significance.

In a study by Walker (1963), predictions about school children were made solely on the basis of their body types. The school children were reliably classified into three categories of body type. Each child's parents were asked to apply the adjectives they thought best described their child's behaviors. Walker was able to confirm two-thirds of the predictions made about each child's behavior. A sex difference was uncovered in the prediction of behaviors. The behavior of the boys was much more difficult to predict, while there were a substantial number of accurate predictions about girls' behaviors with endomorphic or ectomorphic body builds. These results supported the body-type and temperament correlations. The endomorphic girls were eager to please, even-tempered, friendly, relaxed; they were *not* uncooperative, moody, bashful, suspicious of others, or impudent. Ectomorphic girls, on the other hand, were tense, jealous, unpredictable, moody, suspicious, worried, afraid of failure, and not eager to please; they were well-mannered and orderly; however, they did not love physical comfort.

Although the results of numerous studies indicate that there may be a correlation between body build and temperament, we cannot conclude that one's body causes or determines one's temperament. A possible explanation for the relationship between body types and temperaments may be based on the stereotyped perceptions. People clearly associate body builds with personality traits. Whether these stereotypes are accurate or not, they do exist. As a result, people expect a person with a "muscular" body type to be more dominant. Stereotyping about body builds serves to perpetuate self-fulfilling myths about people. If we perceive someone as a leader and treat that person as such, we tend to make the person a leader. By forcing people to fit our definitions of them based on body builds, we may create the corresponding psychological characteristics in them. In other words, people fulfill the role in which we picture them.

Whether we are talking about the perceived characteristics of body types or the actual correlation between the body type and temperament, one conclusion is inescapable: The shape of the body communicates.

Body Weight

People who are happy with their body weight are most satisfied with their bodies. Of the respondents to the *Psychology Today* questionnaire, almost one-half of the women and one-third of the men were very dissatisfied with their weight (Berscheid, Walster, and Bohrnstedt, 1973b). The great concern that society places on a trim figure is reflected in an article appropriately titled "Plump and Loving It" (1977):

> . . . how many women of ample girth appreciate their own sensuous figures? Very few. Invariably you find them plaintively condemning themselves because they haven't been able to whittle their womanly proportions down to fashion model size two.

Women tend to be especially concerned with body weight, so much that the problems of the compulsive weight-watcher has been diagnosed as a distinct disorder called **anorexia nervosa.** Take the case of Laura, discussed in an article entitled "Diet Slowly Murders College Student" (Driska, 1978). Laura decided she was fat and began to diet. At five feet, two inches, Laura weighed 120 pounds and dwindled down to 107. "Everybody kept telling me how great I looked," Laura said. "But I still felt fat, so I kept dieting and by the end of summer I weighed 90 pounds. I still felt fat and I always wanted to lose just five more pounds" (p. 9). In the case of Laura, as with many others, she was unable to readjust her old body concept of feeling "fat" to the new reality of her trim figure. At 75 pounds Laura was admitted to the hospital and fed intravenously.

Anorexia nervosa, in which the distaste for food and refusal to eat lead to excessive weight loss, can eventually result in death. The problem is most commonly found in adolescent and college-age females, from about ten years old to twenty-five years old. The symptoms, although difficult to define because they vary, include the following.

Starvation, which results in excessive weight loss.

Amenorrhea, or total loss of menstruation.

Eating binges, which result in self-induced vomiting.

Obsession with food, in which the victim will spend hours making elaborate meals but will not eat them.

Hyperactivity, in which the individual feels as if she has unlimited energy.

Continual constipation, which causes the victim to become virtually addicted to laxatives and enemas.

Abnormality of body image and perception, in which the victim thinks she is attractive and has no ability to recognize hunger and fatigue.

Body Height

For some time police departments have had minimum height requirements of five feet, nine inches or five feet, eleven inches, thereby excluding more than half of the country's men and nearly all of its women

from police work. In response to equal-employment-opportunity legis-
lation, lawsuits, and 1973 justice department guidelines that denied
federal money to departments with minimum-height standards, many
departments have eliminated the height requirement. Police departments were put to the test of demonstrating that height is an "oper-
ational necessity for designated job categories."

Wilson (1968) looked at height from the perspective of the perceiver. An individual was introduced to several similar groups of students. Each time the individual was introduced as having a different
status—a student, a lecturer, a doctor, and a full professor. The results
suggest that there is a relationship between height and status—the
higher the ascribed status, the higher the judgments of height.

If taller individuals are perceived to have higher status, are both
men and women dissatisfied with their body height? Berscheid,
Walster, and Bohrnstedt (1973a) hypothesized that most men would
like to be tall and most women would be afraid of being too tall. Contrary to their hypotheses, only thirteen percent of both sexes expressed
discontent with their height, and actual height was not related to body
satisfaction.

Skin Color

The color of one's skin has been of concern for centuries. Guilt com-
plexes stemming from a desire to change one's skin color are not uncommon. Brody (1963) reported tragic cases of young black boys who
had great anxiety stemming from their desire to be white. These
detrimental images relating to skin color underscore the fact that the
color of the skin does communicate.

One of the most common methods sought for changing skin color is
by tanning (or in some cases, burning) the skin. The degree of tanning
has communicated different messages over a period of time. When we
lived in a largely agricultural society, a deep tan indicated long hours of
working in the fields. Even Rhett Butler looked with disgust at the
leathery hands of Scarlett O'Hara. During that time, a lily-white complexion indicated that the individual belonged to the wealthy, leisurely
class of society.

During the 1800s, fashionable women everywhere protected their
delicate complexions with sunbonnets that tied under the chin. The
parasol also came in as a protector from the sun. Originating in the
Orient as a mark of high rank, the parasol was copied by the Greeks
from the Chinese, and the Romans copied from the Greeks. Marie de
Medicis brought the sunshade to France, and soon there were parasols
for the sun and parapluies (umbrellas) for the rain. It was not until
post–World-War-I days that the attitude arose that rich, successful

people were usually slightly suntanned. And since most people wanted to appear successful, the parasol was doomed, and tanned skin came into fashion.

Sunglasses replaced the parasol, but technically, these are named incorrectly since the original use was not to block out the sun but to block out bright movie lights. Sunglasses were not popular until movie stars started to wear them, at which time they became a symbol of Hollywood glamour. Actors wore sunglasses because their eyes hurt from the early movie lights (called klieg lights.) In fact, there was a painful condition known as "klieg eyes," resulting from excessive exposure to klieg lights.

The current popular trend is to obtain a tan despite the medical research that suggests that dangers are involved. Once again, in an attempt to be perceived as "beautiful" and/or "wealthy," people have demonstrated that they are willing to risk many things, including their health, in order to communicate a specific message.

Nudity

What does the human body communicate in its natural and uncovered state? The difference between being "nude" and "naked" is that the term nude refers to acceptable instances of undress. Being naked, on the other hand, is considered somewhat vulgar and usually refers to instances of improper undress. Society accepts nudes in art, but naked men and women are considered shocking. In the rock musical *Hair*, performers were permitted to appear on stage nude. In Los Angeles this meant that performers could assume statuesque poses while undressed but could not dance in that condition. According to this definition, the occasionally popular college pastime of streaking would be referred to as "running naked."

Clothing may not be a biological need, according to some anthropologists. On a voyage around the tip of South America, Charles Darwin observed that a native woman, wearing a loin cloth and suckling a baby, was unaffected by a sleet storm or the sleet clinging to her body. It is also reported that women who tend reindeer herds in northeast Siberia are able to sit around in circles on the ground in subzero weather, threading needles and sewing with bare hands. If clothing is not a biological necessity, then perhaps there is an even stronger case for its use as a communicative tool.

Magazines have used various forms of nudity to communicate messages. For example, there is *Playboy* with its nude female centerfold. In 1972, *Cosmopolitan* launched the counterpart to *Playboy* with the partially nude centerfold of Burt Reynolds. Since that time, *Cosmopolitan* has shied away from using the male centerfolds. *Viva* editor Kathy

Keeth stated that her magazine stopped using male frontal nudity because "women get turned on by personality and not physique."

Hair

The United States Army used a persuasive advertising campaign in late 1971 in which it was claimed, "We care more about what you think than how you cut your hair." Apparently, the slogan was too persuasive because servicemen believed it. The army dropped the slogan since regulations for hair length and sideburns were still in effect.

Research on body and facial hair is limited with regard to the correlation between personality characteristics and hair length and color. More plentiful research is available on (1) the perceptions related to hair and (2) the effect of hair on behavior.

Do blondes have more fun? Although we do not have the answer to this question, the very long blonde hair of the woman in the photograph will certainly serve as a nonverbal medium in attracting attention from others.

Characteristics of individuals.   Do blondes have more fun? Nobody really knows the answer to this question, but one study examined hair color in relation to preferences in sports. In a sample of single men under thirty-five in which eighty-five percent were brunettes, eleven percent were blondes, and four percent were redheads, the researchers reported the following sport preferences. Blonde men correlated with an affinity for aerobic sports such as skiing, iceskating, tennis, and hiking. Redheads were above average in involvement with hunting and target-shooting. The only definite preferences for brunettes were roller-skating, bowling, and backpacking. The researchers summarize their findings:

> Do blonde men have more fun? We weren't particularly serious about this subject initially. What we have learned, however, is that there are distinctions to be made in behavior patterns that are related to basic hair color. If we have any conclusion, it is that differences are inherent to one's roots . . . ethnic, not hair. ("Do Blondes Have More Fun?", 1976)

Although we cannot conclude that hair color is related to specific behavioral or personality preferences, there is evidence to suggest that people "perceive" some differences to exist.

Perceptions of individuals.   Literature is complete with references to the attributes of hair color such as "the red devil," "the golden angel," or "the black temptress." Hair communicates messages through (1) color, (2) length, (3) hairstyle and gestures, and (4) the presence or absence of facial hair.

Hair color.   Blonde hair has been the mark of both the princess and the whore. In ancient Rome there were few natural blondes so the state decided to make blonde hair a badge of sin. The wicked "ladies of the evening" were licensed, taxed, and required by law to wear yellow wigs or to dye their hair blonde as a mark of their profession. Messalina, the third wife of Emperor Claudius, threw a wrench in the works when she began wearing a blonde wig. Soon many other women in Rome, aside from the "ladies of the evening," began wearing blonde wigs. The Roman men were distraught and complained that they no longer could tell a lady from a prostitute by the color of her hair. Many centuries later, the German poet Goethe warned of the fair-haired beauty:

> *Beware of her fair hair for she excels*
> *All women in the magic of her locks;*
> *And when she winds them around a young man's neck,*
> *She will not ever let him free again.*

The "dumb-blonde" image has been another common, but unfortunate, association for women who have blonde hair. Perhaps the "dumb-blonde" image was a spin-off from the frenetic post–World-War-I period when the most frivolous of the flappers were also the most likely to experiment with the new platinum-blonde bleaches. Anita Loos summarized the image of blondes in the title of her 1925 book, *Gentlemen Prefer Blondes, But Gentlemen Marry Brunettes.* From 1925 until now, the perception of blondes has remained fairly consistent. In November 1969, the London Daily Mail quoted a well-known psychologist as saying:

> If a man is serious about a girl he wants her to be natural. Anything artificial does not appeal to a serious thinking man who values quality. Generally speaking, a man prefers a blonde for a mistress and a brunette for a wife. Brunettes have more integrity.

It appears as if blondes have varying international reputations. In Japan, black hair is beautiful. When the Japanese encountered Europeans for the first time, they called them "red devils" because of their light hair. Even today a blonde foreigner may elicit sentiments of pity. The Brothers Grimm (1897), on the other hand, praised the blonde maiden: "Rapunzel was the most beautiful child under the sun . . . Rapunzel had splendid long hair, as fine as spun gold."

Redheads also have communicated various messages throughout the centuries. During the fifteenth century, redheads were sometimes burned at the stake as witches. In the twentieth century, Ira Gershwin offered a different perception of the redhead in his lyrics from *Porgy and Bess:* "A redheaded woman makes a choo-choo jump its track, a redheaded woman, she can make it jump right back."* *Glamour* magazine summarized perceptions associated with hair color in this way: Red is tempestuous, brown is wholesome, black is siren-y, and blondes have more fun.

Hair length.   Credibility may be related to the length of your hair, claim researchers Andersen, Jensen, and King (1972). Subjects in two different classes were asked to rate the credibility of a speaker who wore a different hair style when appearing before each class. For the first group, the confederate had his hair combed so it stood out from his head one-and-a-half inches and appeared quite long. This style was similar to that of many of the students in the class. For the second group, the confederate combed his hair flat so that it appeared short. The findings revealed that the short-haired speaker was rated significantly higher on credibility dimensions of competence and dynamism (Andersen, Jensen, and King, 1972). One possible explana-

---

* Copyright © 1935 by Gershwin Publishing Corp. Copyright renewed, assigned to Chappell & Co., Inc. International copyright secured. All rights reserved. Used by permission.

tion for these findings is that males with long hair are perceived to be less serious and less mature when compared to males with short hair.

What about no hair at all? Yul Brynner and Telly Savalas started a trend when they shaved their heads. A New York psychiatrist claims that a "shaved head makes the whole body phallic." The advice for a man who's getting a little wispy and wants to be a sex object might be to "go for broke," either by shaving off all his hair or getting a thick new crop from a wig or transplant (LaBarre, 1976).

Hairstyle and gestures. You already know that hair talks, but what do hair styles say? *Glamour* magazine (1978) tells its readers that:

> . . . long hair says young, and bouffant says matronly . . . who's straightened up her hair has straightened up the mess that's inside; blonde hair says "gee, I'd like to have more fun," and dark roots says, "Oh, what the hell." ("What Your Hair Says," p. 28)

How many women over thirty do you see with hair that falls past their shoulders? Probably not too many, since women tend to believe the myth that long hair should go short after the traumatic age of thirty is reached, perhaps as a symbolic sign that "youth" is over.

Besides hair styles, there are hair gestures—symbolic movements that are used to communicate a particular message. According to Dr. Waters, letting the hair down, especially in one swoop, may be interpreted as both a symbol of abandonment and a striptease. There are also **preening behaviors** that are generally used in the presence of a person of the opposite sex, such as running your fingers through your hair, playing with your hair, or pushing it out of your eyes. These preening gestures provide an invitation for the other person to do likewise—in other words, to play with your hair. How about curling your hair around your finger or nibbling the ends? According to Dr. Waters, those gestures are a type of security blanket that goes back to when we were "little primates clinging to our mother's fur." Even if you play with your hair habitually, with no intention of communicating anything to anyone, your behavior may be mistaken for a sexual invitation ("What Your Hair Says," 1978).

Facial hair. Since ancient times, male facial and body hair has been a symbol of fertility, virility, strength, and most of all, power. The supposition that "a hairy man is a strong man" has been believed by many people over the ages. Ancient Greeks and Romans had a tradition of offering their hair to the gods, thereby symbolically giving some of their own fertility and strength, while hoping for some in return. Ancient Britons defied Caesar's armies by wearing long, drooping mustaches dyed green and blue. King Clovis, who reigned between 481 and 511, describes how his people chose their kings from the hairiest of their

Beards have represented everything from a distinguished look to the look of a depraved individual. The grooming of the beard, color, and personal appearance of the wearer affect these perceptions.

warriors. A king who lacked courage lost not only his throne but his hair also.

The shaving of both beards and head hair has been used as a means of punishment. One poor Spartan, convicted of cowardice in war, was reputed to have been made to wear half a mustache. Defeated enemies suffered a similar humiliation by having their heads and facial hair shaved.

Beards have communicated many different messages. Over 5000 years ago, fastidious men had their beards dyed, oiled, and scented. They also had them pleated, curled, frizzled, or starched. Persian gentlemen of high rank sometimes had their beards powdered with gold dust or laced with gold thread. This custom was not a mere episode in costume history but endured for fifteen centuries. Beards were also used to designate social class in the Roman army, thus providing information about the chain of command. The ancient Egyptians, on the other hand, considered the beard to be unclean. This may in part explain why the Egyptians perceived the bearded Byzantines as ''savages.''

Many centuries later the New York transit authority apparently agreed in part with this negative perception of the ancient Egyptians. In

1965 they ruled that employees who came in direct contact with the public could not wear a beard. A beard on a subway platform, the transit authority stated, tends to scare children and provoke complaints from mothers.

More recent perceptions of men with facial hair are discussed in a study by Pellegrini (1973), in which photos were taken of eight men with varying amounts of facial hair: (1) fully bearded, (2) only with a goatee, (3) with a mustache, and (4) clean-shaven. One hundred and twenty-eight students reviewed these photos and judged the men at various stages in the process of accumulating facial hair. The results showed that the more hair the men had, the more they were judged to be masculine, mature, good-looking, self-confident, dominant, courageous, liberal, nonconformist, and industrious.

In an earlier study by Freedman (1969), a group of undergraduate students were asked how they felt about beardedness. None of the male students wore a beard. The majority of both men and women used adjectives of youthfulness to describe the clean-shaven men. Women described bearded men as masculine, sophisticated, and mature. This description accounted for fifty-five percent of the adjectives used. Twenty-two percent of the men described bearded men as independent, while another twenty percent described them as extroverted. Additional interviews with women revealed that a beard heightens sexual magnetism by making the man appear more masculine and as a result making the woman feel more feminine toward him. Although people will generally stand closer to beardless men, many bearded men themselves report that they are less tense with clean-shaven male strangers than with bearded ones. Freedman explains the social perception of beards in this way: "Beards may be more appealing to women and perhaps help love to blossom. They give men status in the eyes of other men and may increase social distance between two men."

Freedman also reports on a study by Parker in which students were asked to rate a picture of an elderly, unbearded man and a young, serious-looking, bearded man. The catch was that the same man was used in both pictures, except with a beard "drawn on" in one picture. The younger bearded man was perceived as having superior status with regard to masculinity, maturity, self-confidence, and dominance. In another comparison of a bearded man and a clean-shaven man, both were shown with an elderly women. The clean-shaven man was seen as young and troubled. With the addition of the beard, the man was perceived as being in control of the situation.

Hair and beards are perceived to communicate definite, although varying, messages. There is also evidence to indicate that they also affect the behavior of others.

Effects on behavior. Long-haired, bearded comedian George Carlin started out as a comic with a crew cut, who performed for essentially middle-aged audiences. Why the change, his fans asked? Carlin explained that middle-aged Americans were dead-ended intellectually and emotionally and "too busy dropping steaks on each other, throwing whisky, and trying to impress their boss or client." Carlin grew his hair long and wore a beard in order to have a positive effect on young people.

Long hair and beards, however, do not always have a positive effect on others. A placement officer at Stanford University succinctly stated: "The length of a male's hair is directly proportionate to the job opportunities he can find . . . In other words, the longer the hair, the fewer the jobs."

As for women, long hair may have a negative effect in the workplace. Long hair is sexy hair, unless pulled back or up, and may create prejudices. Water (1978) explains:

> Anything that smacks of sexuality engenders resentment among women, and the men think you're incompetent. Also, you're playing into their prejudices. Men are always afraid that women will try to use their sexuality to get ahead; sexual hair feeds their fears. ("What Your Hair Says").

Hair, according to philosophers, poets, and researchers, affects not only the perception but also the behavior of others.

SUMMARY

The body, in all its various shapes and sizes, communicates powerful messages to others. One of the most dramatic ways in which the body communicates is through the degree of attractiveness. Both men and women have suffered untold pains for the privilege of being perceived as "handsome" or "beautiful." Reshaping the body to fit standards of beauty is recorded in both historical and contemporary fashion.

Available research in the area of attractiveness can be classified into three categories: (1) the personality characteristics of the attractive individual, (2) others' perception of attractive individuals, and (3) the effect of attractiveness on the behavior of others. The research available on the characteristics of attractive individuals is limited, although there is some evidence to suggest that attractive persons are more socially skillful and more likable than less attractive persons.

A great deal of research, however, has been conducted on how others perceive the attractive or unattractive individual. Attractive individuals are rated higher on a wide range of socially desirable evaluations such as success, personality, popularity, sociability, sexuality, persuasiveness, credibility, intelligence, and often happiness. When compared to unattractive individuals, attractive persons are also perceived to have more fulfilling lives, happier marriages, and more prestigious occupations.

Since attractive individuals are perceived to have more socially desirable characteristics, what effect, if any, do these perceptions have on behavior? Research findings reveal that attractiveness has a definite effect on behavior in relation to (1) persuasion and manipulation, (2) courtship and marriage choices, and (3) interaction behavior. Attractiveness correlates with greater persuasiveness in the classroom and in the courtroom. Marriage and courtship decisions are also based, in part, on the attractiveness of the partner. People interact and react differently to an individual based on his/her attractiveness. Teachers, for instance, interact less frequently and less positively with an unattractive student. The perceptions of the attractive individual and the effect of attractiveness on the behavior of others communicate important messages.

Body image and appearance are also potent nonverbal communicators. Body-image research focuses on body awareness and body satisfaction with regard to how these factors affect the development of body-concept and self-concept. The degree of which individuals are aware of their bodies will affect whether they experience body distortion, depersonalization, or insecurity about the actual physical boundaries of the body. Awareness and acceptance of the reality of one's body usually produces a state referred to as body satisfaction. The extent to which you are satisfied with your body may be related to events that occurred earlier in your life, such as being called "four eyes" by peers.

Feelings of inadequacy and body dissatisfaction affect one's self-concept and subsequently, one's communication behavior. Also, many therapeutic approaches are directed toward adjusting the structure of the body to release pent-up emotions. The basis for these therapeutic approaches is that the body is always communicating messages about the psychological and physiological self.

Other messages of the body are communicated by body shape, type, weight, height, skin color, nudity, and body and facial hair. The most abundant research in these areas focuses on the perceptions of body shape, weight, and height. For example, people have very definite ideas about the personality characteristics of a heavy-set person. Perceptions may not, and in many cases do not, correspond with the actual attributes of an individual. The communication process, however, is dramatically affected by these perceptions.

The human body, with or without the adornment of clothing and artifacts, continually communicates nonverbal messages. Although the body serves many other purposes, research indicates that it functions as a major communicator about an individual's personality characteristics, attitudes, and self-concept.

REFERENCES

Algozzine, R. "What Teachers Perceive—Children Receive?" *Communication Quarterly*, 1976, 24, 41–47.

Andersen, P. A., T. A. Jensen, and L. B. King. "The Effects of Homophilious Hair and Dress Styles on Credibility and Comprehension." Paper presented to the International Communication Association, April 1972.

Arnaud, S. H. "Some Psychological Characteristics of Children with Multiple Sclerosis." *Psychosomatic Medicine*, 1955, 46, 130–138.

"Attracting the Opposite Sex." *The Arizona Republic*, September 8, 1977, B-55.

Baber, E. *Marriage and Family.* New York: McGraw-Hill, 1939.

Bar-Tal, D., and L. Saxe. "Perceptions of Similarity and Dissimilarity of Attractive Couples and Individuals." *Journal of Personality and Social Psychology*, 1976, 33, 772–781.

Beller, A. S. "Fat's Where It's At." *Time Magazine*, October 24, 1977, 45.

Berscheid, E., and E. Walster. "Beauty and the Beast." *Psychology Today*, 1972, 5, 42–46, 75.

Bercheid E., and E. Walster. "Physical Attractiveness," in L. Berkowitz (ed.), *Advances in Experimental and Social Psychology*, 1974, 7, 158–215.

Berscheid, E., E. Walster, and G. Bohrnstedt. "Body Image." *Psychology Today*, November 1973, 121.(a)

Berscheid, E., E. Walster, and G. Bohrnstedt. "The Happy American Body: A Survey Report." *Psychology Today*, November 1973, 119, 131. (b)

Brislin, L. W. and S. A. Lewis. "Dating and Physical Attractiveness: Replication." *Psychological Reports*, 1968, 22, 1976.

Brody, E. B. "Color and Identity Conflict in Young Boys." *Psychiatry*, 1963, 26, 188–201.

Cortes, J. B., and F. M. Gatti. "Physique and Self-Description of Temperament." *Journal of Consulting Psychology*, 1965, 29, 434.

Dion, K. "Physical Attractiveness and Evaluations of Children's Transgressions." *Journal of Personality and Social Psychology*, 1972, 24, 207–213.

Dion, K., E. Berscheid, and E. Walster. "What Is Beautiful Is Good." *Journal of Personality and Social Psychology*, 1972, 24, 285–290.

"Do Blondes Have More Fun?" *The OGI Times*, October 1976, 1, No. 3.

Driska, M. B. V. "Diet Slowly Murders College Student." *State Press* (Arizona State University), June 22, 1978, 9.

Efran, M. G. "The Effect of Physical Appearance on the Judgment of Guilt, Interpersonal Attraction and Severity of Recommended Punishment in a Simulated Jury Task." *Journal of Experimental Research in Personality.* 1974, *8,* 45–54.

Executive Research Council. *Personnel Management Week,* January 25, 1971.

"Fat Children Suffer Shyness, Rejection" *The Arizona Republic,* February 22, 1978, Section D-1.

Fisher, S. *Body Consciousness.* Englewood Cliffs, N.J.: Prentice-Hall, Inc., 1973.

Freedman D. G. "The Survival Value of the Beard." *Psychology Today,* 1969, *3,* 36-39.

Freud, S. *Psychoanalytische Studien über Werke der Dichtung und Kunst.* Vienna, 1924. Quoted in S. Fisher. *Body Consciousness.* Englewood Cliffs, N.J.: Prentice-Hall, Inc., 1973.

Fugita, S. S., T. A. Agle, I. Newman, and N. Walfish. Attractiveness, Self-Concept and a Methodological Note about Gaze Behavior." *Personality and Social Psychology Bulletin,* 1977, 3, 240–243.

Goldman, W., and P. Lewis. "Good Looking People are Likeable Too!" *Psychology Today,* July 1977, 27. Also reported in *The Journal of Experimental Social Psychology,* 13, No. 2.

Grimm, J. L. K. *Grimm's Fairy Tales.* London: The Hamlyn Publishing Group Limited, 1961.

Gross, A. "How your Mind Shapes your Body and How your Body Reshapes your Mind." *Mademoiselle,* October 1976, 194–198.

Heckenmueller, R. "Researchers Say Society Biased Against Uglies." *Tullahassee Democrat,* November 19, 1972.

Iliffe, A. M. "A Study of Preferences in Feminine Beauty," *British Journal of Psychology,* 1960, *51,* 267–273.

"In Short, Height Doesn't Matter." *Psychology Today,* April 1976.

Jourard, S. M., and P. T. Secord. "Body Cathexis and Personality." *British Journal of Psychology,* 1955, *46,* 130–138.

Kernaleguen, A. P. "Creativity Level, Perceptual Style and Peer Perception of Attitudes Toward Clothing." Unpublished doctoral dissertation, Utah State University, 1968, cited in S. Fisher. *Body Consciousness.* Englewood Cliffs, N.J.: Prentice-Hall, Inc., 1973.

Kleck, R. E., and C. Rubenstein. "Physical Attractiveness, Perceived Attitude Similarity, and Interpersonal Attraction in an Opposite-Sex Encounter." *Journal of Personality and Social Psychology,* 1975, *31,* 107–114.

Kretschmer, E. *Physique and Character,* 2nd ed. New York: Cooper Square, 1970, pp. 18–35.

Kurtz, R., and H. P. Prestera. *The Body Reveals.* New York: Harper & Row Publishers, Inc., 1970.

LaBarre, H. "Men and Hair." *Cosmopolitan,* August 1976, 181, 2, 144–147, 153.

Lavrakas, P. J. "Female Preferences for Male Physiques." *Journal of Research in Personality*, 1975, *9*, 324–334.

Lilly, J. C. *The Center of the Cyclone.* New York: Julian Press, 1972.

"Long-Ago Faces." *Redbook's Be Beautiful.* Winter 1978, 38.

Lowen, A. *Betrayal of the Body.* New York: Macmillan, 1967, p. 5.

"Men—a New Freedom." *Vogue*, December 1977, 220.

Mills, J., and E. Aronson. "Opinion as a Function of the Communicator's Attractiveness and Desire to Influence." *Journal of Personality and Social Psychology*, 1965, *1*, 73–77.

Neen, J. J. "Auto Man." *Road and Track*, December 1976, 94–95.

"Nine Common and Uncommon Ways Women Have Suffered for Beauty." *Good Housekeeping*, October 1977, 5.

"Plump and Loving It." *Cosmopolitan*, October 1977.

Pellegrini, R. "The Virtues of Hairiness." *Psychology Today*, 1973, *6*, 14.

Richards, E. A., and R. E. Hawthorne. "Values, Body Cathexis, and Clothing of Male University Students." *Journal of Home Economics*, March 1971, *63*, 3, 190–194.

Rosenzweig, S. and D. Shakow. "Mirror Behavior in Schizophrenic and Normal Individuals." *Journal of Nervous and Mental Disease*, 1973, *86*, 166–174.

Rudofsky, B. *The Unfashionable Human Body.* New York: Anchor Press, 1974.

Sheldon, W. H. *The Varieties of Temperament.* New York; Hafner Publishing Co., 1942.

——. *Atlas of Man: A Guide for Somatotyping the Adult Male at All Ages.* New York: Harper and Brothers, 1954.

——. *The Varieties of the Human Physique.* New York: Harper and Brothers, 1940.

Sigall, H. "Psychologist Proves Good Looks Helpful." Associated Press Release, 1974.

Singer, J. E. "The Use of Manipulative Strategies: Machiavellianism and Attractiveness." *Sociometry*, 1964, *27*, 128–151.

Singer, J. E., and P. F. Lamb. "Social Concern, Body Size, and Birth Order." *Journal of Social Psychology*, 1966, *68*, 143–151.

Sigh, B. N. "A Study of Certain Personal Qualities as Preferred by College Students in Their Marital Partners." *Journal of Psychological Researchers*, 1964, *8*, 37–48.

Solender, E. N., and E. Solender. "Minimizing the Effect of the Unattractive Client on the Jury: A Study of the Interaction of Physical Appearance with Assertions and Self-Experience." *Human Rights*, 1976, 5, 201, 214.

Solomon, P. "The Surprising Plight of the Handsome, Handsome Man." *Cosmopolitan*, December 1966, *181*, 6, 230–235.

Sontag, S. "The Double Standard of Aging." *Saturday Review*, September 23, 1972, 29–38.

Strongman, K. T., and C. J. Hart. "Stereotyped Reactions to Body Build." *Psychological Reports,* 1968, *8,* 77–78.

Traub, A. C., and J. Orbach. Psychophysical Studies of Body Image, I, The Adjustable Body-Distorting Mirror." *Archives of General Psychiatry,* 1964, *II,* 53–56.

Walker, R. M. "Body Build and Behavior in Young Children: Body Build and Parents' Ratings." *Child Development,* 1963, *34,* 1–23.

Walster, E. V., V. Aronson, D. Abrahams, and L. Rohmann. "Importance of Physical Attractiveness in Dating Behavior." *Journal of Personality and Social Psychology,* 1966, *4,* 508–516.

Warner, S. "An Experimental and Theoretical Approach to Body Image." 1960. Cited in S. Fisher. *Body Consciousness.* Englewood Cliffs, N.J.: Prentice-Hall, Inc., 1973.

Wells, W., and B. Siegel. "Stereotyped Somatotypes." *Psychological Reports,* 1961, *8,* 77–78.

Widgery, R. N., and B. Webster. "The Effects of Physical Attractiveness upon Perceived Initial Credibility." *Michigan Speech Journal,* 1969, *4,* 9–15.

"What Your Hair Says about You." *Glamour,* February 1978, 27–28.

Wilson, P. R. "Perceptual Distortion of Height as a Function of Ascribed Academic Status." *Journal of Social Psychology,* 1968, *74,* 97–102.

Wolff, W. *The Expression of Personality.* New York: Harper & Row, 1943.

3

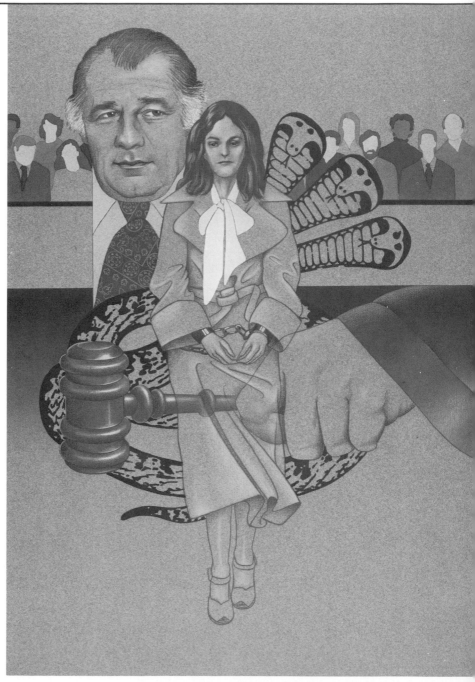

CLOTHING AND PERSONAL ARTIFACTS

In modern civilization there has grown up an immodesty which was lacking in more ancient cultures. We are ashamed of our bodies. Whether the practice of concealing the body is the cause of our uncleanliness of mind, or whether our obscenity is rather the cause of concealment, is a debated question.

DUNLAP KNIGHT

*A*s she entered the courtroom, all eyes locked on her. She was dressed in a coat at least two sizes too large. The collar was grotesquely broad and the sleeves so widely cuffed that they made her manacled hands look small and helpless. Her long hair hung listlessly on her shoulders and appeared deliberately lank. As she moved, her coat parted and one could catch a glimpse of the clothing that literally hung on her body. The neckline of her blouse sagged away from her thin neck, making it appear even thinner. The bow in her blouse was limp and tied low and, as it were, pulled the corners of her mouth down with it. Her skirt, simple and modest, fell slightly below her knees. She appeared to be a frail and vulnerable young woman, perhaps one who had suffered a great deal in the short span of her life.

The above drama did not come from literature. It came from an actual case in a United States courtroom. In this real-life scene, the actress was carefully dressed, and the audience's reaction was carefully calculated to produce the desired response. The producer and director was F. Lee Bailey, one of America's most flamboyant attorneys; the actress, Patty Hearst, was America's alleged kidnapped fugitive. The case of Patty Hearst, the daughter of a wealthy newspaper owner, who traded her position in upper-class society to become a ''bank robber,'' is well known. As Patty's defense attorney, F. Lee Bailey dressed her much in the manner that one would dress a Barbie doll. But in this case, Patty was not dressed for fashion reasons. She was dressed for her life. The clothing worn by Patty Hearst during her long trial was carefully and meticulously selected by her attorney. Bailey knew that Patty's clothing would communicate a message to both the judge and jury. Dressing Patty was to Bailey as legitimate and as important a consideration in her defense as obtaining testimonial evidence from star witnesses.

What specifically did Bailey hope to communicate? The most obvious answer is that he wanted the jury and the judge to *perceive* Patty Hearst as a victim of brainwashing rather than as a bank-robbing radical. Although we can only speculate on what Bailey sought to communicate, it seems clear that definite motives were involved in dressing Patty. But in his choice of costume, Bailey had to be careful. It was common knowledge that his client came from a wealthy family. A coat that was cheap and shabby might be resented by the jury because of the attempt to feign poverty. On the other hand, if the coat were chic, the rich-girl connotation might make the jurors less than sympathetic. The result was that she wore neither an unattractive nor attractive coat. A simple oversized coat that made her appear frail and particularly susceptible was selected.

Moreover, when Patty appeared in the courtroom, she no longer wore the large, dark glasses that she was wearing when apprehended. Perhaps Bailey did not wish to hide the sadness in her eyes. Besides, the large glasses conveyed too much of a radical look. Patty's hair, although groomed, was completely listless, a fact that suggested she was too demoralized by her experience to care about vanity. Upon closer inspection, however, her carefully manicured and polished nails showed some care and some self-involvement. The ill-fitting blouse revealed her thin neck and somehow made it look scrawny. The limp, low-tied bow helped to sweep the lines of her face in a downward direction, causing her to appear melancholy and despondent. The total impression of Patty's appearance was consistent. She never looked particularly feminine or masculine but appeared always neat and always sad.

Most of us are probably aware that if we ever find ourselves on trial in a courtroom, it would be best to *look* a certain way. The guy with shoulder-length hair and a beard, who adamantly insists that he will not cut his hair or shave for anyone, will probably be quick to reverse his decision if he is brought to trial for possession of marijuana. Why? He simply does not want his clothing to communicate what he is verbally denying—that he was not in possession of the drug. If his clothing communicates one message nonverbally and he verbally communicates another, such an inconsistency might turn the jurors against him. And so it is with most of us. Because we believe that others' perceptions of us are to a large extent, based on our personal appearance, particularly the clothing we wear, we are careful to select clothing that conveys the image we wish to project.

The effects of dress on ourselves and others is obviously not limited to the courtroom. Our clothing has a communicative value that permeates all realms of society—the boardroom, conference room, classroom, and bedroom. To explore the communicative value of dress, several questions must be asked. What is the function of clothing in society? How are messages of dress communicated? What are the effects of dress on human behavior? These questions will be discussed in the sections that follow.

FUNCTIONS OF DRESS

"It is impossible to wear clothes without transmitting social signals," claims human behaviorist Desmond Morris (1977). "Every costume tells a story, often a very subtle one, about its wearer" (p. 213). And that includes those people who claim they pay no attention to their clothing with regard to its communicative value. People make quite specific comments about their social roles and, as Morris observes, "their attitudes toward the culture in which they live" (p. 213).

Comfort–protection

According to Morris, clothing serves three functions: **comfort–protection, modesty,** and **cultural display.** Comfort obviously fulfills the utilitarian purpose for wearing clothes. Early human beings evolved in a warm climate, and the body, through its complex physiological processes, regulated its own temperature, thereby making clothing unnecessary. As people began exploring the brutally hot deserts and the icy cold regions of the earth, Morris explains, their bodies proved to be inadequate in adjusting to the changes. At this point the protective function of clothing evolved. Protective clothing, however, created many problems, among which were body odor and disease. Clothing reduced skin ventilation, interfered with removal of sweat from the skin, and provided a perfect haven for small parasites. Fortunately, we know today how to cope with such problems. If human beings needed clothing only to fulfill the comfort and protection function, then there would be little need for costumes, a wide variety of colors and fabrics, or variations in styles. The fact that we do indulge in clothing beyond mere comfort and protection suggests yet another function—modesty.

Modesty

The modesty function of clothing is an attempt to conceal parts of the body. The full frontal exposure of the human body can deny the sexual display only by covering the genital area. "It is not surprising therefore," comments Morris, "to find that the loincloth is culturally the most widespread of all garments. In any social situation demanding costume shedding, it is the last clothing barrier to fall" (p. 215). The one-piece bikini provides a good example, since wearers are willing to forgo the tops but cling, as it were, to the bottoms. Consider your own behavior for a moment. If you were playing strip poker, which article of clothing would you remove last? It would be both comical and absurd to see a group of people playing strip poker with the lower parts of their bodies uncovered and their shirts still on.

History provides us with rich examples of extreme cases of modesty. In the seventeenth century in Armenia, a wife did not remove her veil until she had put her husband to bed and extinguished all lights. Since the wife also rose before her husband, it might be years before he ever caught a glimpse of her. (At this point we will avoid speculation as to whose advantage this was.) But society has deviated from these extremes of modesty by degrees over time. In Hollywood, naked navels were banned before 1930, and it was not until 1960 that naked female nipples appeared on the screen. Even popular magazines with nudes, such as *Playboy,* airbrushed out the pubic hair during the 1960s. The 1970s marked the era of full body exposure in magazines for both males and females.

Cultural Display

The final function of clothing is that of cultural display, as illustrated in the following example. Dagny picks up her date, Mike, for the evening. Dagny is wearing a simple cotton dress and high-heeled shoes, while Mike is dressed in a similar casual fashion in his corduroy pants and long-sleeved cotton shirt. They go to a favorite restaurant to have a relaxing and intimate dinner. There they are greeted by the host, who informs them that they cannot be admitted because Mike is not wearing a necktie. In this case, the necktie serves no other fucntion than that of a cultural badge. It is Mike's admission ticket to the restaurant.

Sometimes the use of clothing as a **cultural badge** is carried to absurd extremes. One of the authors went to the Key Club in New York with three friends. Everyone was dressed casually. One of the men in our group was wearing a short-sleeved suit jacket, and the other man was wearing a sports jacket. Upon entering the club, a big, burly man pulled us aside and explained that long-sleeved jackets were required for men. Rather than take the subway home to change, our friend was given a white jacket. This was fine, except that the sleeves fell six inches past his hands, the shoulders hovered conspicuously over the frame of his body, and the length of the jacket was appropriate only if he wanted to wear it as a dress. This attire, however, was considered acceptable for this "fancy" club, even though it appeared both comical and absurd to wear such ill-fitting clothing.

The use of clothing as a cultural badge can be traced back through history. In earlier centuries, costumes were dictated by law to separate social classes. For example, in the fifteenth century no one under the rank of lord was permitted to wear a tunic that covered the buttocks or to wear shoes with points longer than two inches. If a knight were caught wearing such attire above his station, he would be subject to a fine and/or confiscation of the forbidden articles of clothing. A woman who dressed above her social class in Renaissance Germany might find her neck locked in a heavy wooden collar for punishment. In early New England a woman was forbidden to wear a silk scarf unless her husband was worth at least a thousand dollars. The use of clothing as a cultural badge ranks as clothing's most ancient function, preceding even its protective and modesty roles (Morris, 1977, pp. 216–217).

"I'm sorry, we don't seat anyone without a tie, sir."

Gene Warne

"Is that a table for two, sir?"

Research findings reported by Aiken (1963) suggest that display and decoration are the most important functions of clothing, followed by comfort, interest, conformity, and economy. Concern over clothing for aesthetic purposes was revealed in a study of 500 high school students. Specific uses of clothing were measured by eight Likert scales consisting of eleven statements each. The functions of clothing that were measured were the aesthetic, approval, attention, comfort, dependence, interest, management, and modesty functions. The statements were rated by the subjects on a scale of one to five. Among other findings, the researchers found that high school girls had higher mean scores on each aspect of clothing when compared with high school boys. A possible explanation for this finding is that girls are brought up to place more value on their appearance than boys are. However, aesthetics in dress ranked as the first and most important use of clothing by *both* high school boys and girls. Beyond this point, boys were more concerned with management of clothing than with the remaining uses (Kuehne and Creekmore, 1971).

Sybers and Roach (1962) summarize the current symbolism of clothing as follows:

1. Clothing serves as a symbol of our status.

2. If we fail to dress as expected, we tend to believe that our occupational mobility will be negatively affected.

3. We feel that we have to dress in accordance with our jobs so as to impress other people.

4. We believe that others associate our clothing choices with our socioeconomic status, goals, and satisfactions.

An important function of clothing is that of a cultural display in which the clothing identifies the wearer with a particular group of people.

Our current use of clothing as part of our ceremonial attire suggests that clothes do indeed communicate. The messages clothes communicate about the wearer will be explored next. (Sybers and Roach, pp. 184–187)

COMMUNICATION COMPONENTS OF DRESS

How are messages of dress communicated? The process is not a simple one. To transmit a message about dress involves several components of communication working together. Let's take a look at Linda and Kent and analyze the communication process with regard to Linda's clothing. Linda wants to ask Kent out for Friday night, but she is a little uncertain if he has really noticed her. She decides to buy a new pair of jeans and a halter top. Linda is confident that she can communicate her interest in Kent through her clothes. In order to understand this process, it is important to look at the individual components. Linda is the **source,** the point at which the **message** has originated. Since this chapter is on dress, we will often refer to the source as the wearer. The message in this case is the nonverbal stimulus that serves to evoke meaning in the receiver. Linda's jeans and halter top are the specific nonverbal stimuli, and Kent is the intended **receiver.** The **channel** is the means by which a message is conveyed from the source to the receiver. Linda is engaged in face-to-face interaction with Kent, and the channel is visual. The receiver, Kent, is the person who ultimately acquires the source's message. In many cases we will refer to the receiver as the observer. The process seems pretty direct and simple so far. Obviously, Linda should have no difficulty in getting her message across. Right? Wrong!

Two important components of this process are **encoding** and **decoding.** Since Linda is interested in Kent, she must be careful to encode her message properly. Because of varied experiences and backgrounds, we cannot transmit *meanings* to other people; we can only transmit *messages.* Effective communication depends on proper encoding. If the message that is created does not represent the meaning Linda intends or if it stimulates different meanings in Kent, the exchange will not produce the desired outcome.

The decoding process works in a similar manner. Kent must process the message from Linda and compare it with previous messages and experiences to discover what she means. If Kent has a very different background and different experiences from those of Linda, or if he allows his own biases to enter the decoding process, the exchange will not produce the desired outcome. Since proper encoding and decoding are essential to communication, the transmission of messages becomes a more complicated process.

The final component of a communication system is **feedback.** Generally speaking, feedback tells the source (Linda) how the receiver (Kent) has understood the message. If Kent sees Linda in class and deliberately sits next to her when his usual behavior is to sit alone, Linda has received feedback of Kent's interest in her. An illustration of these communication components can be visualized as follows:

Feedback Loop

Source → Encoding → Message → Channel → Decoding → Receiver
(Wearer: (Clothing) (Visual)   (Observer:
Linda)   Kent)

How does this model apply to the Patty Hearst case? In this instance Patty was the source, the message was the nonverbal stimulus of her clothing, and the receivers were the judge and jury. However, there is another dimension of Patty's communication that must be considered —that of **intentionality.** Did F. Lee Bailey dress Patty in such a way so as to communicate a deliberate message? Do you dress with the deliberate intention of communicating a specific message?

Intentionality and Unintentionality
of Messages

Most nonverbal messages of dress are unintentionally communicated and unintentionally received. Specifically, there are four possibilities with regard to the intentionality of messages.

1. The wearer *intentionally* sends a message that is *intentionally* received.

   For example, a hooker dresses seductively or flashily in order to communicate her profession and services to a potential client. The client looks for these signs in order to identify who is actually a hooker. Imagine the embarrassment of walking up to a person and offering fifty dollars for a session, only to find out that the individual is not in the business.

2. The wearer *unintentionally* sends a message that is *intentionally* received.

   For example, Cheryl is interviewing for a job as vice-president of sales in a large corporation. She is interviewed by a panel of two males and one female. She has deliberately selected her clothing for the meeting, but she has paid little attention to her jewelry. She is wearing a large diamond wedding ring and a watch studded with diamonds. Her interviewers are looking for additional information about her. They presume she is married and in a middle- to upper-income bracket. In this case Cheryl unintentionally communicated a message with her jewelry that was intentionally received by the panel.

3. The wearer *intentionally* sends a message that is *unintentionally* received.

   For example, Dick is teaching at a university for the first time. Because he is so young, people often mistake him for a student. He grows a beard and avoids wearing jeans in an effort to communicate his higher-status position. Other professors and students unconsciously or unintentionally react to this change. They know that something is different, but they cannot specifically identify what it is.

4. The wearer *unintentionally* sends a message that is *unintentionally* received.

   For example, Mike gets dressed for class in his everyday clothing—jeans and a T-shirt. Both the other students in his class and the instructor unconsciously react to his dress. No intentional messages have been sent or received.

Now let's answer the intentionality of messages with respect to Patty Hearst. F. Lee Bailey intentionally wanted to communicate that Patty was not capable of being a bank-robbing radical. Most likely the receivers of this message, the judge and the jury, were unintentionally receiving this message. This process would fit in Box 3 of Fig. 3.1.

The purpose of studying the effects of dress on human communication is to reduce the number of messages in Box 4. Messages that are unintentionally sent and unintentionally received result in communication of which we are unaware. Some popular writers such as John T. Molloy suggest that the best possible world would be one in which we intentionally send a message that is unintentionally received (Box 3 of Fig. 3.1). Perhaps Molloy and others consider the unconscious response to a message to be much like subliminal persuasion. However, we propose that effective communication is conscious communication in which both the sender and receiver are consciously aware of the messages (Box 1 of Fig. 3.1). It is our purpose in writing about the research and information on clothing to increase your understanding and awareness of the communicative value of dress. In so doing, we hope to increase the likelihood that the messages you send and receive about clothing will fall into Box 1—intentionally sent and intentionally received. In an effort to achieve this goal, we will examine the communication effects of dress and **artifacts.**

Figure 3.1
Display of communication possibilities with intentional and unintentional messages.

The clothing we wear is usually accompanied by artifacts, things used to serve an ornamental function, which in turn modify our appearance. Such artifacts include glasses, watches, jewelry, tatoos, masks, badges, and any other objects used for the purpose of ornamentation. Researchers have studied the relation of clothing and artifacts relative to (1) the characteristics of the source–wearer, (2) the perceptions of the receiver–observer, and (3) the effects on the observer and wearer. It is to these three areas of concern that we now turn.

PERSONALITY CORRELATES OF DRESS

Research that has focused on the characteristics of the wearer has been most concerned with the relationship between clothing and personality and demographic variables. For example, do people with a high clothing awareness usually have higher incomes and educational levels than those of people with lower clothing awareness? What type of person wears a small-design pattern on his or her clothing? Much of this research is based on the premise that one's self-image is expressed in the selection of clothing and artifacts. To the extent that certain types of clothing are related to certain personality traits, clothing may communicate the self-image or ideal image of the wearer. F. Lee Bailey, for example, was careful to ensure that Patty Hearst did not wear clothing that was consistent with her wealthy background. In addition, regardless of whether or not she had a poor self-image, Bailey was intent on making the jurors assume that this was the case. This area of research is extremely important since it deals not with the perceived impression of others (such as the jurors' perception of Patty Hearst), but with the actual characteristics of the person wearing the clothes.

Examine your wardrobe and check out the type of clothing you wear. Do you wear bright colors, pastels, large designs, or small designs? Are your clothes unusual or fashionable? "Dressing habits might indicate the mental health of a person," according to Rosencranz (1976). "People who wear very bizarre, strange things might have some kind of problem," says Rosencranz (p. 3). As you read the following studies, consider how your personality and social characteristics relate to the clothing you wear.

Rosencranz examined the characteristics of married women who were high in clothing awareness in an early study in 1962. The findings are not startling and most likely confirm what you would guess to be the case. Married women who were very aware of the clothing they wore were in the upper social classes, belonged to many organizations, had attained a higher level of education, had higher incomes, had higher verbal intelligence, and were, for the most part, married to white-collar workers (pp. 18–22). Since few people would disagree that clothing communicates status, it follows that women who have a high clothing awareness identify with the classes of society that consider appearance to be of the utmost importance.

Aiken (1963) examined the characteristics of the wearer from another perspective. Over 150 women completed psychological examinations and a clothing questionnaire. Aiken's first research question was, "What type of women have an interest in dress?" Such women, he found, were insecure, conscientious, conventional, compliant before authority, stereotyped in thinking, persistent, and tense. The next category dealt with women who were concerned about economy in dress. These women scored as being responsible, alert, efficient, precise, conscientious, intelligent, and controlled. It follows that women who shop for bargains and sales or who at least are careful about the cost of clothing they purchase would have corresponding personality characteristics such as conscientiousness.

Next Aiken looked at women who used decoration in dress. Women in this category tended to be conventional, stereotyped, nonintellectual, sympathetic, sociable, submissive, and conscientious. Women who conformed in their clothing choice were socially conscientious, moral, sociable, traditional, and submissive, and they tended to emphasize economic, social, and religious values and to minimize aesthetic values. The final category that Aiken explored was that of comfort in dress. The findings indicated that women who dressed for comfort were self-controlled, socially cooperative, sociable, thorough, and deferential to authority.

Rosenfeld and Plax (1977) conducted a major follow-up study, which explored responses from both males and females. Their subjects were given a series of personality tests and clothing questionnaires that measured four dimensions of clothing: clothing consciousness, exhibitionism, practicality, and the designer dimension. The responses from the personality tests were matched with the four dimensions of clothing. For example, the statement ''The people I know always notice what I wear'' was used to measure clothing consciousness. ''I approve of skimpy bathing suits and wouldn't mind wearing one myself'' is an example of a statement that was used to measure exhibitionism. Statements such as ''When buying clothes, I am more interested in practicality than beauty'' corresponded to the dimension of practicality. Finally, the statement ''I would love to be a clothes designer'' was used to measure the dimension labeled ''designer'' (pp. 24–31). The question that Rosenfeld and Plax explored was what types of personality characteristics correlate with each of the four dimensions of clothing. We will briefly discuss the results from each category of their study in the following paragraphs.

Males who scored high on the dimension of clothing consciousness were found to be guarded and deferential to authority; they also tended to believe that people could be easily manipulated. Females scoring high in this dimension were inhibited, compliant before authority, and loyal to friends. In this same category, males who scored low were found to be aggressive and independent; they also tended *not* to believe that people could be easily manipulated. Females who scored low were forceful and independent and had low motivation for manipulating others.

Males who scored high on the dimension of exhibitionism were aggressive and confident and had a low self-concept in relation to their familial interactions. On the other hand, females who scored high were radical, detached from interpersonal relationships, and had a high opinion of their own self-worth. Males who were guarded about self-revelation and who had a low self-concept in relation to their familial relations scored low on this dimension. Females who scored low were timid, sincere, and accepting of others.

Who are the people who are more interested in practicality in clothing than in beauty? The Rosenfeld/Plax study indicated that males who felt this way about clothing were inhibited and rebellious and had a low motivation to make friends and that females who had this attitude were clever, enthusiastic, and confident. Males who scored low on this dimension were success-oriented, mature, and forceful. And females who scored low were self-centered, independent, and detached.

Of the males who responded that they would love to be a ''clothes designer,'' characteristics such as cooperative, impulsive, and conforming were correlated. Females who answered in the same way were irrational, uncritical, and expressive. Males who preferred not to be a clothes designer were adventurous, egotistical, and dissatisfied.

Females who expressed no interest in being a clothes designer were efficient, clear-thinking, and easily disorganized under pressure (Rosenfeld and Plax, pp. 24–31).

All clothing has a communicative value. Even those individuals who claim they are not interested in clothing are saying something very definite about the culture in which they live. In a study conducted by Taylor and Compton (1968), the original findings in Aiken's research were confirmed; conformity in dress was related to an individual's desire to be accepted and liked (pp. 653–656). Studies seem to consistently indicate that there are personality dimensions of individuals that are related to the clothing they wear.

In another study by Compton in 1962, design and color preferences and their relation to the personality characteristics of the wearer were examined. In Compton's study, students who preferred deep shades and saturated colors were characterized as outgoing, sociable, and forward. Those preferring small designs were characterized as wanting to make a good impression. Although Compton found no relationship between physical characteristics such as hair color and body size and color and design preferences, he did report several important relationships with occupational interests and personality. The fundamental dichotomy that underlies most of the research conducted on the characteristics of the wearer can be expressed in two questions: "Do we select clothing to express ourselves?" or "Do we select clothing to help build our image of our ideal?" Compton succinctly states: "We express our self through our selection of fabric and color, or looking at the same phenomenon from another perspective, we select fabric and color to help us conform to our image of our ideal self" (pp. 191–195).

The relationship between clothing and the characteristics of the wearer will continue to be the subject of future research. Additional and more sophisticated exploration into these areas will help us to determine whether clothing is a basic extension of who we are or who we want to become. In the meantime, you can try to answer this question for yourself. Does your wardrobe make a statement about "you," your "ideal," or both?

PERCEPTION OF DRESS

The way we see others will have a major impact on the way in which we respond to them. Obviously, F. Lee Bailey was most concerned with how the jurors (the observers) would perceive Patty. In an attempt to play down her wealth, Bailey dressed Patty in a typical middle-class fashion that would be similar to the backgrounds of the jurors. Perceived similarity (i.e., perceived homophily) includes such factors as appearance, background, attitudes, and values. (McCroskey, Larson, and Knapp, 1971). Patty's appearance, specifically her clothing, said a lot about her background, her attitudes, and her values. There is a wealth of research suggesting that observers do perceive clothing and artifacts in a consistent and somewhat stereotypical manner.

Stereotypes

The accuracy with which people can judge others by their clothing depends on what is being judged. Greater accuracy is found in judging sex, age, nationality, socioeconomic status, identification with a specific group, occupational status, and official status. Lesser accuracy is found in judging personality, moods, values, and attitudes. Bailey, for example, was counting on the fact that the jurors would make judgments about Patty's vulnerability and that these judgments in turn would set expectations about the type of behavior in which she would engage.

GOOD GUY—BAD GUY
Is there any question?

Gene Warne

The research that is concerned with how others "perceive" clothing and artifacts is abundant. Many times these perceptions reinforce the stereotypes that we hold, such as "guys never make passes at girls who wear glasses." The following review of this area will be concerned mainly with an examination of clothing, although we will also take a look at the studies on artifacts such as glasses and makeup at the end of this section.

Dress Codes

Even if researchers could not identify conclusive relationships between clothing preference and the characteristics of the wearer, it is doubtful that companies would drop their dress codes for their executives. Why? Most companies know that although clothes may not make the person, they do affect the perception of the person. In other words, it's the appearance that counts.

Thomas J. Watson, Sr., Chairman of the Board of IBM, decided a while back that IBM representatives and executives were to wear white shirts, dark suits, and stiff collars. Of course this formal dress code has changed; today representatives and executives at IBM are no longer required to wear the stiff collars. That's right. The dark suit and white shirts still live on at IBM (Anderson, 1977, pp. 43–45). The IBM uniform is a symbol of conservatism and trustworthiness and, most important, an established company.

IBM is not alone in this dress-code madness. Allied stores, one of the largest department store chains in the country, has a firmly written dress code that governs executive personnel. May Company, J. C. Penney Company, and Sears use similar dress codes. Men are instructed that a suit, shirt, and tie must harmonize. Major executives wear vests and dress very conservatively. According to this policy, if you are not at the top, you may wear a conservative sports jacket. Sorry, no leisure suits or turtlenecks. Brushed denims are all right, but jeans are out, as well as neck jewelry for men. Women, apparently under fewer restraints, are asked to dress to complement the department in which they work. On the other hand, Tiffany and Company is more restrictive with its female employees when compared with other companies. Women are told to wear their skirts slightly above or below the knee. When wearing a pantsuit, the pant legs must cover the tops of the shoes but must not touch the floor. Tops must cover the bottom of the hips, and see-through blouses, tight-fitting sweaters, décolletage, and the braless looks are out (Anderson, pp. 43–45). These major companies are just a few examples of the silent endorsement that clothes do communicate. But exactly what do they communicate? The following studies have attempted to come to grip with this question.

Social Impressions

In an early study conducted by Hoult in 1954, male students were rated on dimensions of "best-looking," "most likely to succeed," "most intelligent," and "best personality." The four men with the highest ratings were told to "dress down," while the four men with the lowest ratings were told to "dress up." Others were told to dress the same. Two weeks later Hoult again obtained ratings and was surprised to see that the clothes had not been influential in changing the ratings (pp. 324–328). After all, it would seem reasonable that the impression of a person who was "dressed up" should change when that person "dressed down." Hoult noticed that the subjects who rated the models had a high social closeness. In other words, they knew the models and had shared social experiences together. This information prompted Hoult to conduct another study in which he used models who were complete strangers to the subjects (raters). These male strangers were rated by fifty-four students. The results clearly demonstrated that high-ranked clothing (i.e., the "dressed-up" look) was associated with an increase in social rank, while low-ranked clothing (i.e., the "dressed-down" look) was associated with a loss of social rank (pp. 324–328). Hoult's studies are important in demonstrating a particular condition under which clothing is not as influential in the perception of others, namely, when people know one another.

In a class assignment, we saw this same principle demonstrated. Our students were asked to dress in a manner that was opposite, or clearly different, from their normal dress behavior on campus. After conducting this experiment for an eight-hour period, the students unanimously reported that their friends tended to react less than anyone else to their change in clothing. This response, or lack of a response, suggests two possibilities. The first is that once impressions are formed, a change in clothing behavior is not observed as critical or even important since information about the person comes from many less superficial areas. The second is that when a person we know behaves differently, such as by wearing "strange" clothing, we tend to make allowances for it. Knapp (1978) concludes the "changes in clothing of a family member or a close friend may indicate a temporary change of mood, but it is likely that we will not perceive any basic changes in values, attitudes, or personality traits unless the clothing change becomes permanent for that individual (p. 178).

Popularity and liking is related to the clothing we wear, according to Williams and Eicher (1966). In response to open-ended questions, female subjects said that clothing was the most important attribute in describing the characteristics of the most popular women. Media and advertising take advantage of this point—if you want to be popular and liked, you need to enhance your appearance via clothing. One magazine, *Hustler*, advertised the "masculine look with Bulger undergear." Basing their entire ad on the fact that perceptions of the observer are important, they stated: "Yes! Now you can have the appearance of size and power that drives women wild with desire. You'll have the same potently virile look as you've seen in Hollywood superstars and heavyweight fighters. Why shouldn't you have the masculine look that women notice immediately?" Magazines geared toward women sell the same "appearances" with just a simple relocation on the human anatomy. "Buy the padded bra that lifts, separates, and gives you that full appearance," an ad reads. Advertisers sell appearances, and we buy them. Most people are interested in any product that will make them look ten years younger. How often have you heard a product advertised that would make you look ten years older? And if there were such products, would you buy them? How others perceive us is the main selling point used by advertisers in the clothing industry.

Another area of perception of dress involves brightly colored clothes. In 1968 Hamid had males and females rate models wearing brightly colored garments with high hemlines. The models were rated as sophisticated, immoral, and physically attractive.

Status and Age

In 1963 still another study found other perceptions that were directly tied to clothing. In this study Douty asked subjects to rate pictures requiring snap judgments of personal traits and status. He found that clothing did affect impressions of both status and personal traits. Douty's findings also indicated that our perceptions may be influenced by things other than clothing such as body or even facial cues (pp. 197–202).

An article entitled, "Giveaways in Age Can Be Found in Clothing" (*New Women Magazine*, 1976, pp. 54–55) explored what types of clothing and artifacts communicate "age." Read the following descriptions and see if you can identify who is the older women and who is the younger woman.

> Lynda is wearing several strands of pearls cascading down the front of her blouse. Her eyes are outlined by simple wire-rim frames. A sporty navy suit jacket with a pleated skirt is her attire, complete with a scarf in her hair and covered with a wraparound coat.
>
> Mindy is wearing an elegant strand of graduated pearls. Her eyes are outlined by discreet blue eyeglasses. A sporty royal blue suit jacket with a straight skirt is her attire. The outfit is completed with a sensible coat with a ranch mink collar and a matching hat.

Based on the above descriptions, who is the "older" woman? If you picked Mindy, you were right. The telltale signs, according to *New Woman Magazine,* can be found in the clothing and artifacts worn. Everything Mindy is wearing communicates "age"—the color, the style, the design, and the fabric.

Age seems to have an important communicative value in clothing, especially if you are in sales. One advertisement asked the direct question, "Are your salesmen fat and unkempt?" Jimmy de Pasquale, the founder of a New York salon for "the complete man," said in 1969 that he would trim men up, change their clothing styles, and freshen their images with haircuts by female barbers and fat-killing injections of pregnant women's urine. Pasquale makes an interesting point about personal appearance:

> Salesmen become old and successful, and they stop trying. They have the same old accounts, they do most of the business over the phone, and they stagnate. Then, they see these young kids coming out of college, with fresh looks and modern clothes, making good money and lots of good impressions, and they can't understand it. "What's wrong with me," they cry. What's wrong is they're pot-bellied, balding and wearing 10 year old suits. (de Pasquale, 1969).

Sexiness and Likability

Recently there has been a great deal of speculation about what type of clothing communicates sexiness or business. Molloy (1977), America's self-acclaimed wardrobe engineer, states rather succinctly that clothes determine whether an individual is headed for the "bedroom" or the "boardroom." In a study that attempted to determine whether sexy clothing and likability go hand in hand, Williamson (1977) gathered twenty-four paired photographs of male and female models. Each set of models was dressed conservatively in one photograph and suggestively in the other. For example, in one pair of photographs the male model had on tight trousers, then baggy trousers; in another pair the male model wore a skimpy bathing suit, then a traditional one. Or a female model might be wearing regular shorts with her shirt buttoned up, then short shorts with her shirt tied above her midriff.

The models were rated for sexiness, attractiveness, and likability. As expected, the students had no difficulty in agreeing on the sexier costume in each pair of photographs. This, however, was the only area of agreement. Students found the women without a bra more sexually suggestive, but not more attractive or likable. An explanation suggested by Williamson was that the braless women appeared to be too threatening. Men reported that the woman who had her shirt buttoned up was slightly less attractive than the woman who left her shirt buttons undone, but they liked her more anyway. Both males and females found men more attractive and likable in tight trousers when compared with baggy trousers. Women rejected men with tight-fitting bathing suits and unbuttoned shirts. Another interesting finding was that women rated all models less likable in sexy clothes. Williamson speculates that women look upon females who dress in sexy costumes as "engaging in unfair competition." Since the men did not seem to dislike sexually suggestive male models, Williamson speculates that perhaps males see sexy clothes as a normal part of *machismo* and therefore do not react competitively (p. 90).

In her book *I'd Love to, But What'll I Wear?* (1977) Polly Bergen claims, like Molloy, that what you're wearing will tell people whether you mean *business* or *monkey business*. Should so-called sexy clothes be worn in business settings? And if they are, how are they perceived by subordinates, equals, and superiors? Molloy presents some very definite opinions on this subject. Although he claims his comments are based on nine years of research, he fails to describe the methodology or analysis used in the studies, thereby making it impossible to assess their validity. However, the ideas presented by Molloy are interesting and important in pointing up the stereotypes that exist about clothing in business.

Stereotypes in Business

Consider the sweater worn by a female in a business setting. Some of us remember that exercise chant from high school, "we must, we must, we must improve the bust, it's better, it's better, it's better for the sweater." Sweaters are best for attracting men, according to Molloy (1975), especially if they're tight and made of soft, luxuriant wool. However, in the office, sweaters spell secretary. "Any woman at any level who wants to move up should not wear a sweater to work," states Molloy emphatically. "In the office, sweaters give out nothing but negative impulses. They say lower middle class and lower" (p. 77).

In the male-dominated business world, men have an acceptable uniform—the suit. Women, on the other hand, have no such designated uniform so they wear skirts and sweaters, pantsuits, dresses, and many other combinations. Not good enough, says Molloy. Women need their uniform in business, as his following example illustrates:

> One woman was particularly steamed up over the fact that when she traveled with her assistant, a man in his early 30's, he got preferential treatment every time. It occurred to me that her assistant had a sign that everyone could read. He undoubtedly wore a suit and tie, and that suit and tie said businessman. I came to the conclusion that there was a real need to develop a sign for businesswomen to wear that is just as effective as the sign worn by businessmen. (p. 35)

Molloy goes on to suggest the symbolic clothing that a woman needs in business—the skirted suit. According to Molloy, the matching-skirt-and-jacket look is professional and, if adopted as the "business uniform" for women, will communicate an official look to others.

Stereotypes in Academia

The communicative value of clothing operates in the academic world as well as in the business world. In the same manner in which an executive must choose his or her clothing carefully, so must a teacher, that is, if the teacher is concerned with how he or she is perceived by the students. Dr. Steven A. Rollmann (1977) of Penn State University showed fifty students three photographs of the same male teacher and the same female teacher dressed in different attire. For example, in one photo the male instructor wore jeans, a sport shirt, and sneakers for casual dress. In the moderately formal condition he wore casual slacks, a sport coat, and a turtleneck sweater. In the formal condition he wore the classic IBM combination of dark suit, white shirt, and tie. Using a list of ten adjectives to rate the various degrees of formality in dress (i.e., fair, sympathetic, knowledgeable, enthusiastic, friendly, flexible, clear, organized, stimulating, and well-prepared), Rollman uncovered some interesting findings. Teachers who were dressed informally were seen as friendly, flexible, more sympathetic, fair, and enthusiastic when compared with the other modes of dress. The other extreme in dress, that of formal attire, communicated that the teacher was organized, knowledgeable, and better prepared.

The study also revealed some differences in the perception of male and female teachers. For the moderately dressed models, the males were seen as stimulating, while both males and females were seen as clear. In the formal attire, males were perceived as most knowledgeable while both males and females were seen as well prepared and organized. Although the findings are inconclusive, they do suggest that sex might be a variable in the perception of clothing. Perhaps conforming to societal stereotypes, a male in formal attire when compared to a female in formal attire was still seen as more knowledgeable.

Group Identification or Uniforms

Clothing in many cases serves as a means of **group identification,** thereby acting as a type of uniform in which the wearers are bound together. Prisons provide a good example of clothing used as a group identification. Writing on prison parlance, Popplestone (1977) observed that "inmates must tune in to a multitude of nonverbal messages to function successfully in this environment. They learn to identify guards by their footsteps and troublesome inmates by their dress" (p. 61).

Based on personal observation and extensive interviews, Popplestone identified the clothing codes in prisons. New inmates, for instance, often wore the blue denim jumpsuits while veteran jailbirds wore brown shirts and trousers. In an effort to establish that they were tough, new prisoners would often go unshaven and act extra tough. Black Muslims could be identified by stocking caps, turned-up cuffs, and short-trimmed hair. Black prisoners from a particular city sported Afro hairstyles and prison trousers deliberately cut six inches short. While homosexuals wore a pair of earrings, prisoners who wore one earring bore the mark of masculinity. Even guards were identified and stereotyped according to the appearance of their clothing. Tough guards had a crisp appearance; easy guards were much more casual in their dress (Popplestone, 1977).

Clothing sets our expectations for the behavior of the wearer—especially if the clothing is a uniform. Popplestone (1977) compared putting on a uniform to providing a protective exoskeleton similar to that possessed by lobsters and turtles. Sometimes people wearing uniforms do have bodies as hard as lobsters or turtles. Uniforms send conspicuous messages. Leathers (1976, p. 92) concludes that "by wearing the uniform of a particular group, a man shows by his clothing that he has given up his right to act freely as an individual and must act in accordance with and under the limitations of the rules of his groups."

Informal uniforms can often be found among people who wish to communicate their political and social attitudes. In analyzing how political and social attitudes were communicated by clothing, Buckley and Roach (1974) collected data from ninety-six students. The subjects were asked to respond to nine questionnaires, which measured (1) each subject's own attitudes toward social and political issues, (2) each subject's perceptions of attitudes of wearers of clothing shown in the stimulus photographs, and (3) each subject's own responses to types of clothing shown in the photographs. Two types of student responses were studied—those from conservatives (i.e., people oriented toward the established American culture) and those from liberals (i.e., people oriented toward a counterculture). Findings indicated that the clothing was perceived as a symbol of people's social and political attitudes. In addition, students who represented the counterculture tended (although not significantly) to prefer clothing that they perceived as communicating attitudes similar to their own. Finally, the results showed that individuals who embraced the counterculture wore clothing that they perceived as being expressive of their political attitudes more often than those individuals who embraced the established culture (pp. 94–102).

A final example demonstrating the fact that the perceptions others have of us based on our clothing are important is the case of juvenile court judge Leodis Harris. The forty-three-year-old judge had a special blue-denim robe made in an effort to relate to the kids in his courtroom. When the juveniles came back with a good report, the judge would wear the denim robe to let them know he was proud of them. The robe was only part of the package. Before dismissing the juvenile, Harris would read the youngster the prediction for his or her astrological sign. In accordance with the researchers, Harris was acting on the fact that perceptions of one's appearance are critical in affecting communication outcomes.

Personal Artifacts

Personal artifacts also contribute a great deal to the perceptions others have of us. Glasses have created a controversy for a long time. The late humorist Dorothy Parker's famous line, ''Men never make passes at

When the glasses come off the face and into the mouth, does it mean that the individual is deep in thought, under pressure, or hungry? The behavior by itself does not provide sufficient information to answer this question. The observer, however, might perceive the removal of glasses as a sign of concentration or as a removal of a barrier to communication.

girls who wear glasses,'' has amused many people. It has also convinced a number of people to stay away from glasses. Over six million
pairs of eyes currently see through contact lenses. And three-fourths of
all contact lense wearers are female. In a recent survey, the American
Optometric Association found that 48.6 percent of all teenage girls who
require prescription lenses are opting for contact lenses instead of
glasses. Obviously, we cannot assume that the reason for the high proportion of contact lense wearers is the unfavorable stereotype about
people who wear glasses. Or can we? In an early study by Thornton
(1944) the stereotyped perceptions of people who wear glasses were examined. Subjects rated slides of people with glasses and people without
glasses. Those with glasses were seen as more intelligent, industrious,
and honest than the nonspectacled individuals. Live models wearing
glasses were also rated as more intelligent and industrious, but not
more honest (Thornton, pp. 203–207).

A Manhattan optician, Alfred Poll (1976), contends that glasses
communicate important information, particularly in business. With a
clientele that numbers more than 100,000 and includes top business
people, jet-setters, and diplomats such as Billie Jean King, Leonard
Bernstein, Isaac Stern, Dustin Hoffman, and Ethel Merman, this
Manhattan optician points out that the way in which glasses are used
can communicate important information. For example, the person who
compulsively folds and unfolds his specs may be indicating boredom.
Or the executive who suddenly removes her glasses and folds them into
the case is indicating that the meeting, or at least the negotiations, are
over. And what about the person who hurls her glasses across the desk?
Poll suggests that this is an obvious show of displeasure. The boss who
wags his spectacles instead of his finger at an errant subordinate is symbolically delivering a softer, more civilized reprimand. Chewing on the
temple tip, according to Poll, is common among people who are tense,
nervous, or under great stress. Because most people are embarrassed
by this habit, Poll has a lot of clients who bring in their glasses claiming,
''Look what the dog did!'' Propping the glasses on the brow and regarding the visitor with the naked eye demonstrates openness and
honesty. Finally, the common pose of propping the spectacles on the
end of the nose and peering over the frames signifies, ''You're putting
me on!'' (Poll, pp. 77–78). The obvious point that Poll is making is that
glasses communicate as much off the face as they do on the face.
Stereotyped perceptions follow the glasses, wherever they might be
placed.

Controversial mirrored sun glasses communicate messages of
anonymity. The protected wearer can look at anything anywhere, and
no one will ever know. Rudofsky (1974) suggests that such mirrored
sun glasses serve yet another purpose: ''Like masks, impenetrable
eyeglasses shift the attention from a woman's face to that part of her

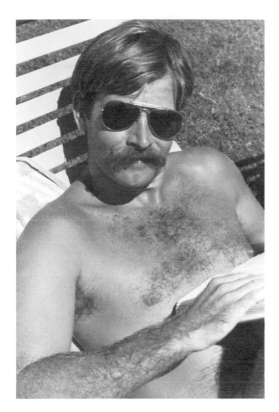

Under the protective covering of the dark sun glasses, you will never know exactly what he is looking at—a freedom coveted by many wearers of dark sun glasses.

body which is next to the eyes, the most eloquent region of female anatomy, the bosom'' (Rudofsky, p. 38). How many females have considered this perception when wearing mirrored shades?

A replication of the Thornton study on glasses was conducted by Hamid in 1968. Using magazine pictures of female figures wearing glasses, he asked subjects to rate each figure. Wearers of glasses were more often rated as religious, conventional, and unimaginative (Hamid, pp. 904–906). This later study suggests an even more negative perception of wearers of glasses when compared with the earlier study by Thornton in which they were seen as intelligent, industrious, and honest.

Hamid (1972) did not stop with the single perception of glasses. He went on to determine the perceptions of makeup cues and the presence and absence of glasses. Using four confederates, all dressed similarly and serving as assistants during a class period, Hamid manipulated the variables. The first female confederate, for instance, wore both makeup and glasses, the second wore makeup without glasses, the third wore glasses without makeup, and the fourth wore neither glasses nor makeup. At the end of the class period, the students were asked to recall what each assistant wore and rate them on various personality traits. Although the confederates were wearing comparable clothes, the two who were wearing makeup were rated as wearing shorter skirts than the two without makeup. This same perception held true for the two without glasses. The perceptions of males and females differed with regard to the confederate who wore glasses and makeup. Males perceived her as artistic, intelligent, self-confident, sophisticated; they ranked her low in shyness, seriousness, and sentimentality. The females' perception of this same confederate are remarkably different. Although they saw her as intelligent, they also perceived her to be both cold and conceited. Both the confederate who wore glasses and no makeup and the one who wore neither glasses nor makeup were perceived as conservative and low in individuality. This finding confirmed Hamid's early study on the stereotypes of glasses. Finally, the confederate wearing makeup without glasses was rated favorably on outward appearance, but unfavorably on personal traits (pp. 279–289). If we want to avoid being stereotyped in one manner, we should take Michael Korda's suggestion and buy a pair of glasses (noncorrective) and keep them with us for those occasions when we want to present a more conservative image (Korda, 1977).

How does lipstick affect our perceptions? That's the question McKeachie (1952) asked in his study. Six male students interviewed six female students and then rated them according to personality perceptions. In these six interviews three women were wearing lipstick, and three women were not. The interviews were structured in such a way that each woman wore lipstick for three of her six interviews. The results were unanimous. The women who wore lipstick were perceived as more frivolous and more overtly interested in males. When asked on what basis the judgments were made, not one of the raters indicated that the presence or absence of lipstick affected his responses (pp. 241–244). This suggests that some of our perceptions occur without our being aware of what is causing the perception. In other words, we unintentionally receive a message from a source. A note of caution should be added to interpreting some of the landmark, but older, research. The current dynamics of fashion would certainly influence many of the findings.

There are countless numbers of artifacts that could be explored. Although the research on artifacts and their communicative value is somewhat sketchy, three items deserve mention: T-shirts, pipes, and briefcases.

Most people do not need research to tell them about the impact of sayings on T-shirts. The message is usually explicit—written for all to see. News writers have speculated that T-shirts reflect "incurable sex on the brain" ("Unsavory T-shirts," 1977). Such writers contend that the G-rated T-shirts are still around, such as those that say "Peace on

"Fred Basset" by Alex Graham © 1980. Associated Newspapers Ltd.
Courtesy of Field Newspaper Syndicate.

Earth,'' but that they have quickly lost popularity to the R- and X-rated slogans. The more popular slogans appearing on T-shirts include ''Free, but not Easy,'' ''So many men, too little time.'' or ''To all you virgins, thanks for nothing.'' One of the most popular T-shirts reads on the front side, ''I'm a virgin.'' The message is completed on the back and says ''This is a very old shirt.''

What do the above T-shirt messages convey to you about the wearer? We can assume that most T-shirt wearers are communicating intentional and humorous messages. The T-shirt messages may even communicate thoughts or feelings that the wearer would not verbalize, such as ''I'm #1''; the wearer lets the T-shirt speak for itself.

What does a pipe smoker communicate to others? The fact is that the pipe smoker gives off some very definite impressions. The owner of one of the largest used-car dealerships in the state of Arizona spoke to one of our nonverbal communication classes. He informed us that car dealers are told to beware of anything that starts with a ''P''— prostitutes, plumbers, and pipe smokers were the examples he offered. Although a strange combination, these ''P'' people are perceived to be poor prospective buyers. Recently, a friend explained that his father told him to ''never hire pipe smokers because they will spend all their time cleaning, filling, and emptying the pipe.'' In addition, other sales personnel have reported that pipe smokers take far too much time to reach a decision and they need a great deal of time to ''turn over'' an idea. Indeed, the very act of cleaning and filling the pipe serves as a mechanism for gaining time. Rudofsky (1974) provides a very eloquent description of the perception and effects of smoking a pipe in the following observation.

A newspaper reporter once quipped that the pipe smoker, during the course of a year on the job, lost one week of time because of tapping, cleaning, filling, and smoking his pipe. The moral: Don't take a pipe to your next job interview.

Originally a container for burning tobacco, today it is used as a tranquilizer that induces slow gesturing and a more accentuated, though less intelligible speech. Men attach as much importance to its shape and color as women do to the right shade of lipstick. Not only does the pipe complement a man's facial features, it greatly bolsters his ego. A pipe in the secure grip of his teeth symbolizes meditative reflection, mature deliberation, and superiority in general. (p. 148)

Another artifact, the briefcase, has become a symbol for both the businessman and businesswoman. A handbag buyer at San Francisco's I. Magnin department store explained that women like to show off the fact that they are in the business world. The briefcase has become a symbol of upward mobility on the corporate ladder. Korda (1977) goes even further and suggests that the briefcase is an important investment requiring sometimes up to a thousand dollars to purchase. In addition, Korda adamantly recommends that a woman carry either a handbag or a briefcase, but never both. What is the concern? Once again, it is with images, with how others will perceive the wearer, or, in this case, the carrier. Briefcases, like many other artifacts, have a high communicative value.

Of course, as fashion changes, the impressions conveyed by various styles of clothing and by personal artifacts also change. At one time, a woman who wore pants was looked upon as "unladylike"; however, pants are now considered to be one of the fundamentals of a woman's wardrobe. Since fashion is dynamic, we must be careful not to assume that research in this area is irrefutable. As different styles and types of dress come into and out of fashion, the impressions created by these clothes will also change. So when we attempt to create a "good" impression through our dress, it is important to remember that current fashion dictates as well as the results of research done in this area. The following section will consider the effects of dress on both the observer and the wearer.

THE EFFECTS OF DRESS

When a waitress was wearing a daisy or a rose in her hair, diners tipped her an average of twenty-six cents extra, according to researchers Stillman and Hensley (1980). The study of flower power was done in a restaurant that primarily served businesspeople, with an average meal cost of $10.20. The six waitresses in the study were asked to wear the same jewelry, perfume, makeup, and hairstyle each night for the four nights the researchers were watching—with one exception. On one of the nights, they were asked to wear a flower.

The results showed that although men tipped more than women did, the flowers had a greater effect on women, who increased their tips an average of thirty-nine cents, compared with the men's increase of fifteen cents. The researchers speculated that women were simply more likely to notice the difference and respond to it.

We will now turn to an examination of the effects of artifacts (such as the flower in the hair) and clothing in terms of both the observer and the wearer. Although the observer and the wearer are two obviously different categories, they both deal with responses, behavioral in nature, to clothing and artifacts.

Effects on the Observer

Clothing does have a persuasive value that influences the behavior of others. Once perceptions have been formed about another person, our subsequent communication will always be mediated by our attitudes. For instance, researchers have found that we are more likely to respond to orders coming from someone in uniform than from someone in civilian clothes. The extent to which we consider another person to be credible may be in part revealed by their clothing. A teacher who wears cut-offs and an old T-shirt to a chemistry class may not appear as cred-

ible a source of information as the instructor who wears more formal attire. In turn, some students may respond more favorably to the instructor wearing the more formal clothing.

The influence of clothing on the behavior of others is a fascinating
area of research. We continually find that clothing is a symbolic
message to which we all respond. The response that F. Lee Bailey
sought in the courtroom was sympathy from the jury for the frail girl
who sat in front of them, rather than rage and hostility directed at a
member of upper-class society who had rejected all of its values. The
perception of Patty's clothing, although unintentionally received,
would most likely affect the jurors' attitudes and behavior in delivering
a verdict.

Although not as plentiful, there is research that demonstrates the
effect of the perceptions of dress on the observer's response. One of the
more dramatic examples has been offered by Lefkowitz, Blake, and
Mouton (1955). They reported that pedestrians would violate the instructions given by a traffic light more often when another person
violated it ahead of them. Clothing made a difference in this behavior;
there were significantly more violations when the original violator was
dressed to represent a high-status person (Lefkowitz, Blake, and
Mouton, pp. 704–706). How about you? Have you ever jaywalked or
violated a traffic light after seeing a well-dressed person do the same?

Clothing does affect the behavior of others, or, as Bickman (1974a)
and others contend, ''Clothes make the person.'' In several studies,
Bickman has explored the influence of high-status and low-status
clothing and uniforms on the behavior of others. In one of Bickman's
studies on the persuasive value of clothing, he had four men stop 153
adults on the streets of Brooklyn. The men's clothing included the
civilian look (sports jacket and tie), the milkman look (uniform, white
pants, and milk bottles), and the guard look (uniform, badge, insignia,
but no gun). The four men asked pedestrians to do one of the following:
(1) to pick up a bag, (2) to put a dime in a parking meter for someone
else, or (3) to stand on the opposite side of a bus stop sign. In each case,
the guard uniforms received greater compliance. Interestingly enough,
eighty-three percent of those who were asked to put a dime in the parking meter obeyed, even after the person in the guard uniform had left
the scene (Bickman, 1974a, pp. 47–61).

The implications for the automatic response to a uniform is critical.
If people are willing to respond to trivial requests from a guard, are they
also willing to respond to more serious, or perhaps deadlier, requests
from other uniformed government agents? In the well-publicized trial
of Lieutenant William L. Calley in the My Lai Massacre of Vietnam, the
question arose as to whether the response to the command was in part
a response to a uniform and whether others would act similarly. In a national survey to measure the attitudes toward the massacre, Herbert C.

Kelman and Lee H. Lawrence asked respondents for their reactions to the trial, their judgment about the behavior of Calley, and their attitudes toward obedience in the military. In the total sample, sixty-seven percent thought that most people would react like Calley, and about half said they, too, would follow orders to shoot men, women, and children (Bickman, 1974b, pp. 48–51).

Does the uniform and implied status speak louder than the person wearing it? In an attempt to explore all avenues to answer this question, Bickman concentrated on status differences in dress. Three male and three female confederates were employed to dress in both high-status and low-status clothing. The high-status males wore suits and ties; the low-status males dressed in work clothes and carried something that would identify them as workers, such as a lunch pail or flashlight. The high-status females wore neat dresses and either wore or carried dress coats. The low-status females, on the other hand, wore inexpensive skirts and blouses and were unkempt in appearance. These confederates were stationed around phone booths in Grand Central Station and John F. Kennedy International Airport in New York City. A confederate would enter a phone booth, place a dime on the shelf, and then leave. After a caller entered the booth, the agent observed the person to see if he or she used the dime, which was in plain sight. After two minutes, the confederate tapped on the phone-booth door and said, "Excuse me, Sir (or Miss), I think I might've left a dime in this phone booth a few minutes ago. Did you find it?" The confederate then recorded whether the subject returned the dime. Although the results showed no relationship between the return of the dime and the sex, race, age, or status of the subject, the mode of dress (i.e., apparent social status) of the confederate did make a significant difference. Seventy-five percent of the people returned the dime to the well-dressed confederate, but only thirty-eight percent returned it to the confederates dressed in low-status clothing (Bickman, 1974b, pp. 48–51).

It is not surprising to find that high-status individuals are treated differently. You have probably experienced different treatment, depending on whether you are dressed up or down. People who do not know you respond differently. If you don't believe that clothing can make a difference, then wear your sloppiest clothing to your next job interview and write us about the results!

Even sports competitors are concerned with their clothing and its possible effects on the judge. "Personal appearance and presentation of the individual gymnast," according to Massimo (1977), "can have a definite psychological effect on an official. . . . Out-psyching one's opponent can be seen in the outfitting shown by participants in events" (p. 60). Just think for a minute about the impact of a tennis player, decked out in a hundred-dollar outfit with Adidas shoes and all the trimmings, on an opponent who is not as well dressed. Clothing is one aspect of "out-psyching" another player.

Claiming that physical costuming is the way of the hard-hearted seductress, Marabel Morgan, author of the controversial best-seller *The Total Woman*, says that the woman's clothes change the man. She explains:

> For an experiment I put on pink babydoll pajamas and white boots after my bubble bath. I must admit that I looked foolish and felt even more so. When I opened the door that night to greet Charlie, I was unprepared for his reaction. My quiet, reserved, nonexcitable husband took one look, dropped his briefcase on the doorstep and chased me around the dining room table. We were in stitches by the time he caught me, and breathless with the old feeling of romance. (1981, p. 76)

It is doubtful that researchers will consider Morgan's experiment as a valid case study, but certainly we have all experienced similar incidents in which our clothing has elicited an observable response. It is strange to think that the colors, fabrics, styles, and artifacts we wear can affect not only the perceptions of others but also their behavior, both verbal and nonverbal, toward us.

But what about the wearer? When you are wearing particular clothing, how does it affect your psychological makeup and feelings? Or does it?

Effects on the Wearer

"Dress changes the manners," Voltaire stated a few centuries ago. Today, many researchers, convinced of the truth of this aphorism, seek to find out how dress affects the wearer. Simply stated, if you wear an outfit in which you're convinced you look "dynamite," do you feel dynamite? If you get up late one morning and don't have time to shower or wash your hair, and you grab the closest pair of jeans and yesterday's shirt, do you wish it were still yesterday? Do you perform better when taking an examination when you are "dressed up" or "dressed down"? Perhaps Bailey hoped that in her oversized clothing, Patty Hearst would feel small, insignificant, and somewhat overpowered by everything going on around her. If, indeed, she felt any of these things, it might be communicated by her slumped posture, her hanging head, and even the pitch and intensity of her voice.

The research in this area completes the communication cycle. The clothing is perceived, it affects the behavior of the perceiver, and finally affects the behavior of the wearer. Hamilton and Warden (1966) found that clothing that is perceived as inappropriate by one's peers can have very negative effects on the behavior of the wearer. Specifically, boys who wore unacceptable clothing, even though their achievement scores were twenty-two percentile points higher than the median score of boys with acceptable clothing, had a lower grade-point average. Students who wore acceptable clothing participated in more extracurricular activities and held more offices than did students with nonacceptable clothing. Boys who wore unacceptable clothing were more consistently in conflict with their peers and society (Hamilton and Warden, pp. 789–791).

Another effect of clothing on the wearer is more direct and is embodied in the phrase, ''When I look good, I feel good.'' Do clothes pick you up, that is, clothes that make you look good? And do clothes get you down, especially when you have to look at the same closetful of old clothes that you've worn for the last year? Most people would say yes; clothes do affect the way they feel. *New Woman Magazine* explained this phenomenon as follows:

> One reason clothes are so compelling to most of us, says one psychoanalyst, is that raiment functions as an extension of the body. Whenever an object is worn on the body, consciousness of the self is extended into the extremities of the object, thereby providing the individual with an increased sense of size, power, and movement. Floating chiffon makes dancers feel more graceful, a girdle makes a women more straitlaced, and a pair of sexy, tight jeans makes the wearer feel more sexual. Clothes, in other words, make you feel more of whatever way you like to feel. When used positively, clothing definitely contributes to your feeling of self-acceptance and self-esteem. (''If I Look Good, I Feel Good,'' 1977)

Much research remains to be done on the effects of clothing on the wearer. In the meantime, experiment with your clothing and carefully observe whether it affects your communication behavior.

SUMMARY

''Whether the practice of concealing the body is the cause of our uncleanliness of mind, or whether our obscenity is rather the cause of concealment, is a debated question,'' explains Dunlap Knight. What we do know is that clothing serves particular functions, both in historical and contemporary society. Historically, clothing served three functions: comfort–protection, modesty, and cultural display. With technological advancement, the need for clothing as comfort and protection has all but disappeared. The two remaining functions, those of modesty and cultural display, are predominant in our society. For example, in terms of the latter function, we still insist that a long, narrow piece of cloth tied in a knot around the neck of a man signifies that he is a gentleman, or at least that he ''looks'' like a gentleman. The use of the necktie functions solely as a cultural badge, as does a great deal of the clothing and artifacts that we wear.

How are messages of dress, such as that emanating from the necktie, communicated? We introduced what at first glance appears to be a simple model. The wearer (source) encodes a message (transmitted by clothing) through a channel (visual) which is decoded by the observer (receiver). The response of the observer, verbal and nonverbal, is referred to as feedback. The encoding and decoding processes are particularly important since the message of dress is based on the perceptions of the observer rather than on any inherent messages of clothing. With our individual and varied life experiences, we may not see the bow tied low on Patty Hearst's blouse as indicative of despair. For some, the low-tied bow may be a sign of inappropriate dress and an indication of a lack of respect for the courtroom.

In addition to this communication model we examined the question of intentionality. There are four possible combinations of intentionality, including (1) messages intentionally sent and intentionally received, (2) messages unintentionally sent and intentionally received, (3) messages intentionally sent and unintentionally received, and (4) messages unintentionally sent and unintentionally received. One of the major purposes of studying the communicative value of clothing and artifacts is to reduce the number of messages that are unintentionally sent and unintentionally received. Messages like these are unconscious, and our awareness of them is either very low or nonexistent. Our goal throughout this chapter has been to increase your awareness of the communicative value of clothing in order to increase the probability of your transmitting and receiving messages intentionally.

One of the most common types of unintentional messages transmitted by clothing has to do with the self-esteem of the wearer. Ali McGraw (1977) explains this relationship as follows:

> When you know who you are then you know how you look—all those little extras just fall into place. You learn about your body. When people present themselves physically, you can tell how they feel about themselves. (p. 24)

In discussing the personality characteristics of the wearer, we introduced several studies that attempted to determine the relationship between what we wear and who we are. One possibility is that we select clothing in an attempt to project our "ideal" self. Additional research in this area may reveal the more complex relationship between emotions, personality, and clothing worn. For example, when you are in a "down" mood, do you wear one of your favorite outfits? There seem to be two responses to this question. Some people answer with a flat no: They would never waste their good clothes on a day when they don't feel good. But other people will answer "yes": They wear their favorites because the clothes help to bring them "up." The question remains, however, whether it is the clothing that elevates an individual's feelings or the responses to the clothing. We began to explore this question with an examination of research on the perceptions of clothing.

The perception of clothing is the process by which an observer (receiver) decodes a message about the source's attire. Dress codes in schools and corporations are based on the assumption that the "perceptions" of the public are important. The research findings indicate that perceptions are made, and in most cases represent, stereotypes about particular clothing and artifacts. For example, many police officers prefer to work in uniform rather than in plain clothes because they receive a more compliant response. Using this same principle, one of our students had his checks printed as "Dr. Caine." Living in a college town he had found out that merchants were sometimes reluctant to take his check. Using his "official" checks and avoiding wearing blue jeans, "Dr." Caine reports the remarkable case with which he can now purchase items from merchants who still refuse to take checks from students. These examples illustrate that perceptions are important. The actual response of the observer, based on these perceptions, introduces another area of research, the effects of dress.

The automatic compliant response to a guard or police uniform is a "real" example of the effect dress has on an observer. Jaywalking after a well-dressed person in front of you has done so is another example of the effect clothing may have on the observer. We not only perceive clothing to communicate a message, but we also respond to it. Therefore, according to our model, we receive the message through a decoding process and then feed back our response to the wearer or the source of the message.

One of the more dramatic effects of clothing, however, is on the behavior of the wearer. "If you wear an outfit you really like," says a pro golfer, "it gives you a psychological lift and you play better." One wife reports that her husband is basically introverted and soft-spoken, that is, before he puts on his police uniform. Her husbands reports that he feels entirely different and in an authoritative role when he is in uniform. Wearers can also be affected indirectly by clothing via the response to the clothing from others.

Continued research is needed in each of these areas, particularly with regard to the effects of artifacts such as pipes or jewelry. In the meantime, we are left with only our speculations as to whether F. Lee Bailey intentionally dressed Patty for the courtroom and whether, in fact, this message of clothing had an effect on the jurors' final decision in the case. Based on the research findings we can conclude that Patty's clothing most likely did have an effect on her own feelings and emotions, on the perceptions of the jurors, and on their response to her. However, it is the nature and degree of that effect that cannot be ascertained at this time.

REFERENCES

Aiken, L. "Relationships of Dress to Selected Measures of Personality in Undergraduate Women." *Journal of Social Psychology*, 1963, *59*, 121.

Anderson, D. "Whatever Happened to the Corporate Dress Code?" *TWA Ambassador*, March 1977, 43–45.

Bergen, P. *I'd Love to, But What'll I Wear?* Ridgefield, Conn.: Wyden Books, 1977.

Bickman, L. "The Social Power of a Uniform." *Journal of Applied Psychology*. 1974, *4*, 47–61.(a)

Bickman, L. "Social Roles and Uniforms: Clothes Make the Persons." *Psychology Today*, 1974, *7*, 48–51.(b)

Buckley, H. M., and M. E. Roach. "Clothing as a Nonverbal Communicator of Social and Political Attitudes." *Home Economics Research Journal*, December 1974, *3*, 2, 94–102.

Compton, N. "Personal Attributes of Color and Design Preferences in Clothing Fabrics. *Journal of Psychology*, 1962, *54*, 191–195.

Douty, H. I. "Influences of Clothing on Perception of Persons." *Journal of Home Economics*, 1963, *55*, 194–202.

Fleming, A. T. "Does the Total Woman Add Up?" *Vogue*, August 1977, p. 76.

"Giveaways in Age Can Be Found in Clothing." *New Woman Magazine*, July–August 1976, 54–55.

Hamid, P. N. "Some Effects of Dress Cues of Observational Accuracy, Perceptual Estimate and Impression Formation." *Journal of Social Psychology*, 1972, *86*, 279–289.

Hamid, P. N. "Style of Dress as a Perceptual Cue in Impression Formation." *Perceptual and Motor Skills*, 1968, *26*, 904–906.

Hamilton, J., and J. Warden. "Student's Role in a High School Community and his Clothing Behavior." *Journal of Home Economics*, 1966, *58*, 789–791.

Hoult, R. "Experimental Measurement of Clothing as a Factor in Some Social Ratings of Selected American Men." *American Sociological Review*, 1954, *19*, 324–328.

"If I Look Good, I Feel Good." *New Woman Magazine*, October 1977, vii, p. 5.

Knapp, M. L. *Nonverbal Communication in Human Interaction*, 2nd ed. New York: Holt, Rinehart and Winston, 1978.

Knight, Dunlap. Quoted in B. Rudofsky. *The Unfashionable Human Body*. New York: Anchor Press, 1974.

Korda, M. *Success: How Every Man and Woman Can Achieve It*. New York: Random House, 1977.

Kuehne, S. H., and A. M. Creekmore. "Relationships among Social Class, School Position and Clothing of Adolescents." *Journal of Home Economics*, October 1971, *63*, 7, 555–556.

Leathers, D. G. *Nonverbal Communication Systems*. Boston: Allyn and Bacon, Inc., 1976.

Lefkowitz, M., R. Blake, and J. Mouton. "Status Factors in Pedestrian Violation of Traffic Signals." *Journal of Abnormal and Social Psychology*, 1955, *51*, 704–706.

Massimo, J. "The Impact of Psychological Factors in the Evaluation Process: Getting to the Judge." *International Gymnast*, June 1977, p. 60.

McCroskey, J. C., C. E. Larson, and M. L. Knapp. *An Introduction to Interpersonal Communication*. Englewood Cliffs, N.J.: Prentice-Hall, 1971.

McGraw, Ali. "On Appearance: One of the Many Determiners of Self-Esteem." *New Woman Magazine*. March/April, 1977, p. 24.

McKeachie, W. "Lipstick as a Determiner of First Impressions of Personality: An Experiment for the General Psychology Course." *Journal of Social Psychology*, 1952, *36*, 241–244.

Molloy, J. T. *Dress for Success*. New York: Warner Books, 1975.

Molloy, J. T. *The Woman's Dress for Success Book*. Chicago: Follett Publishing, 1977.

Morgan, M. *The Total Woman*. New York: Simon & Schuster, 1981.

Morris, D. *Manwatching: A Field Guide to Human Behavior*. New York: Harry N. Abrams, Inc. Publishers, 1977, pp. 213–217.

Poll, A. "Through a Glass Darkly." *Dun's Review*, February 1976, *107*, 77–78.

Popplestone, J. A. "Prison Parlance." *Human Behavior*, April 1977.

Rollmann, S. A. "How Teachers' Dress Affects Students' Opinions." *National Enquirer*, November 1, 1977.

Rosencranz, M. L. "Clothing Symbolism." *Journal of Home Economics*, 1962, *54*, 18–22.

Rosencranz, M. L. Quoted in *Valley Times News*. Phoenix, Arizona, April 6, 1976, 3.

Rosenfeld, L. B., and T. G. Plax. "Clothing as Communication." *Journal of Communication*, 1977, *27*, 23–31.

Rudofsky, B. *The Unfashionable Human Body*. New York: Anchor Press, 1974.

Stillman, J. J., and W. Hensley. "What Tips Tippers to Tip," *Psychology Today*, June 1980, p. 98.

Sybers, R., and M. E. Roach. "Clothing and Human Behavior." *Journal of Home Economics*, 1962, *54*, 184–187.

Taylor, L. C., and N. Compton. "Personality Correlates of Dress Conformity." *Journal of Home Economics*, 1968, *60*, 653–656.

"The Complete Salesman." *Sales Management*, December 1, 1969, pp. 44–45.

Thornton, G. "The Effects of Wearing Glasses upon Judgments and Persons Seen Briefly." *Journal of Applied Psychology*, 1944, *28*, 203–207.

"Unsavory T-Shirts Reflect Incurable Sex on the Brain." *Rocky Mountain News*, August 19, 1977.

Williams, M. C., and J. B. Eicher. "Teenagers' Appearance and Social Acceptance." *Journal of Home Economics*, 1966, *58*, 457–461.

Williamson, L. "Keep Your Shirt On. People Will Like You Better." *Psychology Today*, June 1977, 90.

4

BODY MOVEMENTS AND GESTURES

"Well, this is grand!" said Alice. "I never expected that I should be a Queen so soon—and I'll tell you what it is, Your Majesty," she went on in a severe tone (she was always rather fond of scolding herself). "It'll never do for you to be lolling about on the grass like that! Queens have to be dignified, you know!"

So she got up and walked about—rather stiffly just at first, as she was afraid that the crown might come off: but she comforted herself with the thought that there was nobody to see her. "And if I really am a Queen," she said as she sat down again, "I shall be able to manage it quite well in time."

LEWIS CARROLL

*L*ittle Red Riding Hood set herself up to be mugged. Her first mistake was skipping through the forest to grandma's house. Her second mistake was stopping to pick flowers. At this point, as you might remember in the story, the mean, heavy wolf comes along and begins to check her out. He observes, quite perceptively, that she is happy, outgoing, and basically unaware of any dangers in her surrounding environment. The big bad wolf catches these nonverbal cues and splits to grandma's house. He knows that Red is an easy mark. From this point we all know what happens.

Let's rewrite this scene after Little Red Riding Hood has taken a class in nonverbal communication. Now she walks through the forest with a quick stride, even pace, and determined step. She is clearly goal-directed, and nothing can stop her. She walks over tree trunks and through rivers (at least it seems so). Mr. Bad observes Red's walk and says to himself, "This chick is more heavy than she looks." "If she's so sure of herself," Mr. Bad reasons, "then her grandma may have the punch of Ali." Since he doesn't want to get punched out by an old lady, he goes back to eating berries.

Body movements and gestures reveal a lot of information about a person. Like Little Red Riding Hood, pedestrians may signal to criminals that they are easy targets for mugging by the way they walk. When was the last time you assessed your "muggability rating"? In a recent study two psychologists set out to identify those body movements that characterized easy victims. They assembled "muggability ratings" of sixty New York pedestrians from the people who may have been the most qualified to judge—prison inmates who had been convicted of assault (Rubenstein, p. 20).

The researchers unobtrusively videotaped pedestrians on weekdays between 10:00 A.M. and 12 P.M. Each pedestrian was taped for six to eight seconds, the approximate time it takes for a mugger to size up an approaching person. The judges (prison inmates) rated the "assault potential" of the sixty pedestrians on a ten-point scale. A rating of one indicated someone was "a very easy rip-off," of two, "an easy dude to corner." Toward the other end of the scale, nine meant a person "would be heavy; would give you a hard time," and ten indicated that the mugger "would avoid it, too big a situation, too heavy." The results revealed several body movements that characterized easy victims: "Their strides were either very long or very short; they moved awkwardly, raising their left legs with their left arms (instead of alternating them); on each step they tended to lift their whole foot up and then place it down (less muggable sorts took steps in which their feet rocked from heel to toe). Overall, the people rated most muggable walked as if they were in conflict with themselves; they seemed to make each move in the most difficult way possible" (Rubenstein, 1980, p. 20). It appears that crime victims typically walk around in a daze, oblivious to what goes on around them, very much as Little Red Riding Hood did before her class in nonverbal communication. This dreaminess, the study confirms, is expressed in body movements that criminals read as a clear signal to move in.

In the last few years, there has been an explosion of interest in the study of *kinesics,* popularly referred to as "body language." Authors have told us that if a woman sits with her arms crossed, it "means" she is cold toward other people. If she crosses her legs, it "means" that she is trying to block others out or is sexually frigid. Right? Wrong. Such labeling or stereotyping is one of the problems with current *popular* "research" concerning "body language." It simply overlooks twenty years of formal research as well as the "context" of a given situation. A woman may sit with her arms folded because she is physically cold. Similarly, she may have her legs crossed because she finds this to be a comfortable body position.

Education, social class, geographical background, and habit influence the development of our own individual body gestures and movements. In addition, we cannot forget the social, political, or economic context of a particular communication situation. It is only in the light of the event itself that we can come to determine what is being "communicated" by a certain posture, gesture, or body movement.

This chapter will focus on two major areas of kinesic research: body movement and posture. But first we would like to introduce you to two primary ways in which researchers have classified and studied body movement and posture. The first perspective comes from the research of Raymond Birdwhistell (1970), a noted authority on kinesic research. The second, and more current, approach is found in the work of A.T. Dittman (1971, 1977). We hope that when you finish this section, you will have a general understanding of the current state of the art in kinesic research.

KINESICS: TWO MAJOR PERSPECTIVES

How many times have you heard the expression "we cannot *not* communicate?" Probably several times if you have ever taken any communication classes. As many researchers have noted, we may be able to stop talking in the vocal sense, but we cannot stop sending messages.

Intentionally or unintentionally, our bodies continue to send messages through posture, lean, tension, gestures, and other body expressions.

Ray Birdwhistell was one of the first researchers to conduct in-depth studies concerning the messages we send with our bodies. Birdwhistell believed that kinesics should be studied as a communication system, in much the same way that spoken language is studied—through the use of structural units or building blocks. Figure 4.1 provides an interesting comparison between the structural units of language and those of movement.

As Fig. 4.1 illustrates, **allophones** are the smallest units of analysis in language. An example of an allophone might be the "p" sound in the word "pan." Researchers in language state that there are many ways in which this particular sound may be made. In fact, voice scientists have stated that even the same speaker usually does not pronounce a word in the same way every time. Each of these variations in the "p" sound in the word pan is called an allophone. Likewise, **allokines** are the smallest units of analysis in body language. Each individual variation in one given movement (which can be distinguished from another movement) is termed an allokine.

At this moment you might be asking yourself, "Who cares how many ways you can say the "p" in pan or how many ways you can hold your right index finger and thumb when making the "ok" sign for your best friend who is across the street? In general, researchers would agree with you. These units of analysis are very minute. For that reason, a larger category is usually used in both language and body movement

Figure 4.1.
Comparison of phonetic and kinesic concepts.

analysis. These units are called **phones** in language analysis and **kines** in body language analysis. More specifically, all the ways you can say the "p" sound in the word pan, as well as the ways you can say the "p" sound in the word tapes, are two ways of making two different "phones" of the sound. These "p" phones ultimately come together to form the **phoneme,** (p). As you might guess, the "p" sounds are interchangeable in that any "p" sound may be used without a change in meaning. Likewise, **kinemes** consist of kines, which in turn consist of all possible variations of allokines. These kinemes, much like phonemes, can be interchanged without changes in meaning.

Thus far we have talked only about the small individual sounds and movements that are used in our two language systems. But how do these come together to form the verbal and nonverbal language we use everyday? The answer is quite simple. Rarely do phonemes or kinemes occur without subsequent use of other phonemes or kinemes. Thus when phonemes are used in sequence, they form **morphemes;** likewise, sequences of kinemes are believed to form **kinemorphemes.**

Does the following sequence sound familiar?

> Your friend Leigh is angry. She tosses her head, flips her hair back, clenches her fist, turns, and departs with quick, rapid steps.

Such a sequence of action, in Birdwhistell's system, constitutes the complex language of body movement.*

Birdwhistell's system of analysis of body movement represents one perspective of the study of kinesics. There are, however, researchers who argue with his approach. A.T. Dittman, for example, contends that major differences exist between the language system and the "body language" system. Using American Sign Language and the sign language of American Indians as the basis of his studies, Dittman concluded that body movement as a whole did not merit the criteria for spoken language, although "languages" such as ASL and Indian Sign Language were close to spoken language. More specifically, Dittman argues that body movements in general do not (1) form an alphabet comprised of discrete units and (2) are not governed by explicit, specific rules. On the basis of these findings, he concluded that body movements are not represented by a formalized language code. Body movements do provide valuable information, however, from which we can draw conclusions and make inferences. For this reason, the study of movement is important in the total human communication process.

We hope that at this point you understand the differences between the two major schools of thought concerning kinesics. One view of

---

*For additional information concerning the study of body movement as a structural system of building blocks, see R. Birdwhistell, *Kinesics and Context* (Philadelphia: University of Pennsylvania Press, 1970).

Richard Varney

"Watch out, Rudy's getting ready to raise the ante."

kinesics is that it is a study of the complex structure of body movements, which constitute a formalized language code. The other major perspective denies that there is a "language"; however, adherents of this viewpoint do acknowledge that body movements provide information important to the communication process. We now turn to the study of "body language" as it relates to current research and classification systems.

KINESIC CLASSIFICATION SYSTEM

Ekman and Friesen, two of the foremost researchers in kinesics, divide body movement into the five following categories: emblems, illustrators, regulators, affect displays, and adaptors. The purpose of this section is to provide an understanding of the complementary and independent functions body movements and gestures serve in relation to verbal language.

●

Emblems

It's the end of the fourth quarter of the Superbowl, and the score is tied fourteen to fourteen. The quarterback drops back to pass, throws, and the ball sails high into the air. The receiver catches the pass, zigzags away from three vicious opponents, and finally crosses the goal line. "Bang!" sounds the gun. The referee raises his arms in perhaps the most welcomed gesture he could have made. And the Superbowl is over—another team is victorious.

What sign did the players and fans receive that allowed them to determine that the winning touchdown had been scored? You could say, "Well, that's really obvious; the player crossed the goal line." But what if the referee had not made the body movement signifying a touchdown? He could have made another gesture calling it back. The fact remains that the gesture he made had a definite meaning. Without the use of words, he signified that the touchdown was good.

There are many gestures, other than those used on the football field, that have a specific meaning for those who are either sending or receiving the message. These special kinds of gestures are called **emblems.** What distinguishes emblems from other kinds of gestures? Paul Ekman (1976) explains that an emblem is an act that meets the following criteria:

1. It has a direct verbal translation, usually consisting of one or two words.
2. It is known by most or all of a group, class, subculture, or culture.
3. It is generally used with intent to send a specific message to a receiver.
4. It is received by an individual who realizes both the meaning and the intent of the emblem.
5. It has the sender taking responsibility for having sent the message. (p. 14)

As you can see, an emblem is a gesture that has a very precise meaning. In order to recognize the "ok" sign (formed by placing the index finger on the top of the thumb of the same hand), one need not know who made the gesture, to whom it was sent, why it was sent, or what happened before, during, or after the sign to recognize its meaning (Ekman, 1976, p. 15). We must remember, however, that knowing *some* of these variables helps us to determine more *exact* "meaning." Consider, for example, the response of Americans to an emblem that Khrushchev made when he arrived for a visit to the United States. With hands upraised and clasped over his head in a greeting of friendship, the Russian diplomat stepped off the plane. What was intended as an

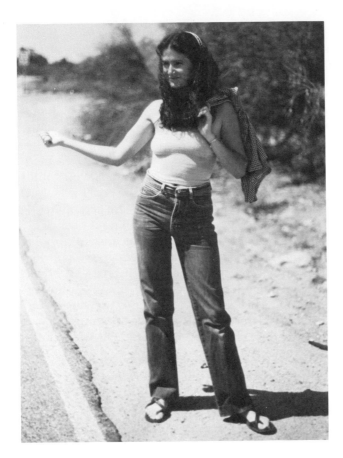

The hitchhiking sign of thumbs-up is an emblem that is widely known. Whether she gets a ride or not may depend on other body cues.

emblem of friendship appeared, instead, to be the American emblem of victory.

This example reminds us that context and geographical background are important in attempting to decode the "meaning" of the message. Likewise, knowing the events that happened before, during, and after an emblem helps to establish whether a sender is serious about the message.

If a friend "flips a bird" or "gives the finger" (formed by making a loose fist and extending the middle finger) to another friend, he probably "means" something different from what the young radical, who is screaming at a political candidate while making the emblem, means. Before we go further, however, you should understand that emblems are made not only with the fingers or hands. Emblems can also include head nods and many other movements of the body. As an exercise, see if you can think of the ''emblems'' that represent the following words or phrases:

shame on you	I don't know
I promise	suicide
hitchhiking	tastes good
peace	what time is it
gossip	it's hot
whoopee	cut it out

An intriguing use of emblematic communication is the unwritten hand-waving protocol that is expected between car drivers. You have probably used many of these gestures yourself, and, like many of us, you have probably failed to use hand-waving gestures when it was appropriate to do so. In order to clarify the guidelines for ''armwagglers,'' we need to establish that indiscriminate waving between drivers is both unacceptable and confusing. Waving is appropriate, however, to signal a thank you to someone who has allowed you to enter his/her lane of traffic. Another type of waving occurs between drivers who share something in common; for example, they may both be driving a purple VW van. The form of the hand wave is extremely important because it communicates a great deal of information. In a 1953 article appearing in *Road and Track* magazine, the author suggested that the following standard be adopted for hand waving:

> Raise the left hand from the steering wheel to the vertical position, keeping fingers loosely joined and palm slightly cupped. Now return the hand to the steering wheel. This movement should be executed smartly and smoothly, but without haste. In a right-hand-drive car, the right hand, of course, is used. (Walsh, 1978, p. 59)

The 1953 article on guidelines for motorists offers several interesting considerations for protocol with regard to hand movements:

1. Waving will be restricted to drivers only, although passengers may be permitted to nod politely in accordance with the same rules that govern waving.
2. Between drivers of opposite sex, a friendly smile may be exchanged, but no hint of a leer will be allowed.
3. Dogs as passengers may be permitted to bark briefly, provided this is done in conformance with the general waving rules. (Walsh, 1978, p. 59).

The next time you are out driving, observe the protocol of hand movements among drivers—or invent some new ones of your own. But beware, or you may be pulled over for using wrong hand movements!

It is interesting to note that we can also have emblematic ''slips'' of the tongue, much as we have verbal slips. As early as 1955, Paul Ekman discovered the phenomenon when he arranged for an interview between the director of a graduate program and one of his students. The student was subjected to several minutes of intense criticism by the director. Ekman noted that the student held ''the finger'' (also known as ''the bird'') on one hand for a few minutes during this difficult interview (Ekman, 1976, p. 25). Perhaps this slip was due to her inability to fight back and the need for her to ''maintain.'' Nevertheless, the study provides some interesting data concerning emblems and emblematic slips. Through our body movements, we communicate unconscious symbols for the thoughts or feeling that we are experiencing but that we are not always communicating verbally. The next time you are ''under fire,'' it is to be hoped that you will (a) be more aware, and (b) smile a little because you will remember this inside information concerning body language!

Illustrators

How would you feel if you could not use your hands when you wanted to give someone directions? What if you had to describe the action of ''zigzagging'' without using your hands? You probably would find yourself less able to make descriptions adequately. As many researchers have noted, language is both linked with and supported by body movement. Body movement can add to the meaning of utterances, provide feedback, and control synchronization of our everyday language. In addition, it can punctuate or display the structure of utterances, emphasize, frame (provide further information), illustrate, and signal continued interaction (Argyle, 1975, pp. 50, 254). Without the use of our hands or limbs, language would at best be less interesting, if not more difficult.

Gestures that are closely linked with language and that help to ''illustrate'' our spoken words are called **illustrators.** Perhaps a logical place to begin a discussion of the role of illustrators is to examine their function in the life of a child.

Piaget, a noted psychologist who worked closely with children and their speech patterns, suggested that for a child under the age of seven or eight, gestures are as important as words and, in fact, constitute the ''real social language of the child'' (in Evans and Rubin, 1979, p. 190). In 1979, Mary Ann Evans and Kenneth Rubin helped to substantiate this theory. Using eight children from kindergarten and grades two and four, Evans and Rubin found that the kindergarten children, when explaining a game to an adult, relied considerably more on hand gestures than the older children, while the older children used more verbalizations. Other researchers have found that although we do decrease our

A verbal statement is being illustrated by one man's hand and extended arm gesture. It appears that the impact of the gesture affects each listener differently.

use of simple hand gestures as we get older, we also increase our use of more complex hand movements (Jancovic, Devoe, and Wiener, 1975, pp. 922–928). There is one exception to this "rule," however. As Ekman (1976) has noted, Americans use a greater number of gestures when they are excited or when they are communicating difficult messages than when they are bored or when they are communicating relatively simple messages (p. 15). In addition, we use more illustrators in face-to-face interactions than in non–face-to-face interactions (Cohen, 1977, p. 54). These findings suggest two functions of illustrators: (1) an encoder function, in which gestures allow us to better encode difficult material, and (2) a decoder function, in which gestures allow the decoder to benefit from use of the gestures. Research from scholars such as Graham and Heywood in 1975 and Cohen in 1977 seems to support the encoder/decoder functions.

In a 1975 experiment, Graham and Heywood found that elementary hand gestures had a negative effect when communicators tried to describe two-dimensional shapes to subjects who had to reproduce them, thus supporting the existence of an encoder function (pp. 189–195). Likewise, using seventy-two males and seventy-two females at Hebrew University of Jerusalem, Cohen (1977) found that more il-

Focusing on the hands provides a great deal of information about tension, impatience, and even anger when the fist is tightly clenched.

lustrators were used in face-to-face interactions than when an intercom was used, thus suggesting the existence of the decoder function of illustrators (pp. 54–63). As you can see, illustrators help us to better encode and decode information. Again, we must remember that results such as these must be evaluated in the context of ethnic or cultural groups to which we belong. Arabs, for instance, have been found to use many more gestures than Americans during face-to-face interactions* (McGough, 1974, p. 111).

Regulators

Before you begin this section, try this experiment. First, put a friend in an adjoining room with the door almost closed. Then, using a monotone voice, try to have an ongoing conversation with your friend. As you may assume, this particular conversation will probably be quite difficult. Without the use of your hands or of paralinguistic cues (voice raised, lowered, etc), it may be almost impossible to speak without be-

---

*See Chapter 11 for more cultural distinctions.

ing interrupted. The purpose of this exercise is to show you the importance of nonverbal behaviors as **regulators** of an interaction, and in this instance, as regulators of a conversation. Although greetings and gestures used when arriving and departing serve as regulators, our discussion will not center on these body movements. Rather, we hope to provide you with some important information on how we use nonverbal behavior to regulate conversation.

Regulators are body movements that help us to interact with another individual. They include head nods, hand gestures, shifts in posture, and many other forms of body movement that allow us to signal the beginning and ending of interactions, as well as when to speak or to shift topics. This **turn system,** as it may be called, acknowledges the importance of signals between a speaker and a listener. The following discussion focuses on the roles of the sender and receiver with regard to nonverbal cues.

The turn system, as Duncan and Fiske described it in 1977, requires that each participant in the conversation sees himself or herself as either a **speaker** or an **auditor** during each second of a conversation. As a result, there are four possible interactions:

1. Speaker–auditor.
2. Auditor–speaker.
3. Speaker–speaker.
4. Auditor–auditor. (Duncan and Fiske, p. 178)

The first two states are considered "normal" states of interaction. If Barb asks Ralph a question, Ralph is the auditor and Barb is the speaker. When Ralph makes a response, he becomes the speaker, and Barb is the auditor. The second two states, however, represent a "breakdown" in the interaction. Perhaps Ralph hasn't read Barb's cues well enough and begins while Barb is still talking. In the fourth state, neither individual takes a speaking turn. Again, there has been a breakdown.

Let us explain further. Mark Knapp (1978) summarized a number of sources and came up with the following breakdown of cues used in the turn system. The first two types of cues are used by a speaker; the second two are used by the auditor.

Using Ralph and Barb again, let's look at these four cues. The first is the **turn-yielding cue.** Ralph has finished speaking and has told Barb what it was he wanted to say. By asking a question, decreasing loudness, or slowing tempo, or simply by using silence, Ralph has cued Barb that it is her turn to speak. Another way Ralph could have cued Barb to speak would have been to terminate or decrease gestures and to relax his posture. If Barb has still not realized that it's her turn to speak, Ralph could touch her on the arm or simply say "Well?"

If Ralph hasn't finished saying what he wishes to say, the way for him to continue is to use **turn-maintaining cues.** Ralph would, according to Knapp, increase loudness, decrease silent pauses, fill pauses with gestures, and avoid allowing his gestures to terminate at the end of phrases or sentences. Knapp also would advise Ralph to lightly touch or use a patting motion that says, ''Just a few more minutes and you can talk.''

When Barb is ready to speak and Ralph hasn't finished saying what he wishes to say, Barb will use what Knapp terms **turn-requesting cues** to adopt the speaker's state instead of the auditor's state. To do this, Barb could use rapid head nods or say ''yeah,'' ''uh-huh,'' or ''I agree'' more frequently. She also could raise her index finger, take an audible breath, or straighten or tense her posture to show Ralph she is ready to speak. Knapp adds that if Ralph continues speaking, Barb can simply begin talking. This would constitute the speaker–speaker state. You probably never realized that turn-taking behaviors in conversations were so complicated!

Another important type of turn-related behavior is **turn denying.** Turn denying would be used when Ralph or Barb do not wish to talk. To remain in the role of the auditor, one simply needs to maintain silence and a relaxed posture. An intent gaze at the environment, smiles and nods, or even some ''um-hums'' thrown in at the appropriate times will show the speaker you would rather remain silent.

It is clear that we use gestures and other nonverbal behaviors to regulate our interactions. One of the purposes of this section is to make you more aware of how we interact with others. Before your next class meeting, take some time to observe how people converse. See how many ''regulators'' you can discover in a conversation between two friends or between two strangers or perhaps at the checkout counter at the grocery store. Increased awareness of nonverbal communication can help us to become better communicators.

Gene Warne

Affect Displays

When was the last time you felt really sad or depressed? Now quickly sketch a cartoon of how you felt, or visualize yourself in your mind, using posture to convey your feelings. Now draw a sketch that represents how you feel when you are happy or excited, again using posture and body parts to represent your feelings. Your sketches might look something like this:

Dale Campbell

Feeling Good   Feeling Bad

If you drew your pictures in some way similar to these, you probably "know" something about the role of **affect displays** and nonverbal communication. Affect displays are those behaviors that reflect the intensity with which we feel an emotion; in addition, they usually can be "measured" by the amount of body tension we are feeling. Think, for example, of the football player who is about to play his first game. Ninety-nine percent of the time you probably would not find this young man slumped over with bowed head. Most of the time he probably would have a rigid and erect posture, with every muscle taut. An increase in muscular tension, in fact, usually is a function of an increase in the emotion being displayed.

Posture is not the only reflection of emotional states. Shifts in body posture, clenching and unclenching our hands, and shuffling or quick movements of the feet also reveal more intensely felt emotions. Have you ever noticed, for example, the person who sits with legs crossed and makes quick, jiggling movements with the foot? What about the person who constantly crosses and uncrosses the legs, shifts around, and moves the body forward and backward? Usually this person is feeling some intensity of an emotion—contempt, disgust, anger, restlessness, or the desire to flee from the situation. However, as we discussed previously, the context of the situation is important in determining the "meaning" of such movements or body language. Without this knowledge, such "meaning" cannot be derived from body movements alone.

It is interesting to note that movements of the body also can be used to determine whether deception is being used by an individual. In the last few years, there has been a growing interest in deception research in the field of communication. As Eakins and Eakins (1978) have noted, the gestures we make with our hands and feet more than those we make with other parts of the body resemble the states we are feeling (p. 163). Research by other people also seems to support the idea that deception cues are often revealed in the lower part of the body.

In addition, when lying was involved in the concealment of emotions, researchers have found that observers were more accurate when they observed the body *only* of a person who was lying than when they observed that person's head and facial expressions (Hocking, Bauchner, Kaminski, and Miller, 1979). This current finding supports earlier research by Ekman and Friesen in 1969 and 1974 and by Ekman, Friesen, and Scherer in 1976. These researchers hypothesized that a sender has better control over facial expressions than over movements of the body or tone of voice. Bugental, Henker, and Whalen (1976) also found similar results and concluded that when deception was involved, the body and voice sent more accurate information than did facial expression with regard to deceptive cues (these studies reported in Rosenthal, 1979, p. 222).

The body sends important information about the intensity of emotion as well as about deception. Try this experiment: Find a friend who hasn't had this course (or one like it) and tell him/her you are going to tell a story (which may or may not be true). Before you begin, ask your friend to watch you closely to see if you are lying. At the end of the story, ask him/her if you were lying or not. See if your friend can tell you exactly why he/she thought you were lying. You might be surprised by the results.

Adaptors

When was the last time you noted a friend's hands move to the throat as she told you something that you knew she didn't really believe? When did you last catch yourself twisting your hair or puffing a cigarette as if you had two seconds left to live? If you can picture any of these scenes in your mind, you probably are "seeing" body movements that psychiatrists and researchers in kinesics have labeled **adaptors.**

Although research concerning adaptors is not currently extensive, several theories and ideas have been tested by researchers. For example, Donaghy in 1980 reported that adaptors are behaviors that we at one time used for our own personal convenience or comfort but that now have become an unconscious habit (p. 14). For example, Jeff constantly adjusts his glasses when in a tense situation; Rosemary incessantly flips her hair over her shoulder when in the same kind of situation. At one time these behaviors may have been necessary (perhaps Jeff's glasses were loose or Rosemary's hair was in her eyes). However, the behaviors now have become a part of their repertoire of body movements.

Other researchers generally have agreed that adaptors are linked with negative feelings, toward either oneself or another person. For example, Ekman and Friesen (1972) found that as psychological discomfort or anxiety increases, such adaptors as picking or scratching behaviors also increase (pp. 353–374). This research was conducted with both psychiatric patients and normal patients, thus revealing that self-adaptors are used in general by people during hostile, aggressive, or other negative states.

Adaptors are not usually exhibited intentionally. They are most often performed in private, and when observed in public they usually take an abbreviated form. For example, although a person may squeeze or pick a pimple in private, when in public he or she will only rub the infection. Since the adaptor appears in an altered or shortened form in public, it is often more difficult to recognize and analyze adaptors and the purposes behind them in a communicative interaction.

Although adaptors are not usually exhibited intentionally, they do communicate to the individual who is receiving the messages. Overall, speech is accompanied by two major types of hand movements: those movements that take place away from the body and those movements that take place on the body, with the clothing, or with its "adornments." Freedman (1972) and Freedman and Hoffman (1967) have labeled the first category of movements **object-focused** and the movements that occur on some part of the body **body-focused** (Barroso, Freedman, Grand, and Van Meel, 1978, p. 321). For example, scratching the blackboard with your fingernails is an object-focused movement, but scratching your head is a body-focused movement. In addition, data from a series of videotapes made by Barroso, Freedman, Grand and Van Meel (1978) suggest that body-focused movements are linked with a cognitive state different from that linked with object-focused movements (movements away from the body). The research team explains the differences in this way:

> Object-focused movements appear to be related to processes involved in representing in spoken language internal experiences as well as external events . . . Body-focused movements seem to be connected to attentional focusing during distraction or interference. In work with different populations, the continuous motions of the hands on the body emerged as signs of attentional disruption and as accomplishments of verbal activity during distracting conditions. (pp. 321–322)

Research by Sousa-Poza and Rohrberg in 1977 also found body-focused movements to be a reflection of uncertainty on the part of a speaker, or encoder. In contrast, object-focused movements were found to occur in relation to the type of information and listener availability (pp. 19–29).

As we have discussed, body movement functions have been divided into five categories: emblems, illustrators, regulators, affect displays, and adaptors. The following section will discuss an additional aspect of kinesics in which researchers have been interested, namely, posture and locomotion. Although some aspects of posture have been included in previous sections, we believe its study is important enough to warrant its own discussion. Included in the discussion are six major topics: (1) an introduction to posture; (2) posture as a reflection of immediacy; (3) posture and status; (4) gender differences in posture; (5) posture and locomotion; and (6) posture and emotions. This discussion will assist you in becoming more aware of the communicative nature of posture, bearing, and locomotion.

POSTURE: AN INTRODUCTION

Every year they come to West Point, a thousand or more, and their posture ranges from not very good to very bad. "On the day they arrive," Colonel James L. Anderson explains, "we begin taking side-view and back-view photographs of each and every man and woman to analyze the position of the head, shoulders, chest, abdomen, back, pelvis, and knees. Good posture has been a major concern at West Point for over 170 years, and West Point probably knows and does more about improving posture than any other institution" (Anderson and Cohen, 1977).

Good posture is more than standing at attention. It applies to the way you move every moment of your life—whether walking, sitting, lifting, or pushing. Long before researchers and scientists began to study body movements and their implication for communication, dancers and artists of mime were aware of the range of communications that could be expressed by body movement and stance alone. Key (1975) has composed a list of terms that gives some idea of the variety of postural stances that we use. We can crouch, sprawl, perch, slump, lounge, repose, loll, stretch out, rest, recline, lean, and stand at attention (p. 77). Can you think of others? If so, see how long you can make the list! It is interesting to note, however, that no matter how long the list, researchers can place every posture or stance you can think of into one of three categories: (1) standing; (2) bent-knee postions, such as sitting, squatting, and kneeling; and (3) lying. In addition, posture may be placed on a type of continuum between gestures and spatial behavior. For this reason, changes in posture may be seen as an extension of gestures or as a method of altering the distance between yourself and another person or object (Argyle, 1975, p. 282). An example is the light-footed boxer who "dances" from his opponent's powerful blows. At the same time that he springs from side to side, he himself levels deadly and accurate punches to his opponent's brow. The boxer's dancing movements are his way of changing the spatial distance between himself and his opponent; the blows he delivers are a form of gesturing. By maneuvering, he will have a better chance of ending the match victoriously.

Although researchers have divided postures into three major categories, the overall range of postures is exceptionally large. Gordon Hewes, a noted anthropologist, has studied postures in many different cultures. According to his work, there are approximately 1,000 different human postures. In primitive cultures, for example, he found almost one hundred common postures, most of which are not used in more advanced cultures. The major factors that influenced posture in these primitive societies were the nature of the ground (whether it was cold or wet) and the clothes that were worn (in Argyle, p. 282).

Another interesting fact is that the culture, as well as subgroups within that given culture, determines both the styles of posture and the situations in which we observe these specific body stances. Key (1975), for instance, noted that not all cultures use the same postures in a given situation. Whereas most people use a sitting or bent-knee postion when eating, some, like the ancient Romans, ate in the lying-down position (p. 78). In addition, from research on 480 different cultures and subgroups, Hewes determined eleven common ways to sit on a chair or chair-like structure, and almost 100 positions of standing and bent-knee positions (Key, p. 78). It seems reasonable to say that culture affects both our postures as well as the situations in which we use them. Although we have our own idiosyncratic body stance, postures, and walks (which are also a function of our body shape), culture dictates the ways in which we will use them. One of the most interesting areas of posture is its relation to immediacy and its impact on interaction, which form the subject of the following pages.

Posture and Immediacy

Picture yourself, for a moment, at a party talking with someone you have just met but would like to get to know better. This person leans forward, gazes into your eyes, and smiles as he or she talks with you. Based on this information, do you (1) think the person likes you; (2) know you must have bad breath; (3) wonder what you said to offend him or her; (4) feel like running and putting on more deodorant? Chances are you figure he or she likes you, right? You're also fairly certain that this very interesting person wants to continue the conversation as much as you do, right? But how do you know this, since this person has not actually verbalized it?

Although you believe it was your stunning personality and wonderfully good looks, researchers would probably disagree—in general. The posture and body movements of the person with whom you interact usually will encourage you to continue or terminate the conversation. Albert Mehrabian, a noted researcher in the area of kinesics, contends that posture communicates our attitudes through two main dimensions: immediacy and relaxation. **Immediacy,** the first dimension, consists of forward leans and other related nonpostural variables such as touching, gaze proximity, and direct body orientation. **Relaxation,** on the other hand, consists of such variables as asymmetrical leg postion, hand relaxation, and backward lean (in Argyle, 1975, pp. 276–277). In addition, openness of limbs usually suggests a more positive attitude on the part of two individuals engaging in conversation. Basically, all positions that reduce proximity or improve visibility between two people suggest a more positive and open attitude. So even if you do have a stunning personality and very good looks (which we know you do), observe body positions closely. They reveal important information about you and others.

Posture and Status

Before you read any further, picture the following scene. It's your first day on the job, and you are about to walk into your boss's office. Although you met her during the interview for the job, you still feel somewhat apprehensive about talking with her. Now freeze. Before you enter the office, which of the following stances would you use: (1) relaxed and open, (2) upright and attentive, or (3) casual and friendly? Most researchers would claim that postures other than an upright stance will probably send a negative message, depending upon the attitudes and personality of your boss. Generally, a relaxed postural style is used by individuals of higher status, while a more upright and tense postural style is reserved for members of lower status. Behavior in the animal kingdom provides interesting support for status- and posture-related behaviors. Argyle (1975) describes status roles of animals:

> The way an animal sits or walks reflects its emotional state and social status. A high-status confident animal sprawls in a relaxed position and struts about in an upright and relaxed manner. Animals lacking confidence are tense, sit with heads drawn into shoulders and curled up, and walk cautiously'' (p. 35).

Goffman, in observing staff meetings at a psychiatric hospital, found that high-status individuals put their feet on the table, slumped in their seats, and in general maintained a relaxed, nontense body position. Lower-status individuals, reported Goffman, maintained a more formal body position and sat straight in their chairs (1961). It is generally accepted that when two strangers meet, the more relaxed one enjoys the higher status (see Goffman, 1961; Mehrabian, 1969; and Mehrabian, 1968). According to Mehrabian (1971, p. 28) the ''one who is powerful, that is, of higher status, can afford to relax, whereas the weak must remain watchful and tense.''

Another interesting finding regarding posture and status is that an individual of equal status will usually assume a posture similar to that of the person with whom he or she is interacting. Sharing a similar posture with another person is referred to as a **congruent body postion,** while dissimilar posture is considered to be an **incongruent body position.** Congruent posture between two persons generally signifies liking and equality. Incongruent posture generally signifies that some difference in status exists (for example, a secretary sitting upright and the employer reclining in a large chair). Group behavior may even display postural changes when an argument occurs. In such cases, postures

By permission of Johnny Hart and Field Enterprises, Inc.

may shift between arguing parties to reflect differences in opinion, while a leader may adopt the postures of both parties to indicate his/her refusal to take sides.

Psychotherapists are aware of the significance of congruent postures or what they refer to as the "postural echo." Davis (1973, p. 91) describes the following technique:

> The late Frieda Fromm-Reichmann would sometimes assume a patient's posture to try to get a better idea of what he was feeling. . . one researcher who analyzed a psychotherapy film for the relationship between posture matching and movements of verbal rapport discovered only afterward that the therapist had deliberately echoed his patient's postures as a way to promote rapport.

As we have discussed, the relaxation dimension of posture usually expresses status and dominance, while the immediacy dimension relates to liking and degree of trust. Scheflen (1964) suggests that we tend to imitate the postural styles of peers during peer interaction (in Key, 1975, p. 80). In addition, a relaxed postural style is used more by females than by males, and more by persons of the opposite sex than of the same sex. We can infer certain status messages from both our own posture and that of others. Observe your posture during the next several days and see how you change when talking with a friend, a professor, or an employer. Also examine your telephone posture and see if you change your posture while talking on the phone to another person, even though that person cannot see you.

Posture and Gender Differences

Take a look at the following two lists and place the term "males" over the column that best represents stereotypical male characteristics and "females" over the column that best categorizes stereotypical female behaviors.

_____	_____
staring	lowering eyes
pointing	smiling
taking more space	cocking head
initiating touch	yielding
head erect	cuddling
upright stance	overting gaze
legs apart	stop talking
hands on hips	blinking

If you know your "stereotypes" you placed "males" over the first column and "females" over the second column. Interestingly enough, these "stereotypes" are somewhat accurate in description for they tend to be consistent with gender differences and, in some instances, actually influence these differences. Eakins and Eakins (1978) support this notion when they state:

> It is considered unfeminine or unladylike for a woman to "use her body too forcefully, to sprawl, to stand with her legs widely spread, to sit with her feet up . . . to cross the ankle of one leg over the knee of the other." And depending on the type of clothing she wears, "she may be expected to sit with her knees together, not to sit cross-legged, or not even to bend over." Although restrictions on women have relaxed recently, these prescriptions of propriety are not fully accepted. (pp. 160–161)

The development of female-submissive behaviors and male-dominant behaviors begins at an early age. It is both surprising and alarming to observe the display of behavioral differences in males and females. Julius Fast (1977, p. 22) reflects on the development of gender behaviors in his children:

> When my daughter was about five, she tended to take much smaller steps than my son did when he was that age. And I remember that even when my son was young, he'd always look me straight in the eye when I yelled at him, while my daughter would lower her eyes at the first sign that I was angry.

Both parents and teachers reward and punish children for appropriate and inappropriate gender behaviors. In *The Female Eunuch* Germaine Greer points out that the little boy "must break his umbilical cord with mother; little boys are encouraged to get out of their mother's way and they eventually 'want to' and are encouraged to do this. Little girls are not" (1971, p. 68).

Female-submissive behaviors represent the continual attempt of females to "shrink" or to take up less space. For instance, Birdwhistell (1970) found that American females keep their legs and feet together while sitting, while males display an angle up to ten to fifteen degrees between the feet. Females hold their upper arms close to the trunk, while males hold their arms five to twenty degrees away from the body. "These gender displays," claims Henley (1977, p. 136), "are acting out female shrinking and male spatial expansion." Other nonverbal behaviors that express femininity through shrinkage are described by Rita Mae Brown:

> Lowering a shoulder in the presence of a man, pulling the body in (literally to take up less space so he can move more), turning the head upward or tilting it to the side, often with persistent eyebrow signals, are motions most non-feminists perform. Such gestures elicit favorable response. (1974, pp. 61–62)

Nonverbal behavioral differences in posture are representative of both individual and societal attitudes about the differences between the

Gene Warne

"DOMINANT" and "SUBMISSIVE" behavior.

sexes. In addition to the influence of stereotypical classifications, posture is also defined by such factors as context, style, the person involved, clothing, and other artifacts. Your own experimentation will reveal how your posture changes depending on the type of clothing you are wearing, from a three-piece suit to blue jeans and a T-shirt.

Posture and Locomotion

Think of the "Charlie Girl" commercial on television. When she strides across the screen, all long legs and swinging arms, you and every other person is supposed to know she's there; she's made it. It's a very stagy walk, but it gets the point across, and she doesn't need to say a word. According to author Gerald Donaldson (1979), "our gait is closely integrated with our personality . . . a 'gaitologist' should be able to cure personality defects by altering the manner of walking" (in Morris, 1979, p. 141). Psychologist Joyce Brothers agrees: "You can change the way you perceive yourself, the way other people perceive you by changing your walk. Assume the posture and walk of someone you'd like to be: self-confident, alert. If you stride out purposefully, people will assume you know where you're going" (Morris, p. 141).

The average walking pace is two steps per second or about three miles an hour. When you walk at an average clip, you have a stride of about twenty-four inches, which stretches as you pick up speed. When was the last time you thought about the way you walk? Today? Last week? Two years ago? If you are not aware of your gait, pace, and posture, you may be missing out on one of the most interesting aspects of body language: the study of **locomotion.**

As you might guess, locomotion is the way we get from one place to another. We can walk, run, skip, jump, hop, dance, trot, crawl, mosey, slide, "make tracks," boogie, or "book it." Each of us has a distinct walk, one that allows our friends (and enemies) to recognize us and that reflects our height, weight, and body structure. In addition, our walk reflects our outlook on life, our attitudes, our emotional states, as well as our cultural or ethnic backgrounds.

One researcher who has studied locomotion in humans found that the way we walk tends to place us in one of three categories: the "pusher," the "puller," and the "balancer" (Birdwhistell, in Key, 1975, p. 92). Our individual walks, however, reflect both variety and style. See if you can find your own special walk from the following list that Birdwhistell compiled. Can you place your friends' walks into any of these categories?

_____ the bent-knee type	_____ the trudger
_____ the straight-knee type	_____ the toe pointer
_____ the bouncer	_____ the flat footer
_____ the glider	_____ the pigeon-toed
_____ the high stepper	_____ the practicer of the duck walk
_____ the foot dragger	_____ the practicer of the Indian walk
_____ the shuffler	_____ the foot stutterer

(adapted from Key, 1975, p. 92)

Not only do our walks reflect our real selves, but our walks also reflect our genders. Although the idea probably does not surprise you, see if you can pinpoint the specific differences in walks between the sexes. Eakins and Eakins (1978) state that the main differences with regard to locomotion between American males and females is that females, when moving, present the entire body as "a moving whole"—from neck to ankle. In contrast, American males "move the arms independently from the trunk, and may subtly sway the hips with a slight right and left movement involving a twist at the rib cage." In short, American males seem to be the more relaxed of the two (p. 159).

Another difference in the way American males and females walk is that the male tends to walk with his legs at a ten-to-fifteen-degree angle and with his arms five to ten degrees away from his trunk. In contrast, American females walk with their legs close together and their arms close by their sides (Eakins and Eakins, p. 160). This research is based on observations of American males and females and does not extend to males and females of other cultures. It would be interesting to compare the walks of individuals from the Soviet Union, Egypt, Australia, Great Britain, and the many other countries of the world. Perhaps such information could help us to determine more about attitudes and personalities, which in turn would allow us to maximize communication efficiency on the international level.

Locomotion plays an important part in the image we portray to others. Although we cannot provide a prescriptive approach to interpreting postures and movement, we can find empirical support to suggest that such behaviors are related to our perceptions of ourselves and to the perceptions others have of us. Your walk is the crowning glory of human body locomotion. "It is an action we all take so much for granted and yet," explains Morris (1977), "when analyzed as a mechanical operation, it emerges as an immensely complex process—so complicated, in fact, that muscle experts are still arguing today over the finer points of how it operates and how we manage to stride along so successfully" (p. 288).

Posture and Emotion

"First you notice the deference people pay her—how humble her colleagues are. Then her large soft eyes look straight at you—almost through you, it seems. Her voice is low and firm. Her white hair is coiled at the crown of her head and is pinned with a fresh flower. Then you might notice her hands resting quietly in her lap. They are large, with massive knuckles, testimony to the work she does. Her cat lies on the floor nearby. Her glasses, hanging by a chain, rest on her bosom. Her hearing is weak, so conversations with her are in raised tones" (Connolly, 1977, p. 17). This is a description of Ida P. Rolf, Ph.D., the well-known and internationally respected founder of the body therapy of structural integration, more commonly referred to as rolfing. This area of therapeutic work is based on the premise that "the body never lies." Rolfers believe that posture, body positions, and areas holding tension say things about one's emotional history, deepest feelings, character, and personality.

What is it that rolfers do? The rolfing practitioner uses his or her fingers, elbows, and knuckles to stretch the connective tissue surrounding those muscles that need lengthening and to separate muscle bundles. When the muscle is not used properly, as a result of trauma and habit, the fascia (the tissue that surrounds the muscle) becomes shorter and thicker and adheres to neighboring fascia (Kurtz and Prestera, 1976, p. 139). The rolfer restores the body to its natural, free-flowing state, thus allowing the person to experience spontaneity of movement, release of deeply embedded emotions, and lengthening of the body. Many people enjoy this aspect of rolfing because it gives them a taller, thinner appearance.

Although somewhat lacking in empirical and laboratory-demonstrated support, body therapies are quickly gaining the attention and respect of the scholarly community. These therapies represent a significant contribution in assisting people with their posture, proper balance, coordination, freedom of movement, and psychological problems. There are six primary body-oriented approaches developed in the West. Structural integration (rolfing) is the first, developed by Ida Rolf as a body-centered approach. Reichian therapy and bioenergetics, developed primarily by Wilhelm Reich and Alexander Lowen, use a psychoanalytic approach and represent the second and third systems. Patterning, the fourth system, grew out of the same theoretical perspective as rolfing and utilizes Rolf's concept of line, symmetry, and gravity. This system was developed by Judith Aston in collaboration with Ida Rolf. The fifth and sixth systems were developed by F. Matthias Alexander and Moshe Feldenkrais and are methods that focus on the functions and movement of the body rather than on the structure.

Gene Warne

"Your depression is contagious."

Most of these body therapies view the body as having fixed muscular patterns that connect with attitudes and predispositions about life. Structural integration, according to certified rolfer Owen Marcus, is "based on a belief that the body is plastic, rather than a fixed unit and that by ordered manipulation of the fascia, the body can resume the anatomically ordered assemblage it's supposed to have. The primary goal is to align the body with gravity" (Johnson, 1980, C-2).

Try an experiment with yourself. Assume various body postures and see what you feel like in each one. Each position will allow you to experience different emotions, ranging from confidence to insecurity and from elation to depression. "On the deepest levels, change always involves the body," according to authors Kurtz and Prestera in their book, *The Body Reveals* (1976, p. 145). "A new attitude means new perceptions, new feelings and new muscular patterns" (p. 145).

Have you ever lost or gained weight? If so, can you recall the different emotional feelings you experienced with the change in your body? Your observations of your body postures and emotional states may provide evidence of the amazing link between the body and the mind.

SUMMARY

History could be changed by altering the nonverbal behavior—especially the body movements and gestures—of particular people. Enter our time portal into the past and let's watch a young boy of fourteen being crowned as king. Many people are unhappy about such a young child being crowned king. Imagine the situation: "Hear ye, hear ye! This is the day young Arthur is to be crowned king before all the greats of the world!" The trumpets are raised in a salute, all eyes turn to the large double doors, and the young boy enters. To the shock of all, Arthur jumps into the doorway, skips down the red carpet, hops with great leaps into the air, and lands in a flip. Finally, with two great bounds he clears the seven steps before the throne and with another jump that would clear the Grand Canyon, he dives into the seat of the throne. Although these are acceptable behaviors for young people, a "king" cannot behave in this way. Many settings have "norms" as to how people are to walk, hold their bodies, and gesture. Body language is critical in terms of situational appropriateness and in depicting the appropriate image of a person.

The study of kinesics or body movements has been a major concern of researchers in psychology, communication, and many other areas.

Birdwhistell and Dittmann offer two perspectives for viewing the structural units of kinesic behavior. Birdwhistell contends that body language should be studied as a communication system, in much the same way that spoken language is studied—through the use of structural units or building blocks. Dittmann, on the other hand, contends that major differences exist between the verbal language system and the body language system. Specifically, Dittmann argues that body movements in general (1) do not form an alphabet comprised of discrete units and (2) are not governed by explicit, specific rules. Both perspectives offer important information and views concerning the study of kinesics and the future research in this area.

The classification of kinesic behaviors assists us in understanding their functional purpose in interaction settings. Researchers Ekman and Friesen divide body movement into the following five categories: emblems, illustrators, regulators, affect displays, and adaptors. Emblems are nonverbal acts that have direct verbal translations usually consisting of one or two words, such as the popular sign of "flipping the bird." Illustrators are closely linked with language and help to "illustrate" our spoken words, such as saying "head north" and pointing in that direction at the same time. Body movements that help us to interact with others are referred to as regulators. Specifically, they include such behaviors as head nods, hand gestures, and shifts in posture. Affect displays are those behaviors that reflect the intensity with which we feel an emotion. And finally, adaptors are nonverbal behaviors that are not as easily defined. Some researchers claim that adaptors are linked with negative feelings toward oneself or another person. Other researchers claim that adaptors are behaviors that we used at one time for our own personal convenience or comfort but that now have become an unconscious habit. In either case, adaptive behaviors represent a different class of movements, which is drawing increasing attention as an area of study.

If you want to look ten years younger and ten pounds thinner, stand up straighter. This simple advice appears in many magazines and books claiming that posture makes an important difference in external appearance and internal functioning of body organs. The discussion of posture in this chapter focused on (1) posture and immediacy, (2) posture and status, (3) gender differences in posture, (4) posture and locomotion, and (5) posture and emotions.

Posture reveals various aspects of immediacy and hence our feelings toward a person and/or a situation. Various displays of immediacy include forward lean, touching, gaze, proximity to another person, and direct body orientation. Status is often expressed through posture, particularly the status of relationships between a superior and a subordinate. Generally, a relaxed postural style is used by individuals of higher status, while a more upright and tense postural style is reserved for members of lower status.

Another interesting study of postural behaviors relates to gender differences. Stereotypically, males exhibit dominant behaviors (e.g., staring, pointing, taking up more space) while females exhibit submissive behaviors (e.g., cocking head, blinking, smiling). In the area of posture and locomotion (the way we get from one place to another), we noted how a person's distinct walk reflects that person's attitudes, emotional states, and cultural or ethnic background.

Finally, the study of posture and emotion raises the question of whether our posture induces particular emotional states or whether certain emotional states trigger a postural behavior. This chicken-or-the-egg phenomenon remains unanswered, but many serious practitioners of body therapies view the body as having fixed muscular patterns that connect with attitudes and predispositions about life. These body therapies include rolfing, Reichian therapy, bioenergetics, patterning, the Alexander method, and Feldenkrais's work. Bernard Gunther shares his insight into the literal and symbolic meanings revealed in our body movement behavior:

> *Body language is literal.*
> *To be depressed is, in fact,*
> *to press against yourself.*
> *To be closed off*
> *is to hold your muscles rigid*
> *against the world. Being open*
> *is being soft.*
> *Hardness is being up tight*
> *cold separate,*
> *giving yourself and other people*
> *a hard time. Softness*
> *is synonymous with pleasure*
> *warmth, flow, being*
> *alive.*
>
> *Are you itching to get at*
> *someone? Is your boss*
> *a pain in the neck?*
> *Are you sore about something?*
> *What is your aching back*
> *trying to tell you.*
> *Is there someone on your back?*
> *What about your ulcer?*
> *Is there someone or thing*
> *you can't stomach.*

What is it that you'd like to
get off your chest?
Your body speaks to you
all the time, telling you
what your own needs are:
LISTEN here. *

REFERENCES

Anderson, Col. J. L., and M. Cohen. *The West Point Fitness and Diet Book.* Rawson Associates Publishers, 1977.

Argyle, M. *Bodily Communication.* New York: International Universities Press, Inc., 1975.

Barroso, F., N. Freedman, S. Grand, and J. Van Meel. "Evocation of Two Types of Hand Movements in Information Processing." *Journal of Experimental Psychology* (Human Perception and Performance), 4, 2, 1978, 321–329.

Birdwhistell, R. *Kinesics and Context.* Philadelphia: University of Pennsylvania Press, 1970.

Brown, R.M. "The Good Fairy." *Quest,* 1974, 1, No. 1.

Carroll, Lewis. *The Complete Works.* New York: Vintage Books, 1976.

Cohen, A.A. "The Communicative Functions of Hand Illustrators." *Journal of Communication,* 27, 4, 1977, 54–63.

Connolly, L. "I. Rolf." *Human Behavior,* May 1977, 17–23.

Davis, F. *Inside Intuition.* New York: Mentor, Plume and Meridian Books, 1973.

Dittmann, A.T. "Review of Kinesics in Context." *Psychiatry,* 34, August 1971, 334–342.

Dittmann, A.T. "The Role of Body Movement in Communication," in A.W. Siegman, and S. Feldstein (eds.). *Nonverbal Behavior and Communication.* Potomac, Md: Lawrence Erlbaum Associates, 1977.

Donaghy, W.C. *Our Silent Language: An Introduction to Nonverbal Communication.* Dubuque, Ia: Gorsuch Scarisbrick Publishers, 1980.

Duncan, S., Jr., and D.C. Fiske. *Face-to-Face Interaction: Research Methods and Theory.* New York: Lawrence Erlbaum Associates, distributed by Halsted Press, 1977.

Eakins, B.W., and R.G. Eakins. *Sex Differences in Human Communication.* Boston: Houghton Mifflin Company, 1978.

Ekman, P. "Movements with Precise Meanings." *Journal of Communication,* 26, 3, 1976, 14–26.

Ekman, P., and W.V. Friesen. "Hand Movements." *Journal of Communication,* 22, 1972, 353–374.

Evans, M.A., and K.H. Rubin. "Hand Gestures as a Communicative Mode in School-Aged Children." *The Journal of Genetic Psychology,* 135, 1979, 189–196.

Fast, J. *The Body Language of Sex, Power, and Aggression.* New York: M. Evans and Company, 1977.

Goffman, E. *Encounters: Two Studies in the Sociology of Interaction.* Indianapolis and New York: Bobbs-Merrill, 1961.

Graham, J.A., and S. Heywood. "The Effects of Elimination of Hand Gestures and of Verbal Codability on Speech Performance." *European Journal of Social Psychology,* 5, 2, 1975, 188–195.

Greer, G. *The Female Eunuch.* New York: McGraw-Hill, 1971.

Henley, N.M. *Body Politics.* Englewood Cliffs, N.J.: Prentice-Hall, 1977.

Hocking, J.E., J. Bauchner, E.P. Kaminski, and G.R. Miller. "Detecting Deceptive Communication from Verbal, Visual, and Paralinguistic Cues." *Human Communication Research,* 6, 1, 1979, 33–46.

Jancovic, M., S. Devoe, and M. Wiener. "Age Related Changes in Hand and Arm Movements on Nonverbal Communication: Some Conceptualizations and an Empirical Exploration." *Child Development,* 46, 1975, 922–928.

Johnson, A. "Rolfing: A New Twist to the School of Hard Knocks." *The Phoenix Gazette,* December 2, 1980, C-2.

Key, M.R. *Paralanguage and Kinesics (Nonverbal Communication).* Metuchen, N.J.: The Scarecrow Press, Inc., 1975.

Knapp, M. *Nonverbal Communication in Human Interaction,* 2nd ed. New York: Holt, Rinehart, and Winston, 1978.

Kurtz, R., and H. Prestera. *The Body Reveals.* New York: Harper & Row/Quicksilver Books Publishers, 1976.

McGough, E. *Your Silent Language.* New York: William Morrow and Company, 1974.

Mehrabian, A. *Silent Messages.* Belmont, Cal.: Wadsworth Publishing Company, 1971.

——. "Significance of Posture and Position in the Communication of Attitude and Status Relationships." *Psychological Bulletin,* 1969, 71, 359–372.

——. "Inference of Attitudes from Posture, Orientation, and Distance of a Communicator." *Journal of Consulting and Clinical Psychology,* 1968, 32, 296–308.

Morris, D. *Manwatching: A Field Guide to Human Behavior.* New York: Harry N. Abrams, Inc., 1977.

Morris, D. "What Your Walk Says About the Way You Think, Work, Love." *Mademoiselle,* July 1979, 141–143.

Rosenthal, R. *Skill In Nonverbal Communication: Individual Differences.* Cambridge: Oelgeschlager, Gunn and Hain, Publishers, Inc., 1979.

Rubenstein, C. "Body Language that Speaks to Muggers." *Psychology Today,* August 1980, 20.

Scheflen, A.E. *Body Language and the Social Order: Communication as Behavioral Control.* Englewood Cliffs, N.J.: Prentice-Hall, Inc., 1972.

Sousa-Poza, J.F., and R. Rohrberg. "Body Movement in Relation to Type of Information (Person- and Nonperson-Oriented) and Cognitive Style (Field Independence)," *Human Communication Research,* 4, 1, 1977, 19–29.

Walsh, D.T. "Armwaggler's Guide." *Road and Track,* August 1978, 59. (Reprint of November 1953 article appearing in *Road and Track.*)

5

FACIAL EXPRESSION AND EYE BEHAVIOR

On the way to his sister's room, in the gallery that united one house to the other, Prince Andrey encountered Mademoiselle Bourienne smiling sweetly. It was the third time that day that with an innocent and enthusiastic smile she had thrown herself in his way in secluded passages.

"Ah, I thought you were in your room," she said, for some reason blushing and casting down her eyes. Prince Andrey looked sternly at her. A sudden look of wrathful expression came into his face. He said nothing to her, but stared at her forehead and her hair, without looking at her eyes, with such contempt that the Frenchwoman crimsoned and went away without a word.

TOLSTOY, WAR AND PEACE

*T*he eyes have a secret language all their own. It has long been known that the eyes can penetrate the invisible bubble that surrounds each one of us. The eyes of another invade our personal space when eye contact is prolonged or inappropriate for a given situation.

Prolonged eye contact or staring is more than a social issue—at the University of Colorado in Boulder it became a legal issue. The publication *National On-Campus Report* claimed that a former student at the University of Colorado in Boulder hired an attorney after being banned from campus for staring at several women in the campus cafeteria. The women who were the recipients of the steady stares complained that this behavior from a complete stranger was unsettling. But the banned student and his attorney claimed that a person has the constitutional right to stare at another person.

Whether staring is constitutional or not, it is a violation of a social norm and upsets people. So the moral of the story is "don't stare; people hate it." An exception might be if the stare is part of a special message that is reciprocated. Julius Fast describes how the language of the eyes alone can determine who will leave with whom at a party. He shares the story of Dana, who exchanged meaningful glances with a man across the room at a cocktail party. The dark-haired, blue-eyed man had arrived with a date, but Dana knew she would leave with him. How did she know? Simple; it was spelled out with eye contact. She caught his eye and looked away, and then she looked back and caught him looking at her. Then he lowered his eyes to his drink, but Dana kept looking. Finally, he looked up again, and they both stared at each other for awhile—just a little too long for it to be innocent. But how was Dana so sure she would be leaving the party with this man? Well, all she did was this: She cast a sideways glance at the room where the coats were hung, then at the clock, then at the door. A simple one-two-three progression that worked. "Now as soon as it's decently possible," Dana said to herself, "I'll excuse myself to our hostess, get my coat, and go to the door. I'm willing to bet two to one that he'll be there with me."

And Dana was right. She spoke to the hostess as the dark-haired man made some excuse to his date and his friends, and they were both at the door together. Coincidence? No, just the language of the eyes at its best (Fast, 1975)!

Your eyes and face communicate important messages. Is your face the *you* that you want to communicate? Many of us don't think so, and we spend millions of dollars each year to alter our facial appearance. In everyday conversation we hear, "I've got to put my face on," "I'm going to cover this mess," and "I can't go out with my face like this." To put our best face forward we buy cosmetics, use medications, apply ointments and creams, and undergo plastic surgery.

You may ask, "Why is so much emphasis placed on the appearance of the face?" Our society stresses the importance of "Beautiful People," and often beauty is associated with the physical characteristics of the face. Every time we turn on a television or open a magazine we see beautiful people. These people may be selling a new scented shampoo or modeling the latest three-piece suit. By using people with attractive faces, advertisers imply that if we use the shampoo or wear the suit, we, too, will be beautiful.

Faces provide us with a wealth of information. Through facial observation we make predictions about the race, nationality, sex, and age of people we meet. Have you ever known identical twins? If you had difficulty in telling the twins apart, imagine each of us with identical facial features. Think of the problems we would have in recognizing each other.

Differences in human faces are limitless, and the differences allow us to recognize each other. Often one facial characteristic helps us to recognize others and acts as a trademark, for example, Marty Feldman's eyes or Barbra Streisand's nose.

From facial characteristics we also make predictions about the type of person someone is or the personality someone may have. For example, when selecting actresses and actors for roles, directors have to take facial features into consideration. Facial features help us to identify the so-called "good guys" and "bad guys"; audiences usually picture hardened criminals with dark, beady, closely set eyes, sunken cheeks,

Richard Varney

small, thin lips, and heavy beards, while damsels in distress typically have large, blue eyes with long lashes, fair complexions, small, well-defined noses, and small, full mouths. Although many performers are indeed selected for their natural facial characteristics, makeup helps build stereotypes.

Some areas of the face give us more cues about the context of a situation and the person's personality than others. One aspect of facial communication that spans different cultures is a form of sign language called tongue showing. Tongue showing usually occurs when tasks or interactions are difficult or undesirable. Notice yourself and others around you the next time you play a game of concentration such as pick-up sticks or bridge.

Tongue display is common in all age groups. While observing children in a nursery school, Smith, Chase, and Lieblich (1974) found that children show their tongues during difficult tasks such as putting a puzzle together and in awkward social settings such as being scolded or embarrassed (p. 46). Another study observed pool players and found that the poor players displayed their tongues more than the better players. This study also found that all players displayed their tongues twice as much on difficult shots as on easy ones ("The Tongue's Own Language," 1973, p. 77).

Facial features also affect interpersonal relationships and judgments in interaction. Can you remember your last blind date and how you rated her/him? Was your first impression based on her/his clothing, body shape, or personality? Probably not. Although we do notice clothing, body shapes, and so on, when forming impressions about others, most of us first judge others by facial features. We respond more favorably to those we find attractive. Generally, physical attractiveness affects our judgments of personality, marital competence, social and professional adjustments, and happiness (Dion, Berscheid, and Walster, 1973, pp. 285–290). Attractive faces are recognized more often than unattractive faces (Sorce and Campos, 1974, p. 79), and physical attractiveness also increases perceived honesty and sincerity. According to research, women with beautiful facial features are less often convicted of crime than men or unattractive women.

However, through continued social interaction we begin to accept and reject others based on characteristics other than facial features. For example, many of us now have close friends whom we disliked at first sight. Although we do form first impressions based on a person's facial features, we also look to the face to provide other types of information about the communication situation and the individual.

The face is a primary nonverbal communicator of feelings and emotion (see chapter sections on emotion). Phrases like "His face was an open book," "It was all over her face," and "His face said it all" give us an indication of how much faces are capable of communication. According to Ekman and Friesen (1967), facial expressions usually communicate the quality and nature of emotions, while body cues tell more about the intensity of emotions (pp. 711–724). The following discussion will examine theoretical aspects of facial expression and facial expression of emotion.

DEVELOPMENT OF FACIAL EXPRESSION

The variety of facial expressions in everyday interactions is limitless. In a matter of seconds we see everything from sympathetic looks on a person's face on learning some sad news to amused expressions on another's face on hearing a good joke. This section will present theories of acquisition, development, and universality in facial expression.

Acquisition

One of the first researchers to take an interest in the types and influences of facial expression was Charles Darwin. Darwin believed that facial expressions were evolutionary processes acquired primarily to establish successful interaction. Primitive peoples, for example, communicated friendliness, dissatisfaction, and other emotions by facial expression when unable to do so verbally. Darwin (1872) suggests that as humans found other methods of communicating (i.e., language), facial expressions developed into a secondary method of communication.

Other theorists identify facial expression as a learned skill connected to language within each culture. They believe facial expressions are used to reinforce verbal messages. Say your friend Ann asked your opinion of her new curly hair style. You decide you don't like it. However, you probably would say that you did like it or that you had to get used to it to avoid hurting her feelings. According to theorists, Ann would doubt you unless your facial expression supported your verbal message. Although some researchers believe in the universality of facial expression, many others believe that similarities are only coincidental.

Tomkins (1962, 1963) suggests that facial expressions are a blend of innate and learned qualities. He believes that there are primary facial expressions that are universal and innate, but he also suggests the existence of cultural variations in their display. For example, young children laugh spontaneously when adults make faces for them, but as they grow up they learn to look ashamed when they've been caught doing something wrong.

Evidence that blind and sighted children have similar facial expressions contributes to the idea that facial expressions are not entirely based on imitative learning (Thompson, 1941, pp. 1–47). Eibl-Eibesfeldt (1970) compared the behavior of blind/deaf children with sighted/hearing children to determine whether facial expressions are innate or learned. He found that spontaneous facial displays of emotions such as surprise, fear, sadness, anger, etc., were not significantly different for blind/deaf children and sighted/hearing children. His contributions support research that indicates facial expressions are only partially based on imitative learning. The following section will explain the developmental processes of facial expression and how facial expressions can be both innate and learned.

Developmental Processes

Facial expressions of parents, relatives, and friends are an important source of information for a developing child. The exact time that infants begin to respond to facial expression in others is uncertain. According to Coss (1974), by the fourth week full-term infants will attempt to visually search for the eyes of the person caring for them (p. 18). Since the infant is helpless, eye contact serves a crucial role in establishing and bonding the relationship between the caretaker and infant (see section on eye contact).

Research also indicates that children begin to perceive meanings behind facial expression before they can demonstrate the facial behaviors themselves (Odom and Lemond, 1972, p. 360). Babies receive cues about moods of those around them, and this may explain why babies are fussy when there is emotional conflict in their home.

According to Stroufe and Waters (1976), infants usually express laughter by the eighth month (pp. 173–189). They express anger even earlier, usually by the sixth month (Ricketts, 1934, pp. 163–171). The ability to express anger is a necessary defense mechanism to signal to others that they are hungry, need their diapers changed, or are sick.

By the end of their first year, normal children usually have recognizable facial expressions. An interesting phenomenon is that facial expressions fail to improve with age. Age does affect the ability to discriminate between emotions but not the accuracy of expression. One reason that children often do not improve in the expression of emotion is that spontaneous facial expressions are often suppressed by cultural norms (Odom and Lemond, 1972, p. 368).

According to Hamilton (1973), children learn to inhibit spontaneous productions of emotion. Society teaches children which expressions of emotion are acceptable and unacceptable. At early ages children are admonished with such expressions as ''Big boys don't cry'' or ''If you don't stop pouting your face will grow like that'' (Hamilton, p. 138).

Sometimes children are punished for displays of inappropriate emotions. For example, if little Laura pouts when her mother tells her to come inside to clean up her room, her mother may spank her. If Laura gets spanked each time she pouts, eventually she'll learn to hide the felt emotion to avoid another spanking.

Although they learn to inhibit their expressions of emotion at early ages, children take quite a while to distinguish between contradictory nonverbal messages. Children take negative messages very seriously, even when accompanied by smiles. If Jason's teacher smiles at him

Sometimes facial expressions clearly express a person's thoughts or feelings.

while telling him he did poorly on a reading assignment, Jason will usually focus on the negative verbal message. Children usually believe
the worst. A teenager can understand that his parents love him even if
they yell at him for coming in late; a small child, however, has difficulty
in believing that she is loved when a parent yells at her for breaking a
lamp (Bugental, Love, and Gianetto, 1971, pp. 6–10).

The previous sections explained how facial expressions are both innate and learned. The following section will discuss cultural differences
in facial expression.

Universality

Some nonverbal behaviors differ across cultures (such as those mentioned in Chapter 11), but most facial expressions are now universally
associated with particular emotions. For example, try to remember the
times you have seen children's faces on posters such as CARE, Project
Uplift, or HUNGER. Was it difficult for you to translate the message,
even though the child's home was in India, China, or Mexico? Researchers have found that observers from the United States, England,
Germany, Spain, France, Switzerland, Greece, and Japan interpret
facial expressions as showing the same kinds of emotion. Observers
from different cultures are also accurate at judging the intensity of the
emotion expressed (Ekman, 1975, p. 35).

Why, then, have researchers differed in their view of the universality of facial expression? One reason is that there are **culture-specific differences** in the causes of emotion, in the acceptability of an emotion,
and in the results of displays of an emotion (Ekman and Friesen, 1969,
pp. 49–98). For example, in the United States children often make facial
expressions disapproving of or questioning actions of their parents,
while in Asian countries such questioning would be highly disrespect-
ful. In middle-eastern countries many men display their emotions (i.e.,
welcoming a friend with a kiss, excitement, etc.), while in America men
are expected to act more reserved. In the United States children might
be punished for frowning at requests from parents, while in some
Oriental cultures the same behavior would cause the child to be
disowned.

Ekman (1971) suggests that it is "likely that there is much more
cultural variability in blends of facial expression than in facial expressions of primary emotions" (p. 223). When observing differing cultures
one must remember that cultural differences depend on the circumstances that elicit an emotion, the consequences of an emotion, and
the display rules that govern the use of facial behavior in particular
social settings.

By now you should have gained a better understanding of the development of facial expression. The next sections of the chapter will examine differences in facial expression of emotion.

EXPRESSION OF EMOTION

Our faces communicate feelings and emotions to others. Spontaneous facial reactions and responses come from environmental stimuli. If you open the door to your apartment, and a group of friends shout "Happy Birthday!" your face will unconsciously express surprise. On the other hand, if you were to open the door to your apartment and find a burglar going through your drawers, your face would probably show fear or apprehensive surprise.

Early research suggested that facial expressions were involuntary reactions, which were thought to be good indicators of emotional states. Since that time further research has revealed that facial cues are only partially reliable or accurate. We have learned to protect ourselves by concealing our true feelings. By controlling the muscles of our face we hide inappropriate or unacceptable responses; such manipulations of facial expressions are known as **facial management techniques.** In the next few sections we will examine facial management, expressions of emotion and their effects, measurement of facial expression, and differences in expression of emotion.

Facial Management

According to Ekman and Friesen (1975), in most social settings four basic management techniques are incorporated. When controlling our facial behavior we usually (1) intensify a felt emotion, (2) deintensify a felt emotion, (3) neutralize a felt emotion, or (4) mask a felt emotion.

Intensifying.   Often societal pressures cause us to respond to the expectations of others, and at times such as these we usually exaggerate our facial behaviors to meet these expectations. Special occasions such as Christmas or birthdays encourage us to intensify felt emotions. We have all had the experience of receiving a gift in the presence of the giver; as we open the gift we express joy, surprise, and excitement even if we have three bottles of the same cologne, hate the color, or don't know what the gift is. The same would be true if you overheard someone mentioning a going-away party for you. Although you now knew about the party in advance, you would probably still show surprise and pleasure so that you wouldn't disappoint your friends. We exaggerate our facial responses to maintain positive social interactions.

Deintensifying. In most social situations individuals also learn to deemphasize facial behaviors to maintain favorable interpersonal relationships; in other words, we monitor normal reactions to respond more appropriately to others. For example, Larry and his best friend Harry both applied for basketball scholarships at a large southern university. After a few weeks, Harry was notified that he had received a full scholarship, while Larry received none. Being sensitive to Larry's feelings, Harry deintensified his normal excitement around Larry by saying he was only lucky. We often try to reduce feelings of anger, also. An employee who is angry at the boss might express the anger, but usually without yelling or using language that he or she might use with someone who is powerless.

Neutralizing. In some situations we avoid showing any emotion. Men and women differ in the emotional displays they neutralize because of cultural norms. Men in the United States, for example, are expected to be strong and brave. Because facial displays of fear or sadness are considered feminine, men may try to neutralize them, even if they are experiencing the emotion at the time. Sometimes, however, covering natural emotions can be detrimental. At the death of his mother, Mike withheld normal expressions of sadness and grief in order to be strong for other family members. Weeks later, doctors diagnosed the cause of his nervous breakdown as the inability to accept or express normal emotions. We neutralize emotions at times when we are unsure of the outcomes. In the popular game show "To Tell the Truth" all of the three players conceal or try to avoid showing emotion on their faces to avoid giving away their true identities.

Masking. We frequently replace felt emotions with emotions thought to be more appropriate. Through masking we try to conceal such emotions as jealousy and disappointment. Girls running for positions in a Homecoming Court eagerly await the decision. As the announcer calls the name of the new Queen, the other girls, though bitterly disappointed, display wide smiles of approval. If you were to surprise someone you were dating with an unexpected visit and found that person having a party in his or her apartment, you might be jealous because you weren't invited. However, you probably would hide this emotion until a later time when the other people were not around.

Some people are better at controlling emotions with management techniques than others. **Affect rules** are culturally learned habits, but rarely do individuals pause to think about which rule to follow (Ekman, 1971, p. 216). The hesitation would destroy the purpose of using facial management techniques. The situation and the people involved determine which display rules will be used. It is important to remember that

Gene Warne

when facial management techniques are used appropriately they are unnoticeable; only when the rules are violated do others become aware of them. If you were to laugh at a funeral, cry when hearing a joke, or smile when someone falls down and gets hurt, others near you would probably give you looks of disapproval or concern.

From this discussion we can see that we manipulate our facial features constantly to achieve desired results. One interesting variable is that we are often unaware of what we are doing; although we do control emotions on our face there are some emotions that are universally recognized. The following section will discuss different types of emotion and their effects.

Facial Movements to Express Emotion

One of the first researchers to develop a procedure for locating and classifying specific facial movements was Paul Ekman (1971). His technique, the Facial Affect Scoring Technique (FAST), divides the face into three areas for coding—brows–forehead, eyes–lids, and lower face (p. 249). Scorers are trained to recognize specific emotions and their corresponding areas of the face. These scorers then determine the beginning and end of each observable facial movement, classify each movement compared to a list of items, and assign a score according to the item the movement most closely resembles (Ekman, p. 248).

From previous research by Ekman with photographs, seven basic emotions have been found to be judged fairly consistently. These emotions include happiness, sadness, surprise, fear, anger, disgust/contempt, and interest.

No one area of the face best reveals emotion. According to Boucher and Ekman (1975), the "value of the different facial areas in distinguishing emotions depends upon the emotion being judged" (pp. 21–29).

They pinpoint anger as the most ambiguous expression of emotion, because unlike the other emotions, anger must be registered in at least two areas of the face, namely, the eyes and the mouth, in order for it to be recognized accurately.

Measurement of Facial Expression

Although emotions can usually be judged accurately, we seldom display pure emotional states. Sometimes we use only one part of the face to show emotion; such expressions are known as **partials** (Burgoon and Saine, p. 215). A kidnap victim trying to remain calm might show fear in the eyes, but not in any other area of the face.

In everyday interactions we express mixtures of the primary emotions. These mixtures are **affect blends** (Ekman, 1971, p. 222). If you open your door and see a friend you haven't seen in five years, you may show surprise in your eye area and happiness in your mouth area.

Affect blends occur often in our interpersonal relationships, but blends are more likely to occur when we try to disguise expression of felt emotions with more acceptable expressions (Ekman, 1971, p. 223). If you were listening with some of your more conservative friends to your favorite comedian tell an off-color joke, your face might show several emotions at once, resulting in a blend.

Sometimes emotions expressed on the face are unobservable in normal conversation. Haggard and Isaacs (1966), while analyzing non-verbal communication between a therapist and patient on a slow-motion film, noticed that facial expressions could change drastically within a few seconds of film. These brief facial expressions are known as **micromomentary facial expressions.**

Micromomentary facial expressions often reveal actual emotional states unidentifiable unless played in slow motion. The slow-motion film reveals many expressions that are incompatible with the person's verbal message and perceived facial expressions. Psychologists and counselors are tremendously interested in micromomentary facial expressions of clients, because they enable them to detect expressions of emotion that they formerly would have missed. If a young woman, observed on slow-motion film, had brief expressions of anger while telling a counselor that she loved her mother, the counselor would probably try to discover what caused the display of anger.

Facial expressions communicate many emotions spontaneously; however, observers must be careful because many factors can influence their interpretation. We have identified emotions that are universally accepted, but now let's look at sex and situational differences.

Sex and Situational Differences

The functions and types of facial expressions are similar for males and females, but differences do occur in interaction behaviors. As mentioned earlier, societal pressures often inhibit a man's expression of emotion. Women usually reveal their emotions more often than men, while men may feel emotions of happiness or sadness very strongly without displaying emotion on the face.

Moreover, males are more often **internalizers** than females. Internalizers are persons who inhibit overt expression of their own feelings. This phenomenon may result from cultural rules such as telling boys not to cry or to show emotion in public (Buck, Miller, and Caul, 1974, pp. 594–595).

Many of us have probably seen the slogan "Smile—and they'll wonder what you've been up to." Often we do wonder if people are smiling because they are happy, covering something, or nervous; however, one reason we do smile is to seek approval. When seeking approval, both sexes smile more often. Research also indicates that women smile more than men, whether or not they are happy. We've all known people who smiled constantly, and we usually questioned their sincerity until we knew them better. For example, the movie "Animal House" well exemplified the stereotype of "plastic smiles" at sorority and fraternity rush parties (Rosenfeld, 1966, pp. 597–605).

In making judgments about facial expressions, we may be accurate or inaccurate. For example, infants expressing negative emotions are more likely to be judged boys and infants expressing positive emotions are more likely to be judged girls (Haviland, 1977, pp. 80–84). The inference, obviously, may not be correct.

Children respond differently to male and female smiles. Even though females smile more often than males, children attribute greater friendliness to male smiles. One reason may be that children interpret a male's smile as being more sincere because males usually smile only when happy or amused. Females, unlike males, are found to smile more often when giving negative messages (Bugental, Love, and Gianetto, 1971, p. 317).

When judging facial expression, neither sex is more accurate at judging its own or the opposite sex's facial expression. However, research does suggest that men make significantly more evaluative errors when judging women speakers. Physical attractiveness, as mentioned earlier, can influence their judgments (Westbrook, 1974, pp. 139–146).

Along with sex differences in facial expression, we must also consider the situational differences that affect our perceptions. Our faces communicate independent information about us and our actions in a given situation. Studies examining whether the context or the facial expressions have greater influence in determining perception are inconclusive. Goodenough and Tinker (1931) state that the situational cues are not more influential than facial expression (pp. 525–536), while Watson (1972) suggests that we rely more on facial expression than on situation (pp. 344–352).

Now that we have discussed sex and situational differences in facial expression of emotion, we turn to the important topic of how facial expressions are judged and how their interpretations affect social interaction.

JUDGMENTS AND INTERPRETATIONS

For years researchers have tried to determine the number of emotions the face is capable of displaying. Seven basic emotions are judged accurately in most social situations, and studies utilize three basic methodologies to identify these facial expressions of emotion: photographs, videotapes, or real-life situations. The use of photographs is the most objective and controlled method of studying facial expression. Photographs help to control outside stimuli but are restrictive because they don't show changes of expression over time (Kleinke, 1975, p. 66).

External factors cause difficulty in interpreting facial expressions of emotion. Factors that complicate judgments include prior exposure to the faces, contextual cues, emotional states of the judges, the methods by which the faces are presented to the judges (videotapes, .photographs, etc.), and characteristics of the faces being judged. For the best results, judges should be trained in evaluation of facial expressions, have prior exposure to the faces, know the context, evaluate simple tasks, and have sufficient time to make the evaluation. If photos are used, the facial expressions should be made by skilled actors and should include the entire face (Knapp, 1978, p. 283).

Taking precautions when studying facial expression is important, but understanding the effects that facial expressions have on social situations is equally important, because facial expressions affect the emotional states of others. If you want someone to empathize with you, you must have the appropriate facial expression. For example, after dinner, Claire's date, John, drove to a low-class motel; obviously, he had planned for the two of them to spend the evening there. Claire told him with a smile on her face that she wasn't that kind of girl and wanted to go home. John failed to believe her until her facial expression reinforced her verbal message (Savitsky, 1974, pp. 346–357).

Decisions are also affected by facial expressions. Emotional displays are powerful interpersonal tools in judicial decision making. According to Savitsky and Sim, the emotional state displayed on the defendant's face helps determine the perceived severity of the crime, the likelihood of recurrent criminal behavior, and the disposition of the defender. These factors may be one reason why more and more trial lawyers are training their defendants in appropriate nonverbal behaviors, i.e., facial expressions, body movement, clothing, etc. (Savitsky and Sim, 1974, pp. 140–146).

Facial muscles can be consciously controlled in all areas of the face except the eyes. Because the eye muscles are unable to be as consciously controlled, the ocular response reveals not only the truth, but also much about a person's individual personality structure. Libby and Yaklevich state: "The lower face may follow culturally transmitted display rules while the eyes may reveal the spontaneous or naked response" (Libby and Yaklevich, 1973, p. 203).

The eyes and eye behaviors have been a source of intense fascination since earliest times. The ancient Greeks believed eyes had special powers; the "evil eye" or fixed stare was believed to have the power to cause physical harm or death (Coss, 1974, pp. 16–17). Even today certain eye behaviors disturb some people. In one study, a supermarket

There is an old Chinese proverb that says "Beware of the man whose belly does not move when he laughs." A hearty laugh is seen not only in the eyes and face but throughout the body.

placed large, frowning eyes in corners of the building and found that shoplifting was drastically reduced (Coss, 1974, p. 21).

Women, sensing the eye's intriguing power, began to find methods of eye adornment. As early as Cleopatra's time, belladonna was used to dilate the pupils, thereby darkening the eyes and increasing attractiveness. Other cultures fastened jewels around the eyes to accentuate them. Today, especially in Western cultures, women spend hours each day applying false eyelashes, putting on mascara, plucking their eyebrows, and applying eye shadow to bring focus to the all-powerful eye!

Many of us have special interest in our eyes because of poor vision. Over half of the population of the United States has corrected vision with the aid of eyeglasses or contact lenses. If you think eyeglasses serve only a functional purpose, millions of people would disagree with you. Eyeglasses reveal much about the people who wear them. A Dun's survey of spectacled businessmen found that businessmen believed that the impressions of their glasses were as important as the suit they wore (Levy, 1976, pp. 77–78).

Americans spend $2.4 billion a year for 52 million pairs of corrective lenses. Fashion giants such as Yves St. Laurent and Oleg Cassini are designing glasses to bring eyes into a more fashionable focus. According to Alfred Poll, a noted optician in New York City, "many people are less concerned with seeing better than with how others see them" (in Levy, 1976, p. 77). More and more ophthalmic prescriptions include a facial analysis to correct physical extremities such as protruding eyes and long noses.

The practice of wearing or not wearing eyeglasses can be used as a protective device. Some people wear sun glasses because they can look at others without revealing interest. Myopic people with eyeglasses report that it is easier to sustain eye contact without wearing glasses. Eye contact becomes less disturbing to them because the images of the eyes are blurred (Coss, 1974, pp. 21–22).

According to *Playboy* magazine, one of the first physical characteristics noticed by males and females is the eyes. Eyes come in all sizes, colors, and shapes, and their uniqueness increases their interest (for example, we see variety in people with protruding eyes, closely set eyes, and slanted eyes). Have you ever sat down and thought about everything that eyes are capable of? Eyes weep, burn, wink, squint, flirt, hurt, and stare.

Recently, even more attention has been given to eyes with respect to medical diagnosis. For years medical authorities have diagnosed diabetes, brain disorders, and some metabolic diseases through retina examinations (Dobson, 1978, pp. 10–19), and now iridology has gained respect. This diagnostic technique, used by the Germans for decades, involves a detailed examination of the iris. The 2,000 proponents in the United States claim that "the iris is virtually an anatomical Etch-a-

Gene Warne

Sketch, capable of revealing through coloration, fiber structure, and tint, the present, past, and future functioning conditions of every organ in the body, including any inherited genetic weaknesses and strengths'' (Dobson, 1978, p. 18). Analysis of the eye is unsuccessful in naming specific diseases, but it does help pinpoint potential weaknesses in the body by matching flaws in the iris. Iridology could have a profound impact on medical diagnosis and treatment; however, most traditional physicians are reserving comment until further research is completed.

With increased interest in eye behavior, principles have been established through a variety of investigations. The remainder of this chapter will examine the functions of eye behavior, the types of eye movement, differences in eye behavior, and pupil dilation and constriction.

Functions of Eye Behavior

A primary function of eye contact is to establish relationships with others. In everyday interactions we notice the eye contact of speakers, share mutual glances with friends, become nervous when confronted

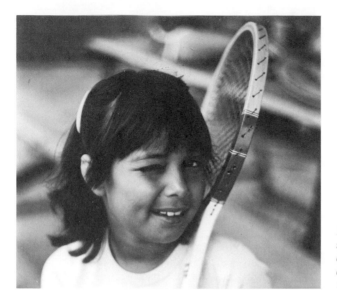

Blinking, twinkling, batting, squinting, or fluttering one's eyes carries a nonverbal message discussed at length by many romantic novelists.

with a penetrating stare, and scan rooms for familiar faces. We communicate by sharing visual interaction, whether it is labeled eye contact, gaze, or glance.

We all know how uncomfortable we feel if eye contact is different from that of our expectations. Think back to situations when a friend wouldn't look at you, when you were uncomfortable speaking to someone with a glass eye or to someone who was blind, or when you had problems in communicating over the phone. We all like to be able to see the other person and to have the other person see us so that we can receive feedback, whether that feedback is positive or negative. Eye contact is an aid to social interaction. In most interpersonal relationships eye contact signals to others that the looker is interested, attentive, and/or willing to listen or develop a relationship (Jellison and Ickes, 1974, pp. 444–450).

If two people engage in eye contact it is known as **mutual gaze** or **other-directed gaze.** Mutual gaze refers to the amount of time that two people spend looking at the eye area of the other person (Wiemann and Knapp, 1975, pp. 75–92). Sometimes individuals will scan other people to see where they are looking, and this eye behavior is known as a **fractional glance** (Coss, 1974, p. 18). The fractional glance is usually used to find mutual eye contact. .

Researchers continually examine the functions of eye contact on human interaction; however, examination is difficult because the functions overlap. Kendon (1967) and Knapp (1978, pp. 297–304) identify four functions of gaze, and we will follow a similar format by examining how eye contact serves (1) to establish and define relationships, (2) to control channels of communication, (3) to display emotion, and (4) to reduce distractions.

Establishing and defining relationships. Eye contact determines the type of interaction that will take place and how the interaction will develop. Merely looking at another person is an indication of interest. Eye contact shows a willingness on your part to admit interest in others and allows others to gain information about you.

The desire to establish relationships through eye contact starts at an early age. Vulnerable infants have an innate survival instinct to search out their mother's eyes in order to have their needs taken care of. At a disco, establishing eye contact can communicate that you want to dance, be left alone, or are with someone else. For example, as Sam enters the nightclub he scans the room, looking for available females. Glancing at the bar, he catches the eyes of a hefty, middle-aged woman and quickly averts his gaze. Finally, he spots an attractive redhead and begins to stare at her. At first she avoids his gaze, but later she acknowledges his eye contact by glancing at the seat next to her. This brief glance signals Sam to join her.

When you make eye contact with someone with whom you want to establish interest or approval, eye contact will increase. Exline (1971) found that we look at a person less often when we dislike the person with whom we are talking, because looking is a signal of liking. When we want approval and attention, we look at the other person more often. For example, during a job interview, college graduates (or graduating seniors) should try to maintain good eye contact to show the interviewer they are interested and alert.

As relationships develop, expectations of eye contact are established. If someone fails to accept or meet the expected standards, conflict may occur. When a female at a laundromat observes a strange male watching her intently, she will avoid his gaze to reduce the possibility of interaction. Increased eye contact is a signal of increased intimacy. If one person looks too often and for too long a time at another, the other person will feel uncomfortable with the height of the intimacy level being established (Coss, 1974, p. 18).

Reactions to differing amounts of eye contact depend on the situation. Research has revealed that love is positively related to mutual glances. One study found that happy couples look more frequently into each other's eyes, while couples in conflict look less. The prolonged looks create power to heighten intimacy. Once the relationship is established (for close friends and lovers), even brief bits of eye contact can be emotionally satisfying as long as the facial expressions are appropriate

(Beier, 1974, pp. 53–56). (See the section on facial expression and contradictory messages.)

A study by Exline, Ellyson, and Long (1975) examined the effects of power and status on eye contact. They found that people of greater status have less direct eye contact than those of lower status, though they may break gaze last. Another study found that all people look more at higher-status persons and that high socioeconomic dyads have more eye contact than low socioeconomic dyads (Levine and Sutton-Smith, 1973, pp. 400–405). Research also indicates that those individuals who need higher affection look more often at and require more eye contact from their associates.

Just as remembering that eye contact helps to establish relationships is important, so is remembering that eye contact is essential in analyzing and monitoring feedback. Through others' visual responses we learn whether to seek out someone at a disco, to keep talking, to look more, or to avoid others' glances.

Channel control.   Eye contact often determines the type of interaction that will take place. How many times have you glanced at your watch when you were late for an appointment, looked down or away when you were embarrassed, or glared at someone who took your seat? These eye behaviors send messages to others and control the communication channels during interaction. Common methods of controlling the communication channel are turn-taking, power displays, and gaze aversion.

You probably have been in a situation in which everyone seemed to be talking at once; one person spoke while another chimed in. These situations are not regular occurrences, but when they do happen interaction can be very frustrating. To avoid this frustration humans have an eye behavior system of signalling to each other when to speak. These eye behavior signals are known as **turn-taking.**

You may ask where and when in the communication process visual interaction takes place. Research indicates that listeners steadily increase speaker-directed gaze and head nods as a role-change strategy. Wiemann and Knapp found that eye contact increased from sixty-one percent in the first third of the conversation to eighty-three percent in the last third of the conversation. When speakers acknowledge the turn-taking cues, they briefly look away from the listener (Wiemann and Knapp, 1975, p. 85). A Kendon (1967) study also indicated that speakers increase the time spent looking at their auditors as their speaking turn approaches completion, and that speakers are less likely to break eye contact before the end of a question.

The purpose of turn-taking behavior is to help define relationships. For turn-taking cues to be successful both of the interactants must make eye contact at or near the exchange point. These cues help us to know when to yield conversation, to obtain and check feedback, or to continue the interaction.

Channels of communication are also used as **power displays.** Have you ever felt someone's stare or felt eyes that could look straight through you? How did you feel? Most people become uncomfortable and want to avoid steady, direct gazes. These gazes are often power displays, and we react to this power with another stare or gaze aversion.

Uninterrupted gaze (a stare) is not necessarily threatening but usually indicates "a demand for a response, and, in a situation where no appropriate response is apparent, tension will be evoked and the subject will be motivated to escape the situation" (Ellsworth, Carlsmith, and Henson, 1972, p. 311). Steady gazes give us a sense of interpersonal involvement and can be interpreted as an invasion of privacy when eye contact occurs among strangers without proper introduction (Coss, 1974, p. 18). When we feel uncomfortable we usually avert direct eye contact.

Hutt and Ounsted (1966) define **gaze aversion** as a biological adjustment to high arousal (pp. 346–356). Gaze aversion begins at an early age. By the fourth week infants will avoid eye contact when fussy, for example prior to bed or feeding (Coss, 1974, p. 18). As children mature they practice gaze aversion by turning their entire heads and bodies. Adults also avert gaze by glancing to one side or the other when wishing to disengage an interaction.

In summary, there are several methods of controlling channels of communication through eye contact. We engage in turn-taking, power displays, and gaze aversion to control interpersonal interactions. An additional eye function, however, is to be found in the actual display of emotion.

Displaying emotion.   Some say that inner emotions are revealed only through the eyes. Even though true emotions may be revealed only in the eye area, most studies measure emotions of the face holistically rather than by focusing only on the eyes. In an attempt to learn more about the function of eyes in displaying emotion, Ekman (1971) conducted a study and found extreme changes in the eye area for the emotions of surprise and fear, but little change for the emotions of disgust and happiness. The study also indicated a difficulty in labeling shame/humiliation through eye behaviors. Other research by Ekman and Friesen (1975) helped to locate and define the configurations of the eye areas while displaying emotion.

Measurement of eye behavior is difficult. For accurate judgments, we must remember to include all facial features and situational cues. Photographs are often used to analyze eye behavior, but photographs allow for no changes over time (see the section on measurement of facial expression). Current theorists suggest a need for more realistic situations to get a better indication of how eyes display emotion.

As with facial expression, individuals try to mask inner feelings with their eye behaviors. As we mentioned earlier, it is difficult, although not impossible, to control eye behaviors, and observers must be trained to recognize microexpressions that give away emotions. When we open an unwanted gift at Christmas or are unsuccessful in attaining public office, we cover looks of dislike or disappointment with microexpressions (see earlier section in this chapter on facial management); these microexpressions are of an involuntary nature and are used to avoid showing some feelings (Ekman and Friesen, 1969a, pp. 88–106).

Just as eyes give us information about the inner emotions of others, they can also serve as a barrier to effective communication. Although contact is used to establish relationships, to control channels of communication, and to display emotions, our eyes can be easily distracted by visual stimuli.

Reducing distractions.   Individuals find it difficult to concentrate when bombarded by too many visual stimuli. Since we need to keep our thoughts on the right track, we must find ways to avoid or reduce these distractions.

The social stimulation of eye contact can be a powerful distraction during interaction. Think of the times that you have looked upward to remember an idea in a speech or looked away to recall an important fact on a test. While looking away or upward we are involved in the nonvisual function of reducing distractions.

Furthermore, we usually avoid eye contact prior to speaking. This gaze avoidance helps us concentrate on what we want to say without visual distraction. Research also suggests that we briefly avert our eyes when asked questions that require reflection. The pause from looking at others helps us to organize our thoughts.

Throughout the preceding discussion we have examined the functions of eye behavior. We have found that eye contact serves to establish and define relationships, to control channels of communication, to display emotions, and to reduce distractions. In the next section we will discuss different types of eye movement.

Eye Movement

When we are asked questions like "Who is your favorite comedian?" or "What is your favorite television program?" we usually move our eyes to the left or the right before answering. Research suggests that these eye movements may be indicators of the mode of information processing we are using (Galin and Ornstein, 1974, pp. 367–376).

According to psychological research the direction of eye movement and the asymmetry of the brain are related. People have two processing hemispheres. The left hemisphere is the rational lobe and is concerned with linguistic, mathematical, and reasoning tasks. The right hemisphere is the intuitive lobe and is used to process spatial, imagistic, and gestalt tasks. For example, if you are right-handed, balancing your checkbook will be a task for the left hemisphere of your brain, while the process of listening to your favorite record album will be a task for the right hemisphere.

Most people can be classified as left or right eye movers. The joint movement of the eyes to the right or left is known as **conjugatelateral eye movement** or **CLEM.** People who shift their eyes to the left would be using the right hemisphere to process information. Research indicates that about seventy-five percent of all lateral eye movement occurs in one direction. To determine whether someone is a left or right eye mover, a simple test may be given. Simply ask a question that will cause your listener to reflect on the answer and watch the direction of his or her eye movement. Possible questions include "How many letters are there in the word Mississippi?" or "How much is 12 times 34?" Besides learning whether a person is a left or right eye mover, recent research suggests personality differences between left and right eye movers (Bakan, 1971, p. 96).

Another interesting area of eye movement is concerned with **blinking behavior.** Observe someone who is trying to solve a problem or who is daydreaming. How often does the person blink? Research suggests that people can't think and blink at the same time. Indeed, one study found that when subjects' blinking is slowed, information is processed from memory more easily. Some theorists suggest that the process of retrieving information from our memory banks is affected by vision ("Blink (Blank)," 1976, pp. 16–17). Thus as we scan our brain for mental pictures, our blinking is slowed.

Slowed blinking is positively correlated to doing well in school. A study by Breed and Colarita (1974) observed that those students who blinked less and looked around less during a lecture scored considerably better on tests (pp. 75–81). Observations also reveal that people tend to blink at the end of sentences when reading and after completing a thought ("Blink (Blank)," 1976, pp. 16–17). If this statement is true, you should be blinking about now.

Differences in Eye Behavior

In examining the functions and types of eye movement and behavior we have made no mention of individual differences. This section will attempt to give insight into the effects of sex, personality, culture, and context on eye behavior.

Sex differences.   The functions and types of eye behavior are similar for males and females, but one must consider sexual differences in terms of the frequency, distance, and duration of eye contact. Sex differences in human interaction are unapparent until about the fourth grade; at approximately this age society's influences begin to affect visual interaction. Little boys learn it is less masculine for them to seek eye contact and to be visually attentive, while little girls are encouraged to make and maintain eye contact.

Environmental influences train women to be more aware of visual cues than men. Women are usually taught to give special attention to dress, color, spatial arrangements, etc. The eye contact of many women becomes an emotional expression of striving to build social relationships (Rubin, 1970, pp. 265–273). Women strive to build social relationships by looking more often, by holding gazes longer, and by looking more while speaking and being spoken to (Libby, 1970, pp. 303–312).

Research also suggests that females look more at people they like, but less when giving false impressions to the person in question. When males increase eye contact while talking they are seen to be more active than females with the same amount of eye contact (Argyle, Lebebure, and Cook, 1974, 4, pp. 125–136). Apparently, both males and females look more at each other as the physical distance increases between them. Argyle and Ingham (1972) found that large distances are more comfortable for women than for men (pp. 32–49). Although there are sex differences that distinguish between men's and women's eye behavior, research has also found personality differences.

Personality differences.   The eyes help to communicate social roles, individual desires, intentions, and spontaneous reactions in social interactions. As the eyes express themselves, much is revealed about an individual's personality structure.

Personality affects the degree to which people return the gaze of another person. Think about those people around you who look you straight in the eye and of those who do not. Do they have any personality similarities? Research indicates that extroverts have greater eye contact and look more frequently than introverts (Rutter, Morley, and Graham, 1972, pp. 371–384). Individuals with greater eye contact are seen as attractive and described with favorable adjectives such as friendly, confident, sincere, and mature, while those subjects showing little eye contact are described as cold, pessimistic, defensive, and immature (Kleck and Nuessle, 1968, pp. 241–246).

Although eye contact is not always an indication of our personalities, we need to be sensitive to what we may be communicating. We must remember that we are seen more positively, whether telling favorable or unfavorable information, when we use greater amounts of

An individual's desires, intentions, and role affect the degree to which people return that individual's gaze.

eye contact (Argyle, Lebebure, and Cook, 1974, p. 126). In learning to become aware of the effects of our eye contact, we should also learn about cultural differences in eye behavior.

Cultural differences. Cross-cultural differences in patterns of eye behavior are a potential problem in social interaction. Misunderstandings and conflicts are often caused by too much or too little eye contact. Effective communication depends upon a shared understanding of behavioral cues.

La France and Mayo (1976) compared the eye behavior between black and white Americans and found a tendency for many blacks to avoid looking others directly in the eyes. They also found that whites in the study judged listeners who did avoid looking them in the eyes as uninterested and withholding. Awkwardness occurs because of dissimilar visual cues. Many visual turn-taking behaviors are different for blacks and whites. For example, in one situation in the study, white listeners were cued to speak when the black speakers paused with a sustained gaze. When the whites did speak they found themselves speaking while the blacks were speaking because of different interpretations of turn-taking cues (LaFrance and Mayo, 1976, pp. 547–552).

Some cultures give more emphasis to the observance of eye behaviors than others. Koreans are especially concerned with expressions communicated by the eyes. Koreans call the awareness of eye behavior "nuichee." Because of status differences and customs most Koreans look to the eyes for real answers of the heart so they will not be embarrassed by unexpected answers to questions they ask. For example, a Korean farmer rented land from a neighbor. His rent was due, but he was unable to pay until he sold his crop. Before the farmer asked for a delay in payment, he searched the eyes of his neighbor for acceptance and approval, for if the neighbor refused his request the farmer would lose face. Finally, the farmer did ask his neighbor for a delay, which he received, but only after reading his neighbor's eye behavior correctly. But besides cultural differences in eye behavior, one must also consider topic and task differences.

Contextual differences.   Eye contact varies according to contextual and situational cues. Some situations create expectations of increased visual interaction while others decrease visual interaction. Think about the gaze behaviors of a small boy caught reading a *Playboy* magazine, a group of friends sharing the latest gossip, or a newly engaged couple discussing marriage plans. Eye contact usually increases when people are comfortable, interested, or happy and decreases when people are embarrassed, guilty, or sad. Since eye contact is a sign of openness, looking away or avoiding eye contact during uncomfortable situations protects the individual.

Gaze also affects how information is received by listeners. Speakers who have greater degrees of eye contact are seen as more skilled, informed, experienced, and friendly. A study by Mehrabian and Williams (1969) found that people trying to persuade others gaze more often at their listeners (pp. 37–58). Studies also reveal that students learn more when their instructors gaze at them more often (Breed and Colarita, 1974, p. 76). Students with high eye contact, instructors reported, scored higher on tests.

Eye behavior is affected by sex, personality, cultural, and contextual differences in human interaction. Another aspect of the eye that affects human interaction is the role of pupil dilation and constriction in interpersonal eye contact.

Pupil Dilation and Constriction

Many of you have stood before a mirror and observed the effects of varying amounts of light on your pupil size, but have you ever noticed differences in your pupil size in other situations? We can control the size of our pupils with light, but we are unable to consciously control pupil dilation and constriction. For this reason true feelings and emotions usually reveal themselves in the depths of a person's eyes.

One of the first people to study the process of pupil dilation and constriction was Eckhard Hess. In one of his preliminary studies, he presented five photographs to male and female subjects (Hess and Polt, 1960, pp. 349–350). The results indicated that pupils enlarged when they were presented a positive stimulus (muscle man and baby for women; nude females for men). Further research also supported Hess's findings that dilation occurs with positive stimuli or things of interest (Borlow, 1969, pp. 587–590; and Hays and Plax, 1971, pp. 316–320).

Along with research concerning positive stimuli, other studies suggest that pupils dilate when involved in either mental or emotional effort (Janisse and Peavler, 1974, pp. 60–63). While taking an exam, telling someone that you love him/her, or working on a favorite craft, your pupil size may enlarge. Even the aniticipation of a difficult problem or an emotional situation can increase pupil size.

Hess (1975) believes that pupillary research is valuable in indicating the degree of individual interest and attention. He also believes that "pupil response in combination with other physiological measures can be a powerful tool in discriminating attitudes which may be relatively hidden even to the consciousness of the individual concerned" (p. 156).

People are more attracted to others with enlarged pupils. Research indicates that men are more attracted to females with large pupils. Most cover layouts and photographs are selected by men (Hess, 1975, p. 95), and if you notice the covers of popular magazines you'll see people with enlarged pupils. According to Andersen et al. (1980), people with dilated pupils are more attractive both physically and socially. However, although you may prefer looking at or socializing with a person with large pupils, that does not mean you would also choose to work with that person. The Andersen study found that pupil size had no effect on a person's attractiveness as a work partner.

Interestingly, research has shown that pupil dilation has a reciprocal effect on the person observing the dilated pupils. Males looking at a photograph of a female with dilated pupils underwent greater pupil dilation than males looking at a photograph of a female with constricted pupils (Hess, 1965; Hess and Goodwin, 1973; Simms, 1967). The same effect was found when females were shown photographs of males with dilated or constricted pupils (Simms, 1967). The females who were shown the pictures of males with enlarged pupils underwent the greater amount of pupil dilation. Apparently, when we look at members of the opposite sex who have enlarged or dilated pupils, we not only percieve them as more attractive but our pupils also dilate.

There are differences in pupil size among different groups. Research has found that the younger one is, the larger the pupils are. Infants and small children have large pupils—a fact that is very advantageous since their enlarged pupils make them more attractive to those who care for them. Experimental research also has shown that blue-eyed people have larger pupillary responses. The popular statement that men prefer blondes may be partially attributed to pupillary response, since most natural blondes have blue eyes, and their pupil changes are easier to perceive.

In the sixties, many groups were interested in measuring attitudes with pupillary research. The advertising industry was particularly interested in individual pupil responses. Much of their enthusiasm vanished when studies failed to support the theory that pupils constrict when observing negative stimuli (Rice, 1974, pp. 55-59). However, in later research, Hess (1975) attributed the contradictions to the lack of proper research applications. Today, advanced technology has increased the reliability of measurement with television pupillometers.

With advanced technology many see bright research possibilities for pupillometry. The largest potential markets will probably be in social attitudes and in clinical and therapeutic procedures. The study of the pupil may be used in all areas—so don't be surprised if your pupillary response is measured in your next job interview.

SUMMARY

Faces and eyes provide a wealth of information and influence interaction by helping you to recognize others, predict personalities, and interpret complex situations. Facial expressions are universally associated with particular emotions because they communicate the quality and nature of emotions. Although there are specific differences within cultures that cause emotions to be expressed, theories of acquisition and development suggest that facial expressions are both innate and learned.

Early research indicated that facial expressions were primarily involuntary reactions to situations, but since that time facial expressions have been viewed as only partially reliable. Through the use of facial management techniques people control facial expressions of emotion by intensifying, deintensifying, neutralizing, or masking felt emotions. Manifestations of partials, affect blends, and micromomentary expressions depend on sex and situational differences. Fear, anger, happiness, surprise, disgust, sadness, and interest are seven basic emotions that can be judged accurately.

Muscles can be controlled consciously in all areas of the face except the eyes. This is one reason why eyes and eye behavior have been a source of intense fascination for thousands of years. A primary function of eye contact is to establish and define relationships with others. Eye behavior also serves to control channels of communication, to display emotion, and to reduce distractions.

Eye movements also transmit information nonverbally. The direction of eye movement is related to brain information processing. Personality differences are associated with right and left eye movers. One type of eye movement, blinking, is often ignored, but research suggests that we can't think and blink at the same time. Good students blink less than poor students. Although eye behavior serves the four different functions noted above, there are individual differences in the frequency, duration, and distance of eye contact. Eye behavior is influenced by sex differences, personality differences, cultural differences, and contextual differences,

A final area of eye behavior concerns pupil dilation and constriction. Pupils characteristically enlarge when positive stimuli are present and grow smaller when negative stimuli are present. Large-pupiled and light-eyed people seem to have an advantage over others because they are perceived as more attractive than others. Although there have been conflicting results when studying pupilometry, advanced technology has increased the reliability and accuracy of pupil dilation and constriction measurement.

REFERENCES

Andersen, P. A., W. R. Todd-Mancillas, and L. D. Clementa. "The Effects of Pupil Dilation as Physical, Social, and Task Attraction." *Australian SCAN of Nonverbal Communication*, 1980, 7–8, 89–96.

Argyle, M., and R. Ingham. "Gaze, Mutual Gaze and Proximity." *Semiotica*, 1972, 6, 32–49.

Argyle, M., L. Lebebure, and M. Cook. "The Meanings of Five Patterns of Gaze." *European Journal of Social Psychology*, 1974, 4, 2, 125–136.

Bakan, P. "The Eyes Have It." *Psychology Today*, April 1971, 64–67, 96.

Beier, G. "Nonverbal Communication: How We Send Emotional Messages." *Psychology Today*, October 1974, 52–56.

"Blink (Blank)." *Science Digest*, October 1976, 16–17.

Borlow, J. D. "Pupillary Size as an Index of Preference in Political Candidates." *Perceptual and Motor Skills*, 1969, 28, 587–590.

Boucher, J. D., and P. Ekman. "Facial Areas of Emotional Information." *Journal of Communication*, 1975, 25, 21–29.

Breed, G., and V. Colarita. "Looking, Blinking, and Sitting." *Journal of Communication*, 1974, 24, 2, 75–81.

Buck, R., R. E. Miller, and W. F. Caul. "Sex, Personality, and Psychological Variables in the Communication of Affect Via Facial Expression." *Journal of Personality and Social Psychology*, 1974, *30*, 4, 587–596.

Bugental, D. E., L. R. Love, and R. M. Gianetto. "Verbal-Nonverbal Conflict in Parental Messages to Normal and Disturbed Children." *Journal of Personality and Social Psychology*, 1971, *17*, 314–318.

Burgoon, J. K., and T. Saine. *The Unspoken Dialogue: An Introduction to Nonverbal Communication*. Boston: Houghton-Mifflin, 1978.

Coss, R. G. "Reflections on the Evil Eye." *Human Behavior*, 1974, *18*, 16–22.

Darwin, C. *The Expression of Emotions in Man and Animals*. London: John Murray, 1872. Reprint, Chicago: University of Chicago Press, 1972.

Dion, K. K., E. Berscheid, and E. Walster. "What is Beautiful is Good." *Journal of Personality and Social Psychology*, 1973, *24*, 285–290.

Dobson, J. "A Closer Look at Eyes." *The Atlanta Journal and Constitution Magazine*, July 1978, 10–19.

Eibl-Eibesfeldt, I. *Ethology: The Biology of Behavior*, 2nd ed. New York: Holt, Rinehart, and Winston, 1975.

Ekman, P. "Universals and Cultural Differences in Facial Expressions of Emotions" in *Nebraska Symposium on Motivation*, Lincoln, Neb.: University of Nebraska Press, 1971, pp. 207–283.

Ekman, P. "Face Muscles Talk Every Language." *Psychology Today*, September 1975, 35.

Ekman, P., and W. V. Friesen. "Head and Body Cues in the Judgment of Emotion: A Reformation." *Perception and Motor Skills*, 1967, *24*, 711–724.

Ekman, P., and W. V. Friesen. "Nonverbal Leakage and Clues to Reception." *Psychiatry*, 1969, *32*, 88–106.(a)

Ekman, P., and W. V. Friesen. "The Repertoire of Nonverbal Behavior Categories, Origins, Usage and Coding." *Semiotica*, 1969, *1*, 49–98.(b)

Ekman, P., and W. V. Friesen. *Unmasking the Face*. Englewood Cliffs, N.J.: Prentice-Hall, 1975.

Ellsworth, P. C., J. M. Carlsmith, and A. Henson. "The Stare as a Stimulus of Flight in Human Subjects: A Series of Field Experiments." *Journal of Personality and Social Psychology*, 1972, *21*, 302–311.

Exline, R. V. "Visual Interaction: The Glance of Power and Preference." In James K. Cole, ed., *Nebraska Symposium on Motivation*. Lincoln, Neb.: University of Nebraska Press, 1971, pp. 163–206.

Exline, R. V., S. L. Ellyson, and B. Long. "Visual Behavior as an Aspect of Power Role Relationships," in P. Pliner, L. Krames, and T. Alloway, eds., *Nonverbal Communication of Aggression*. New York: Plenum Press, 1975, 21–52.

Fast, J. *The Pleasure Book*. New York: Stein and Day, 1975.

Galin, D., and R. Ornstein. "Individual Differences in Cognitive Style-I. Reflective Eye Movements." *Neuropsychologia*, 1974, *12*, 367–376.

Goodenough, F. L., and M. A. Tinker. "The Relative Potency of Facial Expression and Verbal Description of Stimulus in the Judgment of Emotion." *Journal of Comparative Psychology*, 1931, *12*, 525–536.

Haggard, E. A., and F. S. Isaacs. "Micromomentary Facial Expressions as Indicators of Ego Mechanisms in Psychotherapy." In L. A. Gottschalk and A. H. Auerback, eds., *Methods of Research in Psychotherapy*. New York: Appleton-Century-Crofts, 1966.

Hamilton, M. L. "Imitative Behavior and Expressive Ability in Facial Expression of Emotion." *Developmental Psychology*, 1973, *8*, 1, 138.

Haviland, J. M. "Sex-Related Pragmatics in Infants' Nonverbal Communication." *Journal of Communication*, 1977, *27*, 2, 80–84.

Hays, E. R., and T. G. Plax. "Pupillary Response to Supportive and Aversive Verbal Messages." *Speech Monographs*, 1971, *38*, 316–320.

Hess, E. H. "Attitude and Pupil Size." *Scientific American*, 1965, *212*, 46–54.

Hess, E. H. *The Tell-Tale Eye*. New York: Van Nostrand Reinhold, 1975.

Hess, E. H., and E. Goodwin. "The Present State of Pupillometrics. In M. P. Janisse, ed. *Pupillary Dynamics and Behavior*. New York: Plenum Press, 1973, pp. 248–290.

Hess, E. H., and J. M. Polt. "Pupil Size as Related to Interest Value of Visual Stimuli." *Science*, 1960, *132*, 349–350.

Hutt, C., and C. Ounsted. "The Biological Significance of Gaze Aversion: With Special Reference to Childhood Autism." *Behavioral Science*, 1966, *11*, 346–356.

Izard, C. E. *The Face of Emotion*. New York: Appleton-Century-Crofts, 1971.

Janisse, M. P., and W. S. Peavler. "Pupillary Research Today: Emotion in the Eye." *Psychology Today*, February 1974, 60–63.

Jellison, J. M., and W. J. Ickes. "The Power of the Glance: Desire to See and be Seen in Cooperative and Competitive Situations." *Journal of Experimental Social Psychology*, 1974, *10*, 444–450.

Kendon, A. "Some Functions of Gaze-Direction in Social Interaction." *Acta Psychologia*, 1967, *26*, 22–63.

Kleck, R. E., and W. Nuessle. "Congruence Between the Indicative and Communicative Function of Eye Contact in Interpersonal Relations." *British Journal of Social and Clinical Psychology*, 1968, *7*, 241–246.

Kleinke, C. L. *First Impressions: The Psychology of Encountering Others*. Englewood Cliffs, N.J.: Prentice-Hall, 1975.

Knapp, M. L. *Nonverbal Communication in Human Interaction*, 2nd ed. New York: Holt, Rinehart, and Winston, 1978.

La France, M., and C. Mayo. "Racial Differences in Gaze Behavior During Conversations: Two Systematic Observational Studies." *Journal of Personality and Social Psychology*, 1976, *33*, 547–552.

Levine, M. H., and B. Sutton-Smith. "Effects of Age, Sex, and Task on Visual

Behavior during Dyadic Interaction." *Developmental Psychology*, 1973, 9, 3, 400–405.

Levy, R. "Through A Glass Darkly." *Dun's Review*, 1976, 107, 2, 77–78.

Libby, W. "Eye Contact and Direction of Looking as Stable Individual Differences." *Journal of Experimental Research in Personality*, 1970, 4, 303–312.

Libby, W. L., and D. Yaklevich. "Personality Determinants of Eye Contact and Direction of Gaze Aversion." *Journal of Personality and Social Psychology*, 1973, 27, 197–206.

Mehrabian, A., and M. Williams. "Nonverbal Concomitants of Perceived and Intended Persuasiveness." *Journal of Personality and Social Psychology*, 1969, 13, 37–58.

Odom, R. D., and C. M. Lemond. "Developmental Differences in the Perception and Production of Facial Expressions." *Child Development*, 1972, 43, 359–369.

Rice, B. "Rattlesnakes, French Fries and Pupillometric Oversell." *Psychology Today*, February 1974, 55–59.

Ricketts, A. F. "A Study of the Behavior of Young Children in Anger." In L. Jack et al., eds. *Studies in Child Welfare*, Iowa City: University of Iowa Press, 1934.

Rosenfeld, H. "Approval-Seeking and Approval-Inducing Functions of Verbal and Nonverbal Responses in the Dyad." *Journal of Personality and Social Psychology*, 1966, 4, 597–605.

Rubin, Z. "Measurement of Romantic Love." *Journal of Personality and Social Psychology*, 1970, 16, 265–273.

Rutter, D. R., E. I. Morley, and J. C. Graham. "Visual Interaction in a Group of Introverts and Extroverts." *European Journal of Social Psychology*, 1972, 2, 371–384.

Savitsky, J. C. "Aggressor's Response to the Victim's Facial Expression of Emotion." *Journal of Research in Personality*, 1974, 7, 346–357.

Savitsky, J. C., and M. E. Sim. "Trading Emotions: Equity Theory of Reward and Punishment." *Journal of Communication*, 1974, 24, 3, 140–146.

Simms, T. M. "Pupillary Response of Male and Female Subjects to Pupillary Difference in Male and Female Picture Stimuli." *Perception and Psychophysics*, 1967, 2, 553–555.

Smith, W. J., J. Chase, and A. K. Lieblich. "Tongue Showing: A Facial Display of Humans and other Primate Species." *Semiotica*, 1974, 17, 201–246.

Sorce, J. F., and J. J. Campos. "The Role of Expression in the Recognition of a Face." *American Journal of Psychology*, 1974, 87, 1 and 2, 71–82.

Stroufe, L. A., and E. Waters. "The Ontogenesis of Smiling and Laughter." *Psychological Review*, 1976, 83, 173–189.

Thompson, J. "Development of Facial Expression of Emotion in Blind and Seeing Children." *Archives of Psychology*, 1941, 37, 264, 1–47.

Tomkins, S. S. *Affect, Imagery, Consciousness,* Vols. I and II, *The Positive and Negative Affects.* New York: Springer, 1962, 1963.

"The Tongue's Own Language." *Saturday Review of Education,* 1973, *1,* 4, 77.

Watson, S. G. "Judgment of Emotion from Facial and Contextual Cue Combinations." *Journal of Personality and Social Psychology,* 1972, 24, 344–352.

Westbrook, M. "Sex Differences in the Perception of Emotion." *Australian Journal of Psychology,* 1974, 26, 2, 139–146.

"What Your Tongue May Really Be Saying." *Newsweek,* April 1973, 2, 46.

Wiemann, J. M., and M. L. Knapp. "Turn-taking in Conversations." *Journal of Communication,* 1975, 25, 2, 75–92.

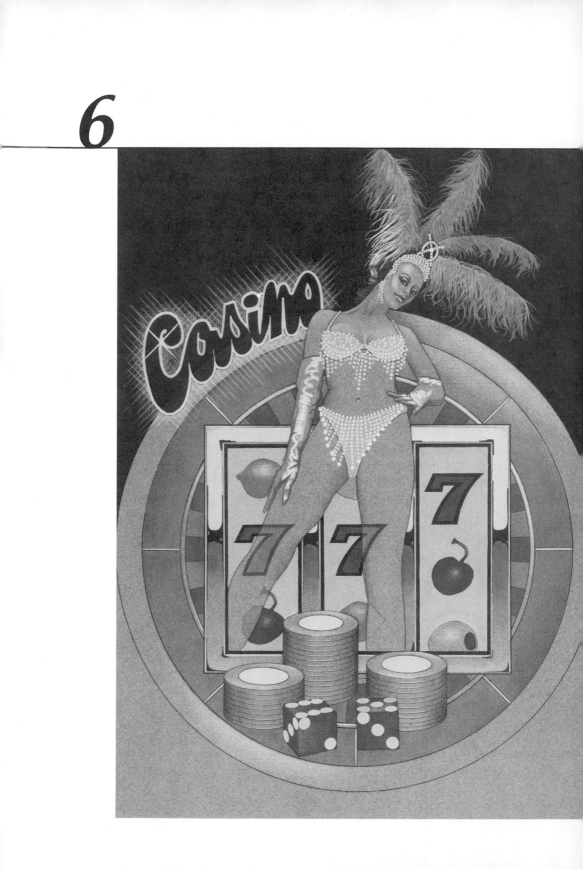

6

ENVIRONMENT

He did not know where he was. Presumably he was
in the Ministry of Love; but there was no way of
making certain.

He was in a high-ceilinged windowless cell with
walls of glittering white porcelain. Concealed lamps
flooded it with cold light, and there was a low,
steady humming sound which he supposed had
something to do with the air supply. . . . ''Do you
know what time of day it is?'' he said.

Ampleforth looked startled again. ''I had hardly
thought about it. They arrested me—it could be two
days ago—perhaps three.'' His eyes flitted round the
walls, as though he half expected to find a window
somewhere. ''There is no difference between night
and day in this place. I do not see how one can
calculate the time.''

GEORGE ORWELL, *1984*

Winston Churchill cogently observed, "We shape our buildings and later they shape us." Buildings are designed to produce a particular "image" or "perception" for the public, and, in turn, they affect our behavior. Las Vegas, for instance, is the archetype of the commercial strip. "The analysis of Las Vegas and its physical structure is as important to architects and urbanists today as were the studies of medieval Europe and ancient Rome and Greece to earlier generations," claim architects Robert Venturi and Denise Brown in their serious inquiry into the architecture in the land of neon dreams (Goldberger, 1978, K-2).

Las Vegas has been designed precisely for the purpose of creating an environment that produces a high arousal level and the emotional state of feeling like a "king" or "queen" entering the palace. One of the most extraordinary visual sights in the world, Las Vegas, contains many elements that exist not for any structural reason but because of the emotional associations they are designed to evoke. As a fairyland, Las Vegas is designed to make us think of palaces and fantasy castles. The wedding chapels look like miniature New England churches or tiny Gothic ones, while restaurant entrances bear a remarkable similarity to Roman temples. Nowhere is light used so fully as a means of defining space. On Fremont Street there are literally blocks of neon signs, several stories high, one running into the next, to create a solid wall of brilliant, dazzling color. In Vegas, one hardly ever knows whether it is day or night. It is one continous plan in motion, with no time constraints. The street is in constant motion, with strips of neon sliding up and down and in and out, yet the overall visual picture, like that of a theater marquee, never really changes. Las Vegas provides an escape trip for grown-ups into a glittering fantasy world where everybody and everything is beautiful. The reality sets in when one leaves Las Vegas poorer than when one arrived (Goldberger, 1978, K-2).

There can be no question that our environment plays an important role in affecting our communication behavior. How we perceive structures and how we respond to environmental manipulation will be explored in the following section.

PERCEPTIONS OF ENVIRONMENT

As in the case of Las Vegas, it is clear that architectural styles may be more than the reflection of the client's and architect's creative and artistic tastes. There are obvious messages intended in the selected design. One of the most dramatic examples of "restructuring" of

Today's modern banking structures represent an architectural comment about the lessening of formality in our once formal institutions.

buildings can be seen in the banking industry. Banks were originally designed to create a solid and conservative image and to impart strength and security. In the past, the design of banks frequently included oversized marble pillars, an abundance of metal bars and doors, tile floors, institutional gray interior, and barren walls. The public saw the banks as cold and impersonal, but also as solid and durable.

Imagine when banks were first introduced into society. If you had never heard of a "bank," could you see yourself driving up to a small, box-like structure, which is now known as the stop-and-go drive-in bank or an "ugly teller," and making a deposit? Could you have confidently handed over your life savings to a woman whose red-and-white-striped blouse matched the awning on the bank? It is unlikely that you or anyone else would have taken the bank seriously, let alone placed your money in it. Before savings insurance was widely available and before money became devalued by inflation, bank executives wanted to assure their customers that their money was safe in a fortress-like building that would survive longer than they would. This image during the early 1900s created the perception that banks were here to stay.

The United States government, also wishing to proclaim its permanence and resistance to overthrow, patterned the architectural designs

The drive-in bank is common today, but years ago most people would never have con-sidered giving their life's savings to someone in this little box-like structure with its striped awning.

of government buildings after classical Roman or Greek styles, as if to say the government would endure as long as those classical styles had endured. Even churches adopted a serious, solid, and foreboding presence by repeating the architectural styles of the medieval period when the church was a very dominant part of the social and political scene in Europe. Twenty years later, dramatic changes had taken place with banks, government institutions, and churches.

Dentistry and oral-surgery practice have paid increasing attention to the perceptions patients have of the environment, both in the wait-ing room and the operating rooms. One oral-surgery practice placed friendly, overstuffed animals in the waiting room and used brightly col-ored and comfortable vinyl chairs. An open-room arrangement was used to reduce patient anxiety. Each operating room, where procedures involving local anesthesia were performed, was painted a light blue to help the patient relax. The operating suites, where general anesthesia was used, was a deeper blue to enhance the somnolent effects of pre-liminary medications. The offices were specially designed to create an informal, private, familiar, and nonconstraining environment for the patients. Here the oral surgeon could relax the patients enough to talk about such personal matters as restructuring their jaws or other facial bone structures.

In another dental practice, a warm and relaxing atmosphere was created in the reception area and a semiprivate area was created for children. The far corner, designated as the "kiddie" area, was partially enclosed with waist-high planters to serve as shelving for books and toys. A ten-gallon aquarium was placed in this area and captivated the attention of the adults as well as the children (Block, 1975, pp. 85–89).

Walking into a dental office to have a tooth pulled or filled creates initial anxiety. The attempt to manipulate the internal and external environment to produce a consistent perception of warmth and relaxation is not limited to dental practice. Environmental design is happening everywhere. The perceptions of our surroundings affect the messages communicated and ultimately our behavior. Knapp (1978) identifies six perceptual frameworks of our environment. We perceive the environment in terms of its (1) **formality,** (2) **warmth,** (3) **privacy,** (4) **familiarity,** (5) **constraint,** and (6) **distance.**

Formality

Is a building structure formal or informal? As we have already mentioned, early banks, government buildings, and churches represented a very formal structure. Winston Churchill's point that we shape our

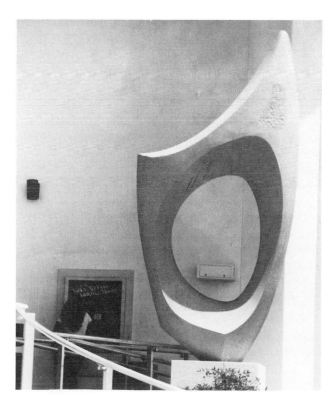

Sculptures and art objects provide an external, decorative structure for many buildings. What do they communicate? It is all in the eyes of the beholder.

buildings and that later they shape us is a reality. The early formal structures of these buildings affected the communication behavior of people within them. A bank teller then was "the keeper of the keys"—very formal, stylized, and impersonal in dealing with customers. Today, with the advent of new informal structures, bank tellers undergo rigorous training programs to improve customer service. These programs teach tellers to be pleasant, use good eye contact, smile, and engage in conversation beyond that of the business transaction.

Warmth

When an environment makes you feel psychologically comfortable or warm, do you have a tendency to relax or linger? Most people do. In fact, restaurants and fast-food chains faced a problem with people lingering too long. In their desire to create a "warm, comfortable, and enjoyable" environment, restaurant owners found that their patrons stayed too long and that profitable turn-over and servicing of customers were greatly reduced. As a result, the Larsen chair was designed to be comfortable enough for eating the meal, but not too comfortable to stay and converse after the meal was finished. Creating warmth in an environment includes the use of carpeting, lighting, sound-proofing, and what the housing industry refers to as colorizing.

Privacy

People usually feel greater privacy in an enclosed environment that accommodates only a few people. Take a look at the cozy corner that promotes conversation. A cozy corner allows a few people to pull apart from the main conversation group at a party or office for their own tête-à-tête. Many restaurants have lost customers after expanding to a larger, more formal dining area from a smaller, more intimate one. In many cases the expansion changed the private and cozy environment so significantly that the original appeal of the restaurant was lost.

The extent to which others cannot enter or overhear the conversation creates a greater feeling of privacy. With increased privacy, the speaking distance between people is reduced and the messages are much more personal, designed and adapted for a specific person rather than "for people in general."

Familiarity

Unfamiliar environments usually produce a high arousal level because we do not know the rituals and norms; visually, the environment is new to the eye and we are hesitant to move too quickly. In a mobile society such as ours, brilliant business executives have designed "chain stereotyped structures" such as McDonald's, Dunkin' Donuts, Holiday Inn, Howard Johnson's, Taco Bell, and many others. The implication is that by maintaining the same environmental structure, external and internal, customers will be readily familiar and comfortable with the surroundings, and the service and/or product will be comparable to what they have had before in another chain. This predictability guarantees that there will be minimum demands placed on customers in terms of adjusting to the environment; the environmental structure is constant. In this way people "feel at home" in a place in which they have never been before.

Constraint

Part of our reaction to an environment is based on our perception of whether (and how easily) we can leave it. Knapp (1978) comments that "the intensity of these perceptions of constraint is closely related to the space available to us and the privacy of this space during the time we will be in the environment" (p. 88).

There is a difference between temporarily confining environments and permanently confining ones. A trip across country in a car is temporarily confining, while a trip in jail is of a much more constraining and permanent nature. Imagine yourself in a tiny room without any means of escape. The noise is endless—people shouting and talking, radio and television blaring. There is no privacy, no way to escape the spatial invasion or the gaze of others. How would you react? This is a description of the basics of jail life according to Barbara Price, co-director of the National Jail Study. She believes that the average middle-class person would find the experience highly traumatic because the perception of constraint generally produces trauma (1977, pp. 27–28).

Distance

How close or far away we are in a conversational setting with another person can affect our communication. This includes actual physical distance (such as the senior executive offices on the top floor and junior executive offices on the floor below) or psychological distance (such as an empty chair between two students working at a table in the library). Office location, as a function of distance, communicates a great deal about power and status, according to Michael Korda. In most cases, Korda (1975) contends, power diminishes with distance from the senior executive's office. He tells a story of Sidney, an assistant to the senior executive who worked in an airless cubbyhole beside the great man's office. No secretary would have worked in that spot, but Sidney chose to stay there because it had a door that led into the executive's secretary, and another door opening out onto the corridor so that he could see everybody coming and going. Sidney tells his story:

> So long as I sat there, I had it made. I got to know everyone who came in; if they had to wait, they came and leaned on my desk, or used my phone to confirm lunch dates, and everybody assumed that I must know everything that was going on.
>
> When I first moved in . . . the only thing I insisted on was a telephone with several lines and an intercom to my boss. I don't think I ever used it, but when he made a call, one of the buttons would light up on my phone, and anyone in my office would have a sense of my being connected to him. It's the proximity to power that counts, not space, a carpet, or a window. (Korda, pp. 69–70)

In Sidney's case, distance served to create the perception of power and access to the head man.

RESPONSES TO ENVIRONMENT

If we grew up in sterile rooms void of objects, color, or movement, we would be far different creatures. Our environment stimulates curiosity and shapes our personality, communication, and performance. Our responses to the environment will be examined with regard to (1) the attractiveness of the surroundings, (2) color, (3) lighting, and (4) sound.

Attractiveness of Surroundings

The young couple had been separated for six weeks and could not wait to be together again. Because of monetary problems they had been forced to rent a dingy, damp, and chilly basement apartment. While they were there, they made love only a few times. The cold dampness of their surroundings, according to the young woman, did not fit the way they felt about each other and somehow affected their sexual life. When they moved to a new, light-filled, and warm apartment, their physical attraction began again. "It was very strange," the young woman said, "I've always enjoyed sex a lot, and I was wild about Jerry, but there was something about that miserable basement that made sex seem beside the point, almost dirty." Dunkell (1978) explains the effect of the environment on the woman's emotional response in the following way:

> For this young woman, it seems clear that the general grubbiness of the furnished flat she and her lover shared had as much to do with turning her off

sexually as did the dampness and cold. For most people, the colors, furniture, and fabrics used in a bedroom are extremely important. For one thing, the environment in which one chooses to live reflects the individuality of the person, and the bedroom is often the room in which that individuality is most clearly evident. (p. 192)

Researchers Maslow and Mintz explored the impact of an ugly, beautiful, and average room on the emotional responses of the participants (1956, p. 247–254). The ugly room was designed to look like a janitor's storeroom, with things scattered everywhere. The beautiful room had carpeting, drapes, and similar effects. Finally, the average room was designed as a professor's office. The subjects in each of the rooms were asked to rate a series of negative print photographs of faces. Given what we know about the effects of the environment, the results were not surprising. The subjects in the beautiful room gave significantly higher ratings to the faces than did the subjects in the ugly room. In addition, subjects in the ugly room engaged in various escape behaviors in an attempt to avoid the unattractive surroundings. They claimed that the room produced monotony, fatigue, headache, discontent, sleep, irritability, and hostility. Subjects in the beautiful room

"You really can't know the real me until you've
seen how I've decorated my bedroom."

Richard Varney

reported feelings of pleasure, importance, comfort, enjoyment, energy and the desire to continue the activity (Mintz, 1956, pp. 459–466).

Another important response to environment focuses on color. The following section will explore the many ways in which color affects our lives.

Color

Did you know

- that sugar won't sell in a green package?
- that beauty aids in brown jars sit on the shelf?
- that kids want cereal in red and yellow boxes?

Advertisers are becoming increasingly selective about their use of colors in promoting products. This was not the case in the time of Henry Ford. It might be said that Henry Ford offered his customers any color automobile they desired—as long as it was black. Today, color merchandising has become big business. A major automobile manufacturer may offer 650 standard color combinations or any kind of color customizing for which the customer is willing to pay.

People react to colors emotionally and physically. One detergent manufacturer sprinkled red granules throughout his white soap powder, and housewives subsequently complained that the detergent was too rough on their hands. He changed the color to yellow, and women said it was easier on the hands but that the clothes were not as clean. Finally, he changed the granules to a blue color, and the women said it was just right. Nothing had changed but the color of the granules.

There are many associations with color. There are blue Mondays and various black days in history. A cowardly person is yellow; an angry person sees red. Some people are green with envy and others are in the pink. Moreover, many specific associations have been made with colors. For instance, red has been associated with more appetite appeal than any other color. Red is usually found somewhere in the decor of restaurants and on the wrappers of many food products. The red-and-white combination has probably sold more toothpaste than any other combination. Blue, violet, and purple have little or no appetite appeal. Green will sell vegetables in the supermarket, but a green wrapper has never been known to sell bread. Mehrabian (1976) claims that the most pleasant hues, in order, are blue, green, red, and yellow, and that red is the most arousing hue followed by orange, yellow, violet, blue, and green.

The symbolic meanings of color have a long history. Colors have been associated with moods and symbolic meanings for a long time. For example, the red-light district is a symbolic phrase that uses red as a hot color. Burgoon and Saine have identified moods and symbolic messages, which are outlined in Table 6.1.

Ketcham (1958) studied three colors in a school setting. One school was left unpainted, a second school was finished in the usual institutional color scheme of light buff walls and white ceilings, and the third was painted in accordance with principles of color dynamics. In the third school the corridors were painted a cheerful yellow with gray doors; classrooms facing north were done in a pale rose; classrooms facing south depicted cooler shades of blue and green; front walls were

Table 6.1 COLOR IN THE ENVIRONMENT: MOODS CREATED AND SYMBOLIC MEANINGS

Color	Moods	Symbolic Meanings
Red	Hot, affectionate, angry, defiant, contrary, hostile, full of vitality, excitement, love.	Happiness, lust, intimacy, love, restlessness, agitation, royalty, rage, sin, blood.
Blue	Cool, pleasant, leisurely, distant, infinite, secure, transcendent, calm, tender.	Dignity, sadness, tenderness, truth
Yellow	Unpleasant, exciting, hostile, cheerful, joyful, jovial.	Superficial glamor, sun, light, wisdom, masculinity, royalty (in China), age (in Greece), prostitution (in Italy), famine (in Egypt).
Orange	Unpleasant, exciting, disturbed, distressed, upset, defiant, contrary, hostile, stimulating.	Sun, fruitfulness, harvest, thoughtfulness.
Purple	Depressed, sad, dignified, stately.	Wisdom, victory, pomp, wealth, humility, tragedy.
Green	Cool, pleasant, leisurely, in control.	Security, peace, jealousy, hate, aggressiveness, calm.
Black	Sad, intense, anxiety, fear, despondent, dejected, melancholy, unhappy.	Darkness, power, mastery, protection, decay, mystery, wisdom, death, atonement.
Brown	Sad, not tender, despondent, dejected, melancholy, unhappy, neutral.	Melancholy, protection, autumn, decay, humility, atonement.
White	Joy, lightness, neutral, cold.	Solemnity, purity, chastity, femininity, humility, joy, light, innocence, fidelity, cowardice.

darker than side walls; the art room was a neutral gray so as to avoid interferring with the colorful work that it contained; and green chalkboards were used to reduce glare. Over a two-year period, behavior in each school was observed. The results were clear; students in the third school showed greatest improvement on several variables measured—social habits, health, safety habits, and scholastic aptitude in language, arts, arithmetic, social studies, science, and music. Those in the unpainted school showed the least improvement in these areas and those in the traditional school fell somewhere in between (1958).

The area of color is complex and is not subject to simple conclusions about psychological and physiological effects. To what extent color affects emotional response is still a question of major concern to researchers.

Lighting

Lighting, like color, also has a pronounced effect on our behavior. Kowinski (1975) has observed, "Most offices are generally overlit—with often twice as much light as they need—while individuals within the office may be working in circumstances that are underlit. The results can be inefficiency, fatigue, and perhaps a sense of dislocation caused mostly by the St. Vitus dance that the pupil of the eye must do to cope" (p. 48).

Gergen, Gergen, and Barton (1973) contrasted and examined behavior in a lighted room and a dark room. Subjects were placed in either a dark or light room to do whatever they wanted for an hour. The room was ten by twelve feet, had padded floors and walls, and contained four male and four female subjects. Verbal behavior was markedly different in the two rooms; there was a continuous stream of talk in the lighted room, whereas subjects in the darkened room spoke very little after about half an hour (pp. 129–130).

Low lights tend to create a relaxed, intimate environment in which people want to linger. Extremely bright lights tend to cause fatigue and a desire to escape. Soft lighting is more flattering to a woman's makeup, so fluorescent lighting is sometimes avoided in offices where women work. Carr and Dabbs found that the combination of intimate questions and dim lighting with nonintimates caused a significant hesitancy in responding, a significant decrease in eye gaze, and a decrease in the average length of gaze (1974, pp. 592–600).

The effects of colored lighting on performance is interesting. Birren (1975) cites evidence suggesting that human reactions are twelve percent faster than average under red lighting conditions. Green lights, on the other hand, seem to generate reactions that are slower than normal. Colored lighting also seems to influence judgments of time, length, and weight. With red lighting, these judgments tend to be overestimated, while a green or blue light appears to generate underestimation.

Fatigue rates rise in direct proportion to the dimming of the visual field. This is a fact, plain and simple. So much of a student's work depends on visual scanning and identification that lowered light levels will decrease his or her efficiency drastically, thereby decreasing the quality and quantity of his or her work (Thompson, 1973, p. 81).

The following are three guidelines for the lighting of the classroom:

1. Maintain high levels of illumination. When students must expend energy just to see, they will have little left to understand what is being said.
2. All areas of the room should be balanced in brightness. Factory and assembly-line workers have their work well illuminated. Industry has known for a long time that eye fatigue plays havoc with production schedules. To avoid sharp contrast, the visual field around the task should be only one-third as bright as the work area. No part of the visual field should be brighter than the immediate vicinity of the task.
3. Avoid glare either from direct light sources or from reflecting surfaces.

Sound

We react emotionally to sound all the time, sometimes without conscious awareness. Since people are accustomed to background sound rather than silence, some companies use a white-noise generator. This generator creates a hum or hiss that sounds similar to an air conditioner and is generated electronically in open office surroundings to mask other background noise. In some cases, the white-sound generator, instead of creating a calm and productive environment, creates frazzled nerves. Paul Harris companies used the generator but had to shut it down because employees found it irritating. On the other hand, a senior designer in a large Philadelphia company reports an office where the generator was too successful. The designer noted that when the white sound went off, everyone thought the air conditioner had broken down. People got warmer and warmer and finally had to go home because everyone was so hot.

Remember the last time you were driving on a rather long trip and began to get a little tired? If you located some music on the radio, you probably noticed that you began to feel more alert and awake almost immediately. If you can recall an incident similar to this, then you realize that music can be a strong stimulant. Mehrabian, however, claims that music has a more immediate effect on our arousal level and pleasure than several cups of coffee. Few will deny that music has an emotional impact; for example, you must know a song that can make you feel a little sad or nostalgic, another that always lifts you up and makes you smile, or still another that makes you want to ''get down'' and ''boogie.''

Although you probably recognize the unique influence music can have upon people, it is important to realize that music is often used to evoke a particular response in them. For example, various types of merchants use music in an attempt to increase the desirability of their products. They use music to create an environment that will elicit a particular response from the customer. A supermarket may raise the volume of music to stimulate more purchases in a shorter period of time. A softly lit restaurant uses soothing music to match the intimate atmosphere. A disco uses flashing lights and music that is loud and has a repeated beat to produce excitement. Each of these businesses uses a different type of music in order to produce a special environment—an environment that will sell their products.

SPATIAL ARRANGEMENTS AND SEATING BEHAVIOR

Power is where you sit, claims Michael Korda. Consciously or unconsciously, people select seats to reaffirm their various roles in groups. In ancient times, seating choice was a matter of self-protection and survival. When a power figure sat at the head of a round table, for instance, it was very important where the next power figure was placed. One natural choice might be to put the next most powerful individual to the right, based on the concept of ''right-hand'' person. This method was not used in ancient times for the simple reason that it was easier to stab to your left with the dagger in your right hand than to stab to your right, again with the dagger in your right hand. It was therefore prudent to place a powerful guest to your immediate left, since in that position he could not stab you, while you were excellently positioned to kill him. The person on your immediate right would be someone of no risk or importance to you. Today, seating behavior requires a choice based not on physical protection but on a need for psychological protection at several levels (Korda, 1975).

The first area of seating behavior and spatial arrangements to be reviewed is the structural setting for interaction, such as the shape and size of the tables used. The following section will examine the research on seating behavior and its effect on communication and interaction.

Structural Settings for Interaction

The story of King Arthur and the Knights of the Round Table is a graphic illustration of power. Presumably, their table was round so that there could be no question of dominance and so that every knight could share equally in the honor of being seated at the table. There was only one flaw in this approach. King Arthur's seat became the status marker, and status decreased as the distance from the king increased. As a result, a knight sitting four seats away from the king was perceived as having lower status in contrast to the knight who sat next to the king. Shapes of tables communicate important information about the nature

Richard Varney

of the interaction, dominance, power, and ultimate control before they are even occupied, as the following example indicates:

> The United States and South Vietnam wanted a seating arrangement in which only two sides were identified. They did not want to recognize the National Liberation Front as an "equal" partner in the negotiations. North Vietnam and the NLF wanted "equal" status given to all parties—represented by a four-sided table. The final arrangement was such that both parties could claim victory. The round table minus the dividing lines allowed North Vietnam and the NLF to claim all four delegations were equal. (McCroskey, Larson, and Knapp, 1971, p. 97)

The round table. A round table, with the absence of distinct edges and sides, expresses unity and equality for all parties. The circle itself has become a symbol of unity and strength throughout the world. A round table, however, does reveal lines of demarcation between individuals. As in ancient times, the direction of the seated power circle reveals status. The order to power is usually clockwise, beginning with the number twelve on a clockface. Power diminishes as it moves around the positions at three o'clock, six o'clock, nine o'clock, and so on. Therefore, the second most powerful person will sit in the one o'clock position, and the least prominent or powerful individual will sit at the eleven o'clock position (Koneya and Barbour, 1976, pp. 58–59).

The square table. What types of games do you play on a square table? How about backgammon, bridge, chess, Monopoly, or any of a number of card games? The square table, with four equal sides, provides excellent corners for the separation of its participants. For a business meeting, the square table signifies equality for each business partner since every person has equal frontage, space, and separate edges. The square table therefore signifies equality and sameness because of the equal length of each side. On the other hand, it does not signify unity because of its distinct sidedness. The square table is excellent for competition because it promotes direct eye contact in all four positions and allows for equal distance between people seated at the table.

The rectangular table. The rectangular table has been a popular shape for boardrooms in business for some time. All types of variations of the rectangular table exist. The rectangular table has some features similar to the square table. It has four distinct sides and does not express the concept of unity because of the separation with the corners. The obvious difference from the square table is the fact that the rectangular table has two long sides and two short sides, with the long and short

sides being of equal length to each other. The short side has traditionally been viewed as the head of the table, particularly when only one
short end is occupied. Who occupies the head seat in your family at
Thanksgiving or Christmas? In many families, the father sits at the head
(the short side of the rectangular table) with the mother sitting opposite
at the other short end.

Salt River Project executives in Phoenix, Arizona, have designed an
interesting variation of the rectangular table. The table has one wide
short side, but grows narrower and narrower toward the end of the
other short side. The reasoning behind this design was to allow board
participants to see the head (President) without craning their necks.
This is an ingenious table design for visual ease, but it leaves something
to be desired for those individuals who get the short end of the table, as
it were. Not only is status diminished with the distance from the head of
the table, but this fact is also accentuated by the reduction in space
toward the end of the table.

Perceptions and Characteristics of
Seating Behavior

In 1977, NBC attempted to give David Brinkley and John Chancellor a
more relaxed conversational relationship with the viewers. So they
moved the set around from behind the desk. After having been sprung
from their imposing desks, the announcers were squeezed into identical chairs with armrests. They sometimes appeared to be as uncomfortable as oversized freshmen trying to keep their legs out of the aisle.
But the point was to change the image or audience perception by manipulating the **seating arrangement** in the set. "I've said for years that
some anchor people tend to become high priests of the news," explains
Chancellor. "They intone it as though they own it. I'm not trying to be a
common-man Joe six-pack. But I think sharing the news this way makes
it more meaningful than just sitting up there and saying this happened,
that happened," (quoted in Carter, 1977b, p. 103).

That's how it happened for NBC. The perception of the viewer was
important in the station's image. Many studies have revealed that certain seating choices may be perceived as leadership positions. In addition, studies have revealed that certain "types" of people, such as
dominant personalities, select particular seats.

Task situations. Sommer (1969) analyzed how students would sit in
various task situations. The study was replicated by Cook in the United
Kingdom with Oxford University students and a sample of nonstudents that included civil servants, school teachers, and secretaries. Sub-

jects were asked to imagine themselves sitting at a table with a friend of the same sex in the following four situations.

Conversation—sitting and talking for a few minutes before class (before work for nonstudents).

Cooperation—sitting and studying together for the same exam (or doing a crossword puzzle or the like together for the nonstudent).

Co-action—sitting and studying together for the same exam (or sitting at the same table and reading for nonstudents).

Competition—competing in order to see who would be first to solve a series of puzzles.

Most pairs who wanted to talk or work together used adjacent chairs. Sommer explains this as the need to have psychological closeness. Subjects gave such explanations as "I want to chat with my friend, not the whole cafeteria, so I sit next to her," and "More intimate, there are no physical barriers between us" (Cook, 1970, pp. 61–76). The results of the study are displayed in Tables 6.2 and 6.3.

Table 6.2 SEATING PREFERENCES AT RECTANGULAR TABLES

	Seat 1	Seat 2	Seat 3	Seat 4	Seat 5	Seat 6
Conversation						
U.S. sample (151 responses)	42%	46%	11%	0%	1%	0%
U.K. (univ.) sample (102 responses)	51	21	15	0	6	7
U.K. (nonuniv.) sample (42 responses)	42	42	9	2	5	0
Cooperation						
U.S. sample	19	25	51	0	5	0
U.K. (univ.) sample	11	11	23	20	22	13
U.K. (nonuniv.) sample	40	2	50	5	2	0
Co-action						
U.S. sample	3	3	7	13	43	33
U.K. (univ.) sample	9	8	10	31	28	14
U.K. (nonuniv.) sample	12	14	12	19	31	12
Competition						
U.S. sample	7	41	8	18	20	5
U.K. (univ.) sample	7	10	10	50	16	7
U.K. (nonuniv.) sample	4	13	3	53	20	7

Reprinted from M. Cook, "Experimentation on Orientation and Proxemics," *Human Relations*, 1970, Vol. 23, pp. 61–76. Used by permission of Plenum Publishing Corporation.

Table 6.3 SEATING PREFERENCES AT ROUND TABLES

	⁺ˣ◯	ˣ◯ₓ	◯ₓ (x top, x bottom)
Conversation			
U.S. sample (116 responses)	63%	17%	20%
U.K. (univ.) sample (102 responses)	58	37	5
U.K. (nonuniv.) sample (42 responses)	58	27	15
Cooperation			
U.S. sample	83	7	10
U.K. (univ.) sample	25	31	44
U.K. (nonuniv.) sample	97	0	3
Co-action			
U.S. sample	13	36	51
U.K. (univ.) sample	16	34	50
U.K. (nonuniv.) sample	24	26	50
Competition			
U.S. sample	2	25	63
U.K. (univ.) sample	15	22	63
U.K. (nonuniv.) sample	9	21	70

Reprinted from M. Cook, "Experimentation on Orientation and Proxemics," *Human Relations*, 1970, Vol. 23, pp. 61–76. Used by permission of Plenum Publishing Corporation.

As the tables reveal, there was a difference in response between the British nonuniversity sample, the United States student sample, and the Oxford University sample. Almost everyone in the studies selected side-by-side choices for cooperative tasks, with the exception of the Oxford group. This might be explained by a misinterpretation of the question by the Oxford group. Since Oxford students are encouraged to do most of their work independently, they may not have realized that the question referred to cooperation with another person. The variety of responses to the co-action question—studying for the same exam or reading at the same table as another—may be the result of the slightly different instructions for the nonuniversity sample. Finally, most persons wanted to compete in an opposite seating arrangement. The American students, however, wanted to sit closer, perhaps to have greater eye contact, body movement, or control, and in general to be more aggressive and competitive. The United Kingdom samples chose a more distant opposite position to protect their task and prevent the other person from spying.

Level of intimacy.   Cook also studied the perceptions of sex and acquaintance (level of intimacy) with regard to seating behavior. Subjects
were asked in a questionnaire to select seating arrangements in two situations—a bar scene and a restaurant scene—when (1) sitting with a
casual friend of the same sex, (2) sitting with a casual friend of the opposite sex, and (3) sitting with a boyfriend or girlfriend. The results are
displayed in Tables 6.4 and 6.5.

As Tables 6.4 and 6.5 indicate, the predominant patterns were as
follows:

1. Corner seating was selected in the bar for same-sex friends and casual friends of the opposite sex.
2. Side-by-side seating was chosen for intimate friends in the bar setting.
3. Opposite seating in the restaurant was chosen for all three variations of sex and acquaintance.
4. Side-by-side seating occurred more with intimate friends in the
   restaurant.

An obvious practical reason for opposite seating in a restaurant is to
avoid crowding while eating and to allow plenty of elbow room. Ap-

*Table 6.4 SEATING PREFERENCES FOR A BAR
OR "PUBLIC HOUSE"*

	×⬜ with x	⬜ with x below	⬜ with x x above	*Other*
Same-sex friend	70%	25%	45%	2%
Casual friend of opposite sex	63	37	29	7
Intimate friend	43	11	82	4

Reprinted from M. Cook, "Experimentation on Orientation and Proxemics," *Human Relations,* 1970, Vol. 23, pp.
61–76. Used by permission of Plenum Publishing Corporation.

Table 6.5 SEATING PREFERENCES FOR A RESTAURANT

	×⬜ with x	⬜ with x below	⬜ with x x above	*Other*
Same-sex friend	30%	73%	34%	4%
Casual friend of opposite sex	43	64	28	4
Intimate friend	40	53	46	2

Reprinted from M. Cook, "Experimentation on Orientation and Proxemics," *Human Relations,* 1970, Vol. 23, pp.
61–76. Used by permission of Plenum Publishing Corporation.

parently, people do attribute certain interaction patterns and relationships to various seating arrangements. At least we know people perceive this to be the case.

Personality characteristics. Herbert Walberg (1969) studied the relationship between seating position and student personality. He found that when a student was given a choice of where to sit, different personalities preferred different locations. For instance, students who were enthusiastic about school as well as about creative activities outside of school chose to sit close to the front in order to see and hear everything. These students, as revealed on tests, felt it was important to be creative and imaginative. They were also task-oriented and frequently thought about values and goals in life. On the other hand, students who selected seats in the back of the room were described as unhappy with school, disinterested in grades and school popularity, and not likely to be organizers or leaders. Students who preferred to sit near a window also disliked school and studying. The majority of students who did not care where they sat had similar characteristics to the group who preferred the front seats. They lacked, however, some of the extremes in enthusiasm that characterized the first group (pp. 64–70).

Dominance. Russo (1967) found that people doing a paper-and-pencil rating of various seating arrangements stated that if one person was at the head and one on the side, there was an unequal situation in terms of status than if both persons were on the ends. This was not a surprising perception of **dominance** or **status** (pp. 37–44).

In a study conducted outside of the classroom environment, Hare and Bales (1963, pp. 480–486), found that people who scored high on a paper-and-pencil dominance test chose a seat at the head of the table or in the center of one of the long sides. Both seating areas facilitated high eye contact and visibility. Similar findings were reported by Sommer (1956) and Strodtbeck and Hook (1961). They observed that leaders are more likely to choose a position at the end of a rectangular table and that individuals who choose the corner seats of a rectangular table contribute the least.

The Strodtbeck and Hook study (1961, pp. 397–415) examined seating behavior in experimental jury settings. The researchers found that the person sitting at the head position was chosen significantly more often as the jury leader, particularly if he/she was perceived as a person from a high economic class. If the choice was between two people sitting at each head position, the one perceived as having higher economic status was selected.

According to researchers Howells and Becker (1962), seating position also determines the flow of communication, which, in turn, determines leadership emergence. Five-person decision-making groups were examined, with three people sitting on one side of a rectangular table and two on the other side. The researchers reported that the side with two people was able to influence the other three (or at least talk more) and, therefore, emerged more often as group leaders (pp. 148–150).

In an analysis of talking frequency in small groups, Hare and Bales noted that people in the end or outside positions were frequent talkers. Subsequent studies revealed that these people were likely to be dominant personalities while those who avoided the central or focal positions by selecting inside seats were more anxious and actually stated that they wanted to stay out of the discussion.

Friendliness. Russo (1967) found that large distances between people generally indicate less acquaintance, less friendliness, and less talkativeness. Russo reported some interesting differences, depicted in Fig. 6.1.

People who were the most friendly toward one another chose the A seating arrangement, while those who were hostile selected the E arrangement. Russo also examined intimate versus unacquainted persons. Seating position B was viewed as more friendly and intimate than position C, C more than D, and D more than E. The same pattern applied when examining the variables of talkative vs. untalkative individuals.

Introverts–extroverts. Cook studied the relationship between the personality variable of extroversion–introversion and seating preference. He found that extroverts chose to sit opposite one another, either across

Figure 6.1
Russo's display of seating arrangements and their effect on interpersonal communication.

Diagram

From N. Russo, ''Connotation of Seating Arrangement,'' *Cornell Journal of Social Relations*, 1967, 2, p. 39. Used by permission.

the table or down the length of it. Many extroverts also chose positions that would put them in close physical proximity to the other person. Introverts, on the other hand, generally chose positions that would keep them more at a distance visually and physically from the other person (Cook, 1970).

Cook also conducted an actual observational study (as opposed to a questionnaire study) to determine interaction behavior. Actual observations of seating in a restaurant validated his questionnaire study. Cook found that most people sitting in bars showed a definite preference for side-by-side seating. The earlier questionnaire had suggested corner seating. Cook suggests that the difference may have been due to the fact that bars are equipped with many seats located against the wall. As a result, this allows persons to sit side-by-side and not have their backs to anyone; therefore, they have a good view of others (Cook, 1970).

Effects

Does the manipulation of objects and seating arrangements produce predictable effects on the outcome of communication events? William Agee, President of Bendix Corporation, thinks so. He recently banished the company's giant wooden table from the boardroom and replaced it with "nothing." The old table was brown and drab and looked like a surfboard, he declared. Besides, it was just a security blanket for directors and had little real purpose. The president believed a boardroom table is a barrier to open and frank discussions and that it exists at most corporations only because of tradition. "If you want to gesture and make a point, it's hard to do it with a table." The fact that the table was removed surprised the directors when they entered the room for a meeting. Of course, when the table was removed the room wasn't left exactly bare. It was furnished with plush new velvet armchairs, which swiveled and rocked, arranged around a handsome $30,000 Oriental rug. The conclusion of the board was that the meeting was more relaxed and highly communicative in the tableless room.

In the business setting the boardroom space was arranged to produce a desired effect on behavior. The same event occurs in the educational content where the teacher exerts behavioral control by arranging the child's environment. One educator asked the question: Why should a youngster smear slime around the classroom when she is supposed to be napping? Why does a youngster punch another child while he eyes a crowded swing set? Why does a youngster like to play near the oven? Children's learning and socialization processes are dramatically affected by the environments in which they occur. Children need boundaries, occasional privacy, and controlled visual and tactile stimulation to learn effectively. The physical environment can often work against learning. For example, youngsters may forego napping for mischief because the environment is too exciting for sleep. Objects in space say "pick me up" while the teacher is saying "listen to me" (Carey, 1978, B-2).

The effects of spatial arrangements and seating behavior on interaction are significant. Whether one is in the classroom or the boardroom, spatial arrangement affects interaction. Studies have demonstrated that the formality and intimacy of communication will change with the manipulation of objects or alternative seating selection.

Classroom space. In a review of studies conducted in college classrooms, Sommer (1969) explains how he became interested in the effects of seating behavior:

> My curiosity about classroom seating had been whetted by teachers' assumptions about students' seating: The front rows contain the most interested students, those in the rear engage in illicit activities, students at the aisles are mainly concerned with quick departures, most absentees come from the rear quadrant most distant from the windows, and the straight-row arrangement inhibits discussion. (p. 119)

Researchers Adams and Biddle (1970) conducted one of the most extensive studies of straight-row seating in the classroom. Their study involved the observation of thirty-two classes and a variety of subject areas. An impressive fact is that their findings were consistent across all teachers, subjects, and grade levels.

The researchers reported that the main determinant of whether a student was actively engaged in classroom participation was dependent on the location of his or her seat. An **action zone,** defined as a center of activity where most interaction occurs, was identified in the typical straight-row seating arrangement. The action zone extends from the front of the room directly up the center line, diminishing in interaction as it moves farther away from the instructor. This zone represents the students who engage in active communication behavior with the teacher, and it also represents the students with whom the teacher converses. Interaction in seminar rooms revealed some interesting findings. Sommer (1969) studied four seminar-room arrangements: open squares or horseshoes, laboratory rooms, a room with no windows, and one described as "light and airy." Participation was the greatest in the seminar room arranged in an open square or horseshoe structure. In the straight-row arrangements the students in the front tended to participate most. Sommer confirmed the Adams and Biddle results when he found that participation is greatest in the front row, as well as in the center of each row. Sommer reported that sixty-one percent of the stu-

The separate study cubicles represent clearly defined space with the small bookshelf and backboard. The latter also limits roaming eyes when studying.

dents in the center of the first row and fifty-seven percent of those at the sides participated; in the last row, forty-eight percent of those in the center and thirty-one percent of those at the sides participated.

Spacing of desks or seats also affects communication behavior in the classroom. Heston and Garner (1972) found that when selecting their own seats, males assume a greater seating distance from each other than do females, with distances between males and females falling between these extremes. In addition, Heston and Garner found that students, when spacing themselves, take up more space. As far as preferences for particular seating arrangements, the semicircle and U-shape are highly preferred over straight rows and circles. This implies a student preference for a seating arrangement that allows the most interaction. The straight-row seating, although the traditional arrangement in the classroom, seems to be inadequate because it does not give students what they intuitively feel they need—interaction with other members of the class.

Office space.   Desks are an important object in promoting or obstructing interpersonal communication. White (1953) conducted an experiment in a doctor's office and reported that the absence or presence of a desk may significantly alter the patient's "at ease" state. When the desk separated the doctor and the patient, only ten percent of the patients were perceived to be "at ease," as compared to fifty-five percent when the desk was moved (pp.256–257).

The desk also plays a significant role in student–teacher relationships. In a study conducted by Zweigenhaft (1976), faculty members were asked to sketch the furniture arrangement in their offices. The sketches were analyzed with other information obtained from the professors along with a school-wide teacher evaluation. Not surprisingly, twenty-four out of thirty-three senior faculty members (full professors and associate professors) put their desks between themselves and their students. On the other hand, only fourteen out of thirty junior faculty members (assistant professors and lecturers) placed the desk between themselves and their students. The most interesting findings were the students' perceptions of how this furniture arrangement affected interaction. The professors who did not use the desk were rated by students as more willing to "encourage the development of different viewpoints by students," more ready to give "individual attention to students who need it," and less likely to display "undue favoritism."

Figure 6.2
Which office affords the greatest power position to its occupant? The third illustration has the desk placed well forward in the room, thus minimizing the space available for the visitor. This gives the occupant greater territorial residence and power.

Figure 6.3
Where would you sit to maintain power and control?

Environmental situations may discourage or facilitate interaction.
Everywhere you go you can observe the effects of seating arrangements
on interaction—be it in a restaurant, library, boardroom, classroom, or
even a theater.

SUMMARY

During the nineteenth century, there was a common tradition of bundling (families huddling together under blankets) in New England,
Wales, and the Hebrides Islands off the coast of Scotland. During cold

weather, usually the only fire in the farmhouse was in the living room or kitchen. Fuel was often in short supply, and the entire family would gather in one room with a fire. This afforded warmth, but did not allow for privacy for a young man and woman who were courting. In order to allow the couple to develop an intimate emotional relationship that would lead to marriage, they were given a special chance to be alone. The young couple was allowed to use the family bedroom to carry on their courtship in private. They were comfortable and warm beneath the covers. Sound good? Well, the couple was prevented from having actual intercourse by one of two methods: placing a wooden board down the center of the bed, or tying the maiden's thighs together with a special knot. Both methods affected the interaction and intimacy of the young couple.

In less obvious ways our environment affects our communication behaviors. Low lighting, for example, increases the probability of self-disclosure, as does soft music. Desks placed between two people in an interaction can create a barrier in the conversation.

In a broader look at environment, various architectural structures produce specific perceptions and effects on our communication behavior. The perception of a bank, for instance, as a solid-form structure may determine the type of customers they will attract. Perceptions of the environment fall into six categories: formality, warmth, privacy, familiarity, constraint, and distance. Each variable reflects how the environment is perceived within the communication setting.

The more dramatic research findings reveal that the environment has a pronounced impact on (1) our emotional responses, (2) our interpersonal behavior (social interaction), and (3) our job performance and productivity. Specific elements of the environment such as color, lighting, and sound have been empirically demonstrated to create both psychological and physiological effects on others. Amos Alonzo Stagg, for instance, had his team's dressing room painted a relaxing blue to calm and rest the players during the half-time period. Last-minute pep talks, however, were a different matter. During these talks, he used an exciting, brilliant anteroom (Ketcham, 1958).

The external environment plays only one role in the impact of objects on us. Spatial arrangements and seating behavior have been the subject of political and social controversy for some time. The various structural settings for interaction, specifically, the shape of a table, encourage different types of interaction. The differences, perceptual and real, between a round table, square table, and rectangular table, are significant.

Seating behavior is related to task situations, the level of intimacy between people, personality characteristics, dominance, friendliness, introversion–extroversion, and the amount of communication among interactants.

What about the effects of the manipulation of objects and seating arrangements? Once again, research findings suggest that these factors affect communication behavior both in classroom and office settings. Where a person sits may determine the extent to which that person interacts in a particular setting.

Finally, our environment, spatial arrangement, and seating behavior is significant with regard to the structural settings for interaction, the perceptions associated with certain seating locations, and the effects on behavior. Clearly, the research demonstrates that our manipulation of microspace is quite revealing.

REFERENCES

Adams, R. S., and B. Biddle. *"Realities of Teaching: Exploration with Video Tape.* New York: Holt, Rinehart and Winston, 1970.

Birren, R. *Color Psychology and Color Therapy.* New York: University Books, 1975.

Block, C. "Design to Dispel Fear of Oral Surgery." *Dental Surgery: The Journal of Dental Practice,* April 1975, 4, 85–89.

Burgoon, J., and T. S. Saine, *The Unspoken Dialogue: An Introduction to Nonverbal Communication.* Boston: Houghton Mifflin Company, 1978.

Carey, S. "Educator Teaches Behavior Control by Arranging Child's Environment." *The Arizona Republic,* September 24, 1978, B-2.

Carr, S. J., and J. M. Dabbs. "The Effects of Lighting, Distance, and Intimacy of Topic on Verbal and Visual Behavior." *Sociometry,* 1974, 37, 592–600.

Carter, M. "NBC News Tries a Cozy Approach." *The Arizona Republic,* September 4, 1977.(a)

Carter, M. "NBC's New Look News." *Newsweek,* September 19, 1977, 103. (b)

Cheek, F. E., R. Maxwell, and R. Weisman. "Carpeting the Ward: An Exploratory Study in Environmental Psychiatry." *Mental Hygiene,* 1971, 55, 109–118.

Cook, M. "Experiments on Orientation and Proxemics." *Human Relations,* 1970, 23, 61–76.

Dunkell, S. "Setting the Stage for Love." *Cosmopolitan,* October 1978, 192.

Gergen, J., M. Gergen, and W. H. Barton. "Deviance in the Dark." *Psychology Today,* 1973, 7, 129–130.

Goldberger, P. "Excessive Neon a Purposeful Ploy." *The Arizona Republic,* April 30, 1978, K-2.

Hare, A. and R. Bales. "Seating Position and Small Group Interaction." *Sociometry,* 1963, 26, 480–486.

Heston, J., and P. S. Garner. "Study of Personal Spacing and Desk Arrangement in the Learning Environment." Paper presented at the Annual Meeting of the International Communication Association, 1972.

Hickey, J. "Colors May Alleviate People's Doldrums." *The Arizona Republic,* February 16, 1978, B-7.

Howells, L. T., and S. W. Becker. "Seating Arrangement and Leadership Emergence." *Journal of Abnormal and Social Psychology,* 1962, *64,* 148–150.

Ketcham, H. *Color Planning for Business and Industry.* New York: Harper and Brothers, 1958.

Knapp, M. *Nonverbal Communication in Human Interaction.* New York: Holt, Rinehart and Winston, 1978.

Koneya, M. and A. Barbour. *Louder than Words . . . Nonverbal Communication.* Columbus, Ohio: Charles E. Merrill Publishing Company, 1976.

Korda, M. *Power! How to Get It, How to Use It.* New York: Random House, 1975.

Kowinski, W. "Shedding New Light." *New Times,* March 7, 1975, 48.

Maslow, A. H., and N. L. Mintz. "Effects of Esthetic Surroundings: I. Initial Effects of Three Esthetic Conditions Upon Perceiving 'Energy' and 'Well Being' in Faces." *Journal of Psychology,* 1956, *41,* 247–254.

McCroskey, J. C., C. E. Larson, and M. L. Knapp. *An Introduction to Interpersonal Communication.* Englewood Cliffs, N.J.: Prentice-Hall, 1971.

Mehrabian, A. *Silent Messages.* Belmont, Cal.: Wadsworth Publishing Company, 1971.

Mehrabian, A. *Public Places and Private Spaces.* New York: Basic Books, 1976.

Mintz, N. L. "Effects of Esthetic Surroundings: II. Prolonged and Repeated Experience in a 'Beautiful' and 'Ugly' Room." *Journal of Psychology,* 1956, *41,* 459–466.

Moskal, M. "Esthetics: More Splash than Substance?" *Industry Week,* June 20, 1977, 83–88.

Orwell, G. *1984.* New York: Harcourt Brace Jovanovich, Inc.: 1949.

Price, B. "A Stretch in Jail—How Would You Handle It?" *Psychology Today,* April 1977, 27–28.

Russo, N. "Connotation of Seating Arrangement." *Cornell Journal of Social Relations,* 1967, *2,* 37–44.

Sargent, W. *The Enjoyment and Use of Color.* New York: Dover, 1964.

Sommer, R. "Further Studies of Small Group Ecology." *Sociometry,* 1956, *28,* 337–348.

Sommer, R. *Personal Space: The Behavioral Basis of Design.* Englewood Cliffs, N.J.: Prentice-Hall, 1969.

Strodtbeck, F., and L. Hook. "The Social Dimensions of a Twelve Man Jury Table." *Sociometry,* 1961, *24,* 397–415.

"The Trouble with Open Offices." *Business Week,* August 6, 1978, 84–88.

Thompson, J. J. *Beyond Words: Nonverbal Communication in the Classroom.* New York: Citation Press, 1973.

Walberg, H. J. "Physical and Psychological Distance in the Classroom." *School Review,* March 1969, *77,* 64–70.

Wexner, L. B. "The Degree to which Colors (Hues) are Associated with Mood-Tunes." *Journal of Applied Psychology,* 1954, *38,* 432–435.

White, A. G. "The Patient Sits Down: A Clinical Note." *Psychosomatic Medicine,* 1953, *15,* 256–257.

Wilson, W. "The New Office Landscape." *Flightime.* April 1978, 34–37.

Zweigenhaft, R. "Personal Space in the Faculty Office-Desk Placement and the Student-Faculty Interaction." *Journal of Applied Psychology,* 1976, *61,* 529–532.

7

PERSONAL SPACE, TERRITORY, AND CROWDING

But we have made a little place in the forest that we may regard as our own. We have sniffed about, recognized a few of its potential resources, found a hiding place or two that seem secure. We have marked out as well as we could the boundaries of our new domain and deposited scent on this tree trunk, that bush, to inform intruders that someone is home. We are predators, of course, and from time to time we shall go out looting and raping and raising general havoc in the surrounding countryside. There will be reprisals, naturally And that is another reason why it will be so good to have some place to stand, some place to regard as ours.

ROBERT ARDREY, *THE TERRITORIAL IMPERATIVE*

211

*E*leven people died in Cincinnati, Ohio, in December, 1979. There was no fire, train derailment, psycho murderer, or natural disaster. Instead, the youths died for lack of something that most people take for granted: space. They were literally trampled to death while waiting for a rock concert. *Newsweek* magazine filed the following report:

> The kids started gathering outside Cincinnati's Riverfront Coliseum at two in the afternoon early last week, six hours before the concert was scheduled to begin. They were waiting to see The Who, the high-voltage British rock group whose combination of controlled rage and frenetic music has electrified rock fans for more than a decade. The doors were supposed to open at 6 p.m., but the four man band was late and needed more time to test the acoustics. By about 7:30 p.m., when the gates finally opened, there were close to 7,000 fans outside—most holding unreserved general-admission tickets, all determined to get close to the stage and all forced to filter through just two banks of doors. As The Who were completing their acoustics check, the sound of their amplified instruments drifted out over the gates. The crowd surged forward, mistakenly believing the show had begun. Glass shattered as impatient fans battered open a locked door—and then the stampede began.
>
> The wild melee lasted only a few minutes. When it ended, eleven people ranging in age from fifteen to twenty-two were dead, suffocated in the crush. (*Newsweek*, December 17, 1979, p. 52)*

The stampede was the product of a variety of factors. The concert-goers were anxious to get inside; many had been waiting for several hours after driving many miles to get to the performance. The general-admission tickets guaranteed only that they would get inside the auditorium; they could not automatically claim seats and so had to fight for them. The crowding may also have influenced their judgment and perceptions. It was so severe that a bystander later reported that he could literally lift his feet off the ground without falling. The pressure of the people around him held him up. The atmosphere became so oppressive that he needed to force himself above others by hoisting himself upon their shoulders to breathe fresh air. Other members of the crowd were fainting because of the lack of fresh air. However, they were not falling down because there was not enough ground for them to fall on. Those who did make it to the ground found it difficult, if not impossible, to get back up. Nancy Tyler told a *Newsweek* reporter,

---

> "I didn't even move my feet. One minute I was maybe 200 feet from the door and the next thing I was stacked up like kindling. I don't know, but I'd bet there were six or eight people under me." (*Newsweek*, December 17, 1979, p. 52)

Although people are rarely crushed to death by crowds of humans, physical space has frequently been a matter of life or death in our history. World War II followed an attack on American soil in 1941, while in 1979 a United States Marine lost his life defending an American embassy in Pakistan. The crisis in Iran during the last months of 1979 came about not only because Iranian students took hostage a group of United States citizens but also because they occupied "our" embassy.

Control of physical space often occurs much more subtly than the armed takeover of an embassy or country. Marilyn was the first to arrive at her dormitory room when school began. She looked at the two beds and immediately claimed one as "hers." Her roommate arrived twenty minutes later and accepted the division without question. For the rest of the school year, each "roomie" took care not to disturb the other's half of the room. Does this sound familiar? Concern over space in dormitories is so great that dorm rules at one southern university forbid roommates from using the other person's side of the room.

A less tangible form of space is the distance people use and control immediately around them. Hank once went out with a woman who sat and stood a little closer to him than he wanted. He liked Cindy but constantly found himself backing or turning away from her. This made her feel "rejected," even though he was only trying to get some breathing room between them. Their use of space communicated different things to each of them.

"Space speaks," according to Edward T. Hall (1959), and **proxemics** is the study of the use of space. Messages ranging from status to liking are communicated through the use of space; they vary according to factors such as sex, age, circumstances, and other nonverbal dimensions such as eye contact, body position, and facial expression. The purpose of this chapter is to introduce the area of proxemics and discuss the ways that "space speaks." The three major topics that will be presented are territoriality, personal space, and crowding.

TERRITORIALITY

Most children are familiar with the story of "The Three Bears." The little girl, Goldilocks, came to the house of the three bears after they went for a walk to let their porridge cool down.

> First she looked in at the window, and then she peeped in at the keyhole; and seeing nobody in the house, she turned the handle of the door. The

door was not fastened, because the Bears were good Bears, who did no one harm, and never suspected that anybody would harm them. So Goldilocks opened the door, and went in; and well pleased she was when she saw the porridge on the table. If she had been a thoughtful little girl, she would have waited till the Bears came home, and then, perhaps, they would have asked her for breakfast. (*The Golden Goose Book.* London: Frederick Warne and Co., Ltd.)

Later the Bears came home from their walk and found Goldilocks in a place where she had no right to be: the bed of the Little, Small Wee Bear. The voices of the Three Bears awakened Goldilocks, and she jumped out the window and ran away, never to be seen again.

The moral of "The Three Bears" is that territory is a very serious matter, not to be taken lightly. "Thou shalt not trespass" might very well be the Eleventh Commandment. Observations of animals have led ethologists such as Robert Ardrey (1966) to conclude that **territoriality** is an innate characteristic, a product of evolution, in both animals and humans. He defines territoriality as "an area of space, whether of water or earth or air, which an animal or group of animals defends as an exclusive preserve" (p. 3).

There is little question that animals, humans included, stake out and defend territories. Male dogs, for example, urinate on bushes and

Gene Warne

"Excuse me, but you're sitting in my seat."

trees to identify them as their own and attempt to chase off other dogs that enter their territory. Similarly, humans erect flags, fences, and "no trespassing" signs to define their territory. They begin wars or call the police to discourage invaders. One man booby-trapped his front door so a gun would shoot anyone who tried to enter uninvited. Unfortunately, he shot a young neighbor who was coming to take care of him when he was ill.

The importance of territoriality in animals is manifested in **homing behavior** (Ardrey, 1966). This is the ability of some animals to travel hundreds or thousands of miles in order to return to a specific location, often for mating purposes. Sea turtles, eels, and pigeons, for example, are able to find exact rivers and bays that are their "territories," although scientists have not yet been able to figure out how they accomplish this feat. "Home" is equally important to humans; as Dorothy stated in "The Wizard of Oz," "There's no place like home, there's no place like home." And although Thomas Wolfe sadly wrote that you can't go home again, thousands of people keep trying. Quests for "roots" are perhaps mythical searches for "home."

For both humans and animals, territory is very important; however, several scientists have argued that Ardrey overstated his case in *The Territorial Imperative* (1966). Especially for humans, they argue, territory is not an "exclusive preserve," and rarely do humans take up arms to defend their personal territory. In fact, humans regularly entertain visitors on their home territory without displaying antagonism (Edney, 1976). Think of the last time you had friends over to your home for a party, to study, or just to watch television. Did you feel hostile and threatened? Probably not. Can you imagine animals "having company"? Humans are unique in this quality.

More importantly, however, human and animal territoriality differ on the criterion of "defense." Animals must actively protect their territory from others that try to take it over. Humans, on the other hand, are rarely called upon to defend their rights to particular holdings; their territoriality is thus much more passive than that found in the animal kingdom. Among humans, children naturally avoid taking their father's chair at the dinner table; bosses naturally avoid sitting at the desks of their secretaries; students naturally avoid taking tables in libraries that appear to be occupied even though the "owner" is not present. We so commonly respect the "territory" of others that any violation rates as a media event. For example, students in the 1960s captured headlines and were televised for taking over the offices of university presidents and administrators.

As a result of societal norms that have been established, human beings rarely use defense to protect their territories. McAndrew and his colleagues (1978) conducted a study in a library to find out whether or not students would protect their tables. One confederate lured twenty students away from their desks by asking their help in answering a questionnaire. While they were away, another confederate moved the belongings of each student to the side and put other books and a jacket in their place. When the students returned from helping the first confederate and found their belongings moved, all twenty of them withdrew to other seats. Not a single student defended his or her table! When territory is invaded, most people would rather switch than fight.

Because human territoriality typically does not involve "defense," it differs from animal territoriality and therefore needs a different definition. As a result, territoriality may be defined as the continuous association of a person or group with certain places (Edney, 1976). The place may be defended by the owner but more often it is simply avoided by others who respect the first person's "claim" to the location.

Territorial rights may be strict or loose, depending on the people involved and their relationship to each other. Rosenblatt and Budd (1975) compared the territoriality of married and unmarried cohabiting couples. Among the unmarried couples, both parties were more likely to have someplace in their home to be alone: Each individual had a special room or location that was "off limits" to the partner. Among the married couples, both parties didn't have any place to be alone, but they more strictly divided up the available territory. They were more likely to have "his closet" versus "her closet," "his chair" versus "her chair," "his drawer" versus "her drawer." Unmarried couples tended to intermingle their belongings more than married couples; they were less territorial. One interesting finding was that couples who lived together and then got married had the characteristics of both groups. Like the unmarried couples, they intermingled their belongings and were less territorial; like the married couples, they did not maintain places to be alone within their homes.

Types of Territories

The United States, a library table at your college or university, a wife's drawers for clothing, a father's chair, the desk you always take in chemistry class—all of these are examples of territory. They are places or locations that are or have been associated with a person or group over a period of time. Several different researchers have attempted to categorize territories, identifying similarities and differences among types. Scheflen (1975) formulated a hierarchy of territories based on their size; he called the smallest territory **spot.** A spot is a space several inches across, just large enough for a glass or an elbow. (Moviegoers stake out a spot on the armrest beside their seats and may have to jostle their neighbors to keep it in their possession.) Scheflen's hierarchy continues with a **cubit,** an eighteen-inch building block of space; several cubits piled up form a **k-space,** which is the amount of territory a person generally occupies. A **location** is the space immediately around a person, while a **module** is a row of locations. (People lined up to buy tickets for a basketball game occupy a module.) Finally, a **nucleus** is at the center of a **region** which is a room-sized territory—large enough for a number of people to occupy.

Although size is only one way to categorize territory, it is extremely relevant to the people who own or control the space. The reason is that the amount of space that a person controls is correlated with the amount of status accorded that person. Henley (1977) argued that nonverbal qualities determine and maintain power structure in society and that territory is an important nonverbal dimension. If you meet someone and learn that he or she owns several houses, property throughout the world, and a dozen classic cars, you will give him or her more respect than if he or she controlled less territory.

Territory is also classified according to its importance to the people who use it. Altman (1975) identified primary, secondary, and public territories. **Primary territories** are those over which a person has exclusive control. Owners of Ferrari racecars often treat them as primary territories, not allowing others to drive them. Personal belongings such as toothbrushes, clothing, and bedrooms are generally primary territories. **Secondary territories** are not the exclusive property of the owner but are generally associated with him or her. The desk you always take in class, the table you always ask for at your favorite restaurant, and the church pew you regularly occupy on Sunday are secondary territories.

Public territories are areas open to anyone; these would include such places as a parking lot, a library, or a beach. Although these areas are "public," an individual may claim **temporary occupancy** over a piece of the territory. Claims are made by stretching out a blanket at the beach or by leaving books and personal belongings on a desk at the library. The items used to define a space as territory in a public setting are called **markers.** Of course, a person's claim to a public territory is not legal and lasts only as long as others respect the markers.

Public territories have also been identified by Lyman and Scott (1967), who have observed that they may be colonized by persons or groups. **Colonization** occurs when a public territory is taken over by a group through continuous usage or defense. Juvenile gangs take over city streets and defend them from other gangs. A fraternity constantly sits at a certain table in a cafeteria, and others come to think of it as the fraternity's domain. Elaine's is a little restaurant in New York City that has become famous because it has been colonized by the rich and famous such as Woody Allen, Ali McGraw, and Norman Mailer.

A public territory that has been colonized becomes a **home territory.** This is an area where a person has relative freedom of behavior

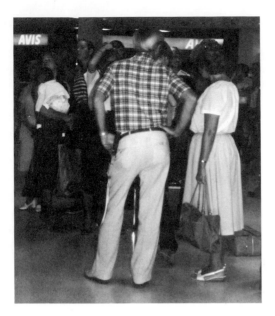

Individuals can claim temporary occupancy of a public territory simply by their stance and stationary positioning.

and control over the territory. This category encompasses both the primary and secondary areas identified by Altman (1975). Lyman and Scott (1967) observed that the distinction between home and public territory is sometimes difficult to make. What is a public territory to one group may be perceived as a home territory to another. Although Elaine's in New York City is "home" for its regular patrons, it is public for others who wander in. Gay bars are home territory for homosexuals, but public territory for others. Lovers may have "their table" in a public restaurant, "their spot" on a public shady lane, "their niche" on a secluded but public beach.

Territory is also given to groups of people who are carrying on a conversation. An invisible boundary surrounds such a group separating it from others. The space inside the boundary is called an **interactional territory** (Lyman and Scott, 1967). Svenn Lindskold and his colleagues (1976) tested the boundaries of groups who formed on a sidewalk outside a store window. Passive groups simply gazed in the window, while interacting groups carried on a conversation. More people went through the passive groups than the interacting groups; pedestrians chose to walk around the interacting groups, thereby preserving their interactional territory.

Invasion of interactional territory depends on the number and status of people interacting. Knowles (1973) found that fewer people walked between two people than between two wastebaskets, and still fewer walked between four people than between two people. The larger the crowd, the less likely it is that it will be invaded. Knowles also controlled the status of the conversationalists by changing their age and dress. Fewer subjects invaded the higher-status than the lower-status people.

The last category of territory identified by Lyman and Scott (1967) is **body territory,** which includes the human body as well as a bubble of space surrounding it. The bubble is classified by some as personal space, and a later section of this chapter will investigate it in greater detail. The body is perhaps one's most sacred territory; access to it is strictly controlled by the owner and by social restrictions. For example, social norms regarding masturbation dictate that a person should not invade certain parts of his or her own body. Because the body is so important in nonverbal communication, several chapters in this book introduce topics such as how it is displayed (see Chapter 3) and the role of touch in communication (see Chapter 8).

Territorial Encroachment and Reaction

Although territorial claims are generally respected by others, trespassing does occur. Lyman and Scott (1967) listed three forms of encroachment: violation, invasion, and contamination.

Violation occurs when territory that belongs to someone else is used without that person's permission. Goldilocks violated the territory of the Three Bears when she sat in their chairs and slept in their beds. A woman in a TV ad asks, "Why is my soap always the smallest bar in the house?" Other people have violated her territory by using it without getting a warrant from her. **Invasion** occurs when someone crosses boundaries and takes over another person's territory. Taking someone's place in line, overrunning an embassy and hijacking a plane are forms of invasion. Territories may also be **contaminated** or rendered impure through the entry or usage of others. Religious fanatics from Saudi Arabia invaded the Mecca in December of 1979 to protest contamination of their country. They called for "a total rejection of Western influences in Saudi Arabia, demanding, among other things, the banning of radio, TV and even soccer" ("The Smoking War on Flight 1410," *Newsweek*, December 3, 1979, p. 65). A growing number of Americans are concerned about the contamination of the air by cigarette smoke. Several states have either adopted or considered laws to prohibit smoking in public buildings. The Civil Aeronautics Board requires airlines to accommodate nonsmokers, much to the chagrin of smoking passengers. An Eastern Airlines flight to New York landed early in Baltimore in December of 1979 because passengers began bickering about the smoking restrictions. Smoking passengers demanded their

By permission of King Features Syndicate Division.

right to smoke, while a nonsmoking passenger insisted on his right to uncontaminated air ("Special Report," *Newsweek*, December 17, 1979, p. 55).

When territory is violated, invaded, or contaminated, the owner may react in a variety of ways (Lyman and Scott, 1967). One alternative is **withdrawal** from the location. This is most likely to happen when the occupancy is temporary in a public territory. People in libraries, cafeterias, and beaches withdraw when their space is attacked. A second alternative is **insulation,** which involves the erecting of boundaries and barriers. Roommates may hang a bedspread or curtain between their beds to separate their sides of a room. Family members may tightly shut and even lock doors rather than let them hang ajar, while students in the library often pile books and belongings between themselves and the people beside them. They insulate themselves by establishing barriers.

The most drastic form of territorial protection is **turf defense,** the active repelling of invaders. The year 1979 saw the immigration of thousands of Vietnamese who were forced to leave their homeland. The immigrants were settled in communities throughout America and often were given training and jobs. Unfortunately, their entry was perceived by many as territorial invasion and some Americans resorted to violence. Several groups of Vietnamese were forced to move again as a result of the turf defense.

Not only do territory owners react to encroachment, but also those who accidentally invade. Efran and Cheyne (1974) examined the nonverbal responses of subjects who walked down a corridor. Sometimes no one else was in the hall; sometimes two people were in the hall conversing and the subject had to walk around them; and sometimes the subject had to walk between two people carrying on a conversation. When the subjects violated the interactional territory by walking between the conversationalists, they lowered their heads, closed their eyes, lowered their gazes, tightened their lips, and pursed their mouths. Subjects who had to walk beside the people lowered their heads and gazes more than subjects who walked down an empty corridor. Invading someone else's territory may be just as annoying as having your own territory invaded.

Factors Influencing Territoriality

A number of researchers have investigated public territoriality and found that it is related to several different factors. Some of the most important factors are sex, intensity of invasion, and desirability of territory.

Sex. Feminine markers are less effective at repelling invaders than masculine markers. Shafer and Sadowski (1975) marked barroom tables with either a man's or a woman's belongings (such as a jacket and briefcase or a sweater and purse) and then observed the results. Tables with feminine markers were invaded sooner and more frequently than tables with masculine markers. Shafer and Sadowski speculated that the feminine markers were less threatening because women would be less likely to try to defend their territory.

Sex also influences invasions of library tables. In one experiment (Krail and Leventhal, 1976), male and female confederates sat down at tables already occupied by students. Students responded to the invasions by leaving, building barriers, leaning away, or challenging the confederate. Responses were fastest if the confederate was of the *same sex* as the student. (Perhaps students hoped they would get a date out of the situation when the invader was of the opposite sex!)

Intensity of invasion. Whether or not a person withdraws from a territory depends on how significantly it is invaded. A dog may not like other dogs to enter his backyard, but he becomes even more territorial when another dog attempts to eat out of his dish. Humans also vary in their reactions according to the seriousness of an invasion. Becker and Mayo (1971) observed territorial behavior in a cafeteria. In one condition, confederates moved fifteen people's belongings and sat in their seats. All fifteen withdrew to other seats. In a second condition, confederates sat beside eighteen reserved seats; sixteen of the eighteen people left. Finally, confederates sat across from fifteen reserved seats; only one person left. In a similar study conducted in a library, Krail and Leventhal (1976) found that students responded sooner if the confederates peered over their shoulder while sitting adjacent to them than if they sat across from them. If you want to meet someone, you should probably sit across from that person rather than beside him or her!

Desirablity of territory. In the same barroom experiment that examined sex differences, Shafer and Sadowski (1975) compared territorial invasions of desirable and undesirable tables. Because bars are social locations, the desirable tables are those that promote interaction with other people while the undesirable tables are more isolated. Consistent with predictions, the researchers found that marked desirable tables were invaded sooner and more frequently than undesirable tables.

PERSONAL SPACE

Alice and Jimmy are facing one another. As she steps backward, he steps forward. Then he takes another step forward, and she turns outward. He then turns outward, and she turns toward him and takes a step in his direction. He turns back toward her and also moves forward. They pause for a second, and each moves backward and turns slightly away from the other.

Have Alice and Jimmy learned the latest disco dance? Were they engaged in an elaborate mating ritual characterized by nonverbal maneuvers? Were they playing tennis or softball? No. Alice and Jimmy were simply carrying on a conversation about their English professor. In addition to expressing their ideas through words, they were communicating nonverbally through their use of space and personal distance. Each was attempting to maintain a certain distance from the other, although their preferred distances were not always the same. Sometimes Alice wanted more space than Jimmy, and sometimes Jimmy wanted more space than Alice. These differences led to the fancy footwork of moving backward and forward, inward and outward. Each person's preferred distance also changed throughout the conversation. When Alice disagreed with Jimmy, he wanted more space; when she flirted, he wanted less distance between them.

The distance or space that Alice and Jimmy were manipulating is called **personal space;** it is a bubble of space surrounding any person that expands or contracts depending on the situation. Personal space is portable territory with invisible boundaries. Individuals carry it around

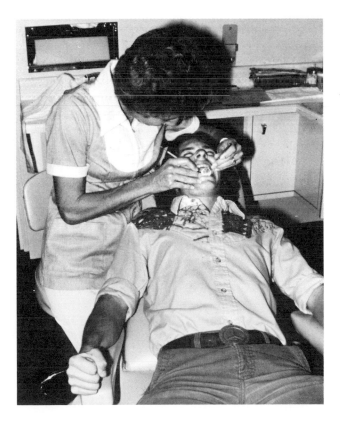

In some professional environments, invasion of personal space is a given. Even though the patient has consented to this invasion, his clenched fist is speaking louder than he can.

with them constantly and position themselves in conversations in a way that will maintain it. Julie has very small personal space needs and is constantly moving closer to people in order to reach the distance she prefers. Sandy, on the other hand, has larger personal space needs and frequently finds herself backed up against walls as a result of trying to move away from people. Each tries to maintain her personal space, not always successfully.

Characteristics of Personal Space

The most important characteristic of personal space is that it is variable. As noted in the example with Alice and Jimmy, some people have larger space needs than others. Furthermore, personal space may vary in size for a single individual depending on the situation, emotional states, and the relationship with the other person. John's space needs are much different when he is lovingly discussing the future with his girl-friend in the back seat of his car than when he is angrily disputing a grade in a professor's office. Some of the most important factors in-fluencing personal space needs will be discussed later in this chapter.

The size and shape of personal space have been analyzed by several researchers. Hall (1963) initially proposed that personal space was spherical or circular. However, later researchers have found that some individuals have larger rear zones than front zones while still others have larger front zones than rear zones. In addition, Hayduk (1978) re-cently suggested that personal space has a vertical dimension. The desired space around the feet may be proportionally smaller than that desired around the head, for example. Figure 7.1 depicts some possible formations of the vertical dimension of personal space. Larger or smaller front and rear zones would alter the size and shape of the bub-ble even more.

The purpose and function of personal space have also been ana-lyzed. Joe stands four feet from his boss, eight feet from his prison war-den, two feet from his mother, and ten inches from his girlfriend. Why is his personal space different for each person? According to **protection theory,** space is a "body-buffer zone" used for protective purposes (Dosey and Meisels, 1969). When an individual is threatened, his or her personal space expands. The threats may be physical or emotional. Ac-cording to this theory, Joe's body-buffer zone is greatest for the prison warden because the warden is very threatening to him. On the other hand, his girlfriend is least threatening to him so he maintains the smallest distance with her.

According to another theory, Joe's personal space varies according to how intimate he wants his interaction to be with another person.

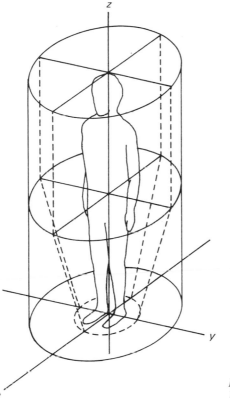

Figure 7.1
Front and rear zones of personal space.

According to **equilibrium theory** (Argyle and Dean, 1965), closer distances establish greater intimacy while greater personal space may decrease intimacy. In addition to personal space, intimacy is also a function of the amount of eye contact and smiling and the intimacy of the topic being discussed. If any one of these is too intimate for a person, he or she may diminish the intimacy of another dimension in order to establish the desired overall level of closeness. If Joe's girlfriend begins a conversation about sex or marriage that is more intimate than he desires, he may move away from her or he may decrease his eye contact or smiling in order to get a level of intimacy with which he feels comfortable. By altering his use of personal space or one of the other dimensions, he reestablishes equilibrium.

A final important characteristic of personal space is that it interacts with other dimensions of nonverbal communication. When Hall introduced proxemics (1963), he determined that it was a function of several different codes. The perception and use of space depends on whether people are standing, sitting, or lying down, and whether they are male or female. It also depends on whether the people are facing or turned away from one another (body orientation), how much touching can and does occur, how much of each other the individuals can see, how loud their voices are, and whether or not body odors or heat can be detected. Sandy may feel "too close" to Paul even though she is six feet away from him. However, even at that distance she can smell unpleasant body odors, her ears are hurting from his loud voice, and she doesn't like the fact that he is looking directly in her eyes. Lee, on the other hand, does not feel very close to Phil, even though they are only eight inches apart. However, they are sitting back to back, cannot see one another, and are having difficulty in hearing one another. Perceptions of personal space and distance are influenced by other dimensions of nonverbal communication.

Personal appearance is another nonverbal dimension that influences personal space. Hartnett, Bailey, and Hartley (1974) asked subjects to approach a tall (six feet, three inches) or short (five feet, four inches) male who was sitting or standing. They found that subjects used less personal space with the short male than with the tall male. Subjects also approached the seated males closer than the standing males, although females stayed further away from the tall male even when he was sitting down.

Physical attractiveness may also influence personal space. Powell and Dabbs (1976) hung pictures of beautiful and ugly male and female models on the wall and asked subjects to approach them. Females moved closer to the attractive pictures rather than the ugly pictures, while males moved closer only to the pictures of attractive females. The researchers also tested the effect of ugly and attractive interviewers on the personal space of pedestrians. They found that the people did not vary the distance they selected according to either sex or attractiveness. Their "real-life" experiment did not confirm the results they found when they used pictures.

Factors Influencing Personal Space

As noted earlier, several different factors are thought to influence personal-space needs. Much research has been conducted on these factors through the use of a variety of techniques for analyzing personal space. Unfortunately, the results of many studies contradict one another, probably because the investigators measured personal space in different ways (Hayduk, 1978). The technique that currently appears to be the most useful for experimental studies is called **stop distance.** Either the subject approaches the experimenter and stops when comfortable or the subject stands still while the experimenter approaches from different angles. The subject instructs the experimenter when to stop, based on how comfortable he or she (the subject) feels with the distance. On the basis of numerous studies, the following factors have been found to influence personal space.

Sex.   Many researchers have assumed that males require more space than females and that male pairs interact at greater distances than female or mixed-sex pairs. Unfortunately, the relationship between sex and personal space is not that simple. Many researchers have found contradictory results. For example, Pederson and Heaston (1972) found that males let people approach them more closely from the front while females let people approach them more closely from the sides. On the other hand, Fisher and Byrne (1975) found that females responded more negatively when invaded from the side while males were more negative when invaded from the front.

Although the contradictory results have not been resolved, recent research indicates that males' and females' use of space depends on the eye contact and facial expression of the other person (Buchanan, Goldman, and Juhnke, 1977; Hughes and Goldman, 1978). Imagine that you are getting on a crowded elevator. Some of the people are looking at you while others are avoiding your glance. Where would you stand? Closer to the people looking at you or closer to those avoiding eye con-

Our culture has taught males to take up more space, while women have been taught to shrink. Males and females use space in fundamentally different ways.

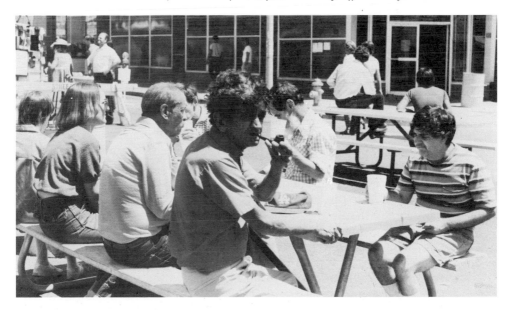

tact? Your answer will probably depend on whether you are male or female. Some researchers found that when people entered elevators containing at least two other people (confederates), males chose to stand closer to the people who were not looking at them. Females behaved similarly when the confederates were male, but chose to violate the space of directly gazing and/or smiling female confederates rather than the space of those who avoided eye contact. Studies such as these point out that males and females use space in fundamentally different ways. Much more research must be conducted before firm conclusions can be stated.

Age.   The effects of age on personal space have been consistently supported (Hayduk, 1978). By the time they are twelve years old, children have learned adult spacing, although even younger children are sensitive to the uses of space. In a test of three- to six-year-olds, Melson (1976) found that even they perceived very close pairs as "friendly," intermediate pairs as "helping," and distant pairs as "angry." Even your little brothers and sisters or nephews and nieces recognize that you are angry when you keep a distance from them and friendly when you move in more closely. Although young children are sensitive to the uses of space, adults have different expectations for five-, eight-, and ten-year-olds (Dean, Willis, and La Rocco, 1976). Imagine that you are standing in line at a theater. A little child approaches you and stands so close that he or she could touch you by moving a couple of inches. How would you react? If you are like the subjects in the study cited above, you would probably respond in a friendly way if the child was a five-year-old. On the other hand, you would respond negatively to a ten-year-old and not at all to an eight-year-old. Perhaps you would expect the older children to "know better" than to stand so close and would thus communicate your expectations to them by responding negatively or not at all.

Expectations established by parents and other adults probably teach children how to use space. Additional evidence suggests that children learn spacing by imitating those around them. Bailey, Hartnett, and Glover (1973) found that fifth- and sixth-graders imitated a popular sixth-grade boy who approached another person at either a very close or a very far distance. Children who did not observe the boy stopped at an intermediate distance. Since personal space is learned by imitating the people around us, much is probably taught in the family. As a result, some families tolerate very near distances for interpersonal interaction, while others prefer larger distances.

Culture.   Latin Americans are very touch-oriented and stand very close together. Italians are also very "close," while Germans and Americans prefer larger distances. Right? Wrong! Many stereotypes exist concerning the personal-space needs of various ethnic and cultural groups. Unfortunately, most are based on anecdotes about only a few members of the culture. As a result, stereotypes emerge. For example, Shuter (1976, 1977) found that not all Latin American cultures are alike. Costa Ricans interact more closely and more directly than Panamanians or Columbians. Furthermore, stereotypes about the Germans and Italians are true for only the men in each culture. Women did not conform to stereotypes.

Cultural differences within the United States have also been studied. Jones (1971) investigated differences in personal space among blacks, Puerto Ricans, Italians, and Chinese in New York City. Although all groups were of the same economic level, he expected differences, especially that the Chinese would interact at a greater distance than the other groups. However, interaction distance was similar for all of them. This led Jones to suggest that personal spacing may reflect socioeconomic differences rather than ethnic or cultural differences. More research needs to be conducted, especially since many existing studies have confused these factors or used only a few subjects (Hayduk, 1978).

Relationship.   Roberto and Sandy are carrying on a conversation while standing ten feet apart. Alice and Norman are standing only six inches apart. Simply by observing the distances between people, inferences can be drawn about their relationships. Most people would assume that Roberto and Sandy do not have a personal relationship, while Alice and Norman are close emotionally as well as physically. Edward T. Hall identified four distinct categories of informal space associated with four different types of relationships. His observations were based on white, middle-class Northeasterners, so the specific distances he found may be different for other cultural groups. The categories he identified are intimate, casual-personal, socio-consultive, and public. **Intimate distance,** from zero to eighteen inches, is used by people who are involved with one another on a personal level, such as Alice and Norman. Lovers interact at an intimate distance. **Casual-personal distance,** from one-and-one-half to four feet, is used for personal business, such as conversations between friends and relatives. When Al and Jack discuss their plans for the evening, they stand about three feet apart. Impersonal business is conducted from four to eight feet, or at a **socio-consultive distance.** Marilyn and Sue have a formal relationship as sales managers for a computer company and stand about five feet apart when discussing company policy. Finally, **public distance** ranges from eight feet to the limits of a person's vision or hearing. Teachers communicate with students at this distance when delivering lectures.

Status is another characteristic of relationships that influences the use of personal space. As we noted in Chapter 6, people of higher rank are given more space than people of lower rank. Dean, Willis, and Hewitt (1975) investigated the role of status and rank in military personnel when they observed personal-space use in 562 conversations. All the observed interactions were informal and took place in the cafeteria, hospital, recreation center, or Navy exchange. As you can imagine, when subordinates approached superiors, they gave more space to those of higher rank than to those of lower rank. However, when superiors approached subordinates, the distance they maintained was not correlated with differences in military rank. Apparently, differences in status are more relevant when approaching superiors than when approaching subordinates.

The amount of *liking* in a relationship also influences how close people stand to one another (Mehrabian, 1969). People who like each other stand closer together than do people who dislike each other. Patty was a student who participated in a class project with several other students, including John, who missed most group meetings. In describing her group, Patty wrote:

> Our topic was relatively intimate, and we liked one another on the whole, so we sat relatively close to each other, especially when seated at a table or with our desks pulled together in a circle. John seemed to have the largest "bubble" of personal space because when he did attend meetings, he was rather alienated. Group members were less tolerant of his invasions of space and less willing to enter into his space than they were with anyone else in the group.

The group disliked John for missing group meetings and communicated with him at a greater personal distance as a result of their feelings.

Pathology and deviance.   Many researchers have studied the effects of personality on personal space. Although interesting, the findings have been inconclusive because most studies have failed to support their predictions or have contradicted the results of other studies (Hayduk, 1978). However, the research has been very conclusive in a related area: People who have been identified as deviant members of society have greater personal-space needs than usual. Deviants include people with histories of mental illness such as schizophrenia, prisoners, other individuals with criminal records, and disruptive high school students. Researchers compared thirty disruptive high school students with thirty "normal" students, using the stop-distance technique (Newman and Pollack, 1973). Disruptive students demanded greater space than nondisruptive students by telling the experimenter to stop approaching them at such close distances.

Violent and nonviolent prisoners in South Africa were compared by Roger and Schalekamp (1976), using the stop-distance technique. Consistent with predictions and previous research, violent prisoners had larger personal zones than nonviolent prisoners. In a related study, Booraem *et al.* (1977) examined the personal space needs of ninety male juvenile delinquents. Those who had committed crimes against people had the greatest personal-space requirements, followed by those who had committed crimes against property. Boys who had committed "victimless" crimes needed the least space. Furthermore, subjects with more psychopathological histories and more prior arrests required greater space than those who were closer to normal.

The research related to pathology and deviance supports the notion that the boundaries of personal space represent "body-buffer zones" used to protect people from emotional and physical threats. Individuals with more serious personality problems see others as threatening and therefore need more space for protection. A current television public-service message suggests that most violent prisoners were abused physically as children. It appears that in response to their physical abuse as children, these prisoners developed larger personal-space needs than most people. As a result, their space is more likely to be invaded by others with smaller needs, thereby causing them to feel "attacked." Thus they are more likely to respond in a pathological or deviant manner.

CROWDING

After learning that her favorite department store was having a gigantic sale, Susie stood in line for an hour for the doors to open, and then jostled with hundreds of other bargain hunters for the best buys. After forty-five minutes of "fighting the crowd," Susie gave up, feeling anxious and "closed in" by the other customers. While shopping, Susie experienced the sensation of "crowding." Jerry experienced the same sensation, although the circumstances were very different. He was at a quiet art museum, admiring the work, when another art lover entered the gallery. Although few people were in the museum and there were many pieces of art to enjoy, the newcomer chose to stand only three inches from Jerry to look at the same painting. The stranger's nearness caused Jerry to feel tense and "closed in"; he also experienced crowding.

Crowding is a psychological experience created when a person becomes aware of spatial restrictions. Both Susie and Jerry became aware of limitations on the space around them, although for different reasons. Susie experienced crowding as a result of **stimulus overload.**

So much was happening around her that she could not cope with everything. She could not process all the stimuli and consequently became fatigued and confused and escaped from the situation. City dwellers may cope with stimulus overload by becoming very aloof and isolating themselves from the people around them.

Jerry's experience of crowding resulted from **behavioral constraint.** By invading his personal space, the newcomer reduced Jerry's freedom of movement, thereby causing him to experience infringement and invasion. Although physical invasion into personal space is a more powerful source of crowding, **surveillance** also creates behavioral constraint (Greenberg and Firestone, 1977). Have you ever felt uneasy because a stanger was watching you for no reason? Or even just because you *thought* someone was observing you? Surveillance can create a sense of crowding and motivate a person to withdraw from a situation.

The negative effects of personal-space invasion have been well documented (Hayduk, 1978). People whose space has been invaded display avoidance and withdrawal behaviors. They may leave the situation entirely, or they may back away or turn away. Invaded individuals may also experience stress and arousal. When Jerry's space was invaded, he experienced stress and quickly moved to the next room in the museum. However, some invasions may have positive consequences. Imagine

There is an acceptable social distance between people as they disembark from an airplane. If you follow too closely on the heels of another person, chances are he or she will signal you to "keep your distance" with a cold facial expression.

how Jerry would have reacted if the invader had been a gorgeous female and he had been looking for a date for that weekend! The violation of his personal space may have caused him to perceive her more positively.

Some researchers have found that invasions of personal space *intensify* interactions (Burgoon, 1978; Schiffenbauer and Schiavo, 1976). Rewarding invaders are perceived more *positively* than noninvaders; punishing invaders are perceived more *negatively* than noninvaders. Imagine that your boss is reprimanding you for being late to work. If she invades your space, your negative feelings for her will intensify. On the other hand, if she is complimenting you for a superior job, your positive feelings for her will intensify if she invades your personal space. The consequences of personal-space invasions depend on the purpose of the communicators.

Density and Crowding

Once upon a time a little mouse from the country decided that his cousin in the city had a better life—better food, more mouse-money, a better job. So the little country mouse decided to move to the city to seek fame and fortune. Unfortunately, when he got to the city, he discovered it was crowded, congested, full of cats—not the paradise he expected. It didn't take long for him to decide that country life was better than city life. He returned home, a lesson learned, and lived happily ever after.

The story of "The Country Mouse and the City Mouse" teaches children a lesson that is common in literature. The city is often presented as a symbol of corruption and decadence, while the country is presented as innocent and good. Scientific researchers have also discovered that contemporary cities breed more crime and delinquency than rural areas. City dwellers engage in more vandalism of property and are less willing to help others than are rural dwellers (Sadalla, 1978).

Crime rates in cities have led researchers to speculate about a relationship between population density and deviant behavior. **Density** is a physical condition and refers to the number of people in an area of space. Accordingly, density may lead to crowding, which may in turn lead to social problems. Remember that crowding is a psychological experience, while density is a physical condition. Many researchers have tried to determine if density leads to crowding; they question whether the physical condition leads to the psychological experience.

One technique (called the "sociological method") for determining a relationship has been to ascertain the density of different cities or areas and then compare their crime rates or mental-illness rates. Unfortu-

COUNTRY DOGS

CITY DOGS

Richard Varney

nately, density may be measured in many different ways: the number of people per acre, per building, per city, per room in a dwelling. It is unfortunate because different measures provide contradictory results. For example, urban areas have more people per acre, while rural areas generally have more people per room in each dwelling. Another problem with sociological studies is that dense urban areas are populated by lower socioeconomic groups. Thus higher crime rates in those neighborhoods may be caused by poverty rather than by crowding. Researchers have found that variables such as race, income, education, and parents' health are more strongly related to social problems than is density (Kirmeyer, 1978).

Although we cannot blame all social ills on density, it has been associated with some problems. High **in-dwelling density** (the number of people living in the same quarters) is associated with decreased socializing. Rohner (1974) compared college students living in a university trailer park. Students with three or four roommates were less happy with the arrangement and socialized less with their roommates than did students with only one or two roommates.

Prison researchers have also learned that high in-dwelling density creates problems. Prisoners who live in dormitory settings are less happy with their environment and have more illness complaints than prisoners who live in one- or two-person cells (Paulus, Cox, McCain, and Chandler, 1975; McCain, Cox, and Paulus, 1976). Density may be more likely to create crowding in prisoners than in other groups because they have larger body-buffer zones. Laboratory experiments have demonstrated that density sometimes creates stress, especially for subjects with "far personal space" (large body-buffer-zone needs). People with smaller personal-space needs are more tolerant of high-density situations (Aiello, DeRisi, Epstein and Karlin, 1977).

Finally, the *opposite* of density may create more significant problems. Living alone is associated with a variety of problems. People who live alone use more drugs to relieve stress and have higher rates of suicide and more admissions to mental hospitals (Kirmeyer, 1978). However, for people who do find themselves in a high-density situation, whether it be rush hour in the city or going home to four roommates, perhaps understanding how personal space and crowding can affect communication will be helpful.

SUMMARY

The use of space, or proxemics, communicates information nonverbally to others. Territoriality, personal space, and crowding are three ways that the use of space speaks to others. Territoriality, an indication of ownership or association with a particular place, affects communication. The amount of space a person controls is associated with that person's degree of status. By identifying similarities and differences in space usage some researchers have categorized territories based on size, importance, and colonization.

Territorial encroachment influences interaction behaviors. When a territory is violated, invaded, or contaminated, people typically withdraw, insulate themselves, or create turf defenses. The sex of the participants, the intensity of the invasion, and the desirability of the territory are factors that influence the success of maintaining your own territory or encroaching on the territory of others.

Personal space, or the portable territories around people, expands and contracts, depending on the situation. The size and shape of personal space vary, depending on the purpose, function, level of intimacy, and other nonverbal communication dimensions. Personal space is also influenced by the sex, age, culture, relationship, status, degree of liking, and pathology or deviance of the people involved.

Crowding, a psychological experience, occurs when people become aware of spatial restrictions. Stimulus overload or behavioral constraint influences the sensation of being crowded. While crowding is a psychological experience, density, or the number of people in a given area, is a phsyical condition. Density and crowding are often associated with deviant behaviors and interpersonal problems. An awareness and understanding of the influence and effects of territoriality, personal space, and crowding should increase communication effectiveness.

REFERENCES

Aiello, J. R., D. T. DeRisi, Y. M. Epstein, and R. A. Karlin. "Crowding and the Role of Interpersonal Distance Preference." *Sociometry*, 1977, *40*, 271–282.

Altman, I. *The Environment and Social Behavior.* Monterey, Cal.: Brooks/Cole, 1975.

Ardrey, R. *The Territorial Imperative.* New York: Dell Publishing Co., Inc., 1966.

Arenson, S. J. "Reactions to Invasions of Marked Seats at a Racetrack." *Social Behavior and Personality*, 1977, *5*(2), 225–228.

Argyle, M., and J. Dean. "Eye Contact, Distance and Affiliation." *Sociometry*, 1965, *28*, 289–304.

Bailey, K. G., J. J. Hartnett, and H. W. Glover. "Modeling and Personal Space Behavior in Children." *The Journal of Psychology*, 1973, *85*, 143–150.

Becker, F. D. and C. Mayo. "Delineating Personal Distance and Territory." *Environment and Behavior*, 1971, *3*, 375–382.

Booraem, C. D., J. V. Flowers, G. E. Bodner, and D. A. Satterfield. "Personal Space Violation as a Function of Criminal Behavior." *Psychological Reports*, 1977, *41*, 1115–1121.

Buchanan, D. R., M. Goldman, and R. Juhnke. "Eye Contact, Sex and the Violation of Personal Space." *Journal of Social Psychology*, 1977, *103*, 19–25.

Burgoon, J. K. "A Communication Model of Personal Space Violations: Explication and an Initial Test." *Human Communication Research*, 1978, *4*, 129–142.

Calsyn, R. J. "Group Responses to Territorial Intrusion." *Journal of Social Psychology*, 1976, *400*, 51–58.

Dean, L. M., F. N. Willis, and J. Hewitt. "Initial Interaction Distance among Individuals Equal and Unequal in Military Rank." *Journal of Personality and Social Psychology*, 1975, *32*, 294–299.

Dean, L. M., F. N. Willis, and J. M. La Rocco. "Invasion of Personal Space as a Function of Age, Sex and Race." *Psychological Reports*, 1976, *38*, 959–965.

Dosey, M., and M. Meisels "Personal Space and Self-Protection." *Journal of Personality and Social Psychology*, 1969, *11*, 93–97.

Edney, J. J. "Human Territories: Comment on Functional Properties." *Environment and Behavior*, 1976, *8*, 31–47.

Efran, M. G., and J. A. Cheyne. "Affective Concomitants of the Invasion of Shared Space: Behavioral, Physiological and Verbal Indicators." *Journal of Personality and Social Psychology*, 1974, *29*, 219–226.

Emiley, S. F. "The Effects of Crowding and Interpersonal Attraction on Affective Responses, Task Performance, and Verbal Behavior." *Journal of Social Psychology*, 1975, 97, 267–278.

Erickson, F. "One Function of Proxemic Shifts in Face to Face Interaction," in A. Kendon, R. M. Harris, and M. R. Key, eds. *Organization of Behavior in Face to Face Interaction*. Chicago: Aldine-Mouton Publishers, 1975, pp. 173–187.

Fisher, J. D., and D. Byrne. "Too Close for Comfort: Sex Differences in Response to Invasions of Personal Space." *Journal of Personality and Social Psychology*, 32, 1975, 15–21.

Frankel, A. S., and J. Barrett. "Variations in Personal Space as a Function of Authoritarianism, Self-Esteem, and Racial Characteristics of a Stimulus Situation." *Journal of Consulting and Clinical Psychology*, 1971, 37, 95–98.

Glassman, J. B., B. R. Burkhart, R. D. Grant, and G. G. Vallery. "Density, Expectation and Extended Task Performance." *Environment and Behavior*, 1978, 10(3), 299–315.

Greenberg, C. I., and I. J. Firestone. "Compensatory Responses to Crowding: Effects of Personal Space Intrusion and Privacy Reduction." *Journal of Personality and Social Psychology*, 1977, 9, 637–644.

Hall, E. T. "A System for the Notation of Proxemic Behavior." *American Anthropologist*, 1963, 65, 1003–1026.

———. *The Silent Language*. Garden City, N.Y.: Doubleday, 1959.

Hartnett, J. J., K. G. Bailey, and C. S. Hartley. "Body Height, Position and Sex as Determinants of Personal Space." *Journal of Psychology*, 1974, 87, 129–136.

Hayduk, L. A. "Personal Space: An Evaluative and Orienting Overview." *Psychological Bulletin*, 1978, 85, 117–134.

Henley, N. M. *Body Politics: Power, Sex and Nonverbal Communication*. Englewood Cliffs, N.J.: Prentice-Hall, 1977.

Hughes, J., and M. Goldman. "Eye Contact, Facial Expression, Sex and the Violation of Personal Space." *Perceptual and Motor Skills*, 1978, 46, 579–584.

Jones, S. E. "A Comparative Proxemics Analysis of Dyadic Interaction in Selected Subcultures of New York City." *Journal of Social Psychology*, 1971, 84, 35–44.

Kahn, A., and T. A. McGaughey. "Distance and Liking: When Moving Close Produces Increased Liking." *Sociometry*, 1977, 40, 138–144.

Kirmeyer, S. L. "Urban Density and Pathology: A Review of Research." *Environment and Behavior*, 1978, 10, 247–269.

Knowles, E. S. "Boundaries Around Group Interaction: The Effect of Group Size and Member Status on Boundary Permeability." *Journal of Personality and Social Psychology*, 1973, 26, 327–331.

Krail, K., and G. Leventhal. "The Sex Variable in the Intrusion of Personal Space." *Sociometry*, 1976, 39, 170–173.

Kuszmonl, B. *Personal Space Invasion in Children*. Unpublished Master's Thesis, University of Missouri, Kansas City, 1971.

Lindskold, S., K. P. Albert, R. Baer, and W. C. Moore. "Territorial Boundaries of Interacting Groups and Passive Audiences." *Sociometry*, 1976, *39*, 71–76.

Lyman, S. M., and M. B. Scott. "Territoriality: A Neglected Sociological Dimension." *Social Problems*, 1967, *15*, 236–249.

Mallenby, T. W., and R. G. Roberts. *A Bibliography of Research on Spatial and Social Behavior*. Winnepeg, Canada: Thomas Todd Press, 1973.

Mazur, A. "Interpersonal Spacing on Public Benches in Contact vs. Noncontact Cultures." *Journal of Social Psychology*, 1977, *101*, 53–58.

McAndrew, F. T., R. M. Ryckman, W. Horr, and R. Soloman. "The Effects of Invader Placement of Spatial Markers on Territorial Behavior in a College Population." *Journal of Social Psychology*, 1978, *104*, 149–150.

McCain, G., V. C. Cox, and P. B. Paulus. "The Relationship Between Illness Complaints and Degree of Crowding in a Prison Environment." *Environment and Behavior*, 1976, *8*, 283–289.

Mehrabian, A. "Significance of Posture and Position in the Communication of Attitude and Status Relationships." *Psychological Bulletin*, 1969, *71*, 359–373.

Meisels, M., and M. A. Dosey. "Personal Space, Anger-arousal, and Psychological Defense." *Journal of Personality*, 1971, *39*, 333–343.

Melson, G. F. "Determinants of Personal Space in Young Children: Perception of Distance Cues." *Perceptual and Motor Skills*, 1976, *43*, 107–114.

Newman, R. C., II, and D. Pollack. "Proxemics in Deviant Adolescents." *Journal of Consulting and Clinical Psychology*, 1973, *40*, 6–8.

Paulus, P., V. Cox, G. McCain, and J. Chandler. "Some Effects of Crowding in a Prison Environment." *Journal of Applied Social Psychology*, 1975, *5*, 86–91.

Pederson, D. M., and A. B. Heaston. "The Effects of Sex of Subject of Approaching Person and Angle of Approach upon Personal Space." *The Journal of Psychology*, 1972, *82*, 277–286.

Powell, P. H., and J. M. Dabbs, Jr. "Physical Attractiveness and Personal Space." *Journal of Social Psychology*, 1976, *100*, 59–64.

Roger, D. B. "Personal Space, Body Image and Leadership: An Exploratory Study." *Perceptual and Motor Skills*, 1976, *43*, 25–26.

Roger, D. B., and E. E. Schalekamp. "Body-buffer zone and violence: A Cross Cultural Study." *Journal of Social Psychology*, 1976, *98*, 153–158.

Rohner, R. P. "Proxemics and Stress: An Empirical Study of the Relationship Between Living Space and Roommate Turnover." *Human Relations*, 1974, *27*, 697–702.

Rosenblatt, P. C., and L. G. Budd. "Territoriality and Privacy in Married and Unmarried Cohabiting Couples." *Journal of Social Psychology*, 1975, *97*, 67–76.

Sadalla, E. K. "Population Size, Structural Differentiation and Human Behavior." *Environment and Behavior*, 1978, *10*, 271–289.

Scheflen, A. E. "Micro-Territories in Human Interaction" in A. Kendon, R. M. Harris, and M. R. Key, eds. *Organization of Behavior in Face to Face Interaction*. Chicago: Mouton-Aldine, 1975, pp. 159–174.

Schiffenbauer, A., and R. S. Schiavo. "Physical Distance and Attraction: An Intensification Effect." *Journal of Experimental Social Psychology*, 1976, *12*, 274–282.

Shafer, D. R., and C. Sadowski. "An Investigation of Territorial Invasion in a Barroom Environment." *Sociometry*, 1975, *38*, 408–419.

Sherman, E. "Listening Comprehension as a Function of Proxemic Distance and Eye Contact." *Graduate Research in Education and Related Disciplines*, 1973, *7*, 5–34.

Shuter, R. "Proxemics and Tactility in Latin America." *Journal of Communication*, 1976, *26*, 46–52.

Shuter, R. "A Field Study of Nonverbal Communication in Germany, Italy, and the United States." *Communication Monographs*, 1977, *44*, 298–305.

Skotkog, V. P., and D. Langmeyer. "The Effects of Interaction Distance and Gender on Self-Disclosure in the Dyad." *Sociometry*, 1977, *40*, 178–182.

"The Smoking War on Flight 1410." *Newsweek*, December 3, 1979, 65.

"Special Report." *Newsweek*, December 17, 1979, 55.

Stokols, D. "The Experience of Crowding in Primary and Secondary Environments." *Environment and Behavior*, 1976, *8*, 49–86.

Tipton, R. M., K. G. Bailey, and J. P. Obenchain. "Invasion of Males' Personal Space by Feminists and Non-Feminists." *Psychological Reports*, 1975, *37*, 99–102.

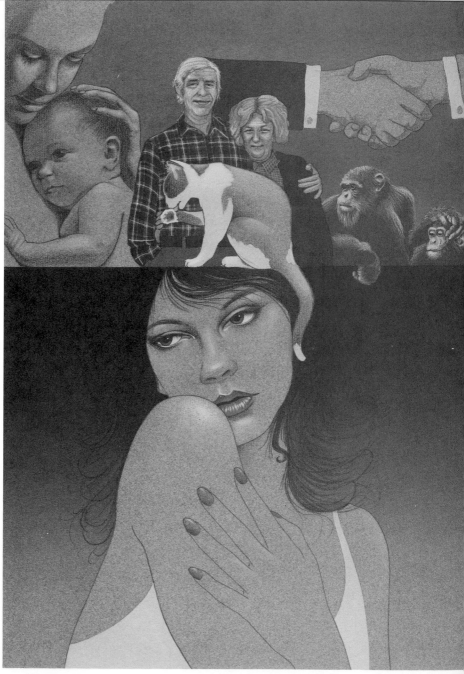

TOUCHING BEHAVIOR

In order to calm her, Goldmund softly rubbed his cheek against her hair and caressed her hip and knee with a quiet hand, the way one caresses a cat. Silent and curious she surrendered to his probing hand, felt the magic with curious reverence, offered no resistance. But while he cast his spell, he also took pains to comfort Lydia, hummed soft, familiar love sounds into her ear and finally made her lift her face and turn it toward him. Soundlessly he kissed her mouth and eyes, while his hand kept her sister spellbound on the other side.

HERMANN HESSE, *NARCISSUS AND GOLDMUND*

*A*nn was a determined toucher. Affection, cuddling, and touching were a critical part of her relationship with a man. Touch was so important in her relationships that in one case the presence of affection prolonged an already emotionally dead marriage and the absence of affection destroyed a relationship. During her marriage, Ann had a husband who was very aggressive in the business world but was a pussycat at home. In their home life, her husband gave Ann a great deal of affection, which allowed her to experience security, comfort, and contentment in their marriage until other factors led to a divorce. After the normal cycle of loneliness following her divorce, Ann fell in love with a man who was her match intellectually and sexually, except for one thing. Ann's new boyfriend did not like to be touched in an affectionate manner. Whenever Ann would touch him, he would ignore the gesture and quietly find a way to move his hand, arm, or leg. Only one thing kept Ann pacified during the absence of affection. "What kept me from feeling like Casper the Friendly Ghost," Ann explains, "was that he was snuggly in the morning before he woke up (when he obviously didn't know what he was doing). It wasn't much to go on, but it was enough to assuage my craving for physical affection."

Things might have been all right if Ann's boyfriend had not changed his job. In his new job, Ann's boyfriend got up at one in the morning and rushed off to work. The result was disastrous. Ann saw him just as much, and even though he was charming and a good sexual companion, an important factor was missing—affection. "I saw him as often as before; he made charming and courtly speeches about how much he liked me, but—try though I might—I had no sense of his being there. When a woman thinks her lover is slipping away, she begins to clutch—to make demands for affection a secure person wouldn't need—and even if the lover hadn't been going anywhere originally, he's soon in full retreat" (Lee, 1978, p. 101).

And that's what happened. By the time Ann's boyfriend was back to his normal working schedule, they had separated. Ann claims that the lack of touch was the main cause of the breakup. "I wanted to feel loved and appreciated and he was a cold, undemonstrative stiff" (Lee, 1978, p. 101).

The truth is that most men and women want, crave, and long to touch each other. Because of our cultural and social tradition, feelings about being touched and desiring to be touched are confused. We even hire "licensed touchers" such as beauticians and masseurs, to take care of our need for bodily contact. Desmond Morris, author of *Intimate Be-*

havior and *Manwatching,* claims that as a touch-starved culture we use many substitutes. Some of these substitutes include petting a dog, stroking a cat, sucking our thumbs, smoking cigarettes, hugging ourselves in distress, and drinking out of bottles that are the same shape and size as baby bottles.

The area of tactile communication has claimed the interest of many researchers during the last decade. The first part of this chapter will review the various functions of touch from a professional setting to an intimate situation and how the type of touch used changes in each interaction setting. For instance, how would you touch a professor, a boyfriend, a girlfriend, your parents? A second area that is explored is the relationship of touch to growth and development. A great deal of research has been conducted with animals in an effort (1) to examine animal behavior and (2) to explore the parallels to human behavior. The role of touch in human growth and development will be explored to determine how touch and touch deprivation affect human development.

We live in a society in which implicit touch norms have been established. There is an acceptable amount of touch we can give others and acceptable areas of the body to touch, depending on our relationship to the other person. In the section on norms of touch, we will explore touch avoidance and factors such as sex, age, race, and religion that may affect the use of touch. In the final section we will focus on the messages of touch and the effects of touch on behavior.

FUNCTIONS OF TOUCH

We touch people in very different settings and for many different reasons. Dr. Richard Heslin has developed a taxonomy of touch that classifies touch from a very impersonal type of touching to full sexual contact. Touch, according to Heslin's system, falls into five categories: functional–professional, social–polite, friendship–warmth, love–intimacy, and sexual arousal (Winter, 1976).

Functional-Professional

You have probably been touched many times for a specific purpose, such as a physical examination. Remember when your physician listened to your heartbeat? He or she probably touched you on the shoulder with one hand, while placing the stethoscope on your chest. In this case, the physician used touch to do something or to perform some act. This type of touch, when used exclusively to serve a professional or functional purpose, is cold and impersonal. **Functional-**

professional touch refers to an unsympathetic, cold, and businesslike touch approach. Generally speaking, when professional touch is used, the other person is treated as an object or nonperson in an attempt to keep any intimate or sexual messages from interfering.

Social–Polite

We use **social–polite touch** as a means of acknowledging another person according to the designated rules of the culture. The handshake is the most common example in the United States, while some European cultures may use kissing for acknowledgment. In all cases social–polite touch serves to recognize the humanity of both parties. The handshake, for instance, signifies that the encounter is starting off on an equal footing. Prior to the handshake, the handclasp was used in ancient Rome for the same purpose.

Friendship–Warmth

The most misinterpreted touching behavior occurs in situations involving **friendship–warmth touch.** We use this type of touch to let other people know that we appreciate their uniqueness and special characteristics. Our society is very cautious about the differences between touching related to friendship and touching related to sex. As a result, there is usually a noticeable decrease in touch when you and your friend are alone. Imagine two friends meeting each other at an airport. Ron throws his arm around Johnny and gives him a big hug. As they walk through the terminal and crowd, they keep their arms around each other. But as soon as they reach the parking lot they end all body contact. Why? There are no more crowds or contextual environment to reinforce the purely friendly nature of their touching behavior. The contact situation, when alone, becomes too immediate and too uncomfortable and may be misinterpreted. In the area of friendship–warmth, there is a lot of cross-cultural variability. The differences among cultures reveal the various approaches to handling potentially illicit or unsanctioned sexuality.

Love–Intimacy

Love–intimacy touch includes different types of touch such as stroking the face of another person. If you do not want to commit yourself to the responsibilities of a love–intimacy relationship, this contact will most likely make you uncomfortable. At this stage, the type of touch used is adapted to the other person, and it is more difficult to identify specific behaviors.

Sexual Arousal

Sexual arousal is the highest level of contact arousal. To most people it is pleasurable because of the stimulation it creates. At the same time, sexual contact can also be frightening and anxiety-producing. Touch behavior in this category is viewed primarily as an expression of physical attraction.

The use of touch communicates many different types of messages as indicated in the categories developed by Heslin. The role of touch in both animal and human growth and development is the subject of the next section.

GROWTH AND DEVELOPMENT

Think back over the last twenty-four hours. How many people have you touched, hugged, patted, stroked, tickled, or kissed? And how many people have touched, hugged, patted, stroked, tickled, or kissed

Gene Warne

'' . . . and that button makes the seatbelt give you
a little hug, if you're feeling lonely.''

you? **Skin hunger,** a common experience for most people from childhood through adulthood, is the result of not receiving enough body contact or touch for psychological well-being.

The physiological and psychological need for touch occurs at the moment of birth, both in the animal and human world. A mother cow, for instance, licks her newborn calf to a standing position and guides the calf to her teats. A female dog's first act of mothering is to bathe the pup with her tongue. An instinctive gesture of a human mother is to reach for her baby and cuddle the baby to her breast, while stroking his or her body tenderly.

These instinctive actions reaffirm the important role of touch in the growth and development of the newborn. Even certain words and phrases in our language demonstrate a preoccupation with touch—"soft touch," "rubbing the wrong way," "getting in touch," "handle with care," "handle with kid gloves," "thick-skinned," "skin-deep," and "touchy."

Touch also functions as a relationship message between people. Its importance in our lives is best understood by an examination of the role of touch in animal and human growth and development.

Animal Growth and Development

An examination of animal touching behavior provides important insights into human behavior. Ashley Montagu (1971), in his best-selling book *Touching*, raises two important questions with regard to the significance of touch in the animal and human worlds. First, what kind of skin stimulations are necessary for the healthy development of the organism, both physically and behaviorally? Second, what are the effects, if any, of the deprivation or insufficiency of particular kinds of skin stimulation? Two specific animal behaviors, gentling and licking, will be examined in light of the questions raised by Montagu. A third area, physical contact among animals and its effect on behavior, will also be discussed.

Gentling. **Gentling behavior** involves the stroking and touching of newborns. A series of studies examining the effects of gentling was conducted by Hammett (1921, 1922) to determine the differences between an experimental group of rats, gentled by human contact, and a standard group that had no tactile contact. The thyroid and parathyroid glands of the rats were removed in an operation, and forty-eight hours later seventy-nine percent of the rats in the standard group died while only thirteen percent of the gentled rats died. In addition to the dramatic differences in mortality rates, Hammett observed that the gentled rats were yielding and not easily frightened, while the nongentled rats were nervous and highly irritable. The researcher concluded that the stability of the nervous system, induced in rats by gentling and petting, produced in them a significant resistance to the loss of parathyroid secretion.

Gentling may play an important role in the chances for survival for animals. Licking has been reported to be another behavior that has particular significance in animal growth and development.

Licking.   Have you ever wondered why a mother cat licks her young? The most common reply is that the mother cat is cleaning her kittens. **Licking,** which is used for cleanliness, also serves as a necessary physiological function for survival of newborns. If a newborn remains unlicked, for example, particularly in the perineal region (the region between the external genitalia and the anus), it is likely to die of functional failure of the genitourinary system. Breeders of chihuahua dogs are very aware of the effects on the puppies when they are not licked. Mothers in this breed of dogs make little or no attempt to lick their young. As a result, there is a high mortality rate among these puppies, caused by failure to eliminate. Unless some substitute for maternal licking such as stroking by the human hand is provided, the newborn has a low probability for survival.

Lisa, a college student, had an interesting experience with a newborn and motherless kitten. The kitten had refused to eat and was not eliminating properly. Lisa had just recently heard a lecture on licking and animal behavior in her class on nonverbal communication, and she decided that the kitten needed a substitute for its mother's licking. She took a cotton swab, dipped it in warm water, and for the next few days, she rubbed the kitten's belly every two hours with the cotton. Soon the kitten began eating and eliminating properly. One can only speculate, but perhaps the simulated licking contributed to the kitten's regained health.

Physical contact.   **Physical contact** plays an important role in animal growth and development. In a series of valuable studies, Harlow (1958, pp. 673–685) demonstrated the significance of physical contact between a mother monkey and her infant. The researcher found that the infant monkey's access to physical contact was a crucial variable in the development of normal behavior. Harlow observed laboratory-raised baby monkeys and found they showed a strong attachment to the folded gauze diapers that were used to cover the hardware cloth floors and cages. In addition, the researcher observed that infant monkeys raised on the floor of a barred and wire-mesh cage survived with great difficulty, if at all, during the first five days of life. Based on these insights, Harlow built a terry-cloth surrogate mother, with a light bulb behind her head that radiated heat. The surrogate was "soft, warm, and tender, a mother with infinite patience, a mother available twenty-four hours a day, a mother that never scolded her infant, and never struck or bit her baby in anger" (Harlow, p. 676).

A second surrogate mother was designed with mesh wire; without the terry-cloth skin this surrogate could not provide vital contact comfort. In the initial experiment, a cloth mother and a wire mother were placed in different cubicles attached to the infant's cage. The cloth mother lactated and the wire mother did not for four newborn monkeys; for another four, this condition was reversed.

The results surprisingly revealed that even when the wire mother provided the milk, the young monkeys spent more time with the cloth mother. Harlow concluded:

> We were not suprised to discover that contact comfort was an important basic affectional or love variable, but we did not expect it to overshadow so completely the variable of nursing; indeed, the disparity is so great as to suggest that the primary function of nursing as an affectional variable is that of ensuring frequent and intimate body contact of the infant with the mother. Certainly, man cannot live by milk alone. Love is an emotion that does not need to be bottle- or spoon-fed, and we may be sure that there is nothing to be gained by giving lip service to love. (Harlow, Harlow, and Hansen, 1963, pp. 260–261)

With the empirical and observational evidence of the significance of touch in the animal world, we may then ask: "Does touch also play an important role in human growth and development?"

Human Growth and Development

"I've had mixed feelings about going back to work," the woman explained. "It's not guilt about the children so much as a sense that something important is now missing from my life. It finally dawned on me that when I was a fulltime mother, one of the kids would climb into my lap to be snuggled a dozen times a day—and I miss that. In fact, at times during the working day I get an almost irresistible urge to hug somebody, but it's not exactly office protocol. Anyway, I've begun to reserve half an hour every evening just for snuggling, and it feels marvelous—to me and to the kids, too" (Davis, 1978, p. 48).

Another person, a divorced man living some distance from his family, attended a massage workshop and found that when it was his turn to be massaged, he had to fight back tears. "It had been such a long time since anyone touched me in a gentle way," he said. "It brought back memories of my mother and my childhood" (Davis, 1978, p. 48). Because touch is such a powerful symbol and signaling system and is closely related to our emotional feelings, it is kept to a minimum in casual encounters.

These are just a few symptoms of the touch-starved culture in which we live. Another sign has been the evolution of encounter groups and experiential workshops that allow limited forms of physical contact to occur. As we mentioned earlier, we use many symbolic forms of "substitute" touch; we hire licensed touchers such as beauticians and masseurs to take care of our need for bodily contact in a socially acceptable way (Morris, 1977). Why do we have such licensed touchers? Morris explains that we are a tribal species, evolved over a million years of living in small tribes. Now we live in groups, surrounded by strangers, and we tighten ourselves up. Social caution creeps into public activities and works against our natural tendency to be friendly and intimate. We button ourselves up and wear a suit of emotional armor, claims Morris.

How does touch affect human growth and development? The following section examines the evolution of touch from historical to contemporary times.

Historical background.   In the nineteenth century, more than half the infants in their first year of life regularly died from a disease called **marasmus** (a Greek word meaning "wasting away"), also known as infantile atrophy or debility. During the period from 1900 to 1919 the death rate of infants under one year of age in various foundling institutions in the United States was nearly one hundred percent. (Montagu, 1971, p. 93).

Dr. Fritz Talbot of Boston, perplexed by the high mortality rate of infants, studied the care of babies in Germany. When doctors in one hospital were unable to help a sick infant, they gave the child to a woman they called "Fat Old Anna." Talbot observed that "Fat Old Anna" would hold, rock, and cuddle the child. Somehow the tactile contact that Anna gave the infants seemed to help them recover. Talbot, after seeing the amazing effect of Anna, brought the idea back to the United States and called it "tender, loving care," which you have commonly heard referred to as TLC (Talbot, 1941, p. 469).

America was influenced for a long period of time, however, by a book written by Dr. Emmett Holt, entitled *The Care and Feeding of Children*. Dr. Holt's book was first published in 1884 and was in its fifteenth edition in 1935. The book was read by millions of mothers and mothers-to-be. Holt claimed that giving the child too much attention would result in spoiling the child. Further, he claimed that sentimentality should be strictly avoided because any show of love or close physical contact made the child too dependent on its parents (Holt, 1935).

It was not until after World War II, when studies were undertaken to discover the cause of marasmus, that it was found to occur quite often among babies in the ''better'' homes, hospitals, and institutions than in poorer ones. This was of great interest since it was thought that these infants were receiving the best physical attention and care. The babies in the poorer homes, however, were receiving more affectionate attention and more touch. Recognizing this fact, Dr. Brennemann in the late 1920s established the rule in his hospital that every baby should be picked up, carried around, and ''mothered'' several times a day. After the institution of this mothering behavior on the pediatric wards at Bellevue Hospital in New York, the mortality rates for infants under one year of age dropped from thirty-five to thirty percent and to less than ten percent by 1938 (Montagu, 1971, p. 94). It is doubtful that the use of touch was the only variable in affecting mortality rates. On the other hand, the fact that touch does have some effect on physical development is more readily accepted.

Early touch: a case study.   Dr. Philip F. Durham Seitz reports a striking example of the significance of touch during an infant's first two weeks of life. The case revolves around a two-and-a-half-year-old white female

We begin receiving touch at an early age in the form of holding, hugging, and cuddling. Children depend on touch and understand its messages.

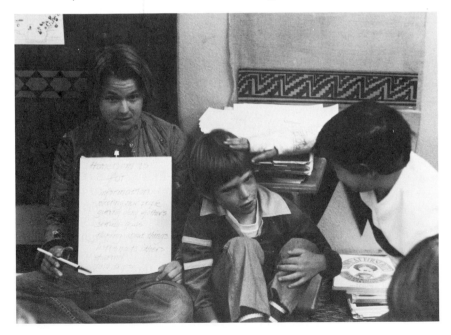

who was referred for psychiatric study by a dermatologist because of a desire to continually pull out her hair.

The doctors could not find a physical reason for the problem, so additional information was collected during the psychiatric interviews. It was observed that the child cuddled herself in the arms of her mother and sucked milk from a nursing bottle. When she was sucking the nipple of the nursing bottle, which she held in her left hand, she searched for her hair with her right hand. When she found a hair or group of hairs, she would pull them out with a twisting motion of her fingers. She then carried the hairs in her fingers to her upper lip where she rolled them against her lip and nose. She continued this pattern as long as she nursed from the bottle. The strange break in the pattern occurred when the nipple was removed from her mouth. At this point she stopped pulling her hair. The mother added that the child pulled her hair only when sucking from the bottle and that hair pulling and nose tickling always occured together.

The psychiatrist conducted additional interviews with the parents and found that for the first two weeks, the mother nursed her baby at her breast but discontinued breastfeeding abruptly during the third week because she thought her lactation was inadequate. During the first year-and-a-half, the child's growth and development was normal. She was weaned from the bottle when she was one year old, after which she ate solid foods and drank liquids from a cup.

At eighteen months old, a punitive program of toilet training was instituted, which involved scoldings and spankings whenever the child soiled herself. During the interviews, the mother realized that after the toilet-training program began, her daughter refused solid foods, insisted on milk from a nursing bottle, and pulled her hair out and tickled her nose while sucking. With this information, can you analyze what was happening to the child?

Dr. Seitz concluded that the child's insistence on drinking milk from a nursing bottle revealed a wish to return to the time when she was breast-fed. As for the nose tickling, the doctor examined the mother's breast and found a ring of long, coarse hairs surrounding each nipple. To test the hypothesis that the child was regressing to the early stage of breastfeeding, a nipple was constructed with a ring of coarse human hairs projecting around its base. This provided an automatic tickling of the child's nose whenever the nipple was held in her mouth. When the child sucked the nipple, she would slowly turn the bottle and brush the upright hairs against her nose and upper lip. This time the hair pulling did not occur. The automatic nose tickling apparently satisfied the child's need to regress to the early experience of breastfeeding.

The importance of this fascinating case is that it demonstrates the significance of human contact during the first few weeks of life. A child who two-and-a-half years later tries to duplicate what she remembers during her first two weeks of life suggests that early tactile contact is critical.

The acceptability of touch in given communication situations is the subject of **touch norms** in our culture. The use of touch is regulated by implicit and sometimes explicit rules about whom you can touch, where, and how much. The touch norms that exist in our culture are discussed in the next section.

NORMS OF TOUCH

The United States is often referred to as noncontact culture. In fact, as one newspaper reporter aptly stated, "More than other folks, pets get loving strokes" (Kaleina, 1979, p. C-2). In a survey of pet owners, a family therapist, Dr. Ann Cain, asked sixty-two persons to tell her who got the most strokes. She defined strokes as "any form of recognition such as physical touch, a look, word, a smile or gesture that conveys 'I know you're there'." The results are interesting. Forty-four percent of those surveyed said their pets got the most strokes, eighteen percent said their children got the most strokes and eighteen percent said family members got equal strokes (Kaleina, 1979, p. C-2). Although there is not enough research available to establish the norms of how often we touch our pets, it may be that our tactile contact with animals is higher than our tactile contact with people.

In examining the norms of touch we will review the topics of the amount and type of touch, touch avoidance, and body accessibility.

Amount and Type of Touch

How does the United States compare with other countries in the amount of tactile contact? Not very well, according to researcher Sidney Jourard. In a study of the rates of touch per hour for adult couples in coffee shops, the researcher reported the following frequency of contact: 180 in San Juan, Puerto Rico; 110 in Paris; 0 in London; and 2 in Gainesville, Florida (Jourard, 1968). One of the norms for adult touching behavior seems to be infrequent and limited contact. The use of touch earlier in life, however, is much more frequent.

Clay found that the highest frequency and duration of touch in mother–infant interactions occur between fourteen months and two years of age, with decreasing rates and duration after that age. Clay also reports that girls receive more acts of affection than boys (Clay, 1966). A different finding was reported by Lewis (1972). Basing his conclusion on the summary of several research studies, he found that for the first six months of life, boys receive more physical contact than girls. After six months, girls are not only allowed, but also encouraged, to spend more time touching and staying near their parents than boys.

Montagu (1971, p. 209) summarizes findings regarding sex differences in the frequency of touch and attitudinal factors. He reports that the following is true in American culture:

1. Mothers tend to be closer to daughters than to sons.
2. Mothers are happier about having girls than boys.
3. Girls receive more attention than boys.
4. Girls are weaned later than boys, a fact that suggests a more indulgent attitude toward girls.

Touch seems to decline from early infancy on, according to researchers Willis and Hoffman (1975). They report that from kindergarten through the sixth grade, the amount of touch steadily declines but still surpasses most adult touching behavior. The trend continues in junior high school, with about half as much touching as in the primary grades. In the Willis and Hoffman study, most touching occurred between same-sexed dyads and black children; females especially exhibited more touching behavior. Touching was initiated in primary grades with the hands, while in junior high school there was more shoulder-to-shoulder contact. Based on a review of studies, Knapp (1978, p. 245) concluded that "following childhood, the American child goes through a latency period in which tactile communication plays only a small role. Then, during adolescence, tactile experiences with members of the same, and then opposite, sex become increasingly important."

There are many limitations on touch contact in our culture. Anthropologist Paul Byers claims that senior citizens suffer the most from touch deprivation. "Perhaps," he speculates, "people are afraid that old age is contagious" (quoted in Davis, p. 48). The actual loss of physical contact must add to the older person's already increasing sense of isolation (Davis, 1978, pp. 48–50). Another popular limitation on touch contact is the difference in physical contact between males and females. Physical contact by a man with another man remains so potentially dangerous and unspeakable for many American males that other than a contained handshake, no one but the dentist and the doctor are permitted to touch the skin surface. Perhaps the involvement of women with the physical care of their children—with bathing, powdering, kissing, dressing, combing, feeding, holding, and carrying them, along with their own body changes and contact—results in fewer taboos against touch. The area of touch avoidance reveals many of these taboos against certain types of touch behavior.

Touch Avoidance

Are you aware that either explicitly or implicitly you ask and receive permission to touch someone else? For instance, a slow dance grants you permission to touch your partner within a limited area. A crowded elevator allows you to have body contact, as long as your arms are pulled in tightly to your sides or are crossed in front of your chest. A handshake is a legitimate means of making contact with another person, as is helping someone across the street. On the other hand, there are some norms that tell you not to touch or to limit your touch. A mother can caress her sons, but fathers are taught to avoid prolonged contact with daughters.

An interesting case of **touch avoidance** was observed on two Manhattan subway lines. Researcher David R. Maines observed that when people were forced to sit within six inches of each other, passengers were less likely to recoil from fellow travelers of the same race and sex. Significant elbow retractions occurred only between blacks and whites and between men and women. Given a little more space, however, most people relaxed their arms, regardless of who was seated next to them. Maines concluded that avoidance appears to follow a predictable pattern, with those who are most like us not really considered untouchable at all ("The Untouchables," *Human Behavior*, November 1978, p. 26).

A study by Jourard (1966) was conducted to find out which regions of the human body are permissible to touch. He divided the body into fourteen areas from the head to the foot, and he asked 300 students to indicate which regions of the body they touched. Subjects were also asked to indicate which areas of the body received touch from same-sex friends, opposite-sex friends, and parents. Jourard concluded that the greatest amount of touch occurred among opposite-sex pairs and that touch was restricted largely to the head, shoulders, and arms. Jourard also reported that the bodies of the father and mother receive little intimate touching, while the mother does a good deal more intimate touching of others. The most touching occurs between friends of the opposite sex. Seventy-six to one hundred percent of the females reported that they touched all parts of their male friends' body, including the genital region, while only fifty-one to seventy-five percent of the males reported that they touched their female friends in the genital area. Another interesting finding was that females were more accessible to touch by all persons than males (Jourard, 1966, pp. 221–231).

Have touch norms changed in a decade's time? Lawrence Rosenfeld and his colleagues repeated the Jourard study in 1976 with 200 new subjects and found very few changes from the earlier study. Parents, for example, continued to limit their touching of sons and daughters primarily to the head and arm regions. Fathers touched their daughters more frequently than their sons but touched them in the same general regions of the body. Mothers, on the other hand, touched both sons and daughters with about equal frequency. The major change from the earlier 1966 study was the significant increase in the percentage of touch to certain areas of the body by opposite-sex friends. The findings revealed that males now received more touch in the chest and hip areas than in the past, and females received more in the chest, stomach, hip, and thigh areas. Overall, this study found that the body is highly accessible to opposite-sex touching (Rosenfeld, Kartus, and Ray, 1976, pp. 27–30).

Sex, age, race, and religion enter into the use of tactile communication. Males are more hesitant to touch members of the same sex while

The body is accessible not only to opposite-sex touching but to touching by members of the same sex. In male-to-male contact, touch usually takes on a "humorist"- or "buddy"-type meaning.

females are more hesitant to touch members of the opposite sex. Another interesting finding is that people reduce their amount of touch to the opposite sex as they increase in age. Also, Protestants avoid touch more than non-Protestants, and older married persons display an avoidance of touching members of the opposite sex (Anderson and Leibowitz, 1978).

The norms for touch in our culture limit both the frequency of touch and the area of the body touched. The variables that determine the frequency and area of touch include sex, race, age, religion, degree of acquaintance, and the family relationship of the interactants.

The use of touch also reveals many messages to the recipient. Touch may signal status messages, emotional messages, body-contact needs, and the need for self-intimacy. These messages of touch are explained next.

MESSAGES OF TOUCH

Physical touch always communicates some type of message. In fact, when we are unable to use physical stroking, we replace it with verbal or symbolic stroking. Our language expresses this when we use phrases such as ''I was so touched by your phone call''; ''That man is touched in the head''; ''I feel for you''; ''I felt as if he'd kicked me in the stomach''; ''He rubs me the wrong way''; or ''Handle with kid gloves.'' Symbolic or real, touch communicates strong messages to both children and adults.

In a national study conducted by Temple University Institute for Survey Research for the Foundation of Child Development, 2200 children aged seven to eleven were asked how they were rewarded for good behavior. Two-thirds said that they were hugged and that they liked it (Welch, 1979, p. 70).

In discussing the impact of touch, Mehrabian observed, ''Even when it contradicts postures, positions, and words, it still determines the total impact of a message'' (Mehrabian, 1971, p. 6).

Emotional Messages

Many emotional messages are conveyed by touch, particularly in greetings and departures. Two researchers, Heslin and Boss (1976), observed people at an airport and found that sixty percent engaged in touching when greeting or saying goodbye to another person. An interesting difference was observed between greeting and departure behavior—there was more emotional feeling displayed in departure. Part of the reasoning might be that there is less embarrassment because the person is leaving. Greeting someone presupposes an additional amount of time spent together afterwards, which might become uncomfortable if there has been a very emotionally charged greeting. Another interesting finding reported by the researchers was that touching behavior was most often initiated by men.

Argyle (1975) claims that touch communicates various interpersonal attitudes such as sexual interest and that it is also used as a status sign. Touch behavior may even be used to regulate the flow of the conversation, or it may be accidental, as in a crowded elevator. The meaning attributed to touch behavior may also be a function of the background of the idividuals involved. Researchers Nguyen, Heslin, and Nguyen (1975, 1976) studied the messages of touch in two separate studies, one with married couples and one with unmarried couples. Subjects were asked to explain what it meant to them to be touched in eleven locations on their bodies. Four different types of touch were used—the pat, the squeeze, the stroke, and the brush. Subjects were to view the touch as coming from an opposite-sex friend as opposed to a parent, sibling, or relative. The scales used to measure the meaning of touch included various degrees of warmth/love, playfulness, friendship/fellowship, pleasantness, and sexual desire. Interestingly, married persons associated touch more often with sex than did unmarried persons, and they also tended to react more positively toward touch.

The type of touch also affected the emotional meaning of a message. Patting, for instance, was associated with play, whereas stroking was associated with warmth/love and sexual desire. Friendliness and sexuality were more closely linked to the location of the touch rather than the type of touch. The hands, regardless of the type of touch, were seen as pleasant, warm, and friendly; the genital area was not seen as playful, regardless of what kind of touch was being evaluated.

There is also a universal relationship between touch and attitudes (Krout, 1942). Cultural expressions of emotions show that touch behavior and positive attitudes seem to go together. So do a lack of touch and negative attitudes. Derision, disrespect, and refusal, as well as other negative attitudes, are shown through the avoidance of touch.

In a series of studies, researcher Alma I. Smith examined the sending and receiving capacity of the skin. In a pilot study, an individual placed his hands on the hands of another individual. They were separated by a screen to eliminate the possiblity of kinesic, proxemic, artifactual, and other cues. The sender was able to convey five different emotions—detachment, mothering, fear, anger, and playfulness (Smith, 1970).

Touch communicates many powerful emotional messages. A mother, for example, may communicate her own feelings about her body as she holds her child. Alexander Lowen (1967) writes:

> The quality of the physical intimacy between mother and child reflects the mother's feelings about the intimacy of sex. If the act of sex is viewed with disgust, all intimate body contact is tainted with this feeling. If a woman is ashamed of her body, she cannot offer it graciously to the nursing infant. If she is repelled by the lower half of her body, she will feel some revulsion in handling this part of the child's body. Each contact with the child is an opportunity for the child to experience the pleasure of intimacy or to be repulsed by the shame and fear of it. When a mother is afraid of intimacy, the child will sense the fear and interpret it as a rejection. The child of a woman who is afraid of intimacy will develop a feeling of shame about its own body. (p. 105)

Status Messages

Touch also reveals status relationships between people. Examine the following list and circle the person whom you think would initiate touch.

Boss   .... Employee

Nurse   .... Doctor

Student .... Professor

Male   .... Female

According to Mehrabian, the person who initiates touch is generally considered to have higher status. Initiating touch increases the immediacy between the persons involved, and it is therefore more common for the boss, doctor, or professor to initiate touch. In the case of the male and female, most sexual initiations are made by males, but in many cases this is changing. The person who initiates touch generally controls the interaction. When was the last time you patted a person of higher status on the back? And how was it received?

Henley (1977, p. 103) reports data that confirm greater touch initiation by men. In conducting an observational study, the observer recorded touch variables in a variety of public settings. Data were collected with regard to who touched whom and whether the touch was reciprocated. Males were found to touch females more frequently (forty-two observations); females did so in twenty-five cases. The number of older people touching younger people was thirty-six compared with a very low figure of seven younger people touching older people.

Based on a review of the literature, Henley (1977, p. 107) drew three conclusions regarding touch and status. First, she claimed that people do have expectations about touching and being touched by others in particular role relationships to them. Specifically, individuals report that they are more likely to exchange touch with those close to them than with more distant others. They also expect to touch subordinates more than superiors and to be touched more by superiors than subordinates. The second conclusion reported by Henley is that touching is affected by the situational context. When one person has some dominance over the other or is attempting to display dominance, that person is more likely to touch the other person. Finally, there is evidence to suggest a link between touching and dominance as a personality characteristic. In other words, persons with dominant personalities may initiate touch behavior.

Messages of Body-Contact Needs

Many messages of touch indicate a need for body contact. Barb strokes her cat, holds him, and cuddles him as a substitute for body contact. Steven strokes his pipe, fills it, stirs it, taps the excess tobacco out—another object-contact need. Rosemary has sex with a man in exchange for being held and touched. Mindy is recently divorced, and one lonely evening she sits and stares at the fire in the fireplace and hugs herself. These are all indications of body-contact needs expressed through different types of touch and object manipulation.

Some historians claim that the Western world was more "snuggle-proned" in the past than it is today and that group sleeping used to be the worldwide norm. In the seventeenth century, British royalty boasted of a bed that could sleep 102 people. In nineteenth-century America, before the forces of religion and hygiene took over, citizens enjoyed one last fling at cuddling known as "bundling." Snuggling in bed with a bundling board between them was a favored ritual for courting couples; others invited friends, even strangers, to bed with them during cold weather. In fact, it was considered polite to invite a guest to share your bed (Jobin, 1978, p. 174).

Body contact needs are expressed through the use of body-contact tie-signs (behaviors that indicate the need or wish to be held) and self-intimacy behaviors.

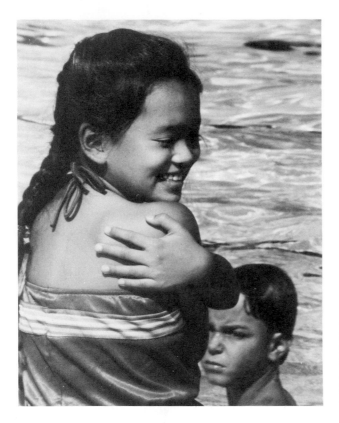

Self-intimacy behaviors such as touching oneself are unconscious mimes of two-person acts, according to author Desmond Morris. In this case the hand would be performing the contact of the imaginary companion.

Body-contact tie-signs. **Body-contact tie-signs** express the bond between two people in the form of physical touching. Desmond Morris identifies fourteen body-contact tie-signs: the handshake, the body guide, the pat, the arm link, the shoulder embrace, the full embrace, the hand-in-hand, the waist embrace, the kiss, the hand-to-head, the head-to-head, the caress, the body support, and the mock attack (Morris, 1977, p. 92). For the purposes of discussion, three selected body-contact tie-signs—the handshake, the body guide, and the pat—will be discussed.

The handshake. In Western culture the handshake is an expected formality, particularly when a personal bond is absent or weak, or when there has been a long separation. The handshake is a modification of the primitive gesture of both hands that indicated no weapons were being concealed. Later this became a greeting of a hand-to-chest gesture, known as the Roman salute. During the time of the Roman empire, men grasped each other at the forearms instead of the hand. The modern handshake takes many different forms and serves basically as a **gesture of welcome;** the palms interlock, signifying openness, and the touching itself signifies oneness.

Various degrees of intimacy are expressed in the handshake. The degree of immediacy of a person is revealed in how they shake hands (Mehrabian, 1971, p. 6). For example, does your handshake change when you contact a male, female, business associate, peer, friend, someone you like, or someone for whom you do not care?

The body guide.   A nonintimate way to guide someone in a particular direction is to point. The **body guide** is a more immediate behavior serving the same purpose. Remember when someone gently placed a hand on your back or when you placed your hand on someone's back to guide him or her in a particular direction? This gentle form of touch guides the person forward without the application of force.

This form of touch is an old parent-to-child behavior, and therefore it is common for a superior to use it with a subordinate. This action implies an ''I-am-in-control attitude.'' Morris (1977) explains:

> Even between spouses, it (the body guide) is an expression of momentary dominance, an act of taking charge of a situation. Used by a wife towards a husband, it presents a pseudo-motherly tie-sign to onlookers. Used deftly by a male, it imparts a masterly air to his actions. Used unwisely it can quickly become pompous and patronizing. (p. 93)

The kiss.   Imagine all the different **types of kisses** you have received—the kiss on the cheek from a doting aunt, the kiss on the hand from an admirer, the kiss on the forehead from a relative, the light kiss on the mouth from a friend, or the full kiss on the mouth from a lover. The wide variety of kisses suggests that each type of kiss imparts a different message. It was not long ago that the ''French kiss,'' in which the tongue would search out the partner's mouth, was frowned upon by adults who warned that it was a clear case of ''upper persuasion for lower invasion.'' Kissing is a form of bonding and is an intimate contact, sometimes more intimate than the sexual act itself. As one male student commented, ''When I like the woman, I will kiss her. When I make love, if it's just sex I don't want to kiss her because it's too intimate.''

Morris describes the messages of public kissing by observing the behavior of young lovers. These lovers, who are just beginning to form a bond, often kiss in public. It is probably safe to assume that a couple engaging in mouth-to-mouth kissing in public is not yet completely tied to one another. By comparison, older couples, who have been together for a time, tend not to kiss in public except at reunions, farewells, and

Although nose-to-nose contact may not appear on a list of courtship behaviors, it is an affectionate sign and in some cultures a very romantic sign.

times of significant emotional experiences such as triumphs, disasters, or even escapes from danger. At these times their emotion overcomes their usual embarrassment at kissing in public.

The cheek kiss is widely accepted as a nonsexual farewell or greeting between friends and relatives. The hand kiss reflects a lower status for the person receiving the kiss, because the hand is lower down on the body than the head. In earlier days, the rigid social formula was for a man to bow down and kiss the woman's hand. A dominant and important male, perceiving this as a lower-status behavior, solved the embarrassing problem of bowing down by raising the woman's hand to his mouth.

The Need or Wish to be Held

The United States is basically a noncontact culture in which touch is legitimate only under certain conditions. One of the most obvious conditions is sex. Sometimes men and women engage in sexual relations for the sole purpose of being held. Each one of us has a **body-contact**

quotient—in other words, a predictable need for a certain amount and a certain type of touch. You can get some idea of your body-contact needs by answering the following questions with "never," "almost never," "sometimes," "almost always," and "always" (Katz, 1976).

1. When you are upset, it is comforting for you to have someone to hold you.
2. If you are not held when you desire closeness, you feel hurt.
3. After sexual intercourse, you like to be held.
4. To get another person to hold you, you use sex.
5. If you have trouble falling asleep, it is helpful to have someone hold you.

The more "always" and "almost always" repsonses you have, the higher your body-contact score and the more you like to be cuddled. These statements are part of a questionnaire designed and administered by Dr. Marc Hollender. Cuddling, claims Hollender, provides feelings of security, protection, comfort, contentment, and love. Women with a high body-contact score are comfortable with their sexuality. They like to eat and talk, and they express their feelings easily.

To date, most of Hollender's research has focused on women. In his questionnaire results, Hollender found that there was a small group of women with extremely high body contact scores that resembled "an addiction." These women tended to be very insecure and were often promiscuous because they found that sex was a very effective way to obtain the body contact they needed. Deprived of tactile stimulation earlier in their lives, these women used both direct and indirect means (i.e., sexual enticement and seduction) to obtain the holding and cuddling they desired. One woman, whose need to be held was compelling, reported:

> I would sooner have him (her husband) hold me every day—not 24 hours every day—but I would sooner have that than a Cadillac convertible, and I have told him that. . . . I was never cuddled or picked up or never had any kind of contact and affection (as a child); therefore, I believe I crave it more than the average person because of a lack of it. (Hite, 1977, p. 75)

A young divorcée, who had had several affairs, expressed her desire for body contact:

> I initiated the sex (with a man in her office). I liked to be close to him because I knew he would touch me. . . .He used to rub my back at the office. I wanted to be even closer than that to him, but it wasn't necessarily that it was sexual, but I thought that that was the only means by which I would be closer to him. (Hite, 1977, p. 75)

Only a handful of women expressed an aversion to being held. The results of Hollender's descriptive study, based on interview data obtained from twenty-seven paid volunteers and twenty-seven psychiatric patients, indicated that the need or wish to be held ranges from indifferent to intense. As one woman explained: "I require hugs, and in exchange give sex; however, I want to stress that often all I really am seeking is for a man to touch me" (Hite, 1977, p. 75).

Body contact commonly provides feelings of being loved, protected, and comforted. Both direct and indirect means are used to obtain the holding or cuddling desired. Sexual enticement and seduction are common means. Women usually separate the wish to be held from the desire for sexual gratification, and for them being held may be an end in itself. Sometimes the message communicated by the need to be held may be misunderstood. "When a man responds sexually to a woman who wants only to be held, she feels put upon. When the woman rebuffs the man's advances, he feels she has misled him. Clearly there are crossed wires in the communication system," writes Hollender (quoted in Stern, 1979, p. 90).

What about men? Originally, Hollender predicted that men would find it easier to acknowledge a need to hold rather than to be held, since American culture places a great emphasis on masculine strength. When a set of identical body-contact tests were administered to groups of male and female psychiatric patients, however, the results showed more similarities than differences between the sexes. The major differences were in the number of men and women with extremely high body-contact scores—the "cuddling addicts." Among the seventy-five people tested, there were ten women with very high body-contact scores, but only one man. "Cultural factors do influence the need to be held in men, but not in the manner originally postulated," Hollender concluded. "Men can acknowledge their longing (to be held), but its intensity either does not reach the height attained by some women or, if it does, it is not reported" (quoted in Stern, 1979, p. 90).

The *National Lampoon* commented that the need for men to touch and to be touched is so great that they go to extraordinary lengths to touch other men. According to the *Lampoon,* war, sports, and health care are the three fields of human endeavor specifically contrived to satisfy men's desire for masculine body contact. The *National Lampoon,* using its unique style of humor, suggests that men who want to maximize touching opportunities should frequent airports. Here it is possible to touch complete stangers all over by pretending to mistake them for arriving relatives.

Touching and affectionate body contact are used as part of the sex-therapy program introduced by Masters and Johnson. The well-known sex therapists help couples overcome problems by having them spend time together simply cuddling and enjoying the preliminary parts of lovemaking without concentrating on or worrying about what's to follow. The couple agrees they will not attempt coitus during this period of therapy. The touch practice works to the extent that it allows a couple to relax without expectations and perhaps to get to know one another in an affectionate way.

Body-contact needs express our degree of liking toward another person. As twenty-four-year-old Sandra observed, "I can have sex with someone I only like, but I can't cuddle with someone I only like" (Jobin, 1978, p. 178). Your hugs may be your most powerful medium of touch communication. By the way, have you hugged someone today?

Self-Intimacy

Picture yourself leaving your apartment or house. You've just locked the door behind you when all of a sudden you realize that you have locked the keys inside. What do you do? Before saying a word, your mouth drops open and your hand goes to your cheek or head as if to say, "Oh no, now what am I going to do?" In that brief moment, your feeling of emotional distress resulted in a self-intimacy contact with your hand. Temporarily, your hand offers you a soothing contact. Self-contact or touching ourselves is what Desmond Morris refers to as **self-intimacy behaviors.** (Morris, 1971, p. 213)

These contacts, although they are individual acts, represent the psychological need for someone else to soothe us at a critical moment, claims Morris. Remember when you were a child and a parent or adult held you or hugged you when you were hurt? Or remember when a friend reached out to comfort you when you were feeling particularly down? When these healing acts of touch are not available from other people, we simulate them ourselves to achieve a similar feeling. Do you remember feeling lonely or sad and hugging your knees, or even cold, both psychologically and physically, and putting your arms across your chest and hugging yourself? "They may appear to be one-person acts," claims Morris, "but in truth they are unconscious mimes to two-person acts, with part of the body being used to perform the contact movement of the imaginary companion" (Morris, 1971, p. 214).

Body intimacies can be classified as resulting from several situations. The first situation is when we feel depressed or nervous. At this time a loved one may give us a comforting hug or squeeze our hand to reassure us. In the absence of a loved one, we may turn to a specialized toucher such as a doctor, who pats our arm and tells us not to worry. If we have only a cat or dog around, we may stroke and pet its furry body.

Body-centered psychotherapists explain that when an individual is in distress the hand will touch that part of the body that is being protected—such as the heart area.

Even as we grow older many of us exhibit "Linus" behavior from the "Peanuts" comic strip; we hug a special blanket or pillow when we are sleeping. And finally, we have our own body that we hug, stroke, and touch in a variety of ways to soothe our emotional states.

Self-intimacy behavior represents a message of a body-contact need. There are many nonverbal gestures that fall into this category. One of the most common is the **hand-to-head behavior.** One action is the hand supporting the head, while the elbow is resting on some surface that offers support for the arm. Some people claim that this gesture is used as a sign of physical exhaustion. It might also be a sign of emotional exhaustion. **Mouth contact** with the hand may substitute for sucking a thumb, which in turn substitutes for breastfeeding. An elaborate form of this contact takes place when the finger or thumb is rubbed sometimes gently and slowly across the lips, recreating the movements of the baby's mouth on the mother's breast. During more intense emotional moments, we may succumb to nail biting. Perhaps during tense or frustrated times, you bite your nails down so far that the nearby skin is almost chewed raw.

In severe distress, simple hand-to-head contacts are not sufficient. Instead, people use **hugging and rocking behavior,** grasping their bodies and shrinking into their own space. Almost everyday we use a variation of this behavior by folding our arms across our chests, and in some cases the message we are sending is ''no one allowed inside.''

Holding hands with ourselves, wringing our hands, clasping our hands, and interlocking our hands provide a form of self-contact. In the absence of being able to interlock our hand with someone else's, we may clasp our own hands together, particularly during tense periods. At these times the clasp may be so strong that the pressure shows white on the flesh.

There are many other self-intimacy behaviors that we use. Simply watch yourself during times of emotional crises or just during the times when you are alone, and observe which forms of self-intimacy behaviors you use. The need for body contact and the wish to be held express themselves continually, and self-contact sometimes provides the temporary answer to this need.

Touch expresses many messages about both the sender and the receiver. The impact of touch behavior, however, does not stop at this point. There is research to suggest that touch and touch deprivation have observable effects on communication interaction. The effect of touch on human behavior and communication will be explored next.

EFFECTS OF TOUCH

We know that touching behavior or the absence of it communicates specific messages of status, body-contact needs, and attitudes, but does touch behavior have an effect on our communication and on our lives? In his book *The Broken Heart*, psychologist James J. Lynch (1977) attributes many diseases, particularly cardiac diseases, to loneliness. He tells a story of a man dying in a coma, who was still wired up to a monitoring machine that recorded his heartbeat. A nurse walked into his room and held his hand for a few moments, and his heartbeat went from rapid and erratic to slow and smooth. Perhaps his heart was literally and figuratively comforted.

A minister began to touch people more and more when he talked with them and found that he could talk much more personally and directly when he touched the other person. He found this to be especially true on sick calls. Does touch make a difference?

In terms of its effect on communication interaction, Aguilera (1967) reports some interesting observations. Nurses who touched psychotic patients were more effective in eliciting verbal responses from them than those nurses who did not touch. Blondis and Jackson (1977) discuss the importance of touch to patients in a hospital:

> In nursing, touch may be the most important of all nonverbal behaviors. Patients are touched as a part of the overall nursing procedure. You touch a patient when you take his temperature, blood pressure, give an injection or bed-bath. In fact, there is not a way to practice nursing without touching. And how you handle and touch your patient says a great deal about the way you feel toward him and his illness. The nurse who is reluctant to squeeze the hand of an aphasic patient may have no aversion to that patient, but merely an upbringing that makes touching situations difficult. Unfortunately, the patient has no way of knowing, and is only aware of her aversion. (p. 6)

Touch deprivation may have an effect on our ability to withstand stress or on our health in general. Dr. Seymour Levine (Hite, 1977) studied sensory-starved rats to determine the effects of three types of situations: (1) where there was touch with the mother; (2) where there was complete absence of touch; and (3) where electrical shocks were used as a form of touch. All rodent litters had plenty of food and water, and all other conditions were consistent across the groups with the exception of the variable of touch. Which two groups would you guess did the best? Not too surprisingly, the totally isolated litter who were deprived of touch were sickly and weak. But the most surprising result was that the group receiving the electric shocks was just as plump and healthy as the rats cuddled by their mothers. Eric Berne, commenting on this startling phenomenon, observed that any social intercourse at all has a biological advantage over none at all.

Does early touch behavior affect later life? There is no conclusive evidence on this point; however, there is some support to suggest that early touch does affect later life and also communication patterns. Sidney Jourard and Jane Rubin (1968) studied touch between friends and family members and found that the degree to which boys are touched by their mother predicts the degree to which they will allow their father and male friends to touch them as adults.

There is no definitive evidence available to tell us precisely the effects of touch and touch deprivation on communication behavior.

Because the study of touch requires a longitudinal approach, that is, a study conducted over time, it is difficult to do. For one thing, it is hard to control the variables. This type of research is important, however, and will have significant impact in helping us to understand the role of touch in human behavior.

SUMMARY

Research in the area of touch has become of increasing interest to such professionals as doctors, nurses, counselors, and educators. The fact that touch plays a significant role in communication and interaction is a well-accepted belief that has some empirical support.

Touch functions as a symbolic means of communication to indicate the nature of the interaction. For instance, a communication setting in which a doctor takes your blood pressure is an example of the use of functional–professional touch behavior. In this case, the touch is used specifically to perform an act. In other situations—a social–polite, friendship–warmth, love–intimacy, and sexual arousal—touch communicates specific information about the relationship between the interactants. Touch may express physical attraction or an important bond of friendship. When you touch another person, consider the type of touch you are using and what you are saying about the nature of your relationship to the other person.

From a very early age we are touched, held, stroked, and rocked. This intimate form of touching also has parallels in the animal kingdom where animals are licked and gentled to aid them in their growth and development. In fact, touch is so important to an animal at infancy that the lack of it may affect the chances for survival. Similarly, some researchers and experts claim that humans suffer from the same effects of touch deprivation. The case of Fat Old Anna in Germany is an interesting example of the use of "tender loving care" in assisting infants back to health. Your own growth and development are important in understanding how touch has affected your life. Were you breast-fed? Did you receive a great deal of touch as a child? Do you enjoy affection as an adult? Are you an affectionate person? Whether your current touch behavior reflects the touching you received early in life is still a matter of speculation. For you, however, it is an important matter of reflection.

Licensed touchers exist throughout our culture. Remember having your head massaged while the hairdresser was shampooing your hair? There are many "illicit" means for achieving touch when we do not receive enough in our own lives. As a culture we have also developed acceptable norms of touch. In other words, we have decided how much we can touch other people and where. In our noncontact culture, you can observe the use of touch in professional and personal settings. Most importantly, you can observe your own use of touch and determine to what extent you engage in tactile communication. Touch avoidance occurs within particular restraints of the norms we have established. Elevators and subways, for example, provide us with interesting and sometimes humorous examples of how we go to extreme lengths to let another person know that we do not mean to touch them.

A very important role that touch plays in communication is in the communication of emotional messages, status messages, messages of body-contact needs, and messages of self-intimacy. Both the sender and the receiver recognize that touch carries messages that are often more dominant than the words we speak.

Finally, there is additional evidence to suggest that touch affects communication and human behavior. More and more, we are finding that touch does make a difference. Exactly what that difference may be is not clearly understood yet. Although the empirical evidence is not available to draw conclusive results, there is testimonial evidence that causes us to reflect on the role of touch in our own lives and the lives of others. A fourteen-year-old girl tells her story of her need for touch:

> Dear Abby:
>
> I am a fourteen-year-old girl. My problem is that nobody ever touches me. My parents haven't hugged or kissed me for a long time, except when I go away for a long time. Close friends outside of the family don't touch me either.
>
> I am outgoing to a degree and sometimes when I really want to hug someone, I just go ahead and hug them, but they always stiffen up or back off. No one ever reaches out to me first. I need someone older to talk to.
>
> I feel like nobody cares about me or loves me. I am intelligent. I don't have a mental problem. I don't smell bad and I'm not ugly. I'm so confused—please help me.*

REFERENCES

Andersen, P. A., and K. Leibowitz. "The Development and Nature of Touch Avoidance." *Environmental Psychology and Nonverbal Behavior*, 1978, 3, 89–106.

Aguilera, D. C. "Relationship between Physical Contact and Verbal Interaction between Nurses and Patients." *Journal of Psychiatric Nursing*, 1967, 5, 5–21.

Argyle, M. *Bodily Communication*. New York: International Universities Press, 1975.

---

*Taken from the "Dear Abby" column. Copyright 1982 Universal Press Syndicate. Reprinted with permission. All rights reserved.

Blondis, M. N., and B. E. Jackson. *Nonverbal Communication with Patients*. New York: John Wiley and Sons, 1977.

Clay, U. S. "The Effect of Culture on Mother–Child Tactile Communication." Ph.D. dissertation, Columbia University, 1966. *Dissertation Abstracts*, 1967, *28*, 1770 B.

Davis, F. "Skin Hunger—An American Disease." *Woman's Day*, September 27, 1978, 48–50, 154–156.

"Even Painful Shocks Were Better than no Contact At All." *New Woman*, September-October 1977.

Hammett, F. S. "Studies in the Thyroid Appratus: I." *American Journal of Physiology*, 1921, 56, 196–204, 199.

Hammett, F. S. "Studies in the Thyroid Appratus: V." *Endocrinology*, 1922, *6*, 221–229.

Harlow, H. F. "The Nature of Love." *The American Psychologist*, 1958, *13*, 673–685.

Harlow, H. F., M. K. Harlow, and E. W. Hansen. "The Maternal Affectional System of Rhesus Monkeys," in H. L. Rheingold, ed., *Maternal Behaviors in Mammals*. New York: John Wiley and Sons, 1963.

Henley, N. M. *Body Politics: Power, Sex and Nonverbal Communication*. Englewood Cliffs, N.J.: Prentice-Hall, 1977.

Hesse, Hermann. *Narcissus and Goldmund*. New York: Bantam Books, 1968.

Heslin, R., and D. Boss. "Nonverbal Intimacy on Arrival and Departure at an Airport." Unpublished manuscript, Purdue University, 1976. Cited in M. K. Knapp, *Nonverbal Communication in Human Interaction*, 2nd ed. New York: Holt, Rinehart, and Winston, 1978.

Hite, S. "What Kind of Loving does a Woman Want?" *New Woman Magazine*, July–August 1977, 75.

Hollender, M. H. "The Wish to be Held." The *Archives of General Psychiatry*, 1970, *22*, 445–453.

Holt, L. E. *The Care and Feeding of Children*, 15th ed. New York: Appleton-Century, 1935.

Holt, L. E., Jr. "Holt's 'Care and Feeding of Children.'" New York: Appleton-Century, 1948.

Jobin, J. "How to Get Your Husband (and other Loved Ones) to Cuddle up a lot Closer." *Redbook*, September 1978, *95*, 174–181.

Jourard, S. M. "An Exploratory Study of Body-Accessibility." *British Journal of Social and Clinical Psychology*, 1966, 221–231.

Jourard, S. M. *Disclosing Man to Himself*. New York: Reinhold, 1968.

Jourard, S. M., and J. E. Rubin. "Self-Disclosure and Touching: A Study of Two Modes of Interpersonal Encounter and their Inter-relation." *Journal of Humanistic Psychology*, 1968, *8*, 39–48.

Kaleina, G. "More than other Folks, Pets Get Loving Strokes." *The Arizona Republic*, March 3, 1979, C-2.

Katz, D. "Body Contact: Cuddle up with Touching Test." *The Miami Herald,* February 17, 1976.

Knapp, M. K. *Nonverbal Communication in Human Interaction,* 2nd ed. New York: Holt, Rinehart, and Winston, 1978.

Krout, M. H. *Introduction to Social Psychology.* New York: Harper and Brothers, 1942.

Lair, J. *I Ain't Much Baby, But I'm All I've Got.* Garden City, N.Y.: Doubleday and Company, 1972.

Lee, A. "The Need for Physical Contact." *New Woman Magazine,* 1978, 101–108.

Lewis, M. "Culture and Gender Roles: There is no Unisex in the Nursery." *Psychology Today,* 1972, 5, 54–57.

Lowen, A. *The Betrayal of the Body.* New York: Collier Books, 1967.

Lynch, J. J. *The Broken Heart: The Medical Consequences of Loneliness.* New York: Basic Books, 1977.

Mehrabian, A. *Silent Messages.* Belmont, Cal.: Wadsworth Publishers, 1971.

Montagu, A. *Touching: The Human Significance of the Skin.* New York: Harper & Row, 1971.

Morris, D. *Manwatching: A Field Guide to Human Behavior.* New York: Harry N. Abrams, Inc., 1977.

Morris, D. *Intimate Behavior.* New York: Random House, 1971.

Nguyen, M. L., R. Heslin, and T. Nguyen. "The Meaning of Touch: Sex and Marital Status Differences." *Representative Research in Social Psychology,* 1976, 7, 13–18.

Nguyen, T., R. Heslin, and M. L. Nguyen. "Meanings of Touch: Sex Differences." *Journal of Communication,* 1975, 25, 92–103.

Rosenfeld, L. B., S. Kartus, and C. Ray. "Body Accessibility Revisited," *Journal of Communication,* 1976, 26, No. 3, 27–30.

Ruesch, J. *Disturbed Communication.* New York: W. W. Norton, 1957.

Seitz, P. F. D. "Psychocutaneous Conditioning during the First Two Weeks of Life." *Psychosomatic Medicine,* 1950, 12, 187–188.

Smith, A. I. "Nonverbal Communication Through Touch." Ph.D. dissertation, Georgia State University, 1970, 1–45.

Stern, B. L. "You Need Body Contact with Others; It Satisfies Skin Hunger." *Vogue,* July 1979, 90.

Talbot, F. "Discussion." *Transactions of the American Pediatric Society,* 1941, 62, 194, 469.

Trow, George W. S. "Touching Moments." *National Lampoon,* 57.

"The Untouchables, Elbow-rubbing Taboos." *Human Behavior,* November 1978, 26.

Walker, D. N. "A Dyadic Interaction Model for Nonverbal Touching Behavior in Encounter Groups." *Small Group Behavior,* 1975, 6, 308–324.

Welch, M. S. "Touching." *Glamour*, July 1979, 70.

Willis, F. N., and G. E. Hoffman. "Development of Tactile Patterns in Reaction to Age, Sex and Race," *Developmental Psychology*, 1975, *11*, 866. *See also* F. N. Willis and D. L. Reeves, "Touch Interactions in Junior High Students in Reaction to Sex and Race," *Developmental Psychology*, 1976, *12*, 91–92.

Winter R. "How People React to Your Touch." *Science Digest*, March 1976, 46–56.

9

VOICE CHARACTERISTICS
AND QUALITIES

The teacher's smiling face didn't help ease the pain
of the message. . . . (Her) voice was an extremely
powerful element in the children's interpretation of
her words: Her voice was negative; the children
heard this, and they didn't like it. ''Her voice was
nasty,'' said some of the children, and so they inter-
preted the message to be a nasty one. What better
way is there to strike back at a nasty message than to
stick out your tongue at the sender?

BARBARA S. WOOD,
CHILDREN AND COMMUNICATION: VERBAL AND
NONVERBAL DEVELOPMENT, 2ND ED.

275

When she spoke, her breathy and unmistakably sensual voice caught everyone's attention. She was a goddess. She was Marilyn Monroe.

When he spoke, his soft but powerful voice commanded the attention of everyone and moved many to the edge of their seats. When the Godfather, played by Marlon Brando, spoke, everyone listened.

Many well-known personalities such as Marilyn Monroe, Marlon Brando, Barbra Streisand, Bob Dylan, and Richard Nixon are highly identified with their voice patterns. Your voice is one of the most important factors affecting your image. The minute you begin to speak, your spoken image becomes dominant and overrides your visual image. When you talk to someone you can either destroy or reinforce the nonverbal messages you are sending via your clothing, gestures, facial expression, posture, and other nonverbal communication channels.

It is not what you say but how you say it that is important. Kevin, for example, has a problem that many people share: His voice and manner of speaking keep him from making a favorable impression on others. His speech is filled with meaningless phrases such as ''you know'' and ''uh''; he rushes his words and sentences together. Sonya has a different but common problem. She speaks so quietly that no one can hear her. In addition, she mumbles many of her words and appears to lack confidence. Both Kevin and Sonya are bright and career-oriented professionals. Their vocal characteristics and qualities unfortunately project an entirely different impression.

Do people really listen to you when you speak? Do you command their undivided attention? The purpose of this chapter is to focus on the impact of your voice based on the message and meaning you convey to others as a result of your vocal characteristics and qualities. This is referred to as the study of **paralinguistics**—the study of all cues in oral speech other than the content of the words spoken.

Vocal cues provide a rich variety of meanings to essentially the same message. Emphasis on one or several words, changes in pitch and rate, and actions such as clearing the throat may limit meaning or change it drastically. If a friend asks you, ''Isn't this day simply marvelous?'' your interpretation of the meaning will depend on both the cues in the friend's voice and other nonverbal information. If his remark is made with a low pitch and slow speed, if he emphasizes the word ''simply,'' and if his facial and posture cues are negative, you might conclude that your friend means that the day is anything but marvelous for him. If, however, his pitch is high and variable, his speed is fast, and his other nonverbal cues are positive, you'll probably perceive his meaning to be consistent with a literal interpretation of his words.

Suppose you happen to meet a friend you haven't seen recently and remark that you'd like to get together to catch up. The friend might answer "Oh," or "Good," or "Yes, let's do that." Whatever the verbal content of the reply, you'll make a decision either to call to set up a time to get together or to forget the whole thing on the basis of paralinguistic and other nonverbal cues. If your friend *sounds* interested, you will make an effort to arrange some time together. Crystal (1978), based on indicators of both everyday observation of people's reaction to language and formal research in the behavioral sciences, has stated that paralinguistic phenomena are frequently the determinants of behavior in interpersonal interaction. Though the prefix *para* suggests that vocal effects are a secondary or optional consideration in communication, paralinguistic phenomena, far from being incidental or marginal, often push the verbal content of the message into a secondary role.

Traditionally, verbal language has been seen as communicating the cognitive aspects of meaning, and nonverbal language, the affective aspects. For example, if I said to you, "I am going to see the play at the theater tonight," my verbal language would give you information about the actual plans for the evening, and my nonverbal language would give you some clues about my feelings toward those plans. In other words, I could give you the impression that going to the play was either a chore or a delight.

Expression of feeling is only one important role of paralanguage. Vocal cues also serve many other purposes. An employer may decide that a job applicant is lower-middle-class and has a pleasant personality on the basis of a telephone conversation. Often the voice reveals information about socioeconomic class, influences our judgments of personality, and determines whether or not we may be persuaded to a different viewpoint. We also use vocal cues to regulate conversation, to deceive and to detect deception in others. For instance, when one person concludes a statement, it is usually done with a low pitch. This is often a cue for the other person to speak. Vocal cues are so critical that therapists and other professionals use them in assessing both mental and physical health.

Precise meanings of paralinguistic messages are difficult to determine. The contrasts in verbal language are somewhat definable and measurable; the verbal content of a message is easier to talk about than the nonverbal content. Writers often discuss paralinguistics in functional terms by trying to answer the questions, "What can vocal cues do?" or "What do paralinguistic phenomena contribute to communication behavior?'' In this chapter we will explore answers to the many questions concerning the nature of paralinguistic behavior, and then we will turn to the uses of vocal cues to identify emotional, demographic, and personality characteristics.

MEANING

Researchers, asking questions concerning the amount and type of meaning carried in the vocal channel, have found few precise answers. For example, Mehrabian's formula, though often quoted to show the relationship between verbal and facial sources of information, is limited in interpretation by the design of the experiment. Using subjects who evaluated a speaker after hearing one spoken word, Mehrabian and Ferris (1967) concluded that total impact = 0.07 verbal + 0.38 vocal + 0.55 facial. Mehrabian later interpreted this to mean that total feeling is equal to ''7% verbal feeling + 38% vocal feeling + 55% facial feeling'' (p. 182).

Listener Judgments

Other researchers, using statements rather than a single word, report different outcomes. Markel (1965), for example, divided judgments of listeners into two categories, evaluation and strength. Evaluative judgments, based on responses to pairs of adjectives involving goodness and likability of a speaker, were found to rely primarily on verbal content rather than on vocal cues. Strength and superiority judgments were based on adjective pairs involving credibility and competence of a speaker. These judgments were often more biased for the listeners who based them on vocal cues than for listeners who based their judgments on verbal content (pp. 306–308).

Using different research methods, Hart and Brown (1974) found that although some evaluative reactions are related to the verbal content of a message, other evaluations such as social attractiveness of a speaker are also related to voice characteristics (pp. 371–380). For example, Nancy is walking across the campus and meets a guy she has seen many times but to whom she has not talked yet. When he speaks to her, he suddenly becomes attractive. The pleasantness of his voice has made a much more positive impression than his rather ordinary appearance. Recently, Hegstrom (1979) attempted to determine the usefulness of Mehrabian's formula. He concluded that it cannot be applied generally and that the sum of verbal, vocal, and facial messages is not equal to the total message impact. Although we have been unable to draw firm conclusions from the differing results, these results do serve to underline the importance of vocal characteristics in conveying a message. In addition to the impact of vocal cues the contributions of paralinguistic phenomena to communication behavior deserve consideration.

Paralinguistic Categories

Trager (1958), an early researcher in paralinguistics, categorized paralinguistics into voice set, voice qualities, and vocalizations (pp. 1–12). **Voice set** is defined as prelinguistics and involves physical and psychological characteristics of the communicator and his or her circumstances. For example, a short, elderly, hunchbacked man who doesn't know where his next meal is coming from will have a very different voice set from a tall, handsome, successful businessman.

Voice qualities, the second category, are defined as recognizable speech characteristics that can be separated from the actual message of the speaker; these include such variables as pitch range, vocal lip control, glottis control, pitch control, articulation control, rhythm control, resonance, and tempo. When John and Fred dropped by Larry's apartment one evening, they were talking rapidly and stuttering over sentence fragments. Larry knew immediately that they were excited. It took longer to understand the verbal content of their speech than the nonverbal content. The nonverbal message told him their emotional state, and the verbal message explained the cause for the state.

The third category, **vocalizations,** includes the following three divisions:

1. **Vocal characterizers,** such as laughing, crying, belching, and yawning;
2. **Vocal qualifiers,** such as intensity, pitch height, and extent; and
3. **Vocal segregates,** which include such vocalizations as ''Uh-huh,'' and ''Shh.''

The uses of vocal cues in the identification of certain emotional, demographic, and personality characteristics is the subject of the following section. In this section we will also examine the effect of vocal cues on learning and persuasion, on turn-taking, and in deception.

VOCAL CUES AND EMOTIONS

Often when you meet a friend, your first remark is to ask, ''How are you?'' Before there is an answer, you may use nonverbal cues to assess your friend's emotional state. After you hear the answer, nonverbal cues are still important, for they will strongly influence your interpretation of the information your friend conveyed verbally. The nonverbal cues that you can see are not the only cues to emotional states, for if you talk with the same friend over the phone, you will probably still be able to guess your friend's mood. The voice conveys emotional cues fairly accurately. Though vocal cues may be useful in encounters with strangers, they are more useful when added to previous knowledge of an individual.

The idea that the human voice transmits cues about emotional states has been relatively easy to support; however, discovering the exact voice features that transmit an emotion is more difficult. In order to study the voice as an expresser of emotion, researchers have found various recording methods that allow them to eliminate the verbal content of speech but to preserve the vocal cues in the message. These technical methods so alter human speech that the listener can hear only the vocal cues. Studies using this **content-free speech** indicate that vocal cues alone convey information about emotional states. Reviews of studies on content-free speech indicate that judges can consistently identify the emotion expressed and can also estimate its strength. Researchers, however, have been unable to identify the exact vocal cues that convey individual emotions (Starkweather, 1961; and Scherer, Koiwunaki, and Rosenthal, 1972).

Researchers have made a few theoretical assumptions. Some believe that pitch level influences evaluative (good-bad) judgments and that volume influences perceptions about the strength of the emotion. The activity level, that is, whether a speaker seems calm or excited, is judged by the extent of change in pitch and volume. If Bob greets Anne with a fairly loud voice and with a great deal of pitch change, she will probably assume that he is experiencing a strong emotion and is feeling excited. If a smile accompanies his vocal cues, she may, with some assurance of accuracy, label the emotion as a positive one. However, she may need more cues of both a verbal and nonverbal nature in order for her to identify the specific emotion that he is experiencing.

Other researchers such as Davitz and Davitz (1961) used recordings of phrases or sentences with the message content retained. They found that speakers expressed active feelings such as anger and joy with a loud voice, a high pitch, and a fast rate. Speakers expressed passive feelings such as despair or boredom with a relatively quiet voice, low pitch, and slow rate (pp. 81–86). Reardon (1971) had six speakers present two sentences, using their voices to express love, happiness, sadness, indifference, fear, or anger. The two sentences were: "There is no other answer. You've asked me that question a thousand times and my answer has always been the same; it will always be the same." He found that the listeners were more accurate in identifying negative expressions of emotion than positive ones and that anger was the most easily identified emotion.

In order to study the relationship between people's ability to observe and control their own expressions of emotion and their ability to accurately identify emotions of other people, Snyder (1974) measured the consistency of an individual's emotional expressions in different situations. He found that individuals differ in the amount of observation and control of their emotions in different situations. **High self-monitors,** that is, those subjects who watched and controlled their own emotions, were found to be especially sensitive to the emotional expressions of other people. Moreover, high self-monitors demonstrated a high level of ability to express emotion intentionally (Snyder, 1974). Think about a person you like to talk to when you feel upset. That person is probably sensitive to your feelings and able to express his or her feelings intentionally.

THE VOICE AND THE IDENTIFICATION OF DEMOGRAPHIC CHARACTERISTICS

We may conclude that the voice does help to express and to identify emotions, whether or not content is an available cue. Furthermore, people who monitor their own emotions efficiently are especially capable of expressing their feelings intentionally and of judging others' emotions correctly.

Gene Warne

Socioeconomic Status

Suppose that you are working on a committee to select upper-class advisers for freshmen and believe it advantageous to match advisers and students by socioeconomic status (SES). Would a telephone conversation aid in searching for this information? Researchers would say yes. Vocal cues can aid in determining demographic characteristics. For example, one graduate student informally investigated the relationship between vocal cues and SES by taping the individual voices of several people reading the same paragraph from a news magazine. The readers included a service-station attendant (working class), a businessman (upper middle class), an office worker (lower middle class), and an insurance executive from a wealthy family background (upper class). Class designation was assigned on the basis of the subject's parent's SES and the subject's own educational level and occupation. The tape was played in a graduate class in speech communication. These students identified each reader's SES with a high degree of accuracy.

Formal research also confirms the presence of SES indicators in speech. In an often quoted 1961 study, Harms established a clear relationship between speech and judgments of status by listeners. Speakers and listeners were classified as having high, medium, or low SES through the use of an established index that took into consideration income, education, and employment. The subjects were instructed to respond to questions printed on cards. The responses, typical of ritualistic conversations during first meetings such as "How are you?" and "I am fine," were then recorded. After the voices were evaluated the results showed that listeners not only gave the speakers the same SES ratings already assigned them by the researchers but also assigned higher credibility ratings to high-status speakers (Harms, 1961).

In replicating this study, Moe (1972) devised voice samples that could be used more consistently for all speakers, thereby helping to eliminate the possible difference in word choices and grammar among the different status groups. With a focus more clearly on the effects of paralinguistic cues, Moe found that SES *is* indicated by a speaker's vocal characteristics. However, other studies indicate that vocal cues sometimes unrealistically influence a listener's opinion of a speaker's SES.

Dialect or Nonstandard Speech

The perception of dialect or **nonstandard speech** is also related to judgments of SES. In one study, teachers were more likely to label children as culturally disadvantaged if their speech contained a noticeable dialect or nonstandard English (Williams, 1970). Speakers of Chicano

English were rated lower on success, ability, intelligence, and social awareness than speakers of standard English (Bradford, Ferror, and Bradford, 1974). A foreign accent also lowers the perceived social status of the speaker. Americans rated less positively Europeans who spoke English than Americans who spoke English (Mulac, Hanley, and Prigge, 1974). Apparently, listeners often infer socioeconomic class on the basis of these vocal cues. However, these inferences may not always be correct. Consider the possible embarrassment if a member of a European royal family or a wealthy Mexican businessman traveling incognito was perceived as having low SES.

Other demographic characteristics are also perceived somewhat accurately through the voice.

Height, Weight, and Sex

Nerbonne (1967) found that such cues as height, weight, and sex, (as well as race, education level, and dialect region) are also available in the voice. Information about height and weight, however, has been found to be less reliable than information on SES if the telephone is the medium of communication. The identification of sex is highly accurate. A rough estimate of age is usually also possible. Consider the dorm adviser who took a telephone message for Bill from his family. Even though the person calling did not identify herself, the adviser guessed accurately that she was Bill's younger sister. Although it seems obvious that the adviser would be able to tell if Bill's caller was a male or female simply by the voice, there is research that suggests that vocal difference between the sexes may be primarily learned. Anatomically, the length and thickness of the vocal folds are in proportion to the size of the larynx, which is directly related to body size. Therefore, a larger larynx will produce a lower pitched voice. However, social conditioning or the wish to sound as people expect us to sound may modify the results of larynx-size difference. One study concerning the identification of sex through vocal cues used boy and girl speakers of approximately the same size. Experimenters took measurements of height, weight, and mandible (jaw) length, and the children were instructed to speak into the telephone in normal voices. Results showed that listeners could identify the sex of the speakers accurately but that the differences in vocal characteristics resulted from socialization and not from physical size. Apparently, these children's voices were more closely related to sexual stereotypes they had observed rather than to body size (Sachs, Lieberman, and Erickson, 1973). Voice therapists observe differences in the pitch best suited to adults' physical equipment and the pitch they actually use most often. Social pressures apparently influence us to try to make our voices sound as we think they should sound.

Lass and Harvey (1976) studied the ability to match pictures of people with samples of their voices. Though the subjects were of different heights and weights, the researcher found that judges were able to match voices with full-length pictures more accurately than with head-and-shoulder shots. Their study pointed out that some relationship seems to exist between height and voice and that social conditioning and/or body size may produce this relationship. A very tall or large person who speaks in a high-pitched or very soft voice is likely to be penalized socially.

To sum up, then, we may say that judgments of SES can be made with considerable accuracy on the basis of paralinguistic cues and that the gender of the speaker can also be determined reliably. Although judgments of age, height, and weight have possibilities of being correct, these judgments should be made cautiously.

THE USE OF THE VOICE IN JUDGMENTS OF PERSONALITY CHARACTERISTICS

When you hear the voice of another person, do you form opinions about the kind of person he or she might be? In other words, do you make judgments about personality characteristics on the basis of vocal cues? Whether we realize it or not, we do often form such opinions about people from their voices. Imagine that a friend has set up a blind date for you; during the crucial telephone call arranging the time and place at which you'll meet, you feel the urge to cancel the plans. What has happened? Probably you have quickly based some opinions about the personality of your prospective date on vocal characteristics. You may also feel a strong liking for this person only to find that, once you meet, he or she is not what you expected. Of course, many factors about the characteristics of others enter into our conclusions, but in empirical research consistency among judges' ratings demonstrates the existence of personality stereotypes precisely related to the voice.

Benevolence and Competence

Let us go back to the question discussed earlier concerning the type of information carried by the voice. We said that evaluative information is based on verbal content and that judgments of social attractiveness and of strength are made on the basis of vocal characteristics. Hart and Brown (1974), reviewing Markel's (1965) study, made this restatement of his ideas: **Benevolence information** is conveyed primarily by content, while **competence information** is conveyed primarily by vocal characteristics. In testing these ideas, Hart and Brown (1974) separated the analysis of verbal content and vocal characteristics by having speakers read a passage that was both uninteresting and free of emotion-laden words and ideas. Such a passage provided a voice sample in a situation in which content was relatively unimportant. The subjects then answered questions, and their answers were transcribed, with mispronunciations and dysfluencies (stammers, breaks) omitted. This method provided a sample of content with vocal cues eliminated (Hart and Brown, 1974).

Another study regarding the positive and negative effects of vocal cues on personality-characteristic judgments was conducted by Addington (1968), who investigated stereotyped judgments of voice qualities, rate of speech, and pitch variety. Four trained speakers were instructed to simulate seven voice qualities (breathy, tense, thin, flat, nasal, throaty, and strong); three rates of speech (normal, fast, and slow); and three pitch varieties (normal, more than normal, and less than normal). Judges listened to the tapes and rated the speakers on personality characteristics. Analysis of the results gave some interesting insights into stereotypical reactions to voice characteristics.

The ratings on voice qualities produced a complex picture. Breathiness in males was identified with artistic personalities and youthfulness, while the same trait in females elicited ratings of beauty and femininity, but also shallowness. Females with thin voices were thought to be immature, but this trait in the male voice was found to be insignificant. Speakers of both sexes using a flat voice were perceived as more masculine, cool, and withdrawn. Nasality provoked ratings that indicated a wide assortment of unpleasant characteristics. Males using increased vocal tension were thought to be older and unyielding, but females speaking with tense voices were thought to be younger, more emotional, and less intelligent. Increased throatiness caused males to appear older, more mature, and more sophisticated, while "throaty-voiced" females were thought to be lazy, ugly, and careless. In general, clear, robust voices produced positive ratings; males with this trait appeared to be enthusiastic and healthy, while females appeared to be lively and gregarious. Females with strong, full voices were thought to be proud and humorless. Ultimately, all speakers were considered more animated and extroverted when they increased the rate of their speech and were thought to have dynamic personalities when they increased variety in their pitch. Males who varied their pitch level were thought to be more feminine and aesthetically inclined, while females using variety in pitch rated high on extroversion (Addington, 1968).

Addington's research suggested that a strong voice, varied pitch, and a lively rate of speech were associated with positive characteristics. Nasality in males and females, a tense voice in males, and a thin or throaty voice in females resulted in negative evaluations.

Anxiety

Anxiety is another personality trait that we often infer from vocal cues. In one study, Mahl (1959) found that as anxiety increases, repetitions, stuttering, omissions, and use of "ums" and "ahs" (**filled pauses**) increase. Fisher and Apostal (1964) found that **unfilled or silent pauses** produced no greater perception of anxiety or of genuineness but did give the impression of more willingness to talk about oneself. The tapes from which the latter judgments were made were simulated counseling sessions, with the ratings being made on the messages of the persons receiving counseling. Since self-disclosure is expected in this setting, pauses might seem more positive than those in a social conversation, and thus the judges may have chosen to rate these voices as self-disclosing rather than anxious.

A survey of anxiety research also revealed some interesting results on pauses and their relation to anxiety (Rochester, 1973). For example, anxiety was found to be positively related to *silent* pauses. In other words, as situational anxiety increases, silent pauses also increase.

The picture is relatively unclear in relation to filled pauses and their relationship to trait anxiety (being anxious or tense most of the time). **Switching pauses** (the silence within a conversation that is counted for the person who ends the silence by speaking) were found to be different for high- and low-trait-anxiety people. Switching pauses are shorter for people who are high in trait anxiety. How does this information affect everyday interactions? Suppose that you are talking with someone who pauses often, stutters, and picks up the speaking role quickly when you stop speaking. You can infer that this person is experiencing anxiety. It is Thursday evening, and Wayne and Ted are chatting about weekend plans over a drink. Ted begins to pause and stutter often. He speaks immediately when Wayne finishes a remark or even before he is finished. Wayne quickly becomes aware that Ted is experiencing anxiety about the weekend plans.

Vocal-quality research is often criticized. Kramer (1964), for example, criticized studies of the voice and its effects on personality evaluation by saying that vocal characteristics are described unclearly and that changing emotional states are not taken into account. Although his point is well made, it seems that we do make stereotypical judgments on the basis of voice. These considerations are useful to remember both when thinking about traits of others and when considering the impression you make on others.

PARALINGUISTICS AND LEARNING

A student taking a vacation in the mountains notices a crude sign near his hotel that says, ''Basket weaving—lessons.'' Since he dropped similar lessons during the school year for lack of time, he decides to investigate. He discovers that the lessons are given by a highly skilled elderly woman who speaks unclearly because she is missing some teeth. He wonders if it is worth his time and money to take the lessons. The answer is yes; he can probably benefit from the lessons in spite of the faulty speech of the teacher.

Effect of Vocal Characteristics on Learning

How do the vocal characteristics of what we hear actually affect our learning? Kibler and Barker (1972) presented three forms of a message to high school students. In the first, no words were mispronounced, in another two percent of the words were mispronounced, and in the third twelve percent of the words were mispronounced. Consistent with earlier studies, the findings showed that the students understood and remembered the content of the different forms of the message equally well.

In an investigation by Wiener (1968) and his colleagues, positive vocal cues were shown to aid children's learning. Given positive vocal cues, the improvement in learning in the lower-class group was dramatic and in the middle-class groups slightly less so. Of course, one must remember that content factors are also involved in improving learning as well as vocal cues.

A class of fourth-graders are making maps of the town they live in. Larry asks the teacher to look at his work. The teacher inspects it and says ''Mmm'' in a moderately loud voice and with a high and falling pitch. A few minutes later the child sitting next to Larry, Susan, calls for the teacher. The teacher has been distracted by a phone call. With the problem from the phone message still on his mind, he looks at the work and says ''Mmm'' in a quiet voice with an even, low tone. Could the teacher's reactions affect the work of Larry and Susan? Common sense and research indicate that reinforcement from the teacher is important to learning.

Closely related to our earlier discussion of the effects of vocal characteristics on estimates of SES (socioeconomic status) is the consideration of the negative effect of minority students' speech on teachers' evaluation of them. Jensen and Rosenfeld (1974) had teachers rate Caucasian,* black, and Chicano students on desirable aspects of classroom behavior. The behaviors included participation, attitude, effort, attendance, courtesy, etc. The teachers were shown tapes (audio, visual, and audiovisual) of students, all neatly dressed, in an interview situation discussing their favorite games and television programs. Results showed that Caucasian students were evaluated more favorably than blacks and Chicanos and that middle-class Caucasians received even more positive ratings when the cues were vocal rather than visual. Therefore, minority students may be receiving less reinforcement simply as a function of their vocal characteristics and other cues of ethnic background.

Time-Compressed Speech

A bright first-year law student is blinded in an automobile accident. Are there any ways to cope with the large volume of reading that must be done? Since we can comprehend at more rapid rates than we normally hear per minute, **time-compressed speech** offers some help by increasing the number of words presented per minute. Orr (1968) summarized research related to time-compressed speech. He concluded that although there is a great deal of difference among people in their ability to comprehend compressed speech, this method has potential as an aid to efficient learning. His summary showed that people *can* understand and learn at some degree of accelerated speech and that practice in listening at faster speeds than usual is useful. His study also showed that although immediate retention is comparable to the retention resulting from speech at normal speed, the retention may be minimal after a few weeks. Although further investigation is needed to determine specific ways in which time-compressed speech can be used efficiently, one can see that it is an important learning tool for the blind. Try to time how long it takes you to read this page silently and how long to read it aloud. You will understand immediately the need of blind students for accelerated recordings of text material.

After considering the research reviewed here, we hope that you understand the importance of paralinguistics to learning. We have seen that we can learn even if pronunciation is less than perfect, that vocal

---

* The study used the designation ''Anglo.'' This term is currently used to designate those who do not fall into the black, Chicano, or Indian ethnic groups.

cues are useful in classroom reinforcement, and that time-compressed speech is an important learning tool for the blind.

PARALINGUISTICS AND PERSUASION

A political rally features two speakers who take opposing views on the Equal Rights Amendment; both are well prepared. Before the speeches, opinion is about equally divided pro and con. Ms. James, who favors ERA, speaks slowly and uses the same pitch most of the time. The opposing speaker, Ms. Brannon, speaks at a lively rate with much variation in pitch. Is the audience more likely to be persuaded by one than the other? Do the rate and pitch variety of the speech and the articulation or style of delivery influence the credibility that listeners assign to speakers? Do these variables contribute to the degree to which listeners are persuaded to the speaker's point of view? Research indicates that these considerations are important to speakers if they want to influence the attitudes of their listeners. The audience will probably feel less favorable toward ERA as a result of the superior speaking skills of Ms. Brannon.

Miller (1976) and his colleagues found that a faster rate of speech is more persuasive; it created more attitude change. The faster rate also produced higher ratings of intelligence, knowledge, and objectivity. Miller interpreted these results to mean that greater credibility was ascribed to the faster speakers.

In another study, **conversational style** and **dynamic style** were compared by Pearce and Conklin (1971). In contrast to the dynamic style, the conversational style had a smaller range of pitch changes, more consistent rate and pitch, and less volume and lower pitch. The conversational-style speaker was rated more trustworthy, better educated, more professional, and more attractive than the dynamic speaker. His dynamic-style delivery was described as more tough-minded, task-oriented, self-assured, and assertive (Pearce and Conklin, 1971). How is such information useful? First, in giving a speech, style should be considered in terms of appropriateness to the purpose of the speech. For example, in speaking to a fraternity or sorority about poor academic performance of their pledges, an officer of the campus panhellenic council should probably choose a more conversational style of delivery. Speaking in a conversational style would give the impression that he or she is trustworthy, professional, and person-oriented. In contrast, a dynamic delivery would be more useful on some occasions. For example, the president of a club for business majors must speak at their annual fund-raising rally. The funds to be raised will be used to provide convention expenses for officers and an annual social function. A dynamic delivery would be a wise choice in this case, because the advantages of impressing this audience that he is toughminded, assertive, and so on, will aid him in achieving his purpose.

In other research, Addington (1968) studied the relationships of speaking rate, pitch variety, voice quality, and articulation to source credibility. Three dimensions of credibility were considered: competence, trustworthiness, and dynamism. The changes in vocal characteristics produced significant effects on all three dimensions; however, judgments of speaker competence were influenced most by the voice changes. A professor who lectures in a monotone voice will not be considered competent by most students. Credibility was also less when speakers used tense voices, nasality, or denasality* (Addington, 1968).

We can conclude, then, that a speaker should give careful attention to voice characteristics in order to have the best opportunity to influence the audience. The style of speaking should be chosen with both the audience and occasion in mind.

THE VOICE AND TURN-TAKING

In the midst of a conversation, how do you indicate that you want to say something? If you think that someone who is quiet could make an interesting contribution, can you encourage this without a verbal question? Yes, there are vocal cues and other nonverbal ways to manage turn-taking in a conversation.

Two commuters are discussing local politics during their morning train ride to downtown offices. After one has explained his views he pauses for the other to speak. His companion nods agreement and remains silent.

A professor shows a student a report completed in the same course the previous quarter, and a moment of silence ensues. The student examines it and then says, "Oh, this is the way you want it done?"

A freshman is at home for a weekend and is making a plea for extra money for the following month. The mother begins to speak by saying, "Now, son. . ." and the father clears his throat. The student attempts "to retain the floor" and to explain by speaking faster and raising his volume.

What do the above examples have in common? Each contains examples of the use of vocal cues in conversational turn-taking.

---

*For explanation of nasality, see section on voice improvement. Denasality is simply lack of nasality on appropriate sounds.

Turn-Taking Cues

What are the types of cues for turn-taking, and how are they used? According to Duncan (1973), in conversation we use turn-yielding cues, back-channel cues, and turn-maintaining cues. Wiemann and Knapp (1975) also include turn-requesting. Let us look at each of these categories of turn-taking behavior.

Speakers use **turn-yielding cues** to let the listener know that they have finished what they want to say and that someone else may speak. Vocal cues that may serve this purpose are intonation, drawl, buffers,* changes in pitch, changes in volume, interrogative inflections, and silence. The last two—interrogative inflections (in which the pitch is raised to indicate a question) and silence—seem obvious, but the others are also frequently used effectively. For example, if someone's speech slows to a drawl and a buffer such as "Well, you know" is interspersed in the heavily content-laden speech, the listener can usually assume that he or she is being given an opportunity to contribute verbally to the conversation. Lower pitch or lower volume and change in the pattern of pitch variation can be used in a similar manner. Carol is in a professor's office to get help with a research paper. She states her opinion on how to handle the issues and finishes with a slowed pace and raised pitch followed by silence. Obviously, she is ready to hear what the professor has to say.

Back-channel cues are used by listeners to indicate that they do not wish to talk even though the speaker is displaying turn-yielding cues. That is, back-channeling is staying in the position of listener in the conversation when there is an opportunity to become the speaker. Vocal cues appropriate for this purpose include reinforcers (e.g., "Mm," "uh-huh"), completion of a sentence by the listener, or requests for clarification. John has had a rough term and is finally home for a holiday. He is pouring out his story of a troublesome roommate and a disloyal girlfriend to his Dad. After talking about the interpersonal problems, he wonders if his Dad is bored, and so he pauses. His Dad's only reply is "Hmm." Encouraged, John continues his tale by talking about difficulties with course work. After a sentence or two his Dad interjects an "Oh" with a rising inflection. John then explains in more detail. Both "Hmm" and "Oh" in this illustration are examples of back-channeling.

Turn-maintaining cues, in which speaking-turn claims are suppressed, are used by speakers to keep their speaking turn. Although hand gestures may constitute the most important nonverbal behavior

---

*Buffers are short words or phrases that are content-free and more or less stereotypical and that either precede or follow substantive statements. Examples include "but uh," "you know," or "uh-well" (Wiemann and Knapp, p. 83).

Gene Warne

for this purpose, some vocal cues may be used alone or may accompany hand gestures. These vocal cues include increased changes in volume and rate of speech in response to turn-requesting cues from listeners. Using more filled pauses (with some form of vocalization, e.g., "Ah. . .") than silent or unfilled pauses is a useful method of turn-maintaining. Don is telling his girlfriend about his admission to graduate school. When she tries to congratulate him, he talks a little louder and leaves no pauses unfilled. He wants to keep the speaking turn because he has more good news. He has also been awarded a fellowship.

Turn-requesting is more frequently accomplished by simultaneous talking. Buffers and reinforcers are also used. Stutter starts are similar to buffers but may reveal a stronger demand to speak than buffers. Stutter starts are also likely to be used if the speaker has had the floor for fifteen to twenty seconds or if the speaker pauses longer than usual. Tim, Sara, and Phil are discussing a proposed change in the local drinking-age law. Tim is expressing his strong opinion that the age should be lowered. Sara wants to disagree with him; therefore, when he pauses she begins with a stutter start, "B-b-but." Phil then tries to take the floor from her with the buffer "Uh. . .well."

For all of the above categories of cues, you should keep in mind that often vocal cues are used in combination with other nonverbal cues. However, the use of more than one cue is probably related to the urgency of the request being made.

VOCAL CUES AND SOCIAL CLASS

Have you ever felt awkward in a conversation with a person whose background or life-style was very unlike yours? Perhaps you were unsure about the specific source of your discomfort. It may have been a difference in nonverbal behaviors, which vary for different socioeconomic statuses. Previously, we noted that vocal cues such as dialect aid listeners in determining the SES of the speaker. Another vocal cue, that of turn-taking practices, helps the listener identify the SES of the speaker. Malcolm is a graduate student in a prestigious university. His responsibility on a research project is to discuss working conditions with road construction workers. He had dressed in work clothes and remembered to use language he learned from summer work experiences. In spite of his efforts to identify with the workers he finds that he feels uneasy in his first conversation with them. Later, when he tries to analyze why he felt that way, he realizes that when they ended phrases without changing pitch and were silent at some points during the conversation, he had reacted with vague uneasiness. The difference in SES had influenced the interaction because of different habits in the use of vocal cues.

In a 1978 study, the subjects were working-class and middle-class high school students recruited from ninth-grade English classes. Each student watched a cartoon while the experimenter ostensibly prepared for the next subject in an adjoining room. After the cartoon was finished, the experimenter returned, said he had not seen it, and asked the subject to tell him about it. Unless the student ended the conversation, for example, by saying "That's all I remember," the experimenter continued to ask questions about the cartoon. The conversation between experimenter and student was videotaped, and afterward judges viewed the videotape and recorded the subjects' eye contact and changes in pitch. The study showed that working-class students used more upward changes in pitch and ended more phrases without changing their pitch than the middle-class students and that they also used more silent pauses. Middle-class students, however, used more pauses filled with some sound (e.g., "Mm") and more downward inflections of pitch. One conclusion drawn was that the upward or interrogative inflection of pitch and the silent pauses of the working class may indicate a lack of confidence and feelings of inferiority. This conclusion seems substantiated by the middle-class speakers' use of cues that are the reverse of those used by the working-class speakers; that is, the middle-class speakers used pauses filled with some sound whereas the working-class speakers used silent pauses. If silent pauses are viewed as cues for turn-taking behavior, that is, as openings where the other person can take over the conversation, then the working-class subjects displayed less resistance to yielding their turn. The predominant use of filled pauses by the middle-class speakers showed their desire to hold on to their turn. Middle-class speakers also used downward instead of upward pitch changes or no pitch change at all at the ends of sentences (Robbins, Devoe, and Wiener, 1978). This behavior is not surprising since we would generally expect that middle-class students would have more confidence and fewer feelings of inferiority than students of lower economic status.

In conclusion, then, we may say that vocal cues are an important part of our turn-taking behavior. We make use of them when we want to keep a speaking turn, gain a turn, pass it to someone else, or pass it up. Furthermore, the specific vocal cues we use will probably be affected by our social class.

THE VOICE AND DECEPTION

Several nonverbal behaviors often accompany deception, but are there useful cues in the voice for detecting untruths? Apparently, one can gain some hints concerning truth or falsity from the voice. We must add, however, that it would be unwise to make a judgment based on voice alone.

Krauss (1975) at Columbia University has identified the following characteristics of speech associated with deception: a slow rate of speech, shifts to higher pitch, inappropriate hesitations, and many dysfluencies. Although Krauss also points out that knowing these characteristics and avoiding them can be useful in improving credibility, they are not really useful in detecting deception because they are just as often signs of nervousness as of untruthfulness.

Suppose your roommate takes a message for you while you are out. The message involves instructions for you to go to a city a couple of hours' drive away for a job interview. You read the note left by your roommate and plan to go; later, however, your roommate gives you a description of the caller's vocal characteristics (stuttering, many oral pauses, and high pitch), and you begin to doubt the wisdom of taking the message seriously. You would be wise to look into the matter further, since the caller may have just been nervous or playing a practical joke.

Although vocal cues to deception that we may use in everyday activities have not been isolated, progress is being made in developing technology for lie detection by voice. For example, spectrographic analysis was performed on voices of subjects replying to questions with one-word low-risk lies. The subjects chose a number and were then asked to respond "No" to all questions about the number chosen. Analysis showed that false responses were shorter, thereby revealing the differences between truthful and untruthful replies. However, when the tapes of the above replies were played to a group of subjects, they were unable to differentiate the true and false answers. Their accuracy was even less than we would expect by chance (Motley, 1974).

Although electronic voice analysis may have possibilities for usage in lie detection, apparently the naked ear is unable to detect deception through vocal cues alone, at least in low-risk lies.

Another interesting development in mechanical voice analysis is a device called *Vopan*, which is being used by the Consumer Response Corporation in New York. It has long been apparent that consumers do not always tell the truth; for example, we hear a great deal of talk about how people detest sex and violence on television, but at the same time, the programs including scenes of sex and violence do well in the ratings. Surveys also show that shoppers believe that nationally advertised brands are superior to house brands, yet the house brands sell very well. *Vopan* is an outgrowth of technology with which the investigative agencies have experimented for a number of years; it can detect slight, inaudible shifts of pitch in the voice. General Motors Corporation marketing personnel compared accuracy in prediction of *Vopan* with attitudinal scales traditionally used to predict brand usage. The attitude scales accurately predicted use of the products being considered only forty-three percent of the time. *Vopan* predicted product use with ninety-two percent accuracy. In another experiment with *Vopan*, a group of women said that they were uninterested in reading any more magazine articles telling them how to improve their sex lives. *Vopan* analysis did confirm that they were bored with the subject ("Detecting Consumers' Fibs," 1978).

It is evident that cues to deception do exist in the human voice. These are unreliably detectable, however, without the aid of modern technology. Shifts to high pitch, excessive pauses, and stutter stops or stammers may be interpreted as evidence of deception, when they actually reflect stress. Suppose you are telling a friend about an incredible incident that you have experienced, and you get stares of disbelief in return. Although your excitement is the cause of stammering, frequent pausing, and pitch changes, these behaviors are being interpreted as signs of deception. Therefore, when you hear someone whose speech is broken and you conclude that he or she is being untruthful, remember to consider that the speech pattern may be caused by stress.

THE USE OF PAUSES

All activity needs to be set against a contrast; a background is needed in order for the material in the foreground to assume importance. Consider the following two situations. A yogi from India is scheduled to speak at a Student Government Association rally on the improvement of study habits. His first statement, "I can teach you a way to improve all aspects of your life," is followed by a pause. Sylvia has had two years of basic college courses and has decided she should major in botany. She is engaged to Don, who is in the third year of an engineering program. Botany is not offered at their university. After a weekend at home to think it over, she broaches the subject with Don by saying, "It looks like I'll have to transfer to another university soon." A pause follows.

Much of the time, brief silences or pauses and longer silences assume the function of contrast or emphasis for spoken language. They serve somewhat the same purpose that the white of this paper does for the print, but they do it in a more dramatic way. Although we accept the blank part of the page without notice, silences of any duration may draw our attention, and sometimes pauses or lengthy silences may become the foreground. Silence then can become the medium for conveying a message.

Pauses

Pauses have already been discussed in connection with turn-taking, personality characteristics, and deception. However, because of their importance, it is worthwhile to give some attention to them as a separate topic.

Pauses occur at grammatical junctures

- at the end of a sentence;
- preceding a conjunction (and, but, if, when, etc.);
- preceding relative and interrogative pronouns (who, which, why, whose, etc.);
- in connection with an indirect or implied question (e.g., "I'm not sure whether I will. . .");
- before adverbial clauses of time, manner, and place (e.g., "I will call you when I arrive in town.");
- at the beginning and end of parenthetical references (e.g., "It seems that those families—the ones on my block—were in favor. . .").

And there are also pauses that are not grammatical. These can occur

- in the middle or at the end of a phrase (e.g., "In all of / / the sections of that course / /. . .");
- in breaks between words and phrases that are repeated (e.g., "The situation with the / / with the athletes in that university. . .");
- in the middle of a verbal compound (e.g., "We are / / going to the convention, and then we will / / stop in New York to. . .");

♦ when a sentence is disrupted by indecision or a false start, (e.g., "We need to remember in planning this function / / I believe the important consideration here is. . .") (Goldman-Eisler, 1968, p. 13).

Actually, the idea of fluent speech is an illusion. In the cartoon study previously mentioned, Goldman-Eisler (1968) found that the speech of her subjects was very fragmented in spontaneous speech and only somewhat less so in practiced speech. In a relaxed situation she found that almost half of her subjects' speech was broken up into phrases of less than three words and that about half of their speaking time was taken up with silence. After they had practiced describing the cartoons, there was only a slight increase in smooth, unbroken phrases.

Fluency is also associated with high predictability of words, while pauses co-occur with low predictability (Goldman-Eisler, 1958b). **Predictability** here refers to the accuracy with which others could guess which word would follow in a sequence. However, all pauses increase with an increase in the degree of abstraction and with the difficulty in encoding (Rochester, 1973). The same occasions would be characterized by low predictability and a high degree of need for encoding. For example, you will notice that if you are finding it difficult to express your thoughts in words (encoding), you will pause more often and for longer periods of time, and your listeners will find it more difficult to predict what you will say next.

For problem solution situations, however, there may be a difference between the usefulness of filled pauses and the usefulness of silent pauses. Subjects in one study were given math problems to do while their behavior was being recorded. Those who exhibited more silent pauses solved the problems in less time than those who used more filled pauses. One researcher argues that filled pauses ("uhh. . .") serve antagonistic functions; that is, although filled pauses increase the speaker's conversational control, they also decrease the quality of production (Livant, 1963). Try asking someone to solve a problem verbally and record that person's filled and silent pauses. Consider the results in reference to this research.

Another important variable in the study of paralinguistics is the speed of speech production, which depends upon the amount of time taken up by hesitation pauses. Variations in overall speed of talking are basically variations in amount of pausing. Chapple (1949) studied the speech tempo of industrial workers playing different roles and found that supervisors spoke faster than the workers "under them" but that they were capable of using a slower pace when the situation demanded. One can see, then, that both the role being played and the type of work influence the speed of speech. Try to notice today whether the speed of your speech varies when you play different roles and do various types of work. Your roles as student, friend, or employee may influence the speed of your speech. Studying, doing handcrafts, and taking care of housekeeping chores will give you opportunities to observe changes in your speech rate. It seems that people who pause less are more capable of spontaneity in formulation of verbal speech; they are speakers who can "think on their feet."

Speed of speech is also an indicator of pathological states. One example of such a state is manic-depressive psychosis. In this state, speech is likely to be rapid and constant. Depression, another state, is characterized by slow speech. In both cases, however, the person is speaking to express an emotional state and is relatively unaware of the listener(s) (Eisenson, 1963).

The speed of speech of a person not suffering from a pathological state follows a similar pattern. In the section on identification of emotions, we mentioned the fast rate of expression of active feelings and the slow rate of expression of passive feelings. In our discussion of the voice and personality, we learned that faster speech gives the impression of being more animated and extroverted.

Pauses serve functions that are useful for both the speaker and the listener. They delineate parts of phrases and sentences, express emotional states, aid in encoding and decoding, and provide time for problem solving.

Silence*

The day has been busy and full. A big decision looms over you. Late in the afternoon you slip away to think. . .alone. . .in silence.

A cathedral is open. Candles are burning. A lone worshiper comes in to kneel. . .to meditate. . .to pray in silence.

Demonstrators camp around the Capitol to protest an action of the senate. For a time they are still and silent, and then they begin to chant.

A director of a social agency makes a lengthy, impassioned appeal for funds to a group that must make allocations of funds to various agencies. A period of silence follows.

Silence appears to be a concept or a process of the mind imposed by people on themselves or on others. Absolute silence does not exist. Even if a person is not talking or listening to external sounds, there may be continuous mental conversation. Bruneau believes that it is a major misconception to treat silence as the opposite of speech. Silence can be considered as an environment surrounding speech or language. Thus it is appropriate to discuss some uses of silence.

---

* This section is largely adapted from Thomas Bruneau, "Communicative Silences: Forms and Functions." *Journal of Communication*, 1973, 23, 17–46.

The process of putting thoughts into words is aided by the imposition of silence on the mind; that is, to encode messages the mind needs relief from other thoughts (the use of pauses in encoding was discussed earlier). Relief from all thoughts may be needed at times in order for the mental processing that occurs below our level of awareness to take place. The common phenomenon of going to sleep while thinking about a difficult problem and waking up with possible solutions in mind illustrates this principle.

Silence is also sometimes necessary to experience awareness of the world around us. Often you may need to go to a quiet place simply to think. If you are not in the habit of doing so, try going to a quiet, peaceful place and avoiding intentional thinking.

Silence can create interpersonal distance. Observe the intense silence of people on a crowded elevator. In other situations, silence can lessen interpersonal distance; an example of such a situation is the understanding silence between longtime friends. Closely related to the silence used to manipulate interpersonal distance is the silence that often follows an intensive sensory event. A beautiful sunset, a tremendous musical performance, or an odor that evokes childhood memories may create a need for silence. Both positive and negative emotions evoke silence, and silence is often the language of the strongest of passions—love, anger, surprise, fear.

Silence is also important for its symbolic relationship to authority. We use silence as an expression of respect and reverence in worship services. Silence, together with continuous repetition or chanting, can remove the mind from distracting peripheral stimuli. Both are often associated with meditative spiritual experiences. A person in authority can use silence to demand respect and to require subordinates to think for themselves. Think of a time when you directed a question to an expert or mentor and felt uncomfortable with the ensuing silence. Afterward, you realized that the time was allotted to give you time to think and answer the question by yourself.

Silence has an important place in psychotherapy, also, in that it allows patients to recuperate and to pull themselves together, so to speak. Greater incidence of silence is often considered a sign of progress; for example, children undergoing psychotherapy seem to need periods of silence to create a field for learning new attitudes. The therapist's silence, too, is important to allow the patient time for free association.

Silence is also used to modify the behavior of others in various situations. Silence is used to punish norm violators; the Amish call this punishment "shunning." You may have experienced the coldness of silence following a blunder. Harry used slang appropriate for his campus at a formal dinner with his dad's business associates. He was treated to silence by all the people sitting near him. Silence is also a convenient way to refuse to reinforce behavior that you consider undesirable. If someone who is sitting next to you in a group continually makes remarks (asides), refusing to answer may stop this behavior. Moreover, people who are deformed or different in some way often experience the nervous silences of others, and a stranger often must bear the burden of breaking a silence or letting it remain. Finally an unexpected or unusual statement may be greeted with silence (Bruneau, 1973).

Silence, then, is useful both as a background for sound and as a means of conveying a message. On a given day, observe how many different uses you make of silence. Is silence really useful? Can you make better use of silence?

IMPROVING THE VOICE

Think about a career that interests you. Mentally list the different occasions on which it would demand oral communication. If you are interested in a career in business or education, the importance of speech is obvious. Your success in almost any career will be enhanced by effective use of your voice. Sandy Linvy (1977), who teaches speech communication to executives, emphasizes that speech is very important to success in business. Obviously, the use of the voice is a major component of the group of behaviors that determine whether one is an effective communicator.

Sarnoff (1970) gives some advice on the improvement of the most common voice problems; the most useful equipment for voice improvement is a tape recorder and a mirror. First, you can listen to your voice and decide whether you want to try to make improvements. Second, your reflection in a mirror will help you to discover tension and failure to open your mouth widely enough. If you have serious voice problems, you should see a speech therapist; however, there are some things you can do on your own.

Nasality

Nasality is a common voice problem. You can probably recall the sound of voices of people who have excessive nasality. The only legitimate nasal sounds in our language are ''m,'' ''n,'' and ''ng.'' Close your nostrils with your thumb and forefinger and talk. You should feel vibration from those three sounds only. If you feel a vibration from other sounds you are talking through your nose; opening your mouth wider and relaxing your jaw may help. If you find it difficult to relax your jaw and other parts of the speech mechanism, try to find someone who can help you with relaxation exercises.

Screeching

Screeching or shrillness in the voice is another common problem. Look in the mirror and see if your neck looks taut. Relaxation is important for this problem, too. Step into a college dining room during exam week and listen to the voices around you. They will likely be shrill and sharp. These students are very tense. Stop to look in a mirror and talk on a day when you are feeling uptight. Then do the same on a day when you are feeling relaxed and note the difference in the appearance of your face and neck.

Softness

Talking in a too-soft voice or whispering can cut off communication. Ask a friend to signal when you are speaking at too low a volume. If this simple tactic does not work, ask someone trained in speech or vocal music to help you learn to use your speech to project your voice more effectively.

Monotone

Monotonous pitch can quickly lose the attention of your listeners. Tape yourself reading aloud. Listen to the playback and concentrate on whether the pitch is varied. Decide what you need to change and then try again. Listen to the voices of those people whose speech you consider pleasant and try to imitate them.

Speed

You also may need to give some consideration to the speed of your speech. Your tape recorder and a good friend will be helpful in this, too. If you are speaking too fast, give some thought to why you are doing so. You may feel insecure or pushed for time. In the same manner, there may be underlying reasons for speaking too slowly. Exploring these reasons with a trusted friend or counselor would be helpful.

Now would be a good time to review the section on stereotypical judgments of personality characteristics in relation to voice. If you want to make changes in your voice, more extensive suggestions are available in books and articles on the subject. Remember that if you are having any serious difficulty with your voice, you should see a physician and a speech pathologist.

After reading this chapter you are probably convinced that the use of your voice is a significant component of your personal communication system. In brief, we have learned the following. Vocal cues are helpful but are inconclusive as evidence in identifying demographic and personality characteristics and emotions. They are important in planning persuasion efforts. Deception is characterized by specific vocal cues but cannot be assumed from voice alone and is often confused with anxiety. The use of the voice is an integral part of turn-taking behavior. Pauses and silences compose a large portion of our communication time and are means of communication in themselves. As with the interpretation of other forms of nonverbal communication, you should keep in mind that literal or rigid translations to verbal language are inappropriate. However, skill in observing and assessing paralinguistic cues is worth your time and effort.

SUMMARY

The study of meaning in oral speech gleaned from cues other than the content of the spoken word is known as "paralinguistics." Vocal variations may suggest several different meanings for the same verbal message. While they answer questions concerning the nature of meaning, vocal cues also help to identify emotional, demographic, and personality characteristics of people. Vocal characteristics also affect learning, persuasion, turn-taking, and deception.

The amount and type of information carried through vocal cues vary from person to person and situation to situation. A person's "voice set," voice quality, and vocalization influence how information and people are interpreted and categorized. It is relatively simple to pick up cues about emotional states through differences in a person's voice, yet researchers have been unable to identify the exact vocal cues for individual emotions. Evaluations are often based on the volume, pitch level, and rate of the speaker. People who monitor their emotions effectively are more capable of expressing intentional feelings through their voice and more accurate at judging emotions of others. Paralinguistic cues are accurate predictors of the socioeconomic status and gender of people, but stereotypical judgments about the personalities of people are often inaccurate.

In spite of faulty speech patterns, students can learn and benefit from them. The vocal cues of teachers play an important role in student classroom reinforcement. Time-compressed speech is a useful aid and learning tool for the blind. Whether a teacher or a politician, speakers with a persuasive purpose in mind should give careful attention to their vocal characteristics. The manner and style of speaking should be suited to both the audience and the occasion.

In conversation, vocal cues help to manage turn-taking through turn-yielding, "back-channeling," turn-requesting, and turn-maintaining cues. Cues are often used in combination, and the urgency is related to the number of cues used. The choice of the specific cues we use in conversation is affected by our socioeconomic class.

The voice is often used as a method of detecting deception, even though it is unreliable without the aid of modern technology. Stammering, frequent pausing, and pitch changes may be caused by factors other than deception. The uses of pause and silence convey as much information as the spoken language. Pauses help to delineate parts of phrases and sentences, express emotional states, aid in encoding and decoding, and provide time for problem solving. Silence is useful as a background for sound and as a means of conveying a message.

The use of the voice is a significant component in your personal communication system. Dissatisfaction with your vocal characteristics can be improved through training and effort.

REFERENCES

Addington, D. W. "The Relationship of Selected Vocal Characteristics to Personality Perception." *Speech Monographs*, 1968, *35*, 492–503.

Bradford, A., D. Ferror, and G. Bradford. "Evaluation Reactions of College Students to Dialect Differences in the English of Mexican-Americans." *Language and Speech*, 1974, *17*, 255–270.

Bruneau, T. "Communicative Silences: Forms and Functions." *Journal of Communication*, 1973, *23*, 17–46.

Chapple, E. D. "The Interaction Chronograph: Its Evolution and Present Application." *Personnel*, 1949, *25*, 295–307.

Crystal, David. "Paralinguistics." In J. B. Pelhams and T. Pelhams, eds. *The Body as a Medium of Expression*. New York: Macmillan & Co., 1978.

Davitz, J. R., and L. Davitz. "Nonverbal Vocal Communication of Feeling." *Journal of Communication*, 1961, *11*, 81–86.

"Detecting Consumers' Fibs." *Human Behavior*, April 1978, 21.

Duncan, S. "Toward a Grammar for Dyadic Conversation." *Semiotica*, 1973, *9*, 24–46.

Eisenson, J., J. J. Auer, and J. V. Irwin. "Affective Behavior (Emotion) and Speech" in J. Jeffrey Auer, ed. *The Psychology of Communication*. New York: Appleton-Century-Crofts, 1963.

Fisher, M. J., and R. A. Apostal. "Selected Vocal Cues and Counselors' Perceptions of Genuineness, Self-Disclosure and Anxiety." *Journal of Counseling Psychology*, 1964, *62*, 247–251.

Goldman-Eisler, *Psycholinguistics: Experiments in Spontaneous Speech*. New York: Academic Press, 1968.

Goldman-Eisler, F. G. "Speech Production and the Predictability of Words in Context." *Quarterly Journal of Speech*, 1958, *10*, 96–106. (a)

Goldman-Eisler, F. G. "The Predictability of Words in Context and the Length of Pauses in Speech." *Language and Speech*, 1958, *1*, 226–231. (b)

Harms, L. S. "Listener Judgments of Status Cues in Speech." *Quarterly Journal of Speech*, 1961, *47*, 164–168.

Hart, R. J., and B. L. Brown. "Interpersonal Information Conveyed by the Content and Vocal Aspects of Speech." *Speech Monographs*, 1974, *41*, 371–380.

Hegstrom, T. G. "Message Impact: What Percentage is Nonverbal?" *Western Journal of Speech*, Spring 1979, *43*, 134–142.

Jensen, M., and L. B. Rosenfeld. "Influence of Mode of Presentation, Ethnicity, and Social Class on Teachers' Evaluations of Students." *Journal of Educational Psychology*, 1974, *66*, 540–547.

Kibler, R. J., and L. L. Barker. "Effects of Selected Levels of Misspelling and Mispronunciation on Comprehension and Retention." *Southern Speech Communication Journal*, 1972, *37*, 361–374.

Kramer, E. "Personality Stereotypes in Voice: A Reconsideration of the Data." *Journal of Social Psychology*, 1964, *62*, 247–251.

Krauss, R. "Improve Your Credibility." *Glamour*, January 1975, 42.

Lass, N. J., and L. A. Harvey. "An Investigation of Speaker Photograph Identification." *Journal of the Acoustical Society of America*, 1976, *59*, 1232–1236.

Livant, W. P. "Antagonistic Functions of Verbal Pauses: Filled and Unfilled Pauses in the Solution of Additions." *Language and Speech*, 1963, *6*, 1–4.

Linvy, S. Reported by Davis, C. "Personal Performance, Proper Speech Affects Your Future, Her Company." *Business*, July 31, 1977.

Mahl, G. F. "Disturbances in the Patient's Speech as a Function of Anxiety." Paper delivered before the Eastern Psychological Association, Atlantic City, N.J., 1956. Reprinted in Pool, I., ed. *Trends in Content Analysis*. Urbana, Ill.: University of Illinois Press, 1959, 89–130.

Markel, N. N. "The Reliability of Coding Paralanguage: Pitch, Loudness and Tempo." *Journal of Verbal Learning and Verbal Behavior*, 1965, *4*, 306–308.

Mehrabian, A. *Nonverbal Communication*. Chicago: Aldine-Atherton, 1972.

Mehrabian, A., and S. R. Ferris. "Inference of Attitudes from Nonverbal Communication in Two Channels." *Journal of Consulting Psychology*, 1967, *31*, 248–252.

Miller, N., G. Maruyana, R. J. Beaver, and K. Valore. "Speed of Speech and Persuasion." *Journal of Personality and Social Psychology*, 1976, *34*, 615–624.

Moe, J. D. "Listener Judgments of Status Cues in Speech: A Replication and Extension." *Speech Monographs* 1972, *39*, 144–147.

Motley, M. T. "Acoustic Correlates of Ties." *Western Journal of Speech Communication,* 1974, *38,* 81–87.

Mulac, A., T. D. Hanley, and D. Y. Prigge. "Effects of Phonological Speech Foreignness upon Three Dimensions of Attitude of Selected American Listeners." *Quarterly Journal of Speech,* 1974, *60,* 411–420.

Nerbonne, G. P. "The Identification of Speaker Characteristics on the Basis of Aural Cues." Ph.D. dissertation, Michigan State University, 1967.

Orr, D. B. "Time Compressed Speech—A Perspective." *Journal of Communication,* 1968, *18,* 288–292.

Pearce, W. B., and F. Conklin. "Nonverbal Vocalic Communication and Perception of a Speaker." *Speech Monographs,* 1971, *38,* 235–241.

Reardon, R. C. "Individual Differences and the Meanings of Vocal Emotional Expressions." *Journal of Communication,* 1971, *21,* 72–82.

Robbins, O., S. Devoe, and M. Wiener. "Social Patterns of Turn-Taking: Nonverbal Regulators." *Journal of Communication,* 1978, *28,* 38–46.

Rochester, S. R. "The Significance of Pauses in Spontaneous Speech." *Journal of Psycholinguistic Speech,* 1973, *2,* 51–81.

Sachs, J., P. Lieberman, and D. Erickson. "Anatomical and Cultural Determinants of Male and Female Speech." In Sheely, R. W., and R. W. Fasold, eds. *Language Attitudes: Current Trends and Prospects.* Washington, D.C.: Georgetown University Press, 1973.

Sarnoff, D. *Speech Can Change Your Life.* Garden City, N.Y.: Doubleday & Co., 1970.

Scherer, K. R., J. Koiwunaki, and R. Rosenthal. "Minimal Cues in the Vocal Communication of Affect: Judging Emotions from Content-Masked Speech." *Journal of Psycholinguistic Speech,* 1972, *1,* 269–285.

Snyder, M. "Self-Monitoring of Expressive Behavior." *Journal of Personality and Social Psychology,* 1974, *30,* 526–537.

Starkweather, J. A. "Vocal Communication of Personality and Human Feeling." *Journal of Communication,* 1961, *11,* 69.

Trager, G. L. "Paralanguage: A First Approximation." *Studies in Linguistics,* 1958, *13,* 1–12.

Wiemann, J. M., and M. L. Knapp. "Turn-taking in Conversations." *Journal of Communication,* 1975, *25,* 75–92.

Wiener, M. Cited in Mehrabian, A. "Communication without Words." *Psychology Today,* September 1968, *2,* 53–55.

Williams, F. "The Psychological Correlates of Speech Characteristics: On Sounding 'Disadvantaged'." *Journal of Speech and Hearing Research,* 1970, *13,* 472–488.

Wood, Barbara S. *Children and Communication: Verbal and Nonverbal Development,* 2nd ed. Englewood Cliffs, N.J.: Prentice-Hall, 1981.

10

TASTE AND SMELL

When you come down to think about it, what change in the landscape occurs when you have made a place of your own. . . . How smells rush to you, the smell of mint—could it be from the brook? Impossible—the smell of leaves green, leaves dampened by dew, but of other leaves also, old leaves, last year's fallen leaves, that sweet, soft odor of death's decomposition. And then there is the muskiness. There is an animal somewhere.

ROBERT ARDREY, *THE TERRITORIAL IMPERATIVE*

*P*ierre fell in love with the beautiful Princess Hélène in an instant. She had been standing very close to him and had bent forward so that a small snuffbox could be passed behind her. Pierre became conscious of her scent and the warmth of her body. Intoxicated with her aroma, their eyes met. Suddenly he knew that Hélène not only could but must become his wife.

At an elegant ball, the Duke of Anjou accidentally wiped his face with the discarded chemise of a young noblewoman. The scent aroused him so much that he could not forget the woman. From that moment on he conceived the most violent passion for her.

After the long and weary days in the battlefield, the soldier would send a messenger with a note for his wife to let her know a few days in advance of his return. The note always read, ''Don't wash, I'll be home soon.''

Pierre and the Princess Hélène are characters in Tolstoy's classic novel *War and Peace*. The Duke of Anjou, according to the French historian Cloquet, lived during the sixteenth century. And the soldier was Napoleon Bonaparte, who sent his messages to his wife Josephine. These anecdotes, whether fictitious or real, illustrate the fact that the sense of smell has the power to move people from one emotional extreme to another. The sense of smell impacts on our emotional response to people, situations, and environments. The first part of this chapter will discuss the nonverbal significance of smell, the process of olfaction, and the measurement and classification of smells.

The area of taste, closely related to smell, also deserves attention as an important area of nonverbal communication. Despite the importance of taste and smell in our lives, especially in our enjoyment of food and wine, surprisingly little information is to be found about how these senses communicate information to ourselves and others.

The second part of this chapter will discuss the sense of taste, from the process of tasting to actual food preferences that you experience.

THE SENSE OF SMELL AND COMMUNICATION: AN OVERVIEW

Everyday we use our **sense of smell** to give us information about the world around us and to send out information about ourselves. As Winter (1976) states, ''We know that in society we can't have bad breath,

Gene Warne

"They say it was love at first sniff."

sweaty underarms, or noticeable genital odor. You can tell people they need a haircut or to wash their faces, but if you tell them they smell, you are really insulting" (p. 16).

Before going on, recall the context in which the word "smell" was used in the preceding paragraph. You probably have noticed several associations with the word. We know that if we "smell" good, we feel confident, and that if we have "bad breath," we feel uncomfortable and must find some means of ridding ourselves of that particular smell. We also use a sense of smell to detect **odors.** Perhaps at this point it would be helpful for our purposes to discriminate between each term in order to have a common understanding of their meanings. From this point on, the word **olfaction** will be used to mean the sense of smell or act of smelling. The smells, or odors, around us will refer in a general sense to **olfactory messages.** With this understanding of the terms, we can now raise the important question, "How are we affected by odors in the world around us?"

According to Bedichek (1960), we all have distinct body odors that are influenced by our chosen life-styles. In addition, these odors are altered by changes in mood, food, living habits, age, or by environmental odors (such as cigarette smoke), which are absorbed from the environment around us by our skin, hair, and clothing. Consider the numerous products such as after-shave lotion and perfume, which we intentionally apply for the sake of odor alteration. The use of perfume, for instance, is not a recent phenomenon. It traces back to the early periods of civilization when people worshipped their gods with the fragrance of incense. Perfume, it was rumored, played an important role in the romances of Cleopatra with Caesar and Anthony. In biblical times, the Queen of Sheba supposedly used perfumes to conquer Solomon. And Catherine de Médicis was said to have had a personal alchemist who mixed exclusive potions just for her. Our preoccupation with perfumes and scents reveals our intuitive knowledge that people react to the human communication of smells.

Russell (1976) has shown that people can reliably detect their own body odors when they are presented among sets of stimuli contributed by other people. In addition, when people are asked to rate the odors on a pleasantness/unpleasantness scale, they consistently relate unpleasant odors with socially undesirable characteristics such as ugliness, obesity, and bad health (reported in Coren, Porac, and Ward, 1979). However, Winter (1976) adds this observation: "Our ability to smell and how we ourselves smell vary with the time of day and, for women, with the time of month as well. Therefore, how we smell and how we smell somone else is strictly personal" (p. 17).

The Russell study also illustrates how odors affect our lives. Subjects in the study reliably discriminated between male and female odors and consistently described male odors as "musky" and female odors as "sweet." This sensitivity to odors begins early in life. Russell noted that two-week-old babies may reliably respond to their own mothers' breasts and not to those of a strange mother (Russell, 1976; cited in Coren, Porac, and Ward, 1979, p. 230).

Such studies have broad social implications. We know that the American preoccupation with the presence of odor is so strong that we spend billions of dollars each year to "freshen" our hair, mouths, armpits, and genital areas, as well as our laundry, kitchens, bathrooms, and carpets. As a result of this obsession with cleanliness and odorlessness, we have repressed our abilities to discriminate smells around us. At the beginning of this section, you will remember that we asked the question, "How are we affected by odors in the world around us?" In answer to the question, we first discussed how people react to human communication of smells in general. In the next section we will address the social implications of the human communication of smells across different cultures, and we will discuss how environmental smells and odors communicate certain messages.

Cultural Smells

In American culture we can illustrate a whole range of attitudes when referring to our noses. As Winter (1976) states, ''When we stick our noses into other people's business, we are interfering. When we stick our noses up in the air, we are snooty. If we thumb our noses at someone, we signify rejection. And, of course, if we rub our noses with someone, we demonstrate affection'' (p. 23). Indeed, the nose plays an important symbolic role in American culture. But this observation also holds for other cultures. Mohammedans, for example, have a ritual in which its people are advised to wash their noses with water each morning to expel the devils that are said to visit the body at night. Similarly, after death, the Eskimo must have their noses plugged up in order to prevent the soul from escaping and becoming restless.

The sense of smell also communicates affection in some cultures. Arabs, for example, are taught to breathe in each other's faces while

Smells good! But why is one odor perceived as pleasant and another unpleasant? Several factors, including association of ideas with some former experience, aesthetics, and spontaneous reaction play important parts in this phenomenon.

speaking; to do otherwise is to deny another one's breath and is considered to be a grave insult. It is also an Arabian custom for a man's relatives to smell a woman before they select her for his bride.

In addition, individuals in many cultures such as the Eskimo, Naori, Samoans, and Philippine Islanders rub noses or place their mouths and noses against the cheek of another person and inhale as a means of communication. Philippine lovers often exchange a piece of clothing on parting to remember each other by smell.

As you might suspect by now, the sense of smell *does* communicate. Yet our sense of smell communicates more than affection or cultural beliefs; it communicates to others racial, cultural, and family traits that help to identify us and to determine an entire range of acceptance and/or avoidance behaviors. The following table of cultural identifications shows how particular scents are associated with different cultures.

Location	Diet/odor
Central Europeans	cabbage, turnips, radishes
Indians	rice and spice
South Sea Islanders	fruit and palm
Americans	butter
Japanese	fish

Winter, 1976, p. 37

As you should note, body odor is associated with the foods we consume. Burton notes that "the odor of Eskimos is due to a diet of fish; Mediterannean people smell of garlic and onions and Northern Europeans have a cheesy, buttery smell. However, within these broad categories, there is much variation and people with a good sense of smell can identify individuals by odors alone, using true body odor and not tobacco, perfume, or other acquired odors" (Burton, p. 113).

In more specific categories, some people claim that they can identify the difference between blonds, redheads, and brunettes by means of their scent. One gentleman, who travels frequently by air, tells how he will often motion a stewardess over and say, "You're a blond, aren't you?" The stewardess is surprised because the man is blind and is also accurate about her being a blond. Her response is usually, "Why yes, I am a blond, but how did you know?" His answer is very simply, "You smell like a blond."

Although you may not have developed the capacity to "sniff out" cultural and subcultural information, your sense of smell is an important medium of communication. Interesting implications in the use of smell for diagnosing a patient's condition and for stimulating learning are also fascinating to study. The following two sections focus on these areas of interest in the study of olfaction.

Smell and the Field of Medicine

The idea of diagnosis by smell seems insane in this computerized and electronically coordinated age. Yet Dr. Thomas Cone, Jr., of the Harvard Medical School urged his fellow colleagues in 1975 to utilize their sense of smell as part of their physical examination process. He especially urged them to listen to the statements of mothers about peculiar odors of their infants, for a number of diseases reveal themselves first in the form of odors (Winter, 1976, p. 60). The notion of diagnosis by smell is not a new one. At one time, such diseases as yellow fever, scurvy, smallpox, typhoid, and diphtheria were diagnosed by smells alone. The following table of diseases and their associated odors reveals the strong correlation between smell and the physical condition of the body.

Disease	Odors
yellow fever	"butcher-shop" odor
scurvy	putrid odors
smallpox	putrid odors
typhoid fever	"freshly baked bread"
diphtheria	very sweet odor
plague	odor of apples

Winter, 1976, p. 59

Today, doctors still use their sense of smell to detect comas in patients brought into hospital emergency rooms. The doctor who smells alcohol or a poison such as cyanide can make a clear diagnosis. But if there is a sweet smell such as acetone, the doctor can deduce that the patient is probably in a diabetic coma. The use of odor detection in schizophrenic patients is perhaps the most intriguing aspect of emotional-odor detection (the odor is especially noticeable in rooms where insulin shock therapy is being administered.)

Smell and the Learning Process

As we have stated, the sense of smell aids in medical diagnosis. In addition, a link between odors and learning has also been established. In one study conducted at the Research Center for Mental Health at New York University, students were given a list of words to learn, some of which were accompanied by odors—and some of which were not. Researchers found that when words and smells were presented together and were related (for example, cheese and the odor of cheese), students retained word lists of substantial length for indefinite amounts of time (Winter, 1976, p. 124).

Because of such research, odors and smells have been used commercially to aid in student learning. For instance, both the Braille Institute of America and the Perkins School for the Blind have adopted scratch-and-sniff labels for books written in braille. Deaf and mute students have also used these learning tools. Smells not only aid in word association, but they also act as rewards (especially the smell of chocolate cake!).

Unlike animals who use their senses of smell for defense, sexual stimulation, and survival, we have made little use of our sense of smell. In general, we are conscious of smells only when they have invaded our personal space and make themselves known as either pleasant or unpleasant (Burton, 1976). We have become reliant upon our other senses such as hearing and seeing, despite the fact that our predecessors used their sense of smell as an aid to the other senses, for example, to find food. As Burton has observed,

> The most important reason for our lack of appreciation of odours is probably that our noses are in the wrong place. The evolution of an upright posture has taken our noses away from the source of many odours. Mice, cats, and dogs walk with their noses near the ground and one can only enter their world by descending to hands and knees, as will be appreciated by a gardener grubbing weeds or a naturalist searching for specimens among the grass stems. (Burton, 1976, p. 109)

However, our sense of smell has not been entirely lost. For example, perfumers have exceptional abilities to distinguish up to 10,000 smells; they can also readily identify half of the 2,000 ingredients they have at their disposal (Burton, 1976, p. 108). These individuals have the ability to "step up" their sensory abilities in olfaction and to use them to affect the lives of others. Moreover, recent research has shown that we are making better use of our sense of smell and that we are beginning to realize that smells affect our behavior. Think about the following questions for a moment. How are we being affected by the odors around us? Do our noses actually send and receive information that alters our behavior? How do our Lysol-disinfected existences differ from those of other cultures? These are some of the issues with which olfaction research deals and as such are the subjects of discussion in the following pages.

Environmental Olfactory Communication

As you begin this section, think back to the last time you walked into a hospital. How did you feel? Do you remember feeling nervous and contracting a case of sweaty palms as you breathed in the smell of ether? Now think of the delicious smells of popcorn you inhaled the last time you walked past a theater. Did the smell of popcorn invite you inside? Perhaps you were flooded with brilliant memories of earlier days when, as a child, you went to the Saturday matinee.

Smells in the environment do communicate. They communicate positive messages, like the popcorn at the cinema, as well as negative messages. An example of the communication of a negative, or warning, message might be the smell of "gas" emitted when a tank of propane is almost empty. Interestingly enough, it is not the actual gas that we are smelling, but an additive, ethyl mercaptan. This additive enables humans to detect the smells of natural gas in order to alert them to its presence.

The addition of this odor to a harmful product is only one example of how odors can be used to communicate in the environment. Because of their chemical composition, many substances can transmit messages of potential harm to the consumer. Cain (1977) points out that people easily recognize odors from memory. In fact, even through time, sensory recognition is extremely stable.

For some people, an attractive display and the aroma of freshly baked donuts is a hard message to resist.

Based on this discussion and the experiences that you have had in the past, you can see that the environment continually communicates olfactory messages. As Wilentz (1968) concludes, "There are many smells to which we, as olfactory receivers, adapt and respond. There are school smells and army smells, laboratory smells and church smells, as well as travel smells such as the clover you smell as you ride the highways. . ., the sage smell of the far West. . ., and briny smells of seaports everywhere" (p. 111). Overall, however, Americans usually believe that their environments should remain odorless. Odors that act as warning agents and those scents generated by perfumes and foods are basically the only exceptions. Americans are constantly attempting to manipulate their olfactory environments.

Having discussed the human and environmental olfactory messages we receive, let's now turn to an examination of how the olfactory process works.

OLFACTION: PROCESS AND PHENOMENA

As you read through the preceding pages, you may have wondered about how the nose actually "knows" when a message has been transmitted. The following section will help describe the *process* of olfaction.

In the olfactory process, the act of smelling begins with an object that emits the odor, smell, or scent. The actual "smell" consists of molecules of volatile (in other words, gaseous) substances that are carried in the air to the olfactory apparatus. This sensitive region in the nose that receives the stimuli is an area of several hundred square millimeters located on the upper surfaces of the nasal cavity. This area is approximately the size of two postage stamps and contains densely packed sense cells.

The brain ultimately receives and interprets the olfactory sensations. Winter (1976) summarizes the entire process in this way:

> When you smell an after-shave lotion or the perfume someone is wearing, you smell the molecules of the scent which have drifted to your nose. The odor molecules are inhaled with the air and dissolved on the wet film of mucus in your nose, and information about the molecules is relayed by sensory cells high in each nasal passage to the olfactory bulb where it is sent along tracts. . . to the brain. You then realize within a thousandth of a second that the person is wearing a particular scent. (p. 154)

Winter informs us that when a smell or scent is pleasurable, "there is a relaxation of the facial muscles, smiling, a pleasant tone of voice, laughing, nodding, opening of the mouth, and deeper respiration"

(p. 154). Conversely, when a smell or odor is unpleasant, there is "a turning away of the head and sometimes of the entire body. The head may be jerked back, the nose wrinkled, and the upper lip raised. The individual speaks with disgust and makes characteristic sounds such as 'ugh' or 'phew.' There may be coughing, compression of the lips, rubbing of the nose, frowning, putting the hand over the mouth, actual spitting, and a waving away of the source of the smell" (p. 154).

Although our sense of smell may not measure up to that of many species of animals, our noses are still extraordinarily sensitive. Our noses also exhibit some common olfactory phenomena, which will be discussed in the next section.

Olfactic Phenomena: Smell Blindness, Smell Adaptation, and Smell Memory

Some people are insensitive to differences in smells, much the same as a color-blind person fails to distinguish between colors. They simply cannot detect certain smells. This phenomenon is called **smell blindness.** Smell blindness, or even variations in sensitivity to certain olfactory messages, is related to the anatomy of the nose. As Burton (1976) states, "In some people the shape of the nasal passage hinders the passage of odorladen air into the nasal clefts" (p. 109). Thus some people may be unaware of certain smells unless they inhale (or sniff) very deeply.

Another phenomenon associated with olfaction is called **smell adaptation.** Smell adaptation occurs every time you walk into a bakery and try to retain the ability to smell freshly cooked bread. Simply stated, when an odor (here meaning any olfactory message) acts as a stimulus, that odor may have an effect on the perception of subsequent stimulations by the same or other odors. In other words, when the same odor follows itself, or when one odor follows another, the second stimulation may be perceived as less intense than the first stimulation. This effect is termed smell adaptation.

Most likely you have experienced smell adaptation on a daily basis. This phenomenon occurs frequently and acts as both a blessing and a curse. Although we would like to be able to enjoy continually the smell of the fresh bread in the bakery or to savor the aroma of an excellent wine for long periods, our ability to adapt to smells will not permit us to enjoy the odor for a long period of time. However, on the positive side, smell adaptation allows us to become less offended by unpleasant odors that we may be exposed to for a long time.

Before you read any further, imagine for a moment the smells you associate with the following environments. If you can, write down a few of these associations:

A bowling alley   _____

A drugstore   _____

A small restaurant   _____

A dentist's office   _____

A spring morning   _____

Christmas   _____

Memories can be instantly recalled if you smell a familiar odor from your childhood: the shampoo your mother used, your father's shaving lotion, your high school locker room, or your classroom. But why does the phenomenon of **smell memory** occur? How can an odor or scent set off a flood of memories?

One explanation of why "odor" or "smell" memory (the two are usually interchangeable) can create such spontaneous recall is that smells are associated with significant emotional experiences in one's personal life. In fact, smells generally have no names of their own but are associated with the names of other things. For example, think of the last time you described a scent or odor without having said it smells like _____." Can you describe some smell now without making a comparison using "like"? Try it.

Engen and Ross (1973) conducted three experiments that reflect the unique quality of smell memory. Overall, they concluded the following:

> Unlike visual and auditory memories, immediate recognition tests for 20 or more odorants produced numerous errors, but there was little further retention loss for periods up to 3 months. . . (and) long term retention held up even when there were no instructions to memorize. (p. 221)

In others words, smell memory seems less influenced by time passage than are auditory and visual memories.*

Other researchers have noted a similar phenomenon that may be associated with smell memory. This phenomenon resembles the "tip-of-the-tongue" phenomenon, in which people are unable to provide a label for a taste experience. In this situation, however, an individual is exposed to a very familiar smell without receiving cues from the other senses. The results of such events suggest that verbal recall of smells is difficult, although olfaction has an excellent recognition memory. As Nebakov summarizes:

> As we know, memory can restore to life everything except smells, although nothing revives the past so completely as a smell that was once associated with it. (Nebakov, 1970, in Engen and Ross, p. 226)

---

* For one of the three experiments, however, the maximum interval in the experiment was only thirty seconds and may have been too short to provide a test of what is meant by odor memory in the literature (Montcrieff, 1970, in Engen and Ross, p. 221).

So far in this chapter we have discussed several aspects of olfaction, including its definition and several phenomena with which it is associated. The next section will be devoted to measurement and classification of odors.

OLFACTION: MEASUREMENT AND CLASSIFICATION

What are some of the ways in which you perceive smells in the environment? Although the answer to this question may appear obvious (just inhale. . .), it is not so simple for researchers who investigate olfaction. One of the basic problems faced by olfaction researchers is inaccessibility to the sensory apparatus that produces the smells being studied. Thus it becomes a difficult task to construct reliable techniques for presenting stimuli to subjects. In everyday life we "sniff" in order to perceive smells. This procedure is also used in the laboratory, but not without some complexity. Usually, there are two methods by which a subject may receive accurate and measurable quantities of odorous materials. The first is through the use of an **olfactometer,** which uses the "sniff" method, and the second is through the **blast-injection method.**

The olfactometer is an instrument that was first proposed and designed by Zwaardemaker, an early researcher in the field of olfaction. Mueller (1965) describes its present structure as consisting of

> a pair of concentric tubes, one of which slides inside the other much like the arm of a slide trombone. The inner surface of the outer tube is coated with the odorous material so that if we slide one of these tubes with respect to the other we change the amount of the surface of the odorous material over which air travels. One end of the inner tube is led to the nostril, so that a sniff will cause air to pass over the material on its way to the nasal cavity. (p. 73)

Although many researchers have noted that this method is crude, results can be reliably obtained when the following variables are controlled: temperature, humidity, purity of the air, and purity of the odorous materials used. With these controls, the olfactometer may be used quite accurately.

The blast-injection method attempts to eliminate some of the uncertainties of the "sniff" method. With this method the experimenter can control the volume of gas, the pressure with which the gas is applied, and the duration of the exposure. Subjects are instructed to hold their breath until the stimulus is administered. At that time they inhale passively, much the same as in normal breathing.

Although the two types of measurements differ in methodology, research has shown that these differences do not generally result in marked changes of sensitivity results. Only differences in experimental procedures lead to large differences in statements about olfactory sensitivity. Thus rigid controls should be placed on procedures in olfactory research.

Classifications of Smells

How many different smells can you name? Quickly jot down a list. How many did you think of? Four? Six? Sixty? Perhaps you can see a problem that many olfaction researchers have confronted. As you might suspect, many of the early classifications were destined to have inherent problems due to a severe lack of data. One of the earliest classifications was suggested by the botanist Linnaeus, to whom we are indebted for the early classification of the plant kingdom. He listed seven primary smell stimuli: aromatic, fragrant, ambrosial, alliaceous, hircine, foul, and nauseous.

Gene Warne

'' . . . this is our superpowered cologne
guaranteed to kill your body odor and any living
creature that comes within ten feet of you.''

Another scheme, and the one to which we most frequently refer, was proposed by Henning. This classification offered the following six-way scheme: spicy, fragrant, putrid, ethereal, resinous, and burned. A third, and more succinct, classification of smells was presented by Crocker and Henderson. They classified smells as fragrant, acid, burned, and coprylic. The three classifications reflect a difference of opinion. Although many of the descriptions might be said to overlap, only "fragrant" smells are included in all three classification systems.

Certainly the differences among the three classifications reflect the amount of organization needed for existing olfactory data, as well as the amount of research still needed. Until more data can be collected, controlled research in olfactics will be difficult.

In the previous section we discussed some of the aspects of the process of olfaction. At this point, we return to the study of olfactory messages as they relate to communication. In the next two sections, we shall discuss olfaction and its effects on fear and sex drives and olfaction and its impact on the perfume industry.

Olfaction and the Drive States

As Cain (1977) notes, "If man does not communicate via chemical secretion, he is an exception to a very general rule. Other primates employ odourous secretions to mark territory, assert dominance, repel rivals, and attract mates. Perhaps the human primate's ability to verbalize his feelings reduced the need to communicate via olfaction" (p. 297). Yet human beings have inherited the necessary characteristics for transmitting meaningful chemical messages. For example, it is our external secretions that allow dogs to distinguish one person from another or to attack. Moreover, cowboys are said to believe that an odor of fear can be detected on humans by horses and often excites them beyond manageability (Bedichek, 1960, p. 142). Some *people* believe that they can detect fear in others through smell. Witch-doctors, for example, are said to have the ability to detect the guilt of suspects. The literature reports that in order to determine the guilt of a person, the witch-doctor lines up all suspects and begins a series of "divinations," which include "sniffing." Provided that the guilty person believes in the "magic," he or she will be frightened—thereby giving away guilt even though remaining outwardly controlled (Burton, 1976, pp. 109–110). There is, however, no tangible proof that aggression, fear, or friendship can be conveyed by odorants.

Before continuing this discussion of olfaction and the drive states, a definition of the term **pheromone** is necessary. The word "pheromone" was coined in 1959 from the Greek *pherein*, meaning "to carry," and *horman*, meaning "to excite" or "to stimulate." Pheromones, unlike hormones, are substances secreted externally that exert a specific effect at a distance on the behavior of another of the same species.

Although there is little evidence supporting the transmission of the message of fear, data do indicate that smells (in this case called pheromones) act as messengers in sexual relationships. The scientists who are studying these pheromones include physicists, biochemists, sociologists, entomologists, sex therapists, physicians, psychologists, and economists.

The effects of pheromones are more easily seen in the mating habits of animals rather than humans. However, in the late 1800s a phenomenon called the French Boarding House Syndrome was reported in medical literature. The case involved girls who were living in a boarding house and who were isolated from males. Results of the report showed that these girls entered puberty later than girls who were exposed to males, even when those "exposed" had had no personal contact with the males. Researchers noted that proximity with males somehow affected the female hormones.

Another study of human pheromones was well documented and reported in a leading scientific journal. This study involved female students living in an American college dormitory. Research showed that the menstrual cycles of close friends became synchronized over time. This effect was said to have resulted solely from time spent together— not from patterns of eating or sleeping, nor from verbal communication. The only conclusion was that some silent communication had taken place. In other words, "since the menstrual cycle is controlled by hormones, there could have been a hormone-linked production of a pheromone, as is known to occur in some mammals" (Burton, 1976, pp. 113–114).

In addition, the study showed that when males were present, the length of the menstrual cycles varied. The general rule seems to be that as exposure to males increased, the average length of female menstrual cycles decreased. Unfortunately, "exposure" to males was not clearly defined but was *suggested* to be no more than physical presence. If "exposure" had included physical personal relationships, there would have been a greater possibility of pheromonal stimulation.

Is there really such a thing as "love at first sniff"? According to a recent study, men preferred the smell of women in the middle of their cycles to that of women who were menstruating. The most popular scent was that of the pregnant woman. Are pheromones responsible? No one knows for sure, but an interesting fact is that the female pheromone level is at its highest level during pregnancy (Von Driska, 1978, p. 69).

Another interesting pheromonal finding has been discovered by a British research team at the University of Warwick. These researchers have announced that they have isolated a steroid in the sweat of males.

When purified, this substance smells like sandalwood oil, which is often used as an ingredient in perfumes. But that's not all. Help is on the way for men who have grown weary of Brut, English Leather, and Old Spice. These researchers claim that the steroid is a male sex pheromone, which has a scent that attracts females. Equivalent pheromones emitted by some female insects, for instance, draw males from miles around. The researchers do not claim, however, that the scent will produce wild results that will revolutionize the laws of attraction. Rather, one scientist unimaginatively notes that the isolated steroid, when refined, creates an immediate empathy between people, even strangers ("Eau de Sweat," *Time*, 1980, 50). At least it's a beginning.

Although there is some documentation of the presence of pheromones in humans and also of their communicative abilities, it is still questionable whether or not males actually secrete pheromones that stimulate females. The only "evidence" of a male sex-pheromone in humans is recounted as follows:

> A young man was reputed to have great success with girls. After a dance, he would wipe the perspiring brow of his partner with a handkerchief that had been carried in his armpit. Apparently his body odor acted as an aphrodisiac, and the young man claimed that his technique was highly successful. (Burton, 1976, p. 113)

Unfortunately, no attempt has been made to substantiate this technique.

Although research has not verified the existence of male sex pheromones, one cannot overlook the extraordinary interest that humans have taken in animal scents and fragrances. Since ancient times we have borrowed animal sexual-scent products such as musk, civet, and castor. Could this interest in "animal sexual scents" say something in support of the existence of the pheromone? Burton implies that this is the case when he reviews the relationship between musky smells, to which females are sensitive, and testosterone, a male hormone (pp. 111–112). The question, however, remains unanswered. We only know that human beings are extremely interested in fragrance—the essence of the perfume industry.

Olfaction and the Perfume Industry

According to British fragrance researcher Juanita Byrne Quinn, one of the world's leading marketing experts,

> fragrance not only has a function of its own, it also is a medium for a message. The messages may be directed to the user about the product or they may be in the product to inform other persons about the user's personality or self-image. (quoted in Winter, 1976, p. 108)

In other words, fragrances are designed to convey messages. Their purpose is *communication*.

Suppose a female college student wants to be considered attractive by male college students. Should she wear perfume to communicate her message? The answer is yes and no. It depends on how she is dressed. Perfume is seen as a come-on when a woman wears it with jeans and a sweatshirt, but not when she wears it with a skirt, blouse, and stockings, according to ninety-four male undergraduates at Purdue University.

In the experiment, a female confederate sat next to a male subject and answered five basic questions such as, "What are your favorite hobbies?" The confederate gave the same standard answers each time, but with half the men she dressed up (blouse, skirt, and stockings); with the other, she wore a sweatshirt and jeans. Half the time, in each outfit, she wore two drops of Jungle Gardenia perfume behind each ear.

Male subjects completed a "First Impressions Form" describing how much they liked the woman and how attractive they found her on a scale from one to seven and rating her on twenty specific traits such as conceited, unconceited; romantic, unromantic; cold, warm; energetic, lazy.

Surprisingly the woman's likability and attractiveness were high when she dressed down and wore perfume and low when she dressed up and wore perfume. Researcher Robert Baron concluded that the combination of formal dress and perfume made the woman seem cold, conceited, and unattainable. One student commented: "I figured that she was all dolled up that way for someone special; there was no chance for me." The experiment shows that perfume and attraction go together in somewhat complicated ways (Horn, 1980, p. 16).

Perfume: a mini-history.   According to Winter, the word "perfume" literally means "through smoke." Primitive people discovered that by burning certain woods and resins they could mask the smells of bloody temple sacrifices. Eventually, the Asian countries taught the Greeks the art of perfumery. In fact, Hippocrates, the famous Greek physician, was known to have prescribed scented baths and massages as well as perfumes for treatment of certain diseases.

Today, the truly talented perfumers in the industry are known as "noses." There are only about twenty such people in the world who are considered great. These individuals push their olfactory abilities to a maximum. Indeed, "noses" are said to have the power not only to distinguish between "orange" and "tangerine" but to detect their respective presences in a mix of a hundred or more scents (Winter, 1976, p. 112).

As you can see, the perfume industry has a long history, beginning with primitive times. However, in relating its history, we have not yet mentioned *why* fragrances have been used, especially in the Western world. The original reason for adding fragrance to such items as soaps, shampoos, detergents, and plastics was to cover the odors inherent in the materials. Then in 1966 Proctor and Gamble set the precedent of adding a fragrance to give consumers the idea of a cleanser's "natural, grease-cutting ability." The product? Joy dishwashing detergent! And the idea caught on.

Since then, the use of fragrance in household products has increased greater than fifteen percent annually (Winter, 1976, p. 106). Today, more than $500 million per year is spent to make products smell good. In fact, marketing experts say that it is more important for a product to smell good than to do its task well.

Thus smells do seem to communicate messages—messages about the environment and about others around us. However, smells are not the only messages that the nose allows us to receive. Our noses allow us to receive messages concerning the foods and liquids that we daily consume. The following section will focus precisely on this issue—the sense of taste and its relation to the sense of smell.

THE SENSE OF TASTE AND COMMUNICATION: AN OVERVIEW

Recall the last time you had a cold or the flu. Did food taste different from the way it tasted when you were healthy? Were there some foods that you couldn't taste at all? The answer to these questions is probably yes! Without the use of our sense of smell, food generally tastes like nothing at all. Unassisted, the sense of taste is able to detect sourness, sweetness, bitterness, and saltiness. It fails utterly to encompass the full flavors of meats, fruits, butter, and coffee. These and nearly all other foods depend for their appreciation mainly on the sense of smell.

Identifying flavor involves many different sensations. Our mouths become the perceiving organs, and the substance that acts as a stimulant is generally edible, drinkable, or smokable. However, it is smell that is primarily responsible for creating flavor. Taste takes on an important secondary role. Having acknowledged, then, the debt that taste owes to olfaction, we turn to the sense of taste as a medium of communication.

Every time we place a substance in our mouths, our sense of taste communicates. Much like the sense of smell, the **sense of taste** acts as a medium that carries messages of pleasure as well as warning to the brain. Think, for example, of bitter foods that you have sampled. Did you immediately enjoy them? Milne and Milne (1962) say probably not. We have long associated bitter flavors with poison, and only through experience do we come to enjoy bitter taste qualities.

Yet bitter qualities make up only one type of message that may be communicated to the brain. Taste is the final arbiter of all that is admitted to our bodies (Milne and Milne, 1962, p. 137). In other words, taste has the ability both to influence and reflect our own physical needs, food preferences, and cultural attitudes toward food preferences.

But what is a sense of taste? How can it "communicate"? To these questions we offer the following sections dealing with a definition and classification of taste.

Taste: A Definition

According to Wilentz (1968), the word "taste" appears to have been taken from the Latin verb "taxare," meaning "to touch sharply," and an intensive form of the Latin verb "tangere," meaning "to touch" or "to appraise." As an added interest, the noun "taste" in Italian means a "trial" or "touch" (Wilentz, 1968, p. 132). Thus taste becomes a "testing of the environment in an intense and intimate way (Wilentz, p. 132). . ." and one that implies both attention and coordinated activity (Wilentz, p. 131).

Classification of Taste Qualities

Unlike the classification of smells, flavors or qualities of taste have evolved into a more formalized classification scheme: the bitter, salty, sweet, and sour taste scheme with which we are familiar. These four, however, have not always been the ones on which classifications have been based. The history of taste is said to date back to the Greek physician Alcameon, who lived during the middle of the sixth century B.C. However, it was not he, but Aristotle, who was said to have first listed the basic tastes. These taste qualities included the categories of sweet, bitter, sour, salty, astringent, pungent, and harsh. By the end of the sixteenth century these seven had changed to the following nine: sweet, sour, sharp, pungent, harsh, fatty, bitter, insipid, and salty. By the end of the eighteenth century, there were additional alterations. If you followed Linnaeus, there were eleven; if you believed Haller to be the authority, there were twelve. Both of their lists were based on the previous sixteenth-century list, but with various changes. Linnaeus dropped pungent and harsh and added astringent, viscous, aqueous, and nauseous. Haller dropped fatty only and added spirituous, aromatic, urinous, and putrid (Geldard, 1972, pp. 504–505).

Finally, in 1927 Hans Henning formalized the present classification of tastes: sweet, salty, sour, and bitter. It is interesting to note that these four had always been present in the classifications. It took the evolutionary process, however, to rule out the ones that did not utilize the sense of taste alone but that used fusion of taste and touch.

The processes and phenomena with which taste is associated will be discussed next. We hope that through this discussion you will be better able to understand exactly how taste communicates certain messages.

TASTE: PROCESS AND PHENOMENA

As with the sense of smell, there are basic processes and phenomena associated with the sense of taste. Indeed, taste is "a chemical touch system—it depends on physical contact with the object that is to be chemically appreciated" (Livingston, 1978, p. 56). Because of the nature of this process, substances that are to be tasted must be soluble in water. Although a taste stimulus initially may take the form of solids, liquids, gases, or vapors, it must go into solution upon contact with saliva (Geldard, 1972, p. 480).

But what happens when the stimuli reach the receptor sites? Is a particular taste quality communicated only with the use of our tongues? These questions and others will be answered next in the discussion of the receptor mechanisms of taste.

Where Do We Taste?

As early as 1750, the belief that the tongue alone was the center of taste was challenged by studies conducted on people without tongues. LeCat, in "A Physical Essay on the Senses" (1750), describes two cases in which children without tongues were able to taste. The first child had been born without a tongue; the second had lost his tongue when gangrene (caused by smallpox) swept through his body. And yet both retained the ability to taste (in Carterette and Friedman, 1978, p. 6).

And so it is that the tongue is not the only site at which stimulation takes place. We respond to taste stimuli in various regions of the mouth. These regions include the palate, the pharynx, the tonsils and epiglottis, the tongue, and in some people, the mucosa of the lips and cheeks, the underside of the tongue, and the floor of the mouth. Children have additional areas of sensitivity to taste stimuli, but with maturity they eventually lose these extra areas.

The tongue: taste buds and sensitivity. Because of the easy accessibility, much taste research has been conducted in the tongue region of the mouth. The tongue consists of taste buds, which are tiny clusters of taste cells that are distributed fairly equally over the tongue. These cells generally measure about 1/360 of an inch; taste nerve endings are "wired into" each tastebud and stimulate many of the taste cells in each cluster. Therefore, "there is interaction between individual taste cells and between taste buds (Livingston, 1978, p. 56.) However, the majority of taste buds group into aggregates that form **papillae,** or the tiny "bumps" you can see on your tongue if you stick your tongue out in front of a mirror.

As you might suspect, taste cells have a relatively short life span—only a few days. This forces the composition of the taste bud into a perpetual state of change, "with some immature cells (around the outside) and some mature cells (near the inside) and some dying cells always present" (Beidler and Smallman, 1965; cited in Coren, Porac, and Ward, 1979, p. 118). No one understands this particular phenomenon,

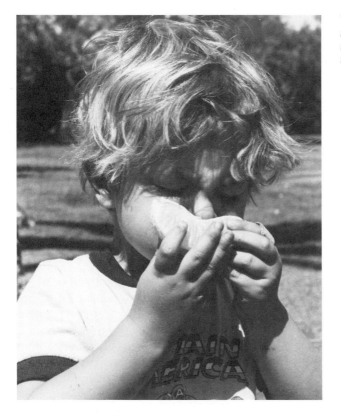

There is nothing more enjoyable than really "getting into" the taste pleasures, as this little boy is experiencing.

but researchers believe that responses to certain stimuli in the mouth may damage the tiny taste cells.

The final level within the taste bud that a stimulus must reach and the place at which the actual stimulation takes place is called the **receptor site.** It is contended that these sites involve the larger molecules on the cell membrane. However, because of the structure of and various locations of these molecules on a given taste cell membrane, there may be many different "sites" per taste cell.

Although taste buds and papillae are distributed relatively equally over the tongue, they do not respond equally to a given stimulus. At one time it was believed that the back of the tongue was more susceptible to bitter taste and that the front and sides were more sensitive to sweet and salty tastes. Researchers have recently found, however, that it is the front of the mouth and especially the palate that have the lowest thresholds for bitterness. Conversely, it is the tip and the back of the tongue that are most sensitive to sweet tastes and the front and sides that are most sensitive to salt (Coren, Porac, and Ward, 1979, p. 222).

As stated earlier, taste buds and taste cells change as we grow older. As children, we have tastebuds "studding the hard palate, soft palate, walls of the throat and the central upper surface of the tongue as well as other regions of sensitivity which adults have" (Milne and Milne, 1962, p. 137). As we grow older, we lose these regions of sensitivity little by little. In an experiment conducted with twenty-seven college students (eighteen to twenty-two) and twenty-nine elderly subjects (sixty-seven to ninety-three), Schiffman found that college students correctly identified food stimuli (e.g., apples, bananas, pears, carrots, corn, potatoes, beef, and pork) more frequently than the elderly subjects (Schiffman, 1977, p. 590). As evidence shows, there is a considerable loss of food recognition and accuracy as one grows into maturity and finally into old age. However, in addition to disintegration of taste sensitivity, there are other phenomena associated with the sense of taste. These include taste blindness and taste adaptation, both of which we shall discuss in the next section.

Taste Blindness and Taste Adaptation

Don't ever take your taste buds for granted. Every year one to two million Americans lose their ability to enjoy eating, according to Dr. Robert I. Henkin of Georgetown University's Taste and Smell Clinic. Many common illnesses, accidents, and experiences can cause impairment of taste and smell perceptions. In fact, an estimated thirty to fifty percent of all expectant mothers temporarily suffer these problems during the first three months of pregnancy (Sobel, 1978, p. 269).

Blindness and adaptation are two phenomena associated with most senses, including the sense of taste. Think for a moment. Are there certain foods that either you or someone you know is unable to taste? When was the last time you had to resalt your food in order to retain the same level of saltiness that you encountered when you began to eat that particular dish?

Taste blindness is the inability to taste a substance that has an ordinary concentration. The common expression ''that smells so good I can practically taste it'' attests to the fact that the senses of taste and smell are linked very closely together. Often, an abnormality in one sense occurs simultaneously in the other. The area of taste blindness can be viewed in very specific terms. A person's sense of taste can be completely absent, diminished, distorted, or perverted. Total loss of taste is referred to as ageusia; a diminished sense of taste is called hypogeusia; a distorted sense of taste is called dysgeusia; and a perverted sense of taste is called cacogeusia. A person suffering from cacogeusia, for example, might experience pleasant-tasting food as foul or obnoxious. The best meats may suddenly taste rotten, omelets may feel like sawdust on the tongue, and even favorite foods may seem to smell like garbage. One writer relates, ''While the loss of the ability to taste or smell is unpleasant, the distortion or perversion of the senses can be downright frightening'' (Scott, 1977, p. 8).

In one experiment, Hall, Bartoshuk, Cain, and Stevens (cited in Coren, Porac, and Ward, 1979) studied taste blindness and the effects of caffeine, or PTC. They found that bitterness in caffeine was barely perceived by one group while a second group could perceive no ''bitter taste,'' even with the caffeine at the same levels of concentration (pp. 223–224).*

A second phenomenon that is associated with taste, as well as with other senses such as hearing and olfaction, is adaptation. Every time you resalt your food at the dinner table, you are displaying ''symptoms'' of **taste adaptation.** In other words, as you eat salty foods, your threshold or sensitivity to salt decreases. In order to retain that level of sensitivity you must add more salt. One way to avoid taste adaptation is simply to eat something else between bites of salty food. Recovery time is only about ten seconds; no matter what amounts of salt you have eaten, you regain your ability to taste salt at lower concentrations.

---

* At this point we want to qualify the use of the term ''blindness'' when speaking of the sense of taste. Unlike visual blindness, people who are taste-blind may actually taste the substance—if the concentration of caffeine (PTC) is increased enough. Visual blindness, on the other hand, is perpetual; no amount of light entering the iris will allow a blind person to see (Coren, Porac, and Ward, p. 223). Nevertheless taste blindness is a phenomena which is considered to be a form of sense blindness.

One of the most interesting effects of the relationship between taste and communication is the phenomenon of **food preferences,** or why we as individuals choose to like or dislike the many different foods that are available. In the next few sections, you will learn some interesting facts about why we have sweet tooths, why we choose certain foods, and why we crave interesting and novel foods at certain times in our lives. It is taste that communicates such messages and that makes us aware of our wants and needs.

The "Sweet Tooth"

Humans turn to foods that are both novel and beneficial when they are experiencing a physiological deficiency. Is this also what happens when we find ourselves experiencing a "sweet tooth"? Researchers say yes. However, when we crave that Hershey bar or chocolate fudge cake, it is **food deprivation** and a need for calories that is responsible. When we experience calorie deprivation, our preference threshold has been lowered and our intake of sugar solution is enhanced (Campbell, 1958; cited in Carterette and Friedman, 1979, p. 110). To be more specific, drag out those brownies!

Food Preferences: What Makes Food Taste Good?

According to research conducted in the field of taste preferences, several factors influence whether we like or dislike certain foods. Although cultural and ethnic backgrounds do influence one's food preferences, several evaluative criteria are applied when decisions of food preference are made. These include expectations, personality, color, textures, and frequency of ingestion.

Food preferences and expectations. How many times have you tasted what you *thought* was Pepsi, but what unexpectedly turned out to be Dr. Pepper or Tab? Were you surprised? Provided you like all three, did the Dr. Pepper or Tab taste as good as they normally would? Some researchers say probably not; our individual expectations do influence whether the taste experience will be pleasant, neutral, or unpleasant. In fact, researchers relate the following observation:

> Classic physics suggests that, by itself, a sweet solution should be found pleasant, and a bitter solution clearly unpleasant (at moderate to high bitterness levels). However, in actual behavior, if (an) individual expects to drink a dry wine, but is served a sweet wine instead, the individual may find the sweet wine to be unacceptable. Bitter-tasting drinks often are preferred to sweet mixed drinks in spite of the fact that bitter solutions are less pleasant than sweet ones. (In Carterette and Friedman, 1978, p. 177)

Expectation has to do with whether you find a taste experience pleasurable or unpleasurable. Your experience also influences food preferences and should not be overlooked.

Food preferences and personality. Another interesting area in food-preference research focuses on food preference and individual personalities. For example, does your preference for certain types of food reveal something about your personality? Research has shown that people who are "sensation seekers" may substitute their taste sensations to avoid boredom. These people prefer chewy foods to soft, spicy foods to bland, and bitter foods to sweet. Other people may seek love and security from their foods. Benjamin Belden, Ph.D., Head of the Chicago Center for Behavior Modification, found in his clinical practice that "obese people prefer mushy foods. Eating a lot can also be a substitute for aggression. You take another bite of chewy or crunchy food, instead of turning and biting what's bothering you" ("Personality and Taste," *Self*, 1980, 22).

Taking an interest in personality and food preferences, the United States Department of Defense also conducted a study of the food preferences of soldiers. The purpose was to establish whether or not there was a relationship between diet and personality traits. The members of the test group were encouraged to select whatever they wanted to eat from a group of 150 foods. Their behavior was studied over a one-month period, and the results showed some fascinating correlations between the foods the experimental subjects preferred and their personality types ("Personality and Taste," *Self*, 1980, 22). Some of the reported findings were as follows:

- Meat eaters were enthusiastic, liked action, and enjoyed selling themselves, ideas, and products.
- Those who preferred fish, fruits, and vegetables for their meals tended to prefer books, music, and art in their recreation hours.
- Those who preferred starchy foods such as rice, mashed potatoes, and spaghetti, were rather complacent and tended to avoid making hard decisions or judgments.
- Those who preferred eating salads were fast-moving types.
- Those who liked desserts above all were excellent officer-types. The study showed that dessert-eaters usually liked to dominate any situation.

You can conduct your own experiment with regard to food preferences and your personality. Observe your preferences for certain types of food when you are active, unhappy, excited, bored, and any other emotional state you experience. When do you like soft foods, salty foods, starchy foods, crunchy foods? The relation of food preferences to personality type raises many important but unanswered questions. In the meantime, you may have to answer these questions based on your own experiences.

Food preferences and color.   How would you feel if you were offered green mashed potatoes? What about an orange filet mignon? Every day, color influences whether we choose to eat certain foods. Not only do we determine whether a food has spoiled by its color, we also use color to tell us whether a food has been cooked as necessary or as desired. Color also determines whether we like or dislike certain foods. For example, Moir (1936) conducted two separate studies concerned with the color of foods. In the first study, he prepared jellies having specific flavors, but he colored them inappropriately (for example, grape jelly might be colored red). When observers were asked to identify the flavors, often they were incorrect, even when they tasted and smelled the jellies (Moir, 1936; cited in Carterette and Friedman, pp. 162–163).

Moir also conducted a second study dealing with color and perception. In this study he prepared a buffet of foods for a dinner with scientific colleagues of the Flavor Group of the Society of Chemistry and Industry in London. As you might suspect, many of the foods were colored inappropriately (for example, mashed potatoes might indeed be green!). Interestingly enough, not only did many people complain about the flavor of the dishes, some also reported feeling sick, even though only the colors of the foods were altered. The foods were perfectly wholesome and had smells, tastes, and textures intact (cited in Carterette and Friedman, p. 163).

Color can affect our perceptions of and preferences for food. Yet there is another evaluative criterion that we apply when determining the foods we will eat—that of texture.

Food preferences and texture.   Recently, in talking with a friend about serving a Jell-o salad as part of a meal to some guests who were coming for dinner, a friend of ours made a face and said that she detested Jell-o. Her reasoning was based on its texture; it simply "didn't go down well." In fact, many of us do decide which foods we prefer on the basis of their textures. Milne and Milne (1962) state:

> All of us judge foods through a delicate awareness in the realm of touch, distributed widely over lips, gums, tongue and palate. This helps us learn of texture, and also to recognize astringent materials which compete for moisture in the mouth. (p. 137)

We perceive texture, then, both orally and visually. Texture affects taste through expectation, but also through the enhancement of or interference with the perception of taste stimuli. Although temperature is important, texture remains an important attribute of a food if it is to be eaten and enjoyed.

Food preferences: "Hamburgers again?"   How many times a week can you eat a hamburger? What about steak? Pizza? Can you eat the latter two as often as you can eat hamburgers? Data suggest not only that people are aware of how often they can consume a particular food, but also that they tend to rate some foods, especially those that they may not be able to tolerate daily, as more acceptable on a pleasantness/unpleasantness scale. It is interesting to note that a food such as bread, which is only moderately liked, can be served more often (even daily) than steak or pizza, which are very well liked but which can be tolerated by most people only once a week. Why does this taste experience occur? Carterette and Friedman (1978) state:

> It is quite possible that foods having very distinct flavors or foods that are very salient in the meal (e.g., the entree) obey cyclical preference patterns. If they have not been eaten for a long time they are highly preferable. After they are eaten they lose their acceptability until a sufficiently long time has elapsed. (p. 167)

Food-preference surveys tend to support this statement. In fact, the usual outcome of such surveys is that respondents prefer to eat simple, familiar foods (e.g., hamburger, mashed potatoes) rather than unfamiliar foods (e.g., chicken tetrazzini) or foods with unusual sauces.

In conclusion, we can state that we all have different taste preferences that depend upon our past experiences, our expectations, the colors of foods, the textures of foods, and the frequency with which we eat various foods.

Food Preferences: Where Do They Come From?

Although the exact origin of food preferences has not yet been determined, researchers believe that our likes and dislikes have biological, educational, and cultural influences. Evidence of a biological genesis for food preference has been provided by such studies as the ones conducted by Desor, Maller, and Turner. In one study they found that one- to three- day-old infants could discriminate a sugar solution from water and displayed a definite preference for the sugar solution (cited in Schiffman, 1976, p. 138).

Other studies add evidence of educational and cultural influences. Although broad preferences may be biological (researchers are undecided at this point), preferences for specific seasonings, spices, and condiments have a basic ethnic origin that is culturally linked.

Cultural influences.   For an American, the response to being offered
sheep's eyes would be similar to that of even the most cultured European when offered the American cheeseburger—both would be simply
revolted. Yet we were not born with these biased food preferences; our
individual cultures helped to bless us with such attitudes. Indeed, the
culture in which we live shapes our individual food preferences. And
yet in this statement lies an irony: Our individual taste preferences
mold and affect our respective cultures and lives. Milne and Milne
(1962) have commented on the relationship between culture and the
sense of taste as follows:

> Our bodies are composed of the molecules of food we eat, and the variety is
> limited. Even if people had genetic heritage as nearly identical as those in a
> colony of inbred laboratory rats, their differences in food habits would go a
> long way toward producing individual characteristics" (pp. 145–146).

As a result, there is a two-way communication that one must consider
when addressing the relationship between taste and culture. Cultural
learning gives us our identities, but in turn, our individuality helps
shape our cultural identity.

In other words, we *cultivate* or *acquire* a "taste" for certain foods.
Perhaps this is the reason why Americans in general do not crave such
"delicacies" as the eyes, brains, and appendages of certain animals.
Give us meat and potatoes!

Food Preferences: Their Influence
on the Selection Process

How do you know which foods you *should* eat? Have you ever had a
craving for a certain food product or for extremely novel foods? As we
know, food is needed to sustain life. More importantly, certain foods
are needed in order for the body to function properly. But how do we
know which foods to eat? One researcher, C. M. Davis, may have
some answers that again reflect how the sense of taste communicates.

In a study conducted with human infants, Davis found that infants
displayed innate abilities to select what was essential from a wide
assortment of natural foods. In addition, he noted physiological crav-
ings of humans with specific food deficiencies. The following excerpt
summarizes several of his findings:

> Children with a parathyroid deficiency sometimes would eat chalk or
> plaster as a source of calcium; (in addition,) the bizarre practices of clay- and
> dirt-eating that are found among the world's poorest and hungriest people
> (may be) derived from needs for minerals in trace elements. (cited in
> Wilentz, 1968, p. 146)

Perhaps the most dramatic case evidencing the need for specific
minerals is the story of a child with an adrenal tumor who kept himself

alive with excessive intakes of salt. The child did so, not knowing that he was losing great urinary amounts of salt because of the tumor. His voluntary ingestion of salts helped to keep him from dying.

Our amazing human system works to maintain physiological balance in diets. Whether we do so innately or whether we have learned to maintain this balance is, as of yet, undetermined. We only know that when we are hungry, the message is communicated, and we "increase rates of injestion, frequency of eating, and rates of bar pressing in an operant situation" (in Carterette and Friedman, 1978, p. 110). In other words, we perform instrumental behavior as our needs for food and food products increase.

All of these discussions bring us back to the question we asked at the beginning of the section: Why do we sometimes find ourselves craving extremely novel foods? According to research, it is a vitamin and/or calcium deficiency that leads us away from familiar foods and into a state called *neophilia,* or a preference for novel foods. As Rozin (1967) has shown:

> In need states, a specific aversion ultimately develops for the familiar but deficient diet which leads to neophilia (i.e., a preference for novelty that enhances extinction of old preferences and the search for new foods. (Carterette and Friedman, p. 113)

As we can see, then, the acceptability of a specific food is not necessarily an attribute of the food or food group itself, but is a direct expression of our needs, our habits of eating, and, of course, hunger. Having discussed these variables that affect our preferences for foods, we turn to a final variable: the very culture in which we live.

SUMMARY

We use the sense of smell to provide information about our environment and others in it. Our personal body odors are unique and are influenced by a variety of factors ranging from the food we eat to the level of sexual arousal. In American culture we tend to "cover up" body odors and replace them with artificial scents such as perfumes and deodorants. In many other cultures, natural smells are not only preferred but are considered essential for close interpersonal communication.

In the field of medicine smells can be used to diagnose several illnesses. In addition, smells can be used to aid in learning—particularly in the case of blind students. Animals use their sense of smell for defense, sexual stimulation, and survival, but humans are usually conscious of smells only when the smells "invade" their personal space or environment.

Smells in environments communicate both positive and negative images and attitudes. Some smells make you want to stay in the environment longer, while others make you want to leave immediately.

The process of olfaction involves the smelling of an object that emits an odor or scent. This odor is interpreted by the brain, and it is labeled and evaluated. In some rare cases, people have smell blindness, a condition that allows them to smell only certain kinds of odors. Smell adaptation is a phenomenon that most of us experience. It involves the gradual inability to perceive smells when we have been exposed to them for a sustained period of time.

The measurement of smells and their classification have intrigued researchers for many years. Although several smell-measuring techniques exist, many are subjective and require additional controls. Classifications of smells have been proposed by several researchers. They tend to overlap but have slight differences—a fact that again reflects the need for refined research methods.

Olfaction can have an effect on both fears and sexual drives. Some researchers suggest that substances called pheromones act as messengers in sexual relationships. These pheromones are secretions of the human body that have a scent associated with them.

In the perfume and deodorant industry, smells mean "big business." Some people who work in perfume factories can actually detect subtle differences among similar smells. However, most of us know that we like or dislike certain smells, but we may have difficulty in differentiating among similar ones.

The sense of smell is also very important in the area of taste. Without smell as an aid, we can taste only four different qualities—sourness, sweetness, bitterness, and saltiness. Tastes can be classified in a variety of ways. Most classification systems include the four basic qualities noted above and add others such as pungent, spirituous, or viscous.

The taste center in the human body is, of course, the tongue. However, we also respond to taste stimuli in various other regions of the mouth such as the palate, pharynx, and tonsils.

Sensitivity to taste of different kinds changes with age. This is because the actual number and size of taste buds tend to change with age. Because of heightened sensitivity to taste, children often are attracted to sweet tastes and are repelled by bitter ones. As children mature, their taste buds change and become more receptive to bitter and sour tastes. As with the sense of smell, we can have taste blindness and taste adaptation. For example, the more salty foods that you eat, the more salt you will need each time you eat such foods when tasting them in the future. Food preferences are affected by many factors such as the color of the food, the texture of the food, the frequency of exposure to the food, and cultural conditioning. And finally, food preferences are probably more cultural than biological in origin.

REFERENCES

Ardrey, R. *The Territorial Imperative.* New York: Atheneum Press, 1966.

Bedichek, R. *The Sense of Smell.* New York: Doubleday & Company, Inc. 1960.

Burton, R. *The Language of Smell.* Boston: Routledge & Kegan Paul, 1976.

Cain, W. S. "Differential Sensitivity for Smell: 'Noise' at the Nose." *Science,* 1977, *195,* 796–798.

Carterette, E. C., and M. P. Friedman, eds. *Handbook of Perception, Vol. 6A.* New York: Academic Press, Inc., 1978.

Coren, S., C. Porac, and L. M. Ward. *Sensation and Perception.* New York: Academic Press, 1979.

Davis, R. G. "Acquisition and Retention of Verbal Associations of Olfactory and Abstract Visual Stimuli of Varying Similarity." *Journal of Experimental Psychology: Human Learning and Memory.* 1977, *3.*

"Eau de Sweat." *Time,* January 14, 1980, 50.

Engen, T., and B. M. Ross. "Long-term Memory of Odors with and without Verbal Descriptions." *Journal of Experimental Psychology,* 1973, *100.*

Geldard, F. A. *The Human Senses,* 2nd ed. New York: John Wiley & Sons, Inc., 1972.

Gorman, W. *Flavor, Taste and the Psychology of Smell.* Springfield, Ill.: Charles C Thomas, Publisher, 1964.

Horn, J. C. "The Scentimental Perfume Put-Off." *Psychology Today,* May 1980, *12,* 16.

Livingston, R. B. *Sensory Processing, Perception, and Behavior.* New York: Raven Press, 1978.

Milne, L., and M. Milne. *The Senses of Animals and Men.* New York: Atheneum Press, 1962.

Mueller, C. *Sensory Psychology.* Englewood Cliffs, N.J.: Prentice-Hall, Inc., 1965.

"Personality and Taste," *Self,* February 1980, 22–26.

Schiffman, H. R., ed. *Sensation and Perception: An Integrated Approach.* New York: John Wiley & Sons, Inc., 1976.

Schiffman, S. "Food Recognition by the Elderly." *Journal of Gerontology,* 1977, *32.*

Scott, M. P. "Is Something Wrong With Your Sense of Taste or Smell?" *Better Homes and Garden,* May 1977, 8–10.

Sobel, D. ''Taste and Smell: What Can Go Wrong.'' *Good Housekeeping*, October 1978, 269.

Von Driska, M. B. ''Love at First Sniff Backed by Sexuality Experiments.'' *Arizona State University State Press*, January 24, 1978, 69.

Wilentz, J. S. *The Senses of Man*. New York: Thomas Y. Crowell, 1968.

Winter, R. *The Smell Book: Scents, Sex, and Society*. Philadelphia: J. B. Lippincott Company, 1976.

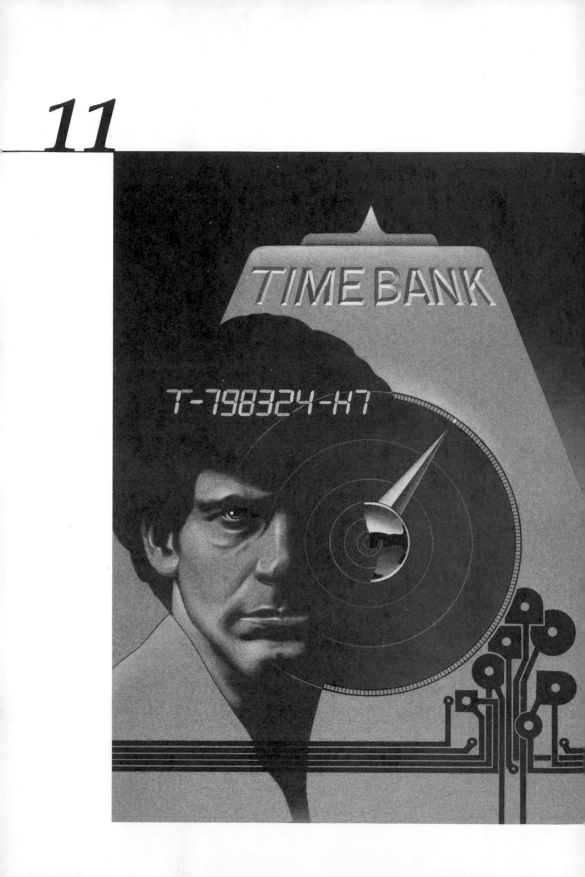

11

CULTURE AND TIME

Man has created a new dimension, the cultural
dimension. However, the relationship between man
and this cultural dimension is one in which both
man and his environment participate in molding
each other. Culture is man's medium; there is not
one aspect of human life that is not touched and
altered by culture.

EDWARD T. HALL, *THE HIDDEN DIMENSION*

*"I*t is understandable that Tom was desperate. Near panic. His time was running out. To be more precise, his account at the Timebank had a balance of one hour, 14 minutes and 27 seconds: 1 hr 14 min 27 sec. If he could not make a deposit within that period, his account would be closed. At that moment, he would stop breathing. He would be dead."* And so begins the fictional story by Lee Falk entitled "Time is Money" (1975, 102). As the story proceeds, the reader begins to realize that fiction can come very close to truth. The main character, Tom, is running out of time, the commodity of exchange used instead of money.

During this future period, all viruses that cause aging have been isolated, and an antibiotic has been developed as a result. This miraculous discovery creates other problems, however, including the threat of overpopulation. The problem is solved with the simple creation of the Timebank. The work ethic, as well as the credit system, is solved. Work is time. Time is life. Life is time. "The most valuable element in the universe became the sole currency of exchange. It had always been the most valuable element in the universe: but never before had its value been so fittingly recognized, so suitably used"* (Falk, 1975, 243).

The story proceeds to explain how the Timebank operated. All newborn infants had a microdevice implanted near their hearts. This mechanism transmitted and received messages from the Timebank that informed them how much time they had left. Some people had amassed millions of years, while others had only months left. If time ran out after poor investments and expenditures (nonproductive deeds or work efforts, as in Tom's case), the tiny implanted device would explode in the left ventricle, and the person would be overdrawn—and dead.

Just imagine a period when being overdrawn (late) would cost you your life. After all, if time is money, then time would be life. Interestingly enough, such an exchange quite aptly reflects the American way of thinking. Guided by a culture that emphasizes the importance of "spending time" wisely—a future-oriented behavior—Americans begin to value at an early age the priceless commodity of time. However, such an ordering of values is not representative of other cultures. As a result, differing conceptions of time may often cause communication problems between individuals of different cultures. It is for this reason that we will begin this chapter with a brief discussion of the effect of

---

* "Time Is Money" by Lee Falk. Copyright © 1975 by *Playboy Magazine*. Reprinted by permission of Brandt & Brandt Literary Agents, Inc.

culture on nonverbal behavior. Indeed, culture affects every aspect of our existence. The perception and use of time is one element that may be affected by the culture in which we live. Culture, indeed, is the guiding force of everyday life.

From our personalities and ways of expressing ourselves to the ways we plan our cities and organize our economic and political systems, culture molds and determines how we will live. Look for a moment at the way in which culturally based behaviors are transmitted. Parents intentionally and unintentionally teach their children the verbal and nonverbal codes of their culture. Children learn these codes by imitation and in turn transmit them to the next generation. In this way culture passes from one generation to another. And yet human beings are not the puppets of culture that we have painted them to be, for they mold culture and in creating their world they determine the kind of organisms they will be (Hall, 1976, p. 4).

But what is culture, and what role does culture play in the study of communication? It is believed that individuals in every society develop their own verbal and nonverbal cues and pass them down through generations. These cues may include meanings of time, body motion, physical characteristics (such as facial expressions), space and proxemics, and touching behavior, each of which helps to set one culture apart from another. In some cases the differences are great, while in others they are indistinguishable. Yet each culture, and each subculture within the culture, has its own patterns and values that help to locate that culture in its own particular time and space. In turn, these patterns and values guide individuals in that culture in the way they think, express emotions, and interact with others. Thus the ways in which individuals from different cultures and subcultures interact are important to study for many reasons. We hope that these reasons will become apparent as you read further. For now, we will limit ourselves to an overview of the chapter.

The aspects of cultural communication presented in this chapter include time, body movement, facial expression, eye behavior, proxemics, and touching behavior. More specifically, the first part of the chapter will be devoted to a study of time. Included in this section will be discussions of 1) the variables of "time," and 2) cultural differences in conceptions and uses of time. After this section, we will present a discussion of cultural differences in 1) body movement and facial expression; 2) conceptualizations and uses of space; and 3) tactile communication. We hope that when you finish this chapter, you will have a greater understanding of how miscommunication may occur between individuals of different cultures. It is important to remember, however, that information presented in this chapter describes behaviors that have been observed in individuals of a culture (or subculture) as a whole, and therefore they should not be generalized to all individuals within a given culture. Indeed, every human being has his or her own unique identity, mannerisms, and style of communicating with others. It is the impact that culture has on the individual that allows the descriptions that are to follow.

CHRONEMICS: THE STUDY OF HUMAN BEINGS AND THEIR TIME SYSTEMS

In this age of advanced and modern technology, the ways we choose to spend our time are of utmost importance. Not only is time money, it is a valuable commodity. We spend it, save it, buy it, and make it, and in general treat it as tangible and divisible. For Americans, years are divided into months, weeks into days, hours into minutes, seconds into milliseconds. And yet, surprisingly enough, this American view of the uses and conceptions of time is unfamiliar to most other parts of the world. Even more surprisingly, there are people who live within the borders of the United States who are unfamiliar with what is believed to be an "American interpretation" of time. For example, the Pueblo Indian, as well as other native Americans, is taught by tradition that an event occurs only when the time is right. As a result, the Pueblo child learns at an early age to remain silent and to give information only when time reveals that it is time for him or her to speak. As a result, the Pueblo Indians and other native Americans may appear more reticent than American Caucasians. However, in reality, it may be prescriptions of the culture that are influencing their interactions. And this American subculture provides only one example. Many other cultures and subcultures do not have such a frenzied, clock-bound existence.

But why do such variations in time perception exist? Do cultural differences with regard to interpretation of and relation to time create many barriers to communication between cultures and subcultures? These are only a few of the questions that exist for researchers in **chronemics,** the study of how we perceive, structure, react to, and interpret time. Perhaps a look at the three existing perceptual levels of time—the **psychological, biological,** and **cultural time orientations**—will allow you to understand why miscommunication between cultures may occur.

The Psychological Time Orientation

From the moment we are born until the time we die, our individual cultures instill in us a partly conscious, partly unconscious concept of the passage of time. Americans, for example, with their preoccupation with death, suggest by their very language the value they place on the passage of time. Many Americans perceive life as unbearably temporal and, as a result, are highly future-oriented. Think of all those "time-saving" devices that have become "essential for Americans to exist," such as dishwashers, calculators, computers, and microwave ovens. Many European cultures, on the other hand, are less conscious of time and are actually past-oriented—they look to tradition and the past for their sense of time. The point to be made is this: All cultures and societies must deal with problems of time, and therefore we must make some preferential statements concerning time. Three psychological alternatives have been reflected in studies of culture and societies. These alternatives include past, present, or future orientations of time.

The **past-oriented society** or culture is one that places a strong emphasis on reliving old times and retelling old stories. These cultures have high regard or respect for their parents and elderly persons in the society. The British, for example, as characteristically close as they are to Americans, place much emphasis on tradition and on the past. The ancient Chinese culture, in which ancestor worship and strong family tradition play strong roles, provides another example of the past orientation of time. Likewise, most North American Indian tribes value tradition and the past. The "powwow" is only one example that reflects the importance of family and tribe to the native American. Families of a given tribe may travel across the country to some specific location—usually on tribal lands—in order to strengthen family and tribal bonds through dance, prayer, and the giving of gifts. During this time spent together, spirits and souls are rejuvenated. Like other past-oriented cultures, these people see events as circular. As Burgoon and Saine (1978) have noted, past events perpetually reoccur in the present (for past-oriented societies) and therefore are applied to similar new situations (p. 100).

Unlike the Americans or the British, many Spanish Americans, Filipinos, and Latin Americans place a strong emphasis on present orientations of time. For these **present-oriented societies,** pleasure is derived from events in the present, and the spontaneity and immediacy of events are viewed as most important. As Prosser (1978) has so aptly noted, " 'Live for today; eat, drink, and be merry, for tomorrow you may die' perhaps best expresses the present value orientation of time" (p. 184). Although the grandfather figure may still be present, in these societies he simply does not have the authority of the grandfather in the past-oriented society.

The third time orientation, and the one with which Americans are most familiar, is that of the future orientation of time. In the **future-oriented society,** the emphasis is placed on tomorrow—a tomorrow that is bigger and brighter only if one works and saves today. One view of the way in which Americans perceive time has been set forth by author and philosopher, P. D. Ouspensky:

> The slaves who toil in . . . offices and factories are invariably barely conscious of their enslavement. If they have any dreams, they are merely of ways of improving their slavery . . . and getting more money. Even if they are dissatisfied with their life, they think only of shortening the hour of work, or increasing their salaries and holidays. (1972, p. 33)

It becomes obvious that various societies view time differently. It is only through an understanding of these views that we can learn to maximize our potential for communication with other societies and cultures.

The Biological Time System

Just as different cultures have different psychological time orientations, the human body has its own time orientations, which are based on natural rhythms. Consider for example, the differences between "owl children" and "sparrow children." "Owl children" are at their best in the late afternoon and evening, while "sparrow children" are at their best in the morning. Everything from our sleeping habits to body temperature and metabolic rate depends somewhat on natural rhythms. It is this variation in rhythms that explains the difference between people who function better at night and those who function better in the morning.

Perhaps the natural cycles we know most about are the physical, sensitivity, and intellectual cycles that make up what is called our **biorhythms.** These three cycles vary in length, with the physical cycle averaging twenty-three days, the sensitivity cycle averaging twenty-eight days, and the intellectual cycle averaging about thirty-three days. According to biorhythm theory, the three biorhythms begin at birth in the positive phase and continue regularly until death. During the first half of each phase our energy is high, and during the second half our energies wane.

The **physical cycle** involves a person's physical energy and alertness. During the first part of the cycle we are at our strongest, and we can work harder and for longer periods of time. During the second half, however, our energies and endurance are at a low, and we spend this time recharging our energy. Think of the last time you really felt drained of energy before the morning was even over. Proponents of biorhythm theory would claim that your physical cycle was at a low point.

The **sensitivity cycle,** on the other hand, is geared toward emotional reactions and fluctuations. As we progress through this cycle, we

Gene Warne

"I would love to go out with you, Herb, but my
biorhythm chart says this is a critical day for me."

first experience a period of cheerfulness and positive outlook; we are
said to get along better with people during this first half of the cycle. As
with the physical cycle, we spend the second half recharging our sensitivity (or emotional) energies. At this time we are less positive and
cheerful and more testy and short-tempered.

The third cycle, or **intellectual cycle,** shows the same positive and
negative movement as the other two cycles. During the first half our
minds are said to be more open and our memories more retentive, and
we tend to better understand and synthesize ideas. In addition, we are
more alert and more adaptable to new situations. During the second
phase of the intellectual cycle, concentration and mental capacities are
at a low ebb—we find it hard to concentrate, to make important decisions, and to deal openly with others. Again, this is the time for recharging intellectual energies.

It is interesting to note that the day on which a cycle shifts can be
especially critical. (In biorhythm language these days are called "critical" days.) On these days, you will find that awareness to your sen-
sitivities will be helpful. A physically critical day may bring greater
susceptibility to fatigue; an emotionally critical day may mean deeper
emotions and periods of high highs or low lows; and an intellectually

critical day may mean greater chances of slow thinking and poor memory. A better understanding of these cycles can alert one to one's individual highs and lows. In addition, an awareness of the ebb and flow of others' energy levels is important for the interpretation of their verbal and nonverbal behavior. The next time you find a friend particularly moody or low in physical energy, think about the functions of biorhythms.* Perhaps this information, plus a little understanding, will help you make your friend more comfortable.

Cultural Time Orientations

The third time orientation is the cultural time orientation. This orientation focuses on the way in which individuals in different cultures view time, and/or the patterns that a given culture has established in using time. As you might expect, understanding time norms of different cultures is not an easy task, even for the most experienced international traveler or businessperson. The reason for the difficulty lies in the existence of three different cultural time systems: technical time, formal time, and informal time.

As researchers have noted, **technical time** is the scientific way in which time is measured and therefore deals with precise measurements of hours, minutes, seconds, and so on. Because technical time is ''nonemotional'' and ''logical,'' it has the least to do with interpersonal or cultural communication processes. An example of this time system would be the tracking of time by the space program, NASA.

Formal time, on the other hand, is not scientific; it is traditional and therefore influences perceptions of individuals who are communicating across cultural boundaries. More specifically, formal time is the traditional way in which a particular culture views time. In our culture, for example, Americans break time into centuries, decades, years, seasons, months, weeks, days, hours, minutes, and seconds. Our formal calendar has 365 days, our week has seven days, and our day has 24 hours. As we stated in the introduction to this section, however, not all cultures view our particular time system as viable. Some cultures, such as farming societies, view time according to natural events such as the phases of the moon or the different crops in a season. In addition, variations in cultural uses of formal time may often be a reflection of religious and philosophical differences among people.

The question you may be asking at this point, however, is what makes formal time different from technical or informal time? In his

---

* Although biorhythm theory is of general interest, it has not been subjected to rigorous scientific research. As a pseudo-science, however, the theory does extend some interesting observations on particular life cycles.

book, *The Silent Language,* Edward T. Hall discusses as many as seven isolates or components of time that distinguish formal time. These include ordering, cyclicity, valuation, tangibility, synthesisity, duration, and depth.

Ordering of events is the first isolate that Hall discusses. This component of formal time focuses on the nature of time as fixed with regard to the ordering of events. Thus "a week is a week not only because it has seven days but because they are in a fixed order" (Hall, 1973, p. 145). However, ordering of events, it must be noted, may vary from culture to culture. Different cultures may vary from lesser to greater degrees on both amount of emphasis on this isolate and ways of ordering of events.

Perhaps the most taken-for-granted isolate in the American formal time system is the cyclical element. This element focuses on our inclination to group days into weeks, months, years, and centuries, and on our perception of the cycling of these units of time. As you might guess, these units of time are perceived as "cyclical" as a function of the limited nature of the units and a given culture's need to segment time.

Two additional isolates that Hall discusses are valuation and tangibility. Valuation is based on the attitude of a culture that time is valuable and therefore should not be wasted nor taken for granted. Similarly, tangibility focuses on a given culture's consideration of time as a commodity (Hall, 1973, p. 145). These two isolates are particularly synonymous with the American perception of time.

Unlike people of some cultures and their perceptions of time, Americans also view synthesisity of time as a major component or isolate of formal time. Synthesisity may be described as the perception of the time as adding up, i.e., the smaller units of time go together to form larger units. For Americans, minutes and hours add up to days and weeks. Since we as a culture begin with the assumption that there is some basic order to the universe (other cultures do *not* perceive the universe in this way), there seems to be no other way to view the basic building blocks of time. As Hall (1973) states,

> We feel it is man's job to discover the order and to create intellectual models that reflect it. We are driven by our own way of looking at things to synthesize almost everything. . . . (p. 147)

Thus whenever we interact with other people whose culture does not emphasize this isolate of time, we often have a difficult time communicating. Should you ever experience such an interaction, the feeling of imbalance that you probably will be feeling is the absence of the synthesisity element in the other person's cultural time system.

Another element of the formal time system in which we function is duration. For most people raised in the European tradition, time is something that occurs between two points. (Hall, 1973, p. 146). It is fixed; it is measurable; it is a quantity. However, as we have seen, this isolate may function to lesser or greater degrees in other cultures. For the Hopi, duration is "the natural process that takes place while a living substance acts out its life drama," says Hall. "It is what happens when the corn matures or a sheep grows up—a characteristic sequence of events (Hall, 1973, p. 146).

The last isolate that Hall discusses is that of depth of time, or the notion that there is a past from which the present emerges. Indeed, we need look no further than the American ideal that we invest in today for a better tomorrow to see the impact that this isolate has on our formal time system.

As we can see, the American time system has several components that are shared to a greater or lesser degree by other societies. However, in all cultures, as Burgoon and Saine (1978) have noted, these concepts are usually learned at an early age. By age six, a child in America knows the days of the week and the values that are placed on them. The child learns, for example, that Monday through Friday are usually workdays and that Saturday and Sunday are usually spent in leisure. By the age of eight, the child has probably learned to tell time by the clock and has learned about the seasons, and by age twelve has usually mastered the formal time system.

The third and most difficult time system to learn and understand is that of **informal time.** Because of its loose definition and its basis on day-to-day practices, informal time systems are unconscious and can only be understood within a situational context. Consequently, this time system is the most difficult for persons outside of the culture to understand.

In the American informal time system, ambiguity plays an important role. When was the last time a friend told you that he or she would be ready "in a minute" or "shortly"? Unless you knew that person, the situation, and the way in which the term was used, you would have had difficulty determining his or her meaning. Words and phrases such as "shortly" or "in a minute" are part of the eight levels of duration in the informal time system in our culture. These eight levels may be described by the following divisions of time in the informal time system in our culture: immediate, very short, short, neutral, long, very long, terribly long, and forever. As you may note, "forever" can vary from the hour you may spend in a very boring class (not this one, of course) to a lifetime and beyond, while "in a minute" or "shortly" may vary from a second to thirty minutes. As you can see, informal time frequently uses the same vocabulary as that of formal time, thus leaving many people confused over meanings. How, for instance, does one determine the nature, or criteria, of "punctuality"?

   Part of the problem of determining criteria for punctuality is that there are two conflicting ways of viewing it. Hall (1972) describes these as the ''displaced point pattern'' and the ''diffused point pattern.'' To explain the two patterns, the ''point'' itself may be defined as the time that a person might expect his or her guests to arrive at a party—say, 7:00 P.M. Hall's hypothesis is that some individuals will arrive at the party anywhere from 6:30 P.M. to 6:57 P.M. (the latter time would be considered as ''cutting it short''), with a majority arriving around 6:55 P.M. These individuals may be said to view time as ''displaced'' and will arrive before the appointed point in time. ''Diffused-point people,'' on the other hand, will arrive anywhere between 6:55 P.M. and 7:15 P.M. These individuals do not see a certain time as fixed in space but view time as scattered and probably will arrive at the party ''around 7:00 P.M.'' The displacement of a point in time, however, is a function of three variables: the type of social occasion and what is being served, the status of the individual who is being met or visited, and the individual's own way of handling time. There is always the possibility that someone

Gene Warne

''When they tell you the party starts at
8 o'clock, that means start drinking then and
roll into the party around 10 or 11.''

intentionally will use punctuality as a message. Often businesspeople will deliberately keep clients waiting to serve as a message of their importance or of their demanding time schedule. The two time patterns would not necessarily cause problems if everyone understood which system others were following.

Although punctuality is not considered an element of the informal time system, four elements of this time system do exist. They include **urgency, activity, variety** (variety is a factor in boredom), and **monochronism** (Hall, 1972, pp. 152–154). The timing of events, for example, may clearly signify urgency. A telephone call, for example, at two or three in the morning communicates something entirely different from a call in the early or late afternoon. Activity and variety, on the other hand, refer to whether or not we are doing something with our time and whether or not we vary the activities in which we engage. A number of other cultures, for instance, the Navajo, Trukese, eastern Mediterranean Arab cultures, Japanese, and many of those of India, include ordinary sitting as activity. For Americans, the attitude toward inactivity is much different: Without activity and variation, boredom will set in.

Perhaps the most important element in the informal time system, in terms of cultural and subcultural implications, is that of monochronism. Monochronism, which is prevalent in the North American culture, is the scheduling of only one activity at a time. Conversely, individuals in "polychronic" cultures, such as Latin America, may schedule several activities or appointments at the same time. Many Americans who have done business with either Latin Americans or Arabs have come home to the United States highly insulted. The reason is that "M-time," or **monochronic time,** emphasizes schedules, segmentation, and promptness, while "P-time," or **polychronic time,** stresses involvement of people and the completion of transactions rather than strict, preset scheduling. People in P-time cultures simply do not allow schedules to get in the way and to place the job in a special category much below courtesy, consideration, and kindness to other people. In most "P-time" cultures many people meet in one room, with the individual in charge moving from person to person.

The problem that many "outsiders" face when communicating with individuals from polychronic cultures is that one must be an insider or else have a friend in the bureaucracy in order to make any headway. People may be kept waiting because they are unknown, and unless they are willing to return repeatedly and meet their hosts outside the office, they have little chance of becoming active members in the P-time social system.* Both time orientations, however, have inherent problems. The problem with monochronic organizations often is that

---

* For further explanation of P-time and M-time, see Hall, 1976, pp. 14–45.

We measure our lives by units of time and often judge others based on their adherence to these artificial constructs.

the M-time people are concerned only with schedules and are blind to the needs of those with whom they are interacting. The polychronic weakness is its dependence on the head person to do everything—scheduling meetings, working with many people at the same time, and simultaneously staying on top of things. If individuals of each of these time orientations are either insensitive to or unknowledgeable about the other, miscommunication can take place.

As you can see from the above discussion, time is inextricably woven into our everyday existence. At times we are unaware of the tremendous impact that time and our view of it have on our lives. Having looked at the different orientations and elements of time, we now turn to a discussion of time and its uses in different cultures.

CULTURAL DIFFERENCES IN CONCEPTIONS AND USES OF TIME

As we said earlier, time in our culture is considered to be a commodity—one that is cherished and bestowed as if it were tangible. As Samovar and Porter (1972) suggest, ''We place a strong emphasis on time as an aspect of history rather than as an aspect of immediate experience. We treat the present as a way-station, an intermediate point between past and future, and an immersion in the present is considered by some of us to be paganistic'' (p. 15).

For Americans a ''long time'' can be almost anything, from a couple of days to ten or twenty years. This orientation, however, does not hold true for other cultures. A person from southern Asia, for example, often equates a ''long time'' with thousands of years or even an endless period. As a result, this person would probably find much humor in our stepped-up, fast-paced age of ''long-term'' projects lasting five to eight years.

Another example of variations in treatment of past and future time is that of the Truk Islanders. This culture is said to treat the past as if it were the present. Because the language has no past tense, all past offenses, grudges, and personal traumas (for example, the murder of a relative many years before the present) are perpetually remembered and are treated as if they just happened. Compliments and gifts are also remembered continually.

Another variation in the uses and interpretations of time is one that is conceptualized by the Tiv culture. According to Hall (1972), the Tiv week varies from five to seven days and is named after the things that are being sold at the nearest market. As Hall notes,

> If we had the equivalent, Monday would be ''automobiles'' in Washington, D.C., ''furniture'' in Baltimore, and ''yard goods'' in New York City. Each of these might be followed by the days for appliances, liquor, and diamonds in the respective cities. This would mean that as you traveled about, the day of the week would keep changing, depending on where you were. (pp. 16–17)

Northern Europeans are perhaps the most similar to North Americans in conceptions and uses of time, although travelers may notice different values being placed on punctuality.

As you can see, conceptualizations and uses of time vary across different cultures and within cultures themselves. A better understanding of the psychological, biological, and cultural conceptions of time as well as information about different cultures can assist us in communicating with people from different cultures and understanding their nonverbal behavior cues. The cultural implications of body movements and facial expressions will be discussed in the following section.

CULTURAL DIFFERENCES IN BODY MOVEMENTS AND FACIAL EXPRESSION

Although research by Paul Ekman (1976) has focused on the existence of universals in facial expressions (we will discuss these in the latter part of the section), other forms of body movement such as emblems, greetings, body position, posture, and dance have not been viewed as universal. In fact, each culture has its own characteristic movements, body positions, and inherited meanings for interpreting them. It is important to remember that within each culture, there also exist many subcultural differences, as well as individual differences. Thus a description of a culture only serves as a generalization and will not always apply to the individual members of that culture.

The purpose of this section is to acquaint you with some of the "cultural differences" of human body movement. After this section, we will introduce the notion of universality of facial expression and its relationship to culture. As we have mentioned, body movement varies from culture to culture. Perhaps a good place to begin a description of these differences is with the greetings that are used by various cultures.

Greetings and Culture

Throughout the various cultures of the world there exist many different kinds and types of greetings. Contrary to American belief, the handshake is not the only means of conveying a greeting. In fact, our handshake may seem quite out of place to some cultures such as the Polynesians, who may greet one another by embracing and rubbing each other's backs. The greeting, which some Americans use, of slapping another person on the back, however, would fit quite nicely into the Northwest Amazonian culture, whose members greet each other in precisely this way.

Another greeting in which the slapping or touching of the back is involved is the one shared by some Spanish Americans with one another. Individuals in this cultural group have almost a "stereotyped embrace"; they place their heads on the right shoulder of the other person, issue three pats on the back, and then place their heads on the left shoulder of the person and issue three more pats of greeting. To most Copper Eskimos, who greet strangers by buffeting them on the head or shoulders with their fists, this greeting would seem most out of place (LaBarre, 1972, p. 172).

Still another greeting used by many members of the Andamanese culture is perhaps the most bizarre when compared with those of the American culture:

> Andamanese greet one another by one sitting down in the lap of the other, arms around each other's necks and weeping for a while; two brothers, father and son, mother and daughter, and husband and wife, or even two friends may do this; the husband (however) sits in the lap of the wife. (LaBarre, 1972, pp. 172–173)

Thus the greetings of various cultural members may differ vastly from those of the North American. There are other nonverbal messages that differ from culture to culture. One such difference lies in the messages of and types of kissing behavior—a great American past-time—which you may not recognize in other cultures.

Culture and the Kissing Ritual

As described by one research team, kissing is Germanic, Graeco-Roman, and Semitic in origin. As they state,

> Greek and Roman parents kissed their children, lovers and married persons kissed one another and friends of the same or different sexes; medieval knights kissed, as modern pugilists shake hands, before the fray. Kissing relics and the hand of a superior is at least as early as the Middle Ages in Europe; kissing the feet is an old habit among various Semites; and the Alpine peasant kisses his own hand before receiving a present, and pages in the French Court kissed any article given them to carry. (LaBarre, 1972, p. 173)

Perhaps the greatest differences in **kissing behaviors,** when compared with those in the continental United States, are those of two other cultures—one with which you are probably familiar and another that you may not recognize. The one with which you are probably most familiar is the nose-rubbing behavior of the Eskimo and Polynesian. The other is the kissing behaviors found in Tierra del Fuego. According to LaBarre (1972), kissing in Tierra del Fuego is performed ''only between certain close relatives and young married couples or lovers; and not lip to lip, but by pressing the lips to the hand, cheek, or arm of the other, accompanied by a slight inward sucking'' (p. 173). Strangely enough, this behavior is similar to most Andamanese good-byes, which, instead of the ''inward sucking'' motion, use a reciprocal, gentle blowing motion on the raised hand of the partner.

Finally, and most interesting, is the fact that kissing in the Orient often is considered in quite a different light. For many Oriental people, especially the Japanese, kissing is an act of private lovemaking, which arouses disgust when performed publicly. Although this fact may not seem so interesting at first glance, one need only think of the American movies that travel from the United States to Japan. Because of this sensitivity toward kissing that many Japanese feel, many of the major love scenes are often censored from the movies.

Beckoning Gestures and Gestures of Contempt

Another set of movements that may vary from culture to culture is that of **beckoning gestures** and **gestures of contempt.** As researchers have observed, simple movements elicit entirely different meanings as we move from culture to culture. Because of this fact, miscommunication between people from different cultures can occur when an emblem symbolizes different messages in two cultures. Perhaps this is especially true of beckoning gestures. In restaurants across America, for example, people often raise the forefinger to summon a waiter or waitress. Outside of these establishments, Americans may make a backward scooping motion toward the body to indicate that another person is wanted for something. In Latin American, however, beckoning gestures differ from American gestures. Many Latin Americans will beckon other individuals with a downward arc formed by the right hand, much like the American gesture meaning "go away with you" (Ekman and Friesen, 1975, p. 175).

The Shans of Burma also have a gesture much different from the American one for summoning others. Placing the palm down, they move their fingers much as if they were playing piano arpeggios. Many individuals in the Boro and Witoto cultures would also be disconcerted by the American gesture, for these two cultural groups beckon "by moving the hand downward, not upward, as with us, in our face-level wrist-flexing, cupped-hand 'come here' signal" (Ekman and Friesen, 1975, p. 175). It is understandable how members of one culture become confused when they visit other cultures. These kinds of problems must

"Hello," "goodbye," "come here"—all can be expressed with a casual flip of the hand. In fact, hand movements convey very precise meanings in some cultures.

be dealt with in order for the cultures of the world to communicate effectively with one another.

Another set of gestures that differs from culture to culture is that of gestures of contempt. Before reading any further, think of the various ways that people in America use to communicate negative feelings such as contempt. Perhaps the two most obvious are the "social finger" (known more commonly as "the bird," performed by the upward thrust of the fist with the middle finger raised) and the slapping of the biceps with the opposite hand resulting in an upraised fist. These two gestures differ from gestures of contempt in other cultures. Perhaps a look at some of these will help you to understand how easily individuals in given cultures miscommunicate feelings and thoughts.

One example of how a culture communicates contempt is that of the Pitta-Pitta aborigines of Australia. Many males of this culture show contempt by biting their beards, while women may insult each other by protruding the abdomen, exposing themselves, and vibrating their thighs together. Another culture, the Menomini Indians, will often use the raising of a clenched fist to show contempt. The hand is placed palm downward, with the thumb and the first two fingers thrown forward (LaBarre, 1972, p. 174). Both of these gestures, however, differ from the "making of horns" or "evil eye," which is made by the extension of the first and little finger, with thumb and other fingers folded. This particular gesture is probably most familiar to Americans, for it is often found in the literature of many countries.

Interestingly enough, gestures of contempt also make use of other parts of the body and often have different meanings in different cultures and within given cultures. Hissing and spitting are two examples. Much as a Malayan Negrito may express contempt by "a sudden expiration of breath," Americans, too, have been known both to hiss and to spit. These gestures, however, may be both positive and welcomed by the Japanese, the Basuto, and the East African Masai. As LaBarre notes, hissing in Japan, which is made by the sudden intake of air, or a sudden breath is often considered "politesse to social superiors, implying the withdrawal of the subjects' inferior breath in the presence of the superior person thus complimented" (p. 177). Likewise, an individual of the Basuto culture may applaud by hissing, and for the Masai spitting may be a sign of both affection and benediction.

Having discussed the various gestures of contempt that exist across cultures, consider the possible miscommunication that can occur when an emblem symbolizes different meanings. To sensitize yourself even more to the problem, consider the dilemma in which two world leaders, Brezhnev and Nixon, found themselves. Brezhnev, unfortunately, was unaware of specific gestures of contempt, and upon entering the United States, insulted the entire nation with a seemingly innocent emblem representing the spirit of détente. What was the emblem? Upraised arms, meeting in a clasp of supposed friendship. Perceived as a symbol of victory, the gesture promoted only hostility for many Americans who watched. Similarly, Nixon is said to have insulted the Brazilian nation when he deplaned with hands upraised in the American "O.K.," or peace emblem. Unfortunately, this emblem for Brazilians was the equivalent of the American "social finger" or "bird" and resulted in an American apology to the Brazilian people. As you can see, movements and emblems are culturally bound and must be dealt with if nations and cultures wish to communicate meaningfully. Posture, locomotion, and body positioning likewise play an important role in understanding non-verbal cultural variations.

According to Hewes (1972), although human postural habits have "anatomical and physiological limitations, . . . a great many choices exist, the determinates of which appear to be mostly cultural. The number of significantly different body attitudes capable of being maintained steadily is probably on the order of one thousand" (p. 193). Indeed, one need look no further than the different body positions of people in conversation to see that culture truly affects our nonverbal behaviors across cultures. Hall (1969) relates a story that clearly illustrates this point. His tale involves an Arab friend with whom he once took a walk.

> After years in the United States, (my friend) could not bring himself to stroll along, facing forward while talking. Our progress would be arrested while he edged ahead, cutting slightly in front of me and turning sideways so we could see each other. Once in this position he would stop. His behavior was explained when I heard that for the Arabs to view the other person peripherally is regarded as impolite, and to sit or stand back-to-back is considered very rude. You must be involved when interacting with Arabs who are friends. (pp. 160–161)

Thus the way people walk may communicate many different variables from status to how they are feeling on a particular day. Although the main purpose of the body and legs is not communication, we can receive messages from the ways in which a person walks, particularly if we are familiar with the person being observed.

Dance: A Reflection of Culture

From the beginning of time, humans beings have heard and felt rhythm. Their own heartbeat was the first rhythm they experienced, and then they encountered the rhythms of the ocean, the rain, and the sound of their own footsteps as they walked. Indeed, the natural development of dance, from a biological point of view, is significant in helping us to understand our human development.

Dance, like other body movements, is culturally bound and reflects natural movement patterns as well as the social and political events of the culture and times. One need look no further than the American dances of the sixties to find evidence of cries for change and revolution. The youth of the country were continually changing their dances to separate themselves from both the masses and the "older generation."

Other cultural messages, however, are also reflected in the dances that the cultures have produced. In Israel, for example, folk dances stress group unity, love of the new land, and faith in youth, and they also reflect the nation's struggle for identity and freedom. These folk dances often are done in a circle with the arms of the participants linked. In addition, each movement of the dance has its own meaning—for example, when the arms are stretched upward, the dancers are symbolizing praise to God.

Like Israel, Japan also reflects its culture through dance, and like other peoples it reflects its culture through a formally organized system of "body communication." Because the Japanese have a great affinity

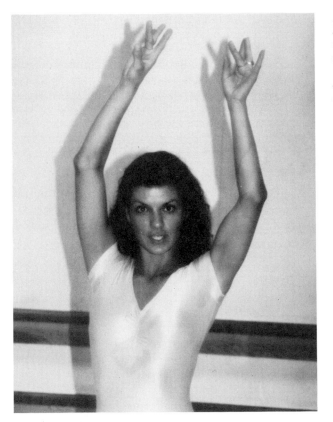

Ballet, disco, country-swing, ballroom, and new-wave dancing not only express natural movement patterns (in some cases "unnatural movement"), but also reflect messages about a culture, group, and way of life.

for the earth, the purpose of its traditional dance is to confirm the existence of the earth itself. Therefore, Japanese dance with a pressing down of the hips and with the knees slightly bent. This action makes the body appear shorter and in closer contact with the ground. The feet slide along, but with strong (foot) beats.

Many other dances could be described with regard to various cultures. The important point to remember is that dance reveals a cultural message, a philosophical view of life. For example, Western dances reflect aspirations toward the heavens, while Eastern dances reflect love for the earth.

Dance and all body movements, in whatever form they take, are bound by culture. Another set of movements involves facial expression and eye/gaze behavior. Before discussing these, however, we will discuss a major methodological question concerning their study: Are facial expressions universal or culturally bound?

Facial Expression and Eye Contact: Universal or Culturally Bound?

As early as the year 1872, with the research of Charles Darwin, the idea of universal facial behaviors for different emotions was existent. Researchers of the twentieth century such as Allport, Asch, Tomkins, Izard, and Ekman were a few who wrote in support of Darwin's view. There were, on the other hand, researchers who argued against universal facial expressions—such investigators as Birdwhistell and LaBarre number in these ranks—and who maintained that facial expressions were "culture bound."

There is today, however, much evidence supporting both views. Facial expressions for the most part appear to be universal with regard to the expression of emotions themselves, but, as Harper, Wiens, and Matarazzo (1978) state, "specific cultural norms may dictate differently how and when they are expressed" (p. 99).* Ekman and Friesen (1975) have done considerable research that supports the contention that facial behavior is both universal and culturally bound. According to these researchers, cultural differences in facial expressions occur for the following reasons:

1. Most of the events, which through learning become established as the elicitors of particular emotions, will vary across cultures.
2. The rules for controlling facial expressions in particular social settings will also vary across cultures.

---

* Although facial expression is often treated as a separate entity in the study of body movement (Harper, Wiens, and Matarazzo, 1978), the authors have chosen to treat facial expression and eye behavior in one subsection for spatial reasons.

3. Some of the consequences of emotional arousal will also vary with culture. (pp. 99–100)

As Ekman (1976) explains, every culture does not have to have an emblem for each emotion, "but those cultures which do have a facial emblem about an emotion are likely to base it upon the universal facial expression of emotion. There still could be a difference. For example, in signifying fear emblematically one culture could draw upon the brow/ forehead part of the universal emotion and another culture could draw upon the lips" (p. 20). Thus research seems to reveal some evidence of universality of facial expressions, but with the stipulation that culture defines how and when they may be expressed. With this understanding, perhaps the best place to turn for a discussion of cultural differences is to **display rules,** or those "unconscious automatic habits that modify or alter facial expression in accordance with the social situation" (Harper, Wiens, and Matarazzo, 1978, p. 101).

In one study conducted by Ekman and Friesen (1975), stress-inducing films were shown in American and Japanese colleges. It was found that Japanese and Americans, when alone, had virtually identical facial expressions. However, when American and Japanese students were placed in the presence of other people (e.g., experimenters), and when cultural rules about the management of facial appearance (appropriate cultural display rules) were applied, there was little correspondence between Japanese and American facial expressions. In addition, the Japanese were found to mask or hide their facial expressions of unpleasant emotions more often than Americans.

Harper, Wiens, and Matarazzo (1978) have also noted variations in display rules across different cultures. Some Mediterraneans, for example, intensify grief and exaggerate expressions of sadness. Many British, on the other hand, are noted for their understatement of emotion; even when sad or grieving, they will show little emotion outwardly.

Americans also adhere to cultural display rules. For example, the display of sadness in the United States is often neutralized, especially in public situations. Perhaps you remember the face of Jacqueline Kennedy at the funeral of former President John F. Kennedy. Her grief was very private—at no time during or after the funeral did she display her feelings to the public. But as much as many Americans may neutralize facial expression, many Japanese go one step further. Individuals in this culture may mask emotion completely; they cover anger, sorrow, and disgust with both laughing and smiling. Again, it is important to remember that not all members of a culture will choose to neutralize or mask an emotion; many will display the exact emotion that they are feeling.

Many differences exist in the display rules of cultures, even though facial expressions in themselves may remain universal. In conjunction with facial expressions, nonverbal differences in eye behavior are a very important aspect of the study of facial movements. Perhaps the most extensive study to date of cultural differences in gaze was performed by O. M. Watson in 1970. Using subject dyads of foreign students conversing in their native language, Watson observed that Arab, Latin American, and southern European subjects focused their gaze on the eyes or face of their dyadic partners. Conversely, Asian, Indian-Pakistani, and northern Europeans were found to have a tendency toward "peripheral gaze" (or an orientation toward the partner but with no direct eye contact with the face or eyes), or no gaze at all (i.e., they would look downward or stare into space). An additional finding was that no correlation existed between gaze behavior and time spent overseas, a fact that suggested that gaze patterns or behaviors may not be expected by environmental–social influences (Watson, 1970, p. 112). In addition to the Watson study, other researchers have noted cultural differences in gaze behavior. One finding, for example, is that British people do not nod their heads to let you know they understand; rather, they will blink their eyes to let you know they have heard you.

Unlike British people, however, many West Africans avoid eye contact to communicate both respect and an acknowledgement of being in a subordinate role. This pattern is also found in some individuals in the Japanese culture, as previously discussed.

Thus you can see that cultural differences exist in all forms of human movement—in emblems, gestures, postures, and movements, as well as in facial expression and gaze behaviors. There are, however, additional areas of nonverbal communication that reveal cultural differences. In the next section, we will discuss another of these areas, that of proxemics.

PROXEMICS: OUR CULTURAL CONCEPTUALIZATIONS AND USES OF SPACE

Unlike the universals that appear to exist in the study of facial expressions, we have no universals for our conceptualizations and uses of space across different cultures and societies. Although we do make use of certain patterned interaction zones (the intimate, personal, social, and public distances that were discussed in another chapter, these, too, differ from culture to culture.

Engebretson and Fullmer offer one reason for the discrepancies. They state that from infancy the child is influenced by social associations that are characteristic for his or her social group. These associations act as a frame of reference for the individual in subsequent social interactions (p. 220). Thus as with other nonverbal behaviors, proxemic or spatial behaviors correspond to the experiences and cultural traditions with which we have lived.

As with other nonverbal behaviors, proxemic behaviors differ from culture to culture. This statement especially holds true for intrusion distances. Hall (1969), for example, makes the following comparison between Western and Arab cultures:

> In the Western world, the person is synonymous with an individual inside a skin. And in Northern Europe, generally the skin and even the clothes may be inviolate. . . .For the Arab, the location of the person in relation to the body is quite different. The person exists somewhere down inside the body. The ego is not completely hidden, however, because it can be reached very easily with an insult. It is protected from touch but not from words. (p. 157)

For most Arab peoples, then, there can be no such thing as an intrusion in public: "Public means public." In this view, if you are standing on a street corner and someone else wants your spot, that person is within his or her rights to do whatever possible to make you uncomfortable enough to move.

In Germany, on the other hand, an individual's "space" may be invaded by as little as a gaze. To many Germans, for example, a person is "inside" a building and has intruded when he or she can be seen from the inside. For these Germans, one does not have to be inside a room to be inside the zone of intrusion, especially if one looks at another person, no matter how far away. The English culture is another culture that may seem to have a strange concept of "intrusion," when compared with that of most North Americans. When an English man or woman feels that he or she needs to be alone, a phone call may be considered an intrusion. In fact, to phone someone in England is often unheard of unless the situation involves business transactions or emergencies. To phone without reason is considered by many to be "pushy" or "rude." If one wishes to communicate other than in person, a letter or telegram is usually considered "less disrupting" than a telephone call (Hall, 1969, p. 140).

Thus different conceptualizations and uses exist for what is termed the **intrusion zone** in proxemic studies. However, there are also cultural differences in definitions of what is considered to be an appropriate **interaction distance.**

In one study conducted by Engebretson and Fullmer (1972), which was designed to determine the consistency of interaction distances within the Japanese, the researchers found that native Japanese had larger interaction distances than Hawaiian Japanese or American Caucasians. American Caucasian males and females were no different, however, than native Japanese in the distances that were maintained with authority figures such as fathers or professors (p. 225).

Many Arabs, on the other hand, have little sense of intrusion in terms of the sense of touch, and they also find an interaction distance of two feet or more to be equivalent to an American approximation of five feet. As Hall and Whyte (1966) note, to Latin Americans we may seem "cold" and "distant," while to us they may seem intrusive and "pushy" (pp. 571–572). Likewise, we often find the Mediterannean and eastern European people to be pushy, when in essence it is a natural tendency for these people to group more closely together. The definitions of interaction distances of these three peoples, along with that of individuals in the Cuban culture, who may stand only eighteen inches apart when talking in quiet, all differ from American definitions of interaction distance.

On the other end of the interaction–distance continuum are the British, British Americans, and black Americans, who traditionally desire large "body buffer zones." According to Scheflen and Ashcraft (1976), the Latin and eastern European Jew may find the British and British-American tendency to stand more than thirty-six inches apart, even in fairly intimate conversations, as a sign of both "coldness" and "detachment" (pp. 90 and 191). As we stated earlier, these latter people would find the Latins exactly the opposite—pushy and highly intrusive.

Perhaps the most extreme conceptualization of interaction distance, when compared with that of Americans, is the one that many Lebanese and Syrian villagers have adopted. Americans have a great problem when attempting to carry on a conversation across a room, but this is not the case in many of these villages, where this kind of interaction behavior may be a way of life. But as Scheflen and Ashcraft (1976) point out, adaptations within a culture are made with regard to activity, density, noise level, and so forth. These variations are, however, made from within the culture itself (p. 91).

The final question to which we now turn in this section is one concerning the different **conceptualizations and uses of office space** that exist in various cultures. The British are quite dismayed and puzzled by the American "need" for secure office space. The two cultures simply disagree on requirements of working space. For example, members of Parliament in England have no special offices in which to conduct legislative business. However, members of Congress in the United States will not tolerate a no-office situation. In their view, constituents, associates, colleagues, and lobbyists simply would not respond properly if they did not have offices (Hall, 1976, p. 53).

Another culture that varies from the American in its definition of office space is that of Germany, where the idea of double doors for sound-proofing is important in offices and private buildings. Many Germans take the door very seriously and find American doors both flimsy and light. Additional problems that Germans find in the American use of office space include the "open-door policy" and the use of furniture arrangements. For many Germans, open doors seem "sloppy" and "disorderly" while closed doors "preserve the integrity of the room and provide a protection boundary between people" (Hall, 1969, p. 135). Similarly, many Germans feel that moving furniture about (especially to move closer to one with whom you are talking) both destroys the order of things and acts as an intrusion on personal space. To illustrate this feeling of intrusion, one German newspaper editor who moved to the United States was reported to have bolted his visitor's chair to the floor "at the proper distance" because he detested the American habit of adjusting the furniture to the occasion. Although this may sound odd, it really is not in light of German experiences. In Germany, furniture is made to be extremely heavy to act as a "deterrent" for those unfamilar with German spatial norms (Hall, 1969, pp. 135–138).

Cultural differences exist in at least three realms of proxemics: intrusion distance, interaction distance, and the uses and conceptions of office space. As we have noted throughout this chapter, the discussion of these differences is based on generalizations, which are not necessarily indicative of all members of the given culture. In addition, we hope that you will see the potential for misinterpretations of nonverbal cues that exists in a world so diverse and rich in cultural definitions of nonverbal behavior. We now turn to a discussion of touching behaviors of various cultures in the final section of this chapter.

CULTURAL DIFFERENCES IN TACTILE COMMUNICATION

Why are some people more prone to touch other people? Most research on tactile communication says that we receive different kinds, amounts, and durations of touch from our parents as infants and that we reflect these differences as adults. Montagu shares similar views regarding tactile differences and adds that it is early tactile relationships, complemented by sound, that determine to a large extent how open, warm, and loving we will be when we reach adulthood (cited in Prosser, pp. 121–122). But what are some of the cultural differences that exist in tactile communication? This question will be addressed in the following paragraphs.

According to Montagu, "Natural and cultural differences in tactility run the full gamut from absolute non-touchability, as among upperclass Englishmen, to what amounts to almost full expression among peoples speaking Latin-derived languages, Russians, and many nonliterate peoples. Those who speak Anglo-Saxon derived languages stand at the opposite pole in the continuum of tactility to the Latin peoples. In this continuum Scandinavians appear to occupy an intermediate position" (cited in Prosser, 1978, p. 120).

The English occupy a position on the nontactile end of the continuum. This orientation may be attributed to the relationships between parents and their children, especially among the English upper classes. At birth, children of upper-class parents in England are usually turned over to nurses, and during their early childhood years they are reared by governesses. Once they have reached school age, they are usually sent away to school. Throughout these years, they have experienced a minimum of tactile experience. Thus you can realize the importance of tactile experience as it relates to cultural differences. Because English upper-class children have a minimum of tactile experiences, they learn to minimize their own giving and receiving of tactile communications.

Another culture that is nontouch-oriented is the Chinese. According to LaBarre, the Chinese people often have a strong aversion to being touched or slapped on the back; they even dislike shaking hands (p. 177). The Japanese and American cultures also may be classified as **nontactile cultures,** but perhaps not to the extent of the Chinese. Although many Japanese and Americans have certain prohibitions concerning interpersonal (tactile) contact in public, the effects of these cultural restrictions are usually restricted only to spatial separation in public (Engebretson and Fullmer, 1972, p. 221).

Even more nontactile than the English, however, are many Canadians of Anglo descent and most individuals of the German culture. Although French Canadians often are as tactilely oriented as the French from whom they have originated, Anglo Canadians are more nontactile than the English. Many Germans, too, are extremely undemonstrative, and as Montagu suggests, their "emphasis on the warrior virtues, supremacy of the hard-headed martinet father, and the complete subordination of the mother in the German family (has) made for a rigidified, unbending character which renders the average German, among other things, a not very tactile being" (cited in Prosser p. 121).

As we stated earlier, the Latin and Russian cultures are highly tactile in nature, as is the Arab, with which Hall deals to a great extent in his research. Hall (1969) has noted, "Americans and Arabs live in different sensory worlds much of the time and do not use the same senses even to establish most of the distances maintained during conversations. . . . Arabs make more use of olfaction and touch than Americans" (p. 3).

Other examples of **tactilely oriented cultures** are the Jewish and Netsilik Eskimo cultures. The Jewish mother, for example, shows deep and unremitting care for her children. Until recently, children were breast-fed on demand, and there was much fondling of the children by the mother, father, and siblings. Interestingly, this description is akin to one that might be used to describe the Netsilik Eskimo (although not quite so extreme in terms of tactile experiences). Prosser (1978) describes this culture in the following depiction of Netsilik life:

> . . . from the earliest orientations and essentially throughout their lives, the Netsilik Eskimos rely virtually upon a sense of touch, and by responding to sensations of touch or contact, learn to find their way in the environment created for the child by the mother. Later, the Eskimo male especially knows instinctively by combinations of touch how to discover a seal hidden beneath a frozen patch of ice, or how to find his way home after a long hunt in a blinding storm. (p. 123)

How different life would seem for us should we be placed in such a culture!

Having described some of the many differences in cultural displays of tactile communication, we should repeat what is perhaps the most important point to be emphasized throughout this chapter: Differences in nonverbal behavior often cause communication breakdowns at all levels of interaction, whether that interaction be at the interpersonal or international level. In addition, you should not forget that when you read descriptions such as these, you should avoid cross-cultural stereotyping of individuals from the cultures. These descriptions are based on cultural generalizations, which in turn are often based on observation alone. Even if descriptions of cultural nonverbal cues are based on rigid experimentation, they cannot represent descriptions of every individual within the culture. Within every culture there are many variations. It is this variation that makes each human being a unique individual.

SUMMARY

Culture influences all aspects of our existence. Cultural interpretations and uses of time, body motion, physical characteristics, proxemics, and touch help to develop and determine behavior. Our conception and use of time has psychological, biological, and cultural influences. In some cultures psychological perceptions of time are past-oriented, that is, emphasis is placed on tradition. Other cultures perceive time as present- or future-oriented. Americans' view of time tends to be future-oriented.

Along with psychological influences, individuals experience biological time orientations. Biorhythm theory suggests that people are affected by physical, sensitivity, and intellectual cycles. Energy is high during the first half of each cycle and low during the second half of each cycle.

Culture also helps to shape perceptions and use of formal, informal, and technical time orientations. The technical time orientation is the most universally consistent. Four elements of an informal time system include: urgency, activity, variety, and monochronism. Although some cultures view time as a commodity, the conceptualizations and use of time vary across and within different cultures.

In addition, cultural factors influence differences in body movement and facial expressions. There are distinct cultural differences in manners of greeting, kissing rituals, beckoning gestures, gestures of contempt, and dance movements. Facial expressions, on the other hand, have been found to be universal for the expression of emotion. Cultural norms and expectations, however, influence how and when they are expressed. Cultural differences also tend to exist in eye behaviors.

Our cultural conceptualizations and uses of space vary across cultures and societies. The intimate, personal, social, and public patterns of interaction distances differ from culture to culture. Proxemic differences exist particularly in intrusion distance, interaction distance, and the uses and conceptions of office space.

One aspect of the use of space, that of touching behavior, also varies from culture to culture. The kinds, amounts, and durations of tactile communication are influenced by cultural norms and expectations. Differences in nonverbal behavior across cultures often cause communication breakdowns. An understanding and awareness of cultural differences should enable individuals to communicate more effectively, both interpersonally and interculturally.

REFERENCES

Burgoon, J., and T. Saine. *The Unspoken Dialogue: An Introduction to Nonverbal Communication.* Boston: Houghton Mifflin Co., 1978.

Ekman, P. "Movements with Precise Meanings." *Journal of Communication,* 1976, *26,* 14–26.

Ekman, P., and V. Friesen. *Unmasking the Face: A Guide to Recognizing Emotions from Facial Clues.* Englewood Cliffs, N.J.: Prentice-Hall, Inc., 1975.

Engebretson, D. and D. Fullmen. "Cross-Cultural Differences in Territoriality: Interaction Distances of Native Japanese, Hawaii Japanese, and American Caucasians." In Samovar, L. A., and R. E. Porter, eds. *Intercultural Communication: A Reader.* Belmont, Cal.: Wadsworth Publishing Co., Inc., 1972, 220–226.

Falk, Lee. "Time Is Money." *Playboy,* December 1975, 102.

Frank, K. "Cultural Patterning of Tactile Experiences." In Samovar, L. A., and

R. E. Porter, eds. *Intercultural Communication: A Reader*. Belmont, Cal.: Wadsworth Publishing Co., Inc., 1972, 200–205.

Gittelson, B. *Biorhythm: A Personal Science*. New York: Warner Books, 1976.

Hall, E. T. *Beyond Culture*. Garden City, N.Y.: Anchor Press/Doubleday, 1976.

Hall, E. Y. *The Silent Language*. Garden City, N.Y.: Anchor Press/Doubleday, 1973.

Hall, E. T. "Proxemics: The Study of Man's Spatial Relations." In Samovar, L. A., and R. E. Porter, eds. *Intercultural Communication: A Reader*. Belmont, Cal.: Wadsworth Publishing Co., Inc., 1972, 205–220.

Hall, E. T. *The Hidden Dimension*. Garden City, N.Y.: Anchor Press/Doubleday, 1969.

Hall, E. T., and W. F. Whyte. "Intercultural Communication: A Guide to Men of Action." In A. G. Smith, ed. *Communication and Culture*. New York: Holt, Rinehart, & Winston, 1966.

Harper, R. G., A. N. Wiens, and J. D. Matarazzo. *Nonverbal Communication: The State of the Art*. New York: John Wiley & Sons, 1978.

Hewes, W. "World Distribution of Postural Habits." In Samovar, L. A., and R. E. Porter, eds. *Intercultural Communication: A Reader*. Belmont, Cal.: Wadsworth Publishing Co., Inc., 1972, 193–200.

Johnson, K. R. "Black Kinesics: Some Non-verbal Communication Patterns in the Black Culture." In Samovar, L. A., and R. E. Porter, eds. *Intercultural Communication: A Reader*. Belmont, Cal.: Wadsworth Publishing Co., Inc., 1972, 181–189.

LaBarre, W. "Paralinguistics, Kinesics, and Cultural Anthroplogy." In Samovar, L. A., and R. E. Porter, eds. *Intercultural Communication: A Reader*. Belmont, Cal.: Wadsworth Publishing Co., 1972, 172–180.

Ouspensky, P. D. *Talks with a Devil*. New York: Alfred A. Knopf, Inc., 1972.

Prosser, M. H. *The Cultural Dialogue: An Introduction to Intercultural Communication*. Boston: Houghton Mifflin Co., 1978.

Samovar, L. A., and R. E. Porter, eds. *Intercultural Communication: A Reader*. Belmont, Cal.: Wadsworth Publishing Co., Inc., 1972.

Sheflen, A. E., with N. Ashcraft. *Human Territories: How We Behave in Space-Time*. Englewood Cliffs, N.J.: Prentice-Hall, Inc., 1976.

Watson, O. M. *Proxemic Behavior: A Cross-Cultural Study*. Hague: Mouton, 1970.

INDEX

371